Sanai y sus amigos rezan por el mundo

Pearl Robinson

Copyright © 2020 Pearl Robinson

Reservados todos los derechos. Ninguna parte de esta publicación puede ser reproducida, almacenada en un sistema de recuperación, o transmitida en cualquier forma o por cualquier medio, ya sea electrónico, mecánico, fotocopia, grabación o cualquier otro, sin el permiso previo por escrito.

Índice de contenidos

Introducción ---------------------------------1

Sanai reza por los Amigos-----------------------3

Oraciones de los Amigos----------------------------6

Escrituras---86

Sobre el autor----------------------------------93

Introduction

Decidí escribir este libro porque quiero que los padres comprendan que está bien que los niños recen. Del mismo modo, quiero que los niños sepan que está bien que recen. Debemos enseñarles que pueden rezar por todo. Cuando tienen problemas en casa, pueden rezar. También, cuando tienen sus problemas, pueden rezar. Creo en lo que dice la Biblia en Proverbios 22:6, que si educamos a un niño en el camino que debe seguir, nunca se apartará de él. Los niños son enseñables cuando son pequeños. Debemos aprovechar todas las oportunidades para enseñarles lo antes posible. Los niños necesitan saber que la oración es la única manera de hablar con Dios. Padres, debemos enseñarles sobre la fe. Enseñarles cuando rezan; también deben creer que . por lo que rezan, Dios responderá según Su voluntad

En este libro, hay versículos bíblicos que los niños pueden leer sobre cómo Dios les protegerá a ellos y a sus familias durante Covid-19 y algunos versículos bíblicos sobre la oración. Quiero que los niños entiendan la importancia de orar. Ruego que los niños sean bendecidos al leer y escuchar este libro en el nombre de Jesús. Amén.

Pearl Robinson

Sanai reza a diario por sus amigos porque cree que la oración es la respuesta a todos los problemas del mundo actual. Sanai quiere que sus amigos comprendan que pueden rezar a Dios por todo. Su oración es que todos los niños se unan y la ayuden a ella y a sus amigos a rezar contra el Covid-19 y otras enfermedades que afectan a la gente en todo el mundo. Sanai cree que nada es demasiado difícil para Dios. Sabe que Dios escucha las oraciones de los niños porque ha respondido a muchas de las suyas. Quiere que los niños sepan que, a veces, Dios no responde de inmediato porque quiere enseñarles la fe, y a veces quiere que esperen. Esperar enseña paciencia y hace crecer su fe en Dios.

Sanai reza para que los niños escuchen a sus padres porque sabe que Dios no responderá a sus plegarias si no obedecen.

A Sanai le encanta rezar por sus amigos, y disfruta oyendo a sus amigos rezar a Dios Padre en nombre de Jesús, pidiéndole ayuda en todas las cosas. Dios desea que todos los niños, de todo el mundo, confíen en Él y dependan de Él.

Glen y Glenda son hermanos. A veces discuten. Quieren que todos los hermanos sepan que, a veces, pueden decirse cosas desagradables cuando están enfadados, pero que siempre deben perdonarse. Después de perdonarse, pueden rezar a Dios y pedirle que les perdone..

Glen y Glenda también quieren que sepas que Dios se siente infeliz cuando no somos amables los unos con los otros. Queremos que Dios esté contento con nosotros. Dios quiere que los hermanos se lleven bien. Cada noche que nos reunimos y rezamos hace que Dios sonría.

SANAI & FRIENDS PRAY FOR THE WORLD

Nathan, el amigo de Melissa, murió el día de su cumpleaños. Ella está de luto por su muerte. Melissa reza y da gracias a Dios por el tiempo que les ha dado juntos en la vida.

También le dice a Dios cuánto echa de menos a Nathan. Melissa quiere que los niños sepan que incluso cuando están sufriendo por la pérdida de un amigo o un familiar, Dios les consolará en su tristeza. Melissa termina su oración pidiendo a Dios que le dé paz y que vele por ella y por sus otros amigos.

.

María, Jeremy, Princesa, Clarice y Carlos se reúnen en oración cada semana. Les gusta rezar por los niños hambrientos de todo el mundo que no tienen comida, ropa ni medicinas. Terminan sus oraciones dando gracias a Dios por todo lo que les proporciona y también por los niños que carecen de estas necesidades en otros países.

Todos se reunieron después de rezar para hablar de cómo podían ayudar. Jeremy dijo que tenía una idea. Los demás se entusiasmaron al oírla. Jeremy dijo: "¿Por qué no recogemos juguetes y se los enviamos a los niños que no tienen juguetes?". Todos pensaron que Jeremy había tenido una gran idea. Clarice dijo: "Me gusta mi vieja muñeca Barbie, pero me han regalado una nueva por mi cumpleaños. Le daré mi vieja Barbie a alguien". Todos donaron algunos de sus juguetes a niños en situación de pobreza de otros países. Sus padres les enseñaron la importancia de dar. A Dios le encanta cuando damos con alegría.

A Sara y Sam les encanta ir a la iglesia. Una de sus partes favoritas del servicio es cuando las familias unen sus manos y el pastor reza por la congregación.

Cuando el pastor termina de rezar, Sara y Sam siguen rezando por muchos de nuestros amigos cuyos padres no asisten a la iglesia. Rezan por ellos porque nos han dicho que les encantaría visitar nuestra iglesia. Le dije a Sara que si continuábamos rezando, Dios respondería a nuestras oraciones. Así que antes de irnos a la cama por la noche, rezamos por ellos. He aprendido de mis padres y del pastor que la oración es la respuesta a todos los problemas del mundo actual.

SANAI & FRIENDS PRAY FOR THE WORLD

A Kai le gusta hacer viajes misioneros con sus padres. Hace poco visitaron Uganda, en África. Durante su estancia allí, conoció a un niño llamado Kimbowa, que le contó que sólo comía una vez al día. Kai no entendía por qué Kimbowa sólo comía una vez al día, mientras que él hacía tres comidas y merendaba al menos dos veces al día.

Le preguntó a su nuevo amigo por qué, y Kimbowa le dijo que no había mucho trabajo en Uganda, así que no había dinero para comprar comida.

Kai reza y pide a Dios que ayude a los padres de Kimbowa con un trabajo para ganar dinero y poder comprar comida para la familia. Kai sabe lo bendecido que es. Quiere que Dios bendiga a Kimbowa con comida y otras cosas que él y su familia puedan necesitar.

SANAI & FRIENDS PRAY FOR THE WORLD

Jeremías sonríe mientras reza, pidiendo a Dios que ayude a todos los niños a ir bien en la escuela. Le gusta rezar por los niños en la escuela porque sabe que algunos de nuestros amigos tienen dificultades en diferentes asignaturas.

Jeremías es excelente en matemáticas, pero sabe que las matemáticas son difíciles para muchos. Su amigo, John, tiene dificultades con las matemáticas, pero le va excelente en inglés. Así que Jeremiah entiende la importancia de rezar por los niños y su trabajo escolar.

Jeremías también reza por los niños de todo el mundo que no van a la escuela porque no tienen dinero. Quiere que Dios les bendiga para que puedan ir a la escuela porque todos los niños necesitan una educación.

Mia, de China, reza para que Dios la sane país del virus que comenzó en China. Pide a Dios que cure a todos los enfermos y ayude a ser felices a quienes han perdido a algún familiar. Mia también reza para que Dios cuide especialmente de su amigo Chang, cuya madre murió a causa del virus Covid-19. Chang es un amigo íntimo, y ella no quiere que esté triste. Chang es un amigo íntimo, y ella no quiere que esté triste.

Mia tries to comfort Chang by telling him that his mother is in Heaven with Jesus. She also wants him to know that she doesn't mind sharing her mother with him. Hearing this made Chang smile. Mia knows how important it is for friends to pray and support each other.

SANAI & FRIENDS PRAY FOR THE WORLD

Zackery reza por su hermanito, que tiene fiebre. Sabe que su hermano no se encuentra bien porque llora cuando está enfermo. Los padres de Zackery van a llevar a su hermano al hospital. No le gustan los hospitales ni los médicos porque dice que hacen daño a los niños con las agujas. Le pide a Dios que proteja a su hermano y lo cure.

Zackery recuerda que lo mejor de ir al médico es que te den caramelos después, pero sabe que su hermano es demasiado pequeño para comer caramelos. Dios escuchó su oración y le aseguró que cuidaría de su hermano. A Zackery le encanta la paz que Dios le da rezando..

Bret, el hermanito de Zackery, llora porque no se siente bien.

Pearl Robinson

Give Thanks!

Tracey, Trevor y Tara saben que es importante rezar antes de comer en la escuela y en casa. Rezan para dar gracias a Dios y pedirle que bendiga su comida. También rezan por los niños hambrientos que no tienen qué comer. Entienden que rezar por otros niños hace feliz a Dios porque no quiere que piensen sólo en sí mismos y no recen por los demás.

La Sra. Clara enseña a sus alumnos de la escuela dominical la importancia de rezar en grupo. Todos pueden pedir oración por sus necesidades personales o por las de los demás. También pueden compartir con el grupo las cosas buenas que Dios está haciendo en sus vidas y en sus familias.

Como grupo, pueden orar tomados de la mano, o pueden orar sin juntar las manos. Otra cosa maravillosa de rezar en grupo es que, cuando todos mencionan su petición de oración, pueden seguir rezando unos por otros. La Sra. Clara también recuerda a la clase que deben seguir rezando por las necesidades del grupo y de los demás.

Enrique no se siente bien; quiere y necesita que sus amigos recen por él. Cuando Enrique está bien, siente alegría al rezar por los enfermos. Se siente mejor sabiendo que sus amigos rezan por él. A Henry le encanta ir al colegio y a la iglesia, pero no puede ir cuando está enfermo, lo que le entristece.

Henry quiere a sus amigos y quiere sentirse mejor porque los echa de menos y quiere volver a jugar con ellos.

Henry reza por sí mismo cuando no se siente bien, y sus padres rezan con él y por él, lo que le hace feliz.

Los padres de Enrique rezan por él. Los padres siempre deben rezar por sus hijos, especialmente cuando no están bien.

Luke pidió a su padre que rezara por su amigo Jacob y su familia. Jacob dio positivo en la prueba de Covid-19. Luke pide a Dios que cure a su amigo porque no quiere que su mejor amigo muera.

No ha visto a Jacob desde que enfermó. Después de rezar, Luke pide a su padre que le explique por qué sufre su mejor amigo. Luego Luke le preguntó a su padre cuándo podrían volver los niños a la escuela. Le dice que tiene miedo. Su padre le abrazó y le dijo que era estaba bien sentir lo que él sentía porque el mundo estaba en crisis; ni siquiera los adultos tenían las respuestas a todo.

El padre de Luke continuó explicándole que sólo Dios conoce la razón del virus y le aseguró que Dios supervisa el mundo entero y puede eliminar el virus en su momento. Dios quiere que recemos unos por otros y que comprendamos que Él es más grande que el virus.

Jacob y su familia

Pearl Robinson

Annabelle reza por su amiga Anna en Australia. Conoció a Anna cuando ella y su familia fueron allí de vacaciones.

Un día, mientras sus padres veían las noticias, Annabelle oyó que el virus se había extendido y que mucha gente estaba muriendo. Inmediatamente se puso a rezar a Dios para que protegiera a Ana y a su familia del virus. Cuando Annabelle terminó su oración, preguntó a sus padres por qué Dios estaba haciendo esto al mundo. Les dijo que tenía miedo de dormir por la noche porque temía que pudieran enfermar y morir.

El padre de Annabelle la sentó en su regazo y le aseguró que las cosas irían bien para ella y para ellos. Annabelle le dijo a su padre que no entendía todo lo que estaba pasando en el mundo. Estaba triste.

Su padre abrió la Biblia y leyó y explicó algunos versículos para ayudarla a entender cómo podía decir lo que decía cuando tanta gente había muerto a causa del virus. Annabelle le dijo a su padre que tenía miedo de volver al colegio. Su padre la abrazó y le explicó que eran cristianos. Le dijo que los cristianos deben confiar en Dios cuando se produce una crisis porque Él sabe lo que hace y por qué.

Salmo 91 "1 Los que viven al abrigo del Altísimo hallarán descanso a la sombra del Omnipotente.

2 Esto declaro del SEÑOR: Sólo él es mi refugio, mi lugar seguro; él es mi Dios, y en él confío.

3 Porque él te rescatará de toda trampa y te protegerá de la plaga mortal.

4 Él te protegerá con sus alas. Te cobijará con sus plumas. Sus fieles promesas son tu armadura y tu protección.

5 No temas los terrores de la noche, ni temas los peligros del día,

6 ni temas la peste que acecha en la oscuridad, ni el desastre que golpea al mediodía.

7 Aunque caigan mil a tu lado, aunque mueran diez mil a tu alrededor, estos males no te tocarán.

8 Pero tú lo verás con tus ojos; verás cómo son castigados los impíos.

9 Si haces del SEÑOR tu refugio, si haces del Altísimo tu amparo

10 ningún mal te vencerá; ninguna plaga se acercará a tu morada.

11 Porque él ordena a sus ángeles que te protejan dondequiera que vayas.

12 Te sostendrán con sus manos para que no tropieces con piedra alguna.

13 Pisotearás leones y serpientes venenosas; aplastarás leones feroces y serpientes bajo tus pies.

14 Dice Yahveh: "Yo rescataré a los que me aman. Protegeré a los que confían en mi nombre.

15 Cuando me invoquen, les responderé; estaré con ellos en la angustia. Los rescataré y los honraré.

.

16 Los saciaré con una larga vida y les daré mi salvación".

Cuando su padre terminó de leer y explicar los pasajes bíblicos, ella le dijo que lo entendía y que se sentía en paz. También le dijo que ya no estaba preocupada por Ana porque sabía que Dios velaría por ella y por su familia. Ellos también son cristianos. Annabelle abrazó a su padre y le dio las gracias por ayudarla a sentirse mejor.

Su padre le dijo que siempre hay que confiar en Dios porque Él lo controla todo.

Pearl Robinson

Jack reza por su amigo Sam y su padre, que se han quedado sin hogar. El padre de Sam perdió su trabajo durante el cierre de Covid-19. Tuvieron que mudarse de casa cuando él perdió su trabajo.

Tuvieron que mudarse de su casa cuando él perdió su trabajo. Jack le pide a Dios que ayude al padre de Sam a encontrar trabajo porque necesitan un lugar donde quedarse.

El amigo de Jack, Sam, y su padre, Jeffery

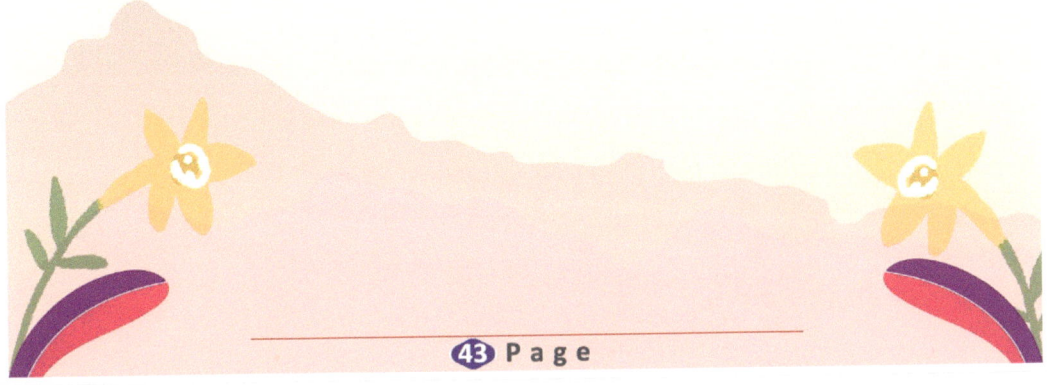

Leo reza y agradece a Jesús lo que hizo en la cruz. Los padres de Leo compartieron la historia del nacimiento de Jesús, cómo nació en un pesebre sucio donde vivían animales.

Le contaron cómo nació Jesús en el mundo. Le contaron sobre la muerte de Jesús y cómo Él murió por todos los pecados del mundo porque Él no quería que Leo y toda la gente muriera y fuera al Infierno.

Leo comparte con sus amigos la hermosa historia de Jesucristo. El reza para que todos acepten la Salvacion de Jesus porque es un regalo que Jesus pago con Su vida en la cruz.

Dio gracias a Dios por sus padres, que compartieron con él la historia más increíble jamás contada. Sus padres le contaron que Jesús resucitó al tercer día y ascendió al Cielo para velar por todos. Por último, pide a Dios que ayude a todos los padres a enseñar a sus hijos sobre Jesús.

SANAI & FRIENDS PRAY FOR THE WORLD

Mary reza por su abuela y por todos los demás abuelos que están en hospitales y residencias. Pide a Dios que cure a su abuela, que lleva mucho tiempo enferma.

Pide a Dios que ayude a su madre porque está triste; su madre está enferma. María escucha el llanto de su madre mientras reza para pedir a Dios que cure a su madre.

María cree en la oración porque sus padres le enseñaron que Dios quiere que le recemos. Ella cree que Dios escucha y responde a las oraciones según Su voluntad cuando oramos. Sus padres le dicen que Dios quiere que confiemos en Él a través de la oración y la fe.

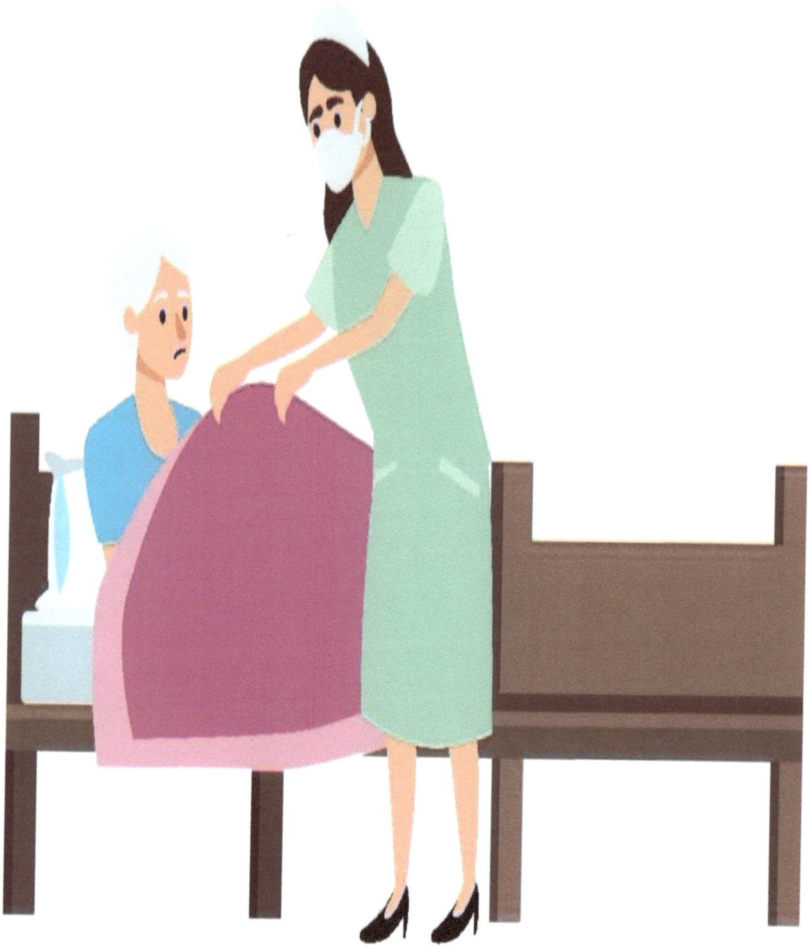

Abuela de Mary

A la pequeña Sue le gusta rezar delante de una cruz porque le recuerda lo que Jesús hizo por ella. Le da las gracias antes de empezar a rezar. Sue reza por todas las escuelas. Le entristece que todas las escuelas estén cerradas a causa del virus.

Muchos niños, padres, abuelos y otras personas están enfermando y algunos están muriendo. Ella reza para que Dios se lleve el virus y sane el mundo.

Sue echa de menos a todos sus amigos y a sus profesores. Le encanta ir al colegio, trabajar en clase y a la hora de comer, cuando juega con su mejor amiga, Sanai. Sue echa de menos llegar a casa para hacer los deberes antes de salir a jugar. Le pide a Dios que le quite el virus. Tiene fe y cree que Dios responderá a su oración.

Pearl Robinson

Jamel reza por todas las personas que están en cárceles y prisiones. Tiene amigos cuyos padres están en la cárcel. Jamel está triste porque él y su padre están muy unidos. A Jamel no le importa compartir a su padre con su amigo.

El padre del amigo de Jamel, Johnny, no hizo nada malo, pero estuvo con la persona que hizo lo malo. Jamel y Johnny son mejores amigos; prometen no estar con nadie que se dedique a hacer cosas terribles porque esto puede meterles en problemas, y podrían pasar tiempo en la cárcel por estar con la persona que hace cosas malas.

El padre de Jamel les habla a él y a Johnny de tomar las decisiones correctas para que no se metan en líos. Johnny siempre da las gracias al padre de Jamel por estar ahí para él.

Jamel y Johnny rezan a diario para que el padre de Johnny salga de la cárcel. Un día, estaban en casa de Jamel en su habitación haciendo los deberes mientras la madre de Johnny le esperaba. La madre de Johnny gritó arriba para que bajara porque tenía buenas noticias para él. Bajó corriendo y vio a su madre llorando mientras la madre de Jamel la abrazaba.

La madre de Johnny le pide que se siente porque tiene grandes noticias para él. Se sentó, temblando de lágrimas mientras Jamel y su madre lo miraban.

La madre de Johnny le pide que se siente porque tiene grandes noticias para él. Se sentó, temblando de lágrimas, mientras Jamel y su madre lo miraban.

La madre de Johnny dijo: "Tu padre vuelve a casa; es libre". Esta es una oración contestada para Jamel y Johnny porque habían rezado para que Dios lo enviara a casa. Los cuatro se abrazaron mientras daban gracias a Dios por responder a las oraciones, y Juanico preguntó a su madre cuándo volvería su padre a casa. Ella respondió: "En dos días".

Johnny y su madre se marcharon alegres, dando gracias y alabando a Dios.

Johnny y su familia

SANAI & FRIENDS PRAY FOR THE WORLD

Jimmy reza por su amigo, Tony, porque toda la familia está enferma con el virus.

El padre de Tony, Harry, es médico. Le encanta cuidar a los enfermos y quiere que todos se recuperen del virus.

El padre de Jimmy fue precavido al ponerse la mascarilla y hacer todo lo posible para evitar que contrajera el virus, pero lamentablemente lo contrajo de todos modos. Pasó 14 días en cuarentena rezando por la seguridad de su familia.

Por desgracia, ya era demasiado tarde. La hermana de Tony, Mary, enfermó; tenía el virus cuando su madre la llevó al médico. El padre de Jimmy, Allen, estaba desolado porque su hija estaba enferma, y puso a dos miembros de la familia en cuarentena.

Unos días después, Tony enfermó.

Su madre le llevó al médico para que le hicieran la prueba; mientras estaba en la consulta, ella también decidió hacérsela porque no se encontraba bien.

Dos días después, Angelia, la madre de Tony, recibe el resultado. Ambos dieron positivo en la prueba del virus. Ahora, todos ellos tienen que estar en cuarentena durante 14 días.

Oír esto no es una buena noticia para Jimmy porque la casa de Tony es como su segundo hogar. Comprendió que no podía ir allí durante un tiempo. Jimmy sabía que debía rezar por la familia. Lo hizo y, al cabo de unas tres semanas, estaban bien.

El padre de Tony quiso estar seguro e hizo que todos se hicieran la prueba de nuevo.

Todas las pruebas dieron negativo. Tony estaba muy contento.

Jimmy agradeció a Dios por responder a sus oraciones; él entiende el poder de la oración. Tony también dio gracias a Dios.

Jimmy quiere rezar por todas las familias. Le dijo a su madre que rezaría por las familias de todo el mundo. Jimmy entiende que con todos los problemas que ocurren en el mundo, todas las familias necesitan oración. Empezó a rezar con y por su familia. Jimmy sabe que la familia que reza unida permanece unida. No reza sólo por las familias de Estados Unidos, sino de todo el mundo. Comprende la importancia de que las familias recen juntas y confíen en que Dios responderá con fe.

Aquí está la familia de Tony después de estar en cuarentena. Se encuentran bien.

El padre de Tony dio las gracias a Dios por salvar a su familia. Se alegró de que Dios cuidara de ellos mientras estaban enfermos, porque el padre de Tony, que es médico, sabe que muchas personas padecen el virus y muchas enfermarán, sobre todo si no siguen las normas establecidas.

Saben que llevar la mascarilla es importante. Se asegura de que su familia las siga porque no quiere que vuelvan a enfermar.

Amos tiene mucho por lo que rezar; está decidiendo por dónde empezar. Mañana empiezan las clases. Así que ha decidido rezar por los profesores y los alumnos. Amos sabe que Covid-19 no ha terminado. Muchos niños tienen miedo de volver al colegio y llevar máscaras.

Está entusiasmado, como muchos otros niños, por volver a la escuela porque verán a sus amigos. Amós reza para que Dios proteja a todos los niños y demás personas que vuelven a la escuela.

Su oración: "Padre Dios, te pido que protejas a todos los niños y mayores que vuelven al colegio. Te pido que todos los niños hagan el bien y escuchen a sus profesores. Te pido que protejas las escuelas de todo el mundo. Mantennos a salvo de las enfermedades y de la gente mala. Te lo pido en nombre de Jesús. Amén"

SANAI & FRIENDS PRAY FOR THE WORLD

Charles reza también por los niños que vuelven a la escuela. Sabe que a Dios le encanta que los niños le hablen porque son muy inocentes y puros. Dios abre rápidamente sus oídos cuando los niños rezan porque quiere que los niños acudan siempre a Él

A Heather le gusta rezar al aire libre. A veces, sale para sentarse, mirar a su alrededor y dar gracias a Dios por haber creado el mundo. Le encanta la hermosa creación de Dios.

Hoy, Heather reza por su padre, que ha perdido su trabajo. Le pide a Dios que les ayude con la comida y con las necesidades de su familia. Heather pide a Dios que ayude a su padre a encontrar otro trabajo porque no quiere que su madre esté triste, ya que no les queda mucha comida.

Heather also has two dogs and a cat that need food. She asks God to help them to be able to keep their pets so that they don't have to be taken away due to lack of food. Heather thanks God for the food they have now.

Heather has a large family. She has three sisters and two brothers. She prays for God to help her mom not to worry about what they are going through.

Heather is also praying for other families whose father does not have a job.

Heather confió y agradeció a Dios por responder a sus oraciones en el nombre de Jesús

Quiere que todos los niños sepan que Dios les escucha cuando le rezan. También quiere que todos los niños se unan a ella en la oración por todas las familias.

Keyona reza para que vuelvan a abrirse las iglesias. Ella y sus padres iban a la iglesia todos los domingos. Pero ahora, desde Covid-19, su iglesia ha cerrado junto con todas las iglesias.

Echa de menos la escuela dominical porque es una parte importante del servicio del domingo, donde puede aprender más sobre Jesús. Keyona echa de menos a su profesora, la Sra. Robinson, que lleva diez años enseñando en la escuela dominical.

Keyona no deja de orar y aprender sobre Jesús porque ella, sus padres, su hermana y sus hermanos tienen un estudio semanal de la Biblia y oran juntos todos los días. Ella entiende que no tiene que asistir a la iglesia para alabar, orar y aprender sobre Jesús. Le encanta leer la Biblia y rezar con su familia. A Keyona también le gusta estar sola en su habitación, orando a Dios.

Al igual que Sanai, Keyona disfruta enseñando a otros a orar en el nombre de Jesús. Sabe que Él la escucha porque Él ha respondido a muchas de sus oraciones. Cuando alguien necesita oración, Keyona es la primera en decir: "Vamos a rezar"

Ann llora mientras reza para que Dios cure a todos los niños enfermos de cáncer. Comprende que hay muchos niños enfermos de cáncer en el hospital.

La abuela de Ann murió de cáncer y la echa mucho de menos. Ann también tenía un primo que murió de cáncer. Sus muertes la entristecen, pero sabe que están en el Cielo con Jesús. Ella reza por la cura del cáncer.

Ann comprende que Dios escucha su clamor a través de la oración. Mientras reza, le pide a Dios que la proteja a ella y a su familia del cáncer. No quiere que nadie más muera de cáncer. Sabe que sólo Dios puede curar al mundo de todas las enfermedades.

Sabrina tiene un árbol precioso en el jardín de su casa bajo el que le encanta rezar. Dice a sus padres que se siente cerca de Dios cuando reza allí. Reza temprano por la mañana mientras sus padres la observan. A sus padres no les importa que rece fuera si uno de ellos la vigila.

Hoy, Sabrina ora por la salvación de todos. Ella quiere que todos los niños y adultos acepten a Jesús como su Señor y Salvador. Sabrina quiere que todos sepan que si creen que Jesús murió en la cruz y resucitó al tercer día, pueden ir al Cielo y estar con Él.

Ella quiere que todos sepan que Jesús murió en la cruz por todas las cosas terribles que hemos hecho y haremos. Pero, cuando le aceptamos con fe, podemos pedir perdón, y Él nos perdonará. Les dice a sus amigos que lo único que tienen que hacer es creer en su corazón y confesar con su boca que Jesús es el Salvador del mundo, y podrán ir al Cielo.

Juan 3:16

Nueva Versión Internacional

16 Porque de tal manera amó Dios al mundo, que ha dado a su Hijo unigénito, para que todo aquel que en él cree, no se pierda, mas tenga vida eterna.

Jesús murió en la cruz.

Jesús está vivo hoy. Él nos am.

Sabrina está de nuevo bajo su árbol favorito para rezar. Sus padres han ido a visitar a un miembro de la iglesia que está en la cárcel. Jessica, la hermana mayor de Sabrina, la está cuidando.

Hoy reza por las personas que están en la cárcel y en prisión. No puede imaginar cómo alguien puede ser feliz encerrado entre rejas. Le pide a Dios que les deje salir y que no vuelvan a hacer cosas terribles.

Sabrina puede identificarse con el sentimiento de soledad que pueden sentir algunos de ellos. Sabrina sabe cómo se siente cuando se mete en líos en el colegio o no hace caso a sus padres. La mandan a su cuarto a pensar en lo que ha hecho.

Odia estar sola en su habitación. Se siente sola. Pero sabe que para la gente que está en la cárcel y en prisión, la soledad dura más que la suya porque ella puede salir de su habitación, pero la gente que está en prisión puede estar encerrada durante mucho tiempo.

El corazón de Sabrina desea rezar por ellos y hacer paquetes de ayuda para enviar a las cárceles. Le pide a Dios que los consuele y les dé paz.

Le gustaría enviar Biblias, lápices y blocs en sus cajas para que puedan escribir cuando se sientan tristes y solos. Le gusta escribir poesías sobre Dios.

Ahora, por supuesto, Sabrina sabe que necesitará ayuda. También le pide a Dios que la ayude con formas e ideas para llevar a cabo su deseo. Sabrina comprende que el primer paso es hablar con sus padres sobre lo que ha estado pidiendo. Ellos pueden tener algunas ideas sobre lo que ella necesita hacer para empezar.

Si sus padres dicen que sí, empezará a hablar con algunos amigos que quizá quieran ayudar donando y recaudando dinero para comprar las cosas que necesitan para meter en los paquetes de ayuda.

Sabrina, emocionada, volvió corriendo a casa para explicar sus oraciones a su hermana. Su hermana se alegró y le dijo que donaría dinero para ayudarla. Las dos se abrazaron y Sabrina levantó la vista y dijo: "Gracias, Dios"

Sanai quiere que todos sepan que Dios creó el mundo en seis días y luego descansó. Además, Dios ama a todos los habitantes del mundo. Le encanta que sus amigos Christopher, Tonya, Jacob, Lucy, Luke, Sara, Isaiah y Leah comprendan la importancia de rezar por el mundo.

Sus padres les enseñaron a rezar por todas las cosas. Entienden que cuando la gente hace cosas terribles, rezan. Cuando la gente hace daño a los demás, rezan. Este grupo de niños se reúne cada semana y reza por el mundo. Su oración es que Dios sane el mundo algún día.

Que tú y tus amigos hagáis lo mismo. Dios quiere oír a todos los niños y a sus padres rezar por el mundo.

Las oraciones hacen sonreír a Dios porque así es como Él nos escucha.

Sanai preguntará a algunos amigos más y a sus padres a su casa. Quiere crear un grupo de oración.

Sanai está orando para que sus padres y los padres de sus amigos acepten reunirse en oración. Ella desea tener un grupo de niños y un grupo de adultos orando. Después podrían ver una película, comer palomitas y jugar.

Sanai cree que la oración es lo que el mundo necesita hoy. ¿Te unirás a Sanai y a sus amigos y rezarás mientras ellos rezan por el mundo?

Oración Versículos (NLT)

Jeremías 29:12

"Entonces me invocaréis, e iréis y oraréis a mí, y yo os escucharé"

Mateo 7:7-8

"Pedid, y se os dará; buscad, y hallaréis; llamad, y se os abrirá: Porque todo el que pide, recibe; y el que busca, halla; y al que llama, se le abrirá."

Mateo 18:19

"Otra vez os digo, que si dos de vosotros se pusieren de acuerdo en la tierra acerca de cualquier cosa que pidieren, les será hecho por mi Padre que está en los cielos."

Juan 14:13-14

"Y todo lo que pidiereis en mi nombre, yo lo haré, para que el Padre sea glorificado en el Hijo. Si pedís algo en mi nombre, yo lo haré".

Salmo 118:5

"Invoqué a Jehová en la angustia: Jehová me respondió y me puso en lugar espacioso".

Romanos 12:12

"Gozosos en la esperanza; pacientes en la tribulación; constantes en la oración".

Mateo 6:7

"Pero cuando oréis, no uséis vanas repeticiones, como hacen los paganos; porque piensan que serán oídos por su mucho hablar."

Marcos 11:25

"Y cuando estéis orando, perdonad, si tenéis algo contra alguno; para que también vuestro Padre que está en los cielos os perdone vuestras ofensas."

Mateo 6:6

"Pero tú, cuando ores, entra en tu aposento, y cerrada la puerta, ora a tu Padre que está en secreto; y tu Padre que ve en lo secreto te recompensará en público."

Filipenses 4:6-7

"Por nada estéis afanosos, sino sean conocidas vuestras peticiones delante de Dios en toda oración y ruego, con acción de gracias. Y la paz de Dios, que sobrepasa todo entendimiento, guardará vuestros corazones y vuestros pensamientos en Cristo Jesús."

Mateo 6:9-13

"Así pues, orad de esta manera: Padre nuestro que estás en los cielos, santificado sea tu nombre. Venga a nosotros tu reino, hágase tu voluntad en la tierra como en el cielo. Danos hoy nuestro pan de cada día. Y perdónanos nuestras deudas, como también nosotros perdonamos a nuestros deudores. Y no nos dejes caer en la tentación, mas líbranos del mal: Porque tuyo es el reino, y el poder, y la gloria, por todos los siglos. Amén".

Salmo 17:1

"Oye la derecha, oh Jehová, atiende mi clamor, presta oído a mi oración, que no sale de labios fingidos".

Proverbios 15:8

"El sacrificio de los impíos es abominación a Jehová; pero la oración de los rectos es su delicia."

Salmo 34:17

"Claman los justos, y Jehová oye, y los libra de todas sus angustias."

Salmo 102:17

"Tendrá en cuenta la oración de los indigentes, y no despreciará su plegaria"

Sobre el autor

Pearl Robinson es esposa, madre, abuela y bisabuela. Enseñó en la escuela dominical para niños y también fue líder del ministerio infantil en su iglesia durante muchos años. Siente una pasión desenfrenada por enseñar a los niños. Ella cree que el mejor regalo que uno puede dar a los niños es enseñarles acerca de la gracia y el conocimiento de Jesús y llevarlos a aceptar el regalo de la salvación de Jesús mientras son jóvenes; ella escribe desde su corazón debido a su amor por Dios y su pueblo. Ella es verdaderamente una escritora inspirada por Dios.

Padre Dios, te pido que bendigas este libro, en el nombre de Jesús. Amén.

Ingram Content Group UK Ltd.
Milton Keynes UK
UKHW051135250623
423979UK00001B/2

Travellers guide to the PARKS & RESERVES of Western Australia

SECOND EDITION

Simon Nevill

Introd

Western Australia is vast, covering over one third of Australia with a population of just 1.8 million people of whom 80% live in Perth. This has one big advantage for the traveller; it allows you to visit many areas in the State where one can often be the only visitor, and this is a rare privilege in this over crowded world.

The options of where to travel are limitless. In the far north is the Kimberley, one of the finest wilderness areas in Australia.

In the north west is the Pilbara region with huge parks like Karijini National Park with its spectacular deep gorges lined with multi-coloured layers of rock or the Rudall River National Park with its wild timeless beauty.

There are the marine parks of Shark Bay, Ningaloo Reef and Coral Bay that provide stunning contrasts between the red desert sands that meet the turquoise clear waters of the Indian Ocean.

The south west has its tall Karri and Jarrah forests, rugged wild coastlines and mountains. This region also has one of the richest floras in the world where you can walk amongst a sea of colour in the wildflower season.

The Goldfields offer the visitor examples of early colonial history with its many old character gold mining towns. Here lie some of the most extensive eucalypt woodlands in Australia and beyond this are the vast open plains of the Nullarbor.

Chichester Range–Pilbara region

uction

This book attempts to show not only the stunning beauty of so many of our parks and nature reserves but to give the reader detailed information and sketch maps of every single park illustrated; also how to get there and what special features occur there. I have been fortunate enough to visit every park except the distant Rowley Shoals Islands, so you will know that much of the information is first hand.

Although the book is geared to help promote the various recreational activities that one can enjoy in our parks, a major underlying theme is the importance of conservation and preservation of our natural heritage.

Many people are under the illusion that we have a vast percentage of land gazetted as national parks, the reality is that Western Australia has only 7% of its total landmass vested in national parks and reserves. As a comparison South Australia has nearly as much land vested in national parks and reserves as Western Australia but is only one third the size. Tasmania has 26% of its land vested in national parks and reserves. So it is vital that we strive to protect what reserves Western Australia has.

The wonderful parks illustrated in this book are your parks, so travel far and wide and enjoy the many natural wonders they have to offer, in this peaceful corner of the world.

Karijini National Park, Pilbara region

How to Use this Book

This book is divided into three sections. The first section between pages 8 and 17 contain general pre-travel information that may assist you in planning your holiday.

The second section between pages 18 and 177 contains the major part of the book, comprising of all the main national parks and reserves to be found in Western Australia. This section is divided into 9 geographic regions: Perth, South West, South Coast, Wheatbelt, Goldfields, Nullarbor, Mid West, Pilbara and Kimberley. The individual parks within each region have text, a location sketch map and an illustration depicting the park. The sketch maps are a guide only to the location of each park but it would be wise to carry detailed maps of each region when travelling. The parks are not placed in alphabetical order but mostly positioned geographically so that travel planning is made easier. Within the text, not only is each park described in general terms but included is a description of the various wildlife that can be found there. The Latin names have been included for most plants and animals but birds are described by their common name only.

The government Department of Conservation and Land Management that manages Western Australia's parks has been abbreviated throughout the text to DCLM.

The final section, from page 178 to page 192 contains ancillary information for the reader's interest.

Please note this a second edition. Editing is a massive task and many changes to text and maps have taken place. However, changes to roads and park facilities are taking place on a continual basis, so do check with the various authorities.

'Natures Window', Kalbarri National Park–Mid West Region

Contents

SECTION 1
Pre-Travel Information — 8

SECTION 2
Perth — 18

South West region — 54

South Coast region — 72

Wheatbelt region — 94

Goldfields region — 108

Nullarbor region — 118

Mid West region — 124

Pilbara region — 142

Kimberley region — 160

SECTION 3
Ancillary Information — 178

SECTION 1
Pre-Travel Information

Travel planning & preparation

PLANNING WHERE TO GO

As mentioned in the introduction Western Australia is vast, if you were travelling from Albany in the south to Kununurra in the north you would have to drive over 3700km, which is a lot of driving, taking several days at the very least. So any travelling to distant areas requires careful planning in terms of distance and time on the road.

The most common problem when people are planning long trips, particularly the classic 'around Australia tour', is that they completely underestimate how long they require in each area–for example the Kimberley alone can take a minimum of 3 weeks. Unless you have the luxury of an unlimited time frame, you will invariably run out of time and the final stages of the holiday become a very rushed affair, with the final days being spent covering long distances to get back to your base, which is not a wise move.

This problem is not necessarily the fault of the traveller, as often they have never experienced long distance holidays and there is the temptation to look at books and maps and say "let's see it all". It really is best to try and concentrate on one region, by spending quality time there, getting to know the many aspects of a region.

If you live in Perth, then try to make short journeys that radiate out from the city in all directions, getting to know the south west well. You will gain valuable experience with driving techniques and what suits you best.

Then start longer trips that may take you to the 'Goldfields' or the mid west. Then finally the longer trips doing first the Pilbara then another longer journey where you slowly pass through the Pilbara and spend quality time in the Kimberley.

The book is designed to cover the majority of parks and reserves found in the main geographic regions of the state. This allows the reader to plan visits to each region with a multitude of options.

There has been no 'star rating' for parks based on degrees of worth, as even the smallest reserve can give immense pleasure to some people. The largest body of text in this publication, for example, is centred on one small reserve in the Wheatbelt, namely Dryandra Woodland Reserve. The fact that few people know about it, or that it possesses no mountains, waterfalls, beaches or lakes does not detract from its immense natural wealth. The reason why so much has been written on a reserve only a few kilometres wide, is to demonstrate that when we really look, there is so much to see in any park or reserve, however large or small.

BEST TIME OF YEAR TO VISIT EACH REGION

Not only is the state huge in size but its weather patterns and temperatures vary greatly from region to region. I am often asked "when should I go there and what's the weather like?". Well after travelling to every corner of the State for nearly 30 years and running wildlife tours for 14 of them, I've developed some understanding of what one is likely to expect in an area, often learning the hard way. Please note that the following is a guide only to the weather patterns and as we all know, unseasonal weather can come at any time of the year and also some people feel the cold and some love the big heat. As an overall guide, though, let's look at each region individually.

Kimberley: The Kimberley lies well above the Tropic of Capricorn and experiences tropical weather patterns with dry mild winters and hot, sometimes very wet summers. To many who live in the Kimberley, their favourite time of year is the 'Wet Season', or more to the point, when the 'Wet' actually comes, as prior to the 'Wet' the weather can be intolerable, with no rain and very high humidity.

For those who live in the temperate zones, the tropics can be very debilitating in the summer months, with the temperatures between November and March averaging 34°C and the humidity reaching 90% at times.

The ideal time to travel is in the winter months June to August, even then the beginning of June or even the end of August can be hot, particularly when on long walks. However the disadvantage is that the highest concentration of travellers are on the road at that same time, but you will find many areas if you do your homework well, where you can get to quiet spots.

Mid May can have quite bearable weather and there are fewer people on the road, but the Gibb River Road can sometimes be closed to most traffic around Gibb River Station as late as early June some years.

July is the best time, as the weather is cool in the evening and mild and sunny in the day with no rain. Also there should be water in many of the smaller water holes. If you are still in the Kimberley in late September and October, the water holes will often be dry and temperatures will be getting hot during the day. The main thing to do, besides visiting the main tourist areas is to try to make contact with the cattle stations that allow camping. There are fees involved but most of the locations are well worth the small payment. On these properties there are many areas you can visit that most travellers will never see and some of them you can have just to yourselves.

The Pilbara: Much of this region also lies above the Tropic of Capricorn and summers can be very hot with cyclonic rain storms, so it is not a wise move to travel between November and April. However the period of pleasant mild weather is slightly longer than the far north and end of May to late September can be very pleasant. In mid June–July even though the days may be sunny, there can be bitterly cold winds blowing from the desert region east and the night temperatures in Karijini can fall below 0°. So do take adequate sleeping gear. The ideal period is mid-August to late September; the temperature is warming up and if there have been reasonable winter rains the everlastings and other flowers will be in full bloom.

Cyclones can occur quite often in the Pilbara region particularly between January and mid March.

This book does not include the desert reserves except the remote Rudall River National Park. Many people travel the southern desert regions in mid-winter but they can be bitterly cold both day and night so again try to travel in the deserts either in mid-May or mid-August to mid-September. These are very precise times being given but that is the difference between very cold weather that can occur in July and hot weather that can come as early as mid October both making holidays not so pleasant.

The Mid West: This is similar to the Pilbara regarding weather with longer periods of mild weather. Mid April to May is pleasant but it is autumn and there will be far less wildflowers in bloom. June and July can have lovely sunny days but often cold particularly at nights. The best period is from mid-August to mid-October. For coastal activities the summer months can be pleasant.

Perth Region: The Darling Range hills are best to visit in spring, between mid-August and late October, with mid-September normally having the highest concentration of flowering plants. It is great time to go walking in the Jarrah and Wandoo woodland. The Perth coastal region is pleasant for marine activities from November through until March, with the occasional summer cyclonic weather.

South West Region: Springtime normally comes later in the south west starting in late August and going through till early November. However, in this region, particularly on the deep south west and southern coastal areas, the summer months can be very mild at times. It pays to check the long range forecasts. In the height of the summer, when Perth is experiencing a week of very hot weather, Albany can have weather that does not exceed 29° and even then, if it does have a hot day reaching say 35°, it rarely lasts more than a day – so travel.

South Coast: Again the weather is similar to the south west, except that east of Albany the rainfall drops considerably particularly only a few kilometres inland. Towns like Esperance often have magic weather either in winter or summer and generally it remains sunny most of the year. So any time of the year except say the very middle of winter can be rewarding. It can however have a few very hot days in summer, so again, check the long range weather forecasts.

Wheatbelt: The winters are mostly dry but can be very cold and inland temperatures drop below freezing point at night. So if you are camping between June and early August rug up. The midday however can be mild and sunny. Spring is a wonderful time here from August to mid-October – still cool but great for wildflowers viewing and other bush activities.

The Goldfields: Similar to the Wheatbelt but often very cold mid-winter and freezing at night particularly in the southern areas. So mid August to mid October is best for travelling. The summers can be extremely hot and this is not a wise time to travel the Goldfields, especially in the northern areas where temperatures in the shade can reach the high forties.

The Nullarbor: This has almost identical weather patterns to the Goldfields, except on the very coast where temperatures can drop quite considerably. For example, the weather at Eyre Telegraph Station on the coast can be only 28°C mid-day in summer but only 50km inland on the Nullarbor proper, the temperature can be in the high 30's. Best time to travel is mid-August to end of October.

Type of accommodation

This book is primarily about national parks however, I have included some guidelines that may assist the reader. For in-depth information regarding four wheel driving, camp cooking etc there are more detailed publications available.

Before we discuss the various aspects of planning a trip, the big questions, is what vehicle will you be taking and what type of accommodation you will use. You probably have a vehicle and that is what you will be taking. However some points should be raised, as what you take will certainly have a bearing on what you can do and where you can go.

Many of you may be retired and possess one of the current six cylinder two wheel drives and your chosen preference is to take your home with you and that normally takes the form of a caravan; this is quite a natural decision.

The benefits of this mode of travel are that you can base yourselves at a caravan park having most of the luxuries that home has to offer. There is a temptation to pull very large caravans that obviously emulate one's home but these are often a great strain on the vehicle and if unbalanced, lower the back of the vehicle, making the steering very light, which is extremely dangerous for road-holding ability.

So ask yourself, do you need to have so much space? There are now some very good compact caravans with the added facility of pop-up canopies. There are several advantages to these caravans; firstly they are light in weight needing less fuel to tow them. They are more manoeuvrable, particularly when reversing. There is less height, so the wind resistance drops dramatically, allowing for greater average speed. There is more stability with less likelihood of jack-knifing. There is greater visibility, both for the driver and for vehicles trying to overtake.

Many accidents are caused by large caravans being towed in convoy, where the drivers stay close to their buddy in front, creating no room for overtaking vehicles to pull in. It is highly selfish and very dangerous particularly on winding roads, so leave lots of room if you must tow large vans.

Off road trailers: There are some very good off road camper trailers on the market. They are not cheap, but can carry a fair amount of additional gear as well as having the luxury of a built-in tent that extends out from the trailer. The advantage is that they allow you to travel to many remote areas except the high sand dune country or very rugged 4WD tracks with steep creeks. They are fairly quick to erect and free you up to drive off leaving a semi permanent base to which to return to at night. The disadvantage is they cannot take you everywhere, use slightly more fuel and are difficult to reverse in boggy situations.

Tents fitted to vehicle roof racks that fold out: These are very useful, there are some that extend out from the side of the vehicle. Some that can extend over the back, with the rear of the vehicle being used as the kitchen area and you climb up to the bed via a ladder. The benefits are that they are reasonably cheap compared with trailer campers. Do not have to be towed. Take up little storage space. Very quick to erect and do not need ground pegs. The disadvantages are that you can not leave them as a base camp to return to as you must re-pack and fold away.

Free standing tents: These come in all shapes and sizes, some so huge you need almost a year to erect them. Seriously, you should select tents that will give you the basic minimum layout you require having countless awnings and flaps may look impressive but if you have to erect them on a regular basis on tour, they can be most frustrating. The author uses the simple stand up tent that is used by commercial tour operators, being 2.4m x 2.4m and requires in firm ground only 4 pegs. It has one single pole, full length mosquito netting at front and a window at rear and takes only 2 minutes to erect from taking out of bag to, to placing the four pegs and erecting the single pole. Why have such a basic tent, well they are the fastest tent to erect, you can stand up in it, sleep two and one small child if you had to, a second or third can be used for other family members, who need their own space. They require just one simple pole and four pegs (more can be used if required in stormy conditions). They require little space on the roof rack or inside the vehicle. Many camping grounds in parks do not allow the vehicle to drive right up to the actual tent site, so lugging a huge tent is not ideal, these are relatively light. However they can not be used for back pack hiking. For awnings that protect you from the sun, you can extend a tarp from the roof rack with just two extendible poles with two guy lines using the rear of the vehicle as a kitchen.

The most common problems seen in camping grounds is that some travellers take far too long erecting tents and unload from their vehicles far too much unnecessary gear. The author has arrived at camping grounds after others and has erected the tent, laid out the table and chairs and the cooler, gone to have a shave and shower and come back to see people still unloading gear. The more one travels, the more one learns and the less one carries. If you have been privileged to walk and sleep out under the stars with desert Aborigines, you realise how much unnecessary gear we take. It would not be the author's chosen form of travel but it certainly puts things into perspective.

The Aussie Swag: A great way to travel. Relatively portable and you can sleep under the stars. However, a fast stand up tent allows more freedom with no mosquitoes to annoy you and your gear does not get so dirty but try and tell that to a true stockman or bikie and they'll just laugh.

Accommodated: There are so many forms of accommodation and this book does not intend to cover them in detail, suffice to say that on page

204, there is a full Western Australia map with the names of some 'Station and Farm Stay' locations. There are many chalets, lodges, hotels, farm stays, Station Stays and Caravan Parks too numerous to mention in this book. A short word on Station Stays and Farm Stays, in general the people who run these properties are some of the finest people we have on the land and are most hospitable. Even if you are on a fairly restricted budget, try and take a break and stay on a farm or station, they don't charge much and they often have different levels of accommodation to suit your needs. Sometimes they cater for evening meals and it is a great way to get to know how they live on the land.

2WD'S or 4WD'S

2WD: Having owned 4WD's and travelled throughout Australia for nearly 30 years, one naturally becomes biased towards that mode of travel. However, 2WD's with adequate clearance will take you to most places. If you do get stuck in sand, you can deflate your tyres down to say 12lbs. There is a good chance that with adequate preparation, like clearing sand in front of the tyres and if possible laying some form of more solid material under the tyres, you would get out but this is obviously no way to travel and enjoy yourself. So only travel where there is firm ground.

2WD have the advantage of being cheaper. If the expenditure of 4WD's is an issue, there are some small saloon type vehicles that have the 4WD facility. One vehicle stands head and shoulders above most and that is the Subaru. They are well made, travel long distances at maximum speed limits with ease, handle most 4WD situations well and have reasonable storage space, very maneuverable in cities, use less fuel than the big 4WD's. However they do not have the heavy-duty chassis and suspension of the more robust 4WD vehicles and must be driven with care on rough roads. The storage area is less than the larger 4WD's. The engine requires petrol, which is not always available in remote area and has a limited towing capacity. Other than that, it is great value.

4WD: What do the robust 4WD's give, they certainly give you a good deal of security when you're in the middle of the Canning Stock Route looking up at a 20metre sand dune and also a great respect for their 4WD abilities if driven well.

The main benefit that robust 4WD's give you, is surprisingly, not their 4WD ability as in fact one rarely needs to engage 4WD in most areas. No, the major advantage is that they are built tougher, having stronger chassis and heavy duty suspension. This allows you to cover great distances over the years on very rough roads without normally major breakdowns in the suspension and chassis, the two areas that take the real punishment. I am of course talking about the legitimate heavy duty 4WD's not the many 'toys', that now fill the market place.

There are so many advantages of a 4WD but some of the main features are that they can tow heavy loads, carry heavy loads and be used in difficult 4WD situations. On the point of heavy loads, they will not do the impossible and the most common problem that occurs with many travellers, is that of over loading. It is not hard to do particularly when making long, desert trips, where extra fuel, water, food, retrieval gear etc are required.

The best solutions are twofold, first 'beef' up the suspension, there are several methods of doing this and you should approach good 4WD accessory stores for advice, or better still join a 4WD club for a while and learn what really works. The other factor to lessen suspension damage is to pack the bare essentials, try and live by the motto 'less is more'.

Petrol or Diesel: Again I'm biased here, petrol driven vehicles are cheaper and can give you faster take off speeds although the new breed of turbo-diesels almost match them. They tend to use more fuel especially the big V8's. Diesel engines on the whole last longer; the engines are more reliable although if they do break down, you can have bigger troubles. Diesel engines particularly need clean fuel and definitely no water getting in to them. Diesel is available more in the remote areas. For those who really do wish to travel in remote desert regions, there is a thing called Spinifex (scientifically, it is not a spinifex but a member of the grass family known as Triodea). In the winter and spring months the plant seeds and on the remote tracks where few vehicles go, the plant grows quite tall, particularly in the middle of the track, after a while the vehicle starts to collect the stems underneath the vehicle and clumps of the grass build up. With the heat generated by the hot exhaust pipe the grass can start to smoulder, with diesel it is not such a problem but with petrol it can have disastrous consequences, so be very careful and for both diesel and petrol, stop every few kilometres and remove the build up. Also cover the radiator grill or bull bar with wire mesh, it does not cut and seeds are removed much easier. If you don't do this, the radiator will clog up and over heat.

Good, well known petrol or diesel driven 4WD's will both, in general serve you well, the choice is yours.

Petrol engines can be hazardous in spinifex country

Planning the journey

Check the distances you have to travel and try and break the overnight stops into manageable driving distances between stops, allowing plenty of time to have adequate meal breaks.

As mentioned previously, there is a tendency to plan too many stops and do too much. Take it easy, your tour should be a holiday not an endurance test. If you wish to get to distant regions and you only have limited time, then it is best to cover reasonable distances, making sure though that you have a break every two hours. Then plan to have quality time in the region you wish to travel. It is always best to have at least a few two night stops. There is nothing worse than travelling on long tours where you have to pack up gear on a daily basis, having two night or longer stops allows you to radiate out from a base camp with leisure and really get to know an area.

Try and plan your stops to allow you to get in one hour before dark, there is nothing worse than looking for a campsite in the dark. It takes twice as long to erect tents as you are forever looking for the odd peg or something else. A useful item is to have a rear low wattage light that can be turned on from the dash, so that when you pull up after dark, you can reverse into areas easily and set up camp quite easily having the whole rear area lit up. You can not use it for long stops if you are not using the vehicle, as it will drain the battery.

Take out the maps and check where the fuel stops are if it is a remote areas and check the kilometres you will travel knowing your fuel capacity. There is no point in filling the long range tanks if you know you are stopping well before one tank load, Even if fuel is expensive in remote areas, the added cost is far out weighed by reducing the heavy load of an additional 80 litres. However it is always wise to have 20 litres in the spare tank.

Knowing the time of year you are travelling, check the local weather conditions, it is pointless heading into the Goldfields say, if there have been heavy rains unless you intend to stay on sealed roads. It is also silly to visit the deep South West if heavy rains are imminent for a few days when the Mid West may be dry and pleasant.

Try and read up on areas you intend to visit, so you are fully conversant with what you can see and do in each area, saving precious holiday time. Remember some busy areas may require pre bookings to get in.

Check if you will be entering Aboriginal or station country, do you need permits or permission. If taking pets on a long tour, remember most parks do not allow Cats or Dogs in them and you won't win a popularity vote with the ranger if caught.

Good maps are worth their weight in gold and there are many quality ones available. The Hema, West Print Maps and DCLM maps are exceptionally good. The more detailed, the more you will enjoy your travels.

Children

Holidays are such special events for children and can remain in the memory well into adulthood. How you plan for their journey can have a great bearing on how the journey will pan out for every one. The long drives required to cover the longer tours will obviously affect children. Different ages will require different needs. Make sure a box of 'goodies' that each child likes is packed in the rear easily accessible, containing items like story books, sketch pads, crayons, felt pens and pencils, small tape recorders with head phones with music or story tapes. The items will vary with the age but do make provision. From your initial short tours, try and develop codes of conduct and basic rules of does and don'ts, like do not unlock doors while travelling, definitely no fighting particularly whilst driving as the driver will be distracted and an accident may occur. Do not lean out of windows, etc. You will know your children but the message is do plan for them too and make sure they get adequate breaks. And get to stretch their legs on the route.

On a final note try and introduce children to the world of nature, showing them different animal's and birds, you may encounter. This may sow the seed that has a bearing on how they view the planet, for they are its future and ultimately will have a great bearing on how it develops.

Packing & storage

There is a phrase, 'the plan did not work, because there was no plan' and whether planning a trip short or long, this could never be more true It is very important that you take everything you require but basically the bare essentials. The biggest mistake is to take far too much and over load the vehicle.

Packing and Storage: Having selected a vehicle and knowing the mode of accommodation you will have, comes the planning process. Try having your equipment purchased well before very long trips because it is well worth taking a few short journeys to check what equipment you really need. Try and organise the packing so that it is easy to get to items. Equipment like recovery gear, long term canned food stuffs, additional wheels, tubes and tools can go up front of the roof rack and be packed separately, knowing that you may not require them for several days or weeks. Make sure the rear of the vehicle allows you to access gear for mid day stops and meals, without pulling out heaps of gear that you don't require until the evening stop. Try and have storage boxes that contain set groups of items so you can avoid the "where did I put it" situation. Try not to have them too big, as a box full of cans will weigh a lot. It is a common problem putting one's back out by trying to lift heavy boxes while leaning forward.

Having fine tuned the equipment you require, make a complete list for short trips and long trips, having the list split into sections like vehicle tools, spares and recovery gear, cooking gear, camping gear, clothing gear etc.

Before leaving for a long trip, pack most of your gear the day before. Try not to leave it till the afternoon, as it takes several hours if you have a lot of gear. Make sure either a spare car is available to pick up some last minute items or if only the tour vehicle is available, get the odd things on the journey. The only last minute items to pack should be frozen foods for the cooler and vegetables if it is summer. It stands to reason, that it is not wise to leave a fully packed vehicle out on the street particularly with gear on a roof rack. So park in a secure area and leave the very valuable items till the morning. Alarms are of course a major deterrent.

Regarding the roof rack and tying down gear, try not to use ropes. The reason being they work loose, as the load moves with travel and it takes so long to tie down and worst of all you have to do this on a daily basis if you need items on the roof.

The best system by far, is to use a custom built heavy duty plastic tarp that fits squarely over the roof rack load and has rubber stretch straps that run through eyelets and are pulled down to hooks rivetted to the roof rack supports. The elastic cords allow different loads and adjust to the continuing movement of gear. It takes only two minutes to go around the vehicle pulling down the cords over the hooks.

To really secure the load however, the author uses two medium heavy-duty truck stretcher straps that have a simple ratchet system. One is thrown over the front third of the roof rack load, to stop any flapping and pull down the load and the other does the same at the back third of the roof rack load. It only takes a further two minutes but nothing ever moves.

Some useful equipment

Useful equipment
- vehicle air compressor for tyres
- latest approved plastic fuel container
- portable gas light
- cooler
- top loading freezer
- heavy duty storage boxes
- traditional swag
- compact gas cooker with cartridge gas unit
- fire extinguisher
- first aid kit
- canvas storage bag
- axe
- collapsible shovel
- shackles for winch cables
- snatch strap
- leather gloves
- kangaroo jack
- geared hand winch
- exhaust lifting air bag jack

Driving technique

2WD: Not too much to say in this area, suffice to say, do not drive too long with out breaks. Try not to tow caravans or trailers beyond the capacity of the vehicle. Try not to enter 4WD territory you may get hopelessly bogged. Do take two spare wheels for longer trips around Australia and have your vehicle well serviced prior to departure, check where the nearest main service centres are for your make of vehicle in the remote case of major break downs. Have adequate poundage in the tyres if carrying heavy loads.

4WD: This book is certainly not intended as a manual for 4WD's. Some general comments may help though.

Try and engage 4WD particularly low range once in a while on rough roads, even if it is not required, it helps lubricate the cogs and bearings and wears in the gearbox.

Sand: In soft sand the main thing is to keep moving. Second gear in high range is good. The essential thing is letting tyres down to about 20 psi. In very soft sand, take the pressure even lower say 14–15 psi. Try to avoid turning in soft sand, keep going until you strike firmer ground. Stay in existing tracks where sand has already been compressed. Where you have to negotiate steep long dunes, then build up speed, not too fast and keep the revs up.

On tracks like the Canning Stock Route travelling from the north, people have made numerous tracks way into the bush to try and get a run up. Not only is it damaging the environment but also it is completely unnecessary. It is simply that they haven't let tyres down. With skillful driving you do not need to drop below 25 psi on these tracks with most loads.

If you have been having trouble, then get up really early and head off, as the heavy morning dew helps hold the sand together for a while.

Rocky Tracks: On the most rugged tracks that you may encounter, like in the Kimberley on private cattle station tracks, go into low range and use even first gear and take it really slowly. When you see bigger boulders that rise up in the middle of the track, take the nearest tyre side and drive right over it. This will avoid damaging the diff or sump. Do not do this on tracks that drop away steeply to the side.

Be careful on loose gravel roads

Driving through water: Always get out and take your boots off and check the depth of water. Often the middle although deeper can be firmer, as the sides of the track can be waterlogged mud. Most vehicles can drive through 60 cm of water. However if you are crossing flooded highways, this can be dangerous, if the water is running fast as it can hit the side of the vehicle and just take it over the edge of the road. If you have to drive through very deep water, then cover the front of the vehicle with a tarp and drive in second high range, keeping up a constant speed creating a bow wave. Remember petrol and water do not mix well and the combination can be disastrous for the engine.

Recovery equipment: This book will not cover this complex area but approach a good 4WD accessory store or do a 4WD course if you need advice.

Driving on Dirt Roads: Do be careful on straight gravel roads. There is a tendency to still try and drive at high speeds, the same as on sealed roads. At some stage one of the wheels will lose traction and the other will still grip, this causes the driving wheel to turn the vehicle. The driver panics and overcompensates with the steering wheel. The next moment the whole vehicle goes into a spin and the car can end up anywhere.

The other problem is bends. If you approach a bend too fast on gravel you will slide on the loose stones and the vehicle may go completely out of control.

So do slow down on dirt roads.

General camping notes

Setting up camp

If you are in commercial or regulated park camping ground then much of the following will not apply, as you have little choice in where you can go. If you do get to a commercial camping ground park near the entrance and walk around first. Then come back to the front office and request an area of your choice, most times the managers will be most accommodating.

If fires are allowed in park campsites, pick up your firewood a few kilometres before the camping ground. I place it on the roof load and tie it down. If you have a trailer, you can strap it down on the front bars, driving to the camp very carefully.

Bush campsites

Unlike much of the east coast we are still fortunate enough to have areas where we can get away to quiet areas all to ourselves.

When looking for a campsite, do not leave it till after dark if you can help it.

Try and get well off the road. Select a flat area, preferably on higher ground if rain is imminent. Do not camp in creeks, even if the ground looks easier to do so, you never know when water may flow down. In the bigger river systems, flash floods can occur in areas where it may be bright and sunny but the waters have come from hundreds of kilometres away.

The gathering and lighting of firewood is frowned on by a few, nowadays but if you have camped in the back blocks for years, it is something that is hard to let go of. Obviously small reserves are very fragile areas where fallen wood is scarce, then get that gas stove out.

If however weather conditions are safe and there is plenty of wood and few people have camped in the area, then gather your wood but select only dead fallen timber. One of the first things you can do when pulling up at a campsite is gather wood, and get the fire going first, don't use lots of wood. The desert Aborigines find it amazing how much wood white people use for cooking. If they had lit fires over the last 40,000 years like some of us, we would not have a single stick of firewood in the dryer regions left to burn. Don't forget to clear the loose-leaf litter away from the fire area, so you have bare ground.

Come back to the fire after a while and put two heavier pieces on. These will burn slowly and give you good hot cooking ash. You don't want to cook on a fire with large flames.

Sleeping Bags

There is a huge range available and each will have a different thermal rating, generally speaking the price will dictate the quality. It really is not worth buying a cheap sleeping bag. The author uses a sleeping bag but in a different way than most, it is used fully open over a thin high-density foam mattress and above this, a doona is used, which allows one to stretch right out at night. It is vital that you have warm bedding below you as well as above. The doona and open sleeping bag is also used as insulation over all the back gear in the vehicle. This keeps items surprisingly cool from the mid day sun. Don't cover a fridge if you have one running but keep it well ventilated. A fridge is one of the many luxuries I don't use.

A word about winter camping, especially in the Mulga and desert areas. The mid day temperatures may be 18°C, but the night temperature may drop to 3 or 4 degrees below freezing, that's cold. If you have a tent, make sure there is a small opening for fresh air but close up the big open mesh windows, that will bring the temperature up one or two degrees. It sounds funny, but having thermal underwear gear can make a big difference. The trick is to wash, if you can, in the last day light hour, while it is not too cold around the fire. Put on new woollen/nylon socks and your thermal gear and be ready for the cold night ahead. Washing late at night when the temperature has dropped dramatically can take a lot of your body temperature away.

When you go to bed you will be still warm but one final item, that will definitely keep you warm when temperatures drop to freezing is to wear a 'beanie' (woollen hat). You can lose up to 30% of your body heat through your head, so keep it warm.

Bush Camping Rules

In the cities we are so used to seeing volunteers or road workers clearing the rubbish from highways thrown out the window by the most mindless individuals. Also along the roads that lead away from country taverns, we see the stubbies and cans littering the road side verge, but to drive up to an otherwise pristine camp site and see previous campers litter is really depressing.

Keep to the main rule of taking your rubbish with you, until you get to the nearest town. It does not have to be much, as tins can be thrown on the fire and then crushed with the steel peg mallet. Unused vegetables, paper containers can be burned and buried with the ash. Don't burn plastics as they give off toxic fumes. I place the rubbish in heavy-duty plastic bags, strapped up on the roof to unload at the earliest stop.

With toilet requirements dig deep and bury, making sure you are away from even dry creeks. A word on hygiene, especially when travelling with a group. Make sure a bowl with disinfectant and water and scrubbing brush is placed near the toilet shovels and paper and make sure every one is made aware they must use them. In the 14 years of running camping tours, we never had a hygiene problem. I know of one group who went out in the Victoria Desert and nearly every member came down with gastroenteritis from one persons slack hygiene methods—needless to say the group who paid good money were not impressed.

Don't use soap, shampoos or toothpaste in rivers but collect water in a bowl and take away from the river or pool.

Try to use existing fireplaces where possible, do not start new ones.

Do stay on already formed tracks, do not create new ones.

Please respect pastoral or Aboriginal lands by doing the right thing, most Aboriginal communities and many pastoralists, will let you camp on their property if you take the time to approach them. All they wish for is for you to ask, as they may have cattle in a particular area and will guide you to another location. Obviously do not camp near dams and water troughs, station owners will not be impressed, as the stock will often not come in to drink.

Do leave all gates as you find them, either closed or open. Do ask if you can light a fire on a station, as one station I know south of Broome, was set alight by slack visitors. Needless to say no one is ever allowed to camp on that property ever again, while the present owner is there, thanks to a few idiots not putting out a fire or even informing him that they were there.

On a final note do obey the various park signs they are there to protect your parks.

Bush survival

Again there are good publications on this subject. But a few words may help. Most people know the rule never leave your vehicle when in remote areas but still people do it, and alas sometimes they die. A German couple, who got badly bogged east of William Creek on the edge of Lake Eyre, one survived staying with the vehicle and one tragically died trying to walk out. Always make it clear to people where you are going. I always phone back to a buddy in Perth and let him know when I am about to enter a remote area I give an estimated time of return to a main town and add several days onto that. I also inform the local police station if possible. If you say you will let them know when you come out from a remote region, do it. It is easy to forget when the pressure is off but they haven't, as they have it on record, so do the right thing. I nearly always carry enough water and food, for at least 2-3 weeks and can extend this period if things get bad. Radio Flying Doctor or Satellite phones are a bonus if you have them but still don't use them as a crutch, they still can break down.

If you are stuck, avoid the heat of the day, create shade wherever possible and try and keep cool. Drink most fluids in the morning, do not leave it to mid day, as you will never catch up on your thirst. There is a lot written about making desert stills, where water gathers from condensation. but unfortunately it can take a lot out of you, by having to dig. It is best to carry a minimum 60 litres of water on remote trips and more if you know you are travelling where there is no water.

To draw the attention of rescuers, in the cool of the morning gather as much green live bushes into an open cleared area. Pile it up and clear a large area free from flammable material. Set light to it, making sure you definitely cannot start a bush fire. The green leaves will let off dark gray smoke. At night burn timber. The fire can be seen for many miles from the air. Do not start this process until after the deadline you have given people for returning to civilisation.

On a humourous note, a Japanese motorbike tourist was told "If you get lost you can light a fire" he certainly did that, he set light to one of our finest parks, Needless to say he was found, but understandably, DCLM were certainly not impressed.

First Aid

Make sure you carry an up to date first aid kit and if possible do a short Red Cross first aid course and learn some basics. You never know when it will come in handy.

Basic camp
COOKING EQUIPMENT

Basic camping and cooking equipment
- plastic water containers
- folding chairs
- plastic storage box
- stainless steel flask
- gas cylinder
- gas cooker
- steel open mesh collapsible grill stand
- stainless steel saucepans and billy
- large steel handle frying pan
- large slice
- long tongs
- stainless steel plates
- plastic mug
- leather gloves
- head torch
- essential cutlery, don't forget a quality tin opener
- small camp oven
- hanging basket steel rod for pot removal
- long handled shovel–used also for vehicle recovery

Cooking

There are many great bush cooking books that will help those who love cooking. Many are based on the camp oven. I rarely use my camp oven, because of time and the attention required getting the right heat and keeping the right quantity of ash going. The bush is what many of us have come to see and the more time one is out there in it the happier most of us are. Some tips however for fast cooking may not go amiss. Firstly the most important item is the grill stand, illustrated in the photograph. Some people buy a half mesh, half plate grill. They use the plate for barbecues but a full mesh is best, as you may want two or three saucepans on the grill and you won't have space with half being a plate, as you require so much wood to heat the plate and still boil water. A large frying pan is great and will still pre cook your meat and you can sling it on the grill to finish off. Do not use one with a wooden handle, you will certainly burn it off with time. To protect your self from hot handles, keep a pair of leather welding gloves close by. If the handle is very hot, just grab it quickly with the gloves and remove off the grill and place on the ground. Do not keep holding the handle, as even the heavy leather will burn.

Why have a grill, well if you don't sure enough when you wedge your saucepan in the fire or balance it on the timber it will tip over and all your evening meal becomes grilled whether you like it or not.

Stir-fries are great; they are fast and very nourishing. Try and mix foods on a time basis, i.e. get the rice on boil first. Do other tasks, and then come back drop a few vegetables in, thicker ones first. Quickly put the frying pan on, having diced some garlic and ginger drop in some olive oil (don't have pan too hot). Drop in very thin diced meat or cubes of fish. After three minutes drain the rice and vegetables and chuck in the frying pan with the meat or fish and stir pouring in some soy sauce.

"What about the steak and spuds" I hear you cry. Well they don't take long either but to speed things up, slice the potatoes thin and pre-boil, while cooking the meat and vegetables, you can then sling the potatoes in the pan to crispen up if you choose. There are a multitude of meals that can be done that take no more than half an hour.

The author doesn't even make deserts but uses either fresh or canned fruit with fruitcake or similar pre purchased. No time for baking unless there is a chef on board who just loves spending time cooking.

A few small useful hints, use a garden hanging basket rod as a cooking pot or billy remover if things are really hot, then use the gloves later.

There is nothing like billy tea, but to get the best results, make sure you have what we call a rolling boil, where the water is really bubbling. Pick up the tea leaves with four fingers and toss into the billy, have a clean bush stick handy and stir vigorously for a good 15 seconds, then grab the hook and pull off the fire tapping the sides of the billy. The leaves will settle right to the bottom if you had a real hot rolling boil. It's the most thirst quenching drink even on the hottest day.

Cooking over an open fire can get you really hot, if you stay for any length of time. Stay back from the fire and when you want to turn or stir items, grab the leather glove, pull off the fire and stir on the ground away from the fire, then put it back on the hot fire, you will not get so hot.

As mentioned previously, a rear light turned on from the dash that lights up the cooking area makes everything much easier. You can see what you are eating, then when the eating is done, one can turn off the light and drink a drop of wine or a beer around the glowing coals, the best part of a long day and one of the privileges we can enjoy in Western Australia.

Before retiring to bed, make sure the fire is just a small pile of coals and if you think the night is going to be windy, then pile some earth over the ash, they will still be hot in the morning to re start the fire. When departing dig and bury the fire, making sure everything is well out and covered as if you had never been there.

MASTER PARKS LIST

No.	Park	Page Number	Phone Number	Admission Fees	Camping/Fees	Caravans	Barbecues	Picnic Site	Toilets	Ranger	Walks/Trails	Km.s from Perth
	PERTH REGION											
1	Araluen Park	48	08 9490 3460	●			●	●	●▼		●	30
2	Avon Valley N.P.	40	08 9571 3066	●	▼		●	●	●	●	●	80
3	Bibbulmun Track	53										18
4	Bibra Lake	30	08 9431 6500				●	●	●		●▼	18
5	Bickley Brook	47									●	24
6	Bold Park	38	08 9387 0800								●	7
7	Booragoon Lake	31	08 9431 6500								●	11
8	Boulder Rock	51	08 9390 5977					●			●	44
9	Bungendore Reserve	47	08 9390 5977								●	33
10	Canning River R.P.	34	08 9405 1222				●	●	●▼		●	15
11	Christmas Tree Well	48	08 9390 5977				●	●			●	72
12	Churchman's Brook Dam	52	08 9397 5286				●	●	●	●	●	23
13	Ellis Brook Reserve	46						●			●	25
14	Forrestdale N.R.	32	08 9390 5977				●	●	●		●	25
15	Fred Jacoby Park	46	08 9295 1955				●	●	●		●	37
16	Gleneagle	53	08 9390 5977				●	●	●		●	55
17	Gooseberry Hill	42	08 9298 8344									16
18	Herdsman Lake	32	08 9405 1222				●	●	●		●	7
19	Hills Forest Discovery Centre	45	08 9295 2244				●	●	●	●	●	37
20	John Forrest N.P.	43	08 9298 8344	●			●	●	●▼	●	●	26
21	Kalamunda N.P.	42	08 9298 8344								●	18
22	Kings Park	37	08 9480 3600				●	●	●▼	●	●▼	2
23	Karakamia	44	08 9572 3169	●				●	●	●	●	52
24	Langford Park	48	08 9538 1078				●	●	●		●	54
25	Lesmurdie N.P.	46	08 9298 8344				●		●		●	22
26	Manning Reserve	30	08 9411 3444				●	●	●▼		●	24
27	Marmion M.P.	25	08 9432 5111							●		25
28	Mt Dale C.P.	51	08 9390 5977				●	●				64
29	North Ledge	45	08 9295 1955				●	●	●		●	40
30	Paruna Sanctuary	44	08 9572 3169	●				●	●		●	52
31	Penguin Island C.P.	22	08 9432 5111					●	●▼	●	●▼	43
32	Rottnest Island	23	08 9432 9111	●	▼		●	●	●▼	●	●▼	30
33	Serpentine N.P.	50	08 9525 2128	●			●	●	●	●	●	55
34	Shoalwater M.P.	27	08 9432 5111							●		41
35	South Ledge	45	08 9295 1955				●	●	●		●	42
36	Spectacles N.R.	31	08 9431 6500					●	●		●	28
37	Star Swamp Reserve	33									●	18
38	Sullivan's Rock	49	08 9390 5977				●	●			●	65
39	Swan Estuary M.P.	34	08 9431 6500								●	2
40	Thomsons Lake N.R.	31	08 9405 1222								●	34
41	Walyunga	41	08 9571 1371	●			●	●	●▼	●	●	40
42	Whiteman Park	38	08 9249 2446				●	●	●▼	●	●▼	18
43	Woodman Point	27	08 9431 6500				●	●	●▼		●	22
44	Wungong Dam	52	08 9399 2212				●	●		●	●	35
45	Yanchep N.P.	35	08 9561 1004	●			●	●	●▼	●	●▼	51
46	Yellagonga R.P.	33	08 9405 1222				●	●	●		●	17
	SOUTH WEST REGION											
47	Beedelup N.P.	69	08 9776 1207	●			●	●	●		●	308
48	Canebrake Pool	62	08 9787 2322		●	●	●	●	●▼			254
49	Capel Wetlands	58							●		●	209
50	Chapman Pool	62	08 9757 2322		●	●	●	●	●			282
51	D'Entrecasteaux N.P.	70	08 9776 1207	●	●		●	●	●	●	●	376
52	Forest Heritage Centre	60	08 9538 1078	●					●▼		●▼	96
53	Gloucester N.P.	66	08 9776 1207	●			●	●	●▼	●	●	332
54	Hoffman Mill	61	08 9729 1505		▼	●	●	●	●▼			143
55	Hut Pool	62	08 9840 1027				●	●	●		●	274
56	Lane Poole C.P.	60	08 9538 1078		▼	●	●	●	●▼	●	●	106
57	Leeuwin-Naturaliste N.P.	63	08 9752 1677	●	●	●	●	●	●▼	●	●▼	250
58	Leschenault Peninsula C.P.	58	08 9797 0552		▼		●	●	●▼	●	●	160
59	Mandalay Beach	69	08 9840 1027					●			●	421
60	Shannon N.P.	71	08 9776 1207	●	▼	●	●	●	●▼	▼	●▼	351
61	Stirling Dam	61	08 9729 1505				●	●	●	●	▼	155
62	Sues Bridge	62	08 9757 2322		▼	●	●	●	●			268
63	Tuart Forest N.P.	59	08 9752 1677				●	●	●			217
64	Yalgorup N.P.	57	08 9582 9333		▼		●	●	▼	●	●	96
65	Warren N.P.	66	08 9776 1207	●	●		●	●	●▼	●	●	350
	SOUTH COAST REGION											
66	Cape Arid N.P.	93	08 9075 0055	●	●	●	●	●	●	●	●	840
67	Cape Le Grand N.P.	92	08 9075 9022	●	▼	●	●	●	●▼	●	●	746
68	Centre Road	74	08 9840 1027	●			●	●	●		●	403
69	John Rate Lookout	76	08 9840 1027				●	●	●			417
70	Esperance Lakes N.R.	91	08 9071 3733								●	721
71	Fernhook Falls	75	08 9840 1027		▼		●	●	●			395
72	Fitzgerald River N.P.	87	08 9835 5043	●	●		●	●	●	●	●	479
73	Mt Frankland N.P.	75	08 9840 1027		●		●	●	●		●	370
74	Porongurup N.P.	82	08 9853 1095	●			●	●	●	●	●	377
75	Recherche Archipelago N.R.	91	08 9071 3733									728
76	Stirling Range N.P.	84	08 9827 9230	●	▼	●	●	●	●	●	●	338
77	Stokes Inlet N.P.	90	08 9076 8541	●	▼	●	●	●	●	●	●	636
78	Tree Top Walk	77	08 98401826	●					●▼	●	●▼	438
79	Torndirrup N.P.	80	08 9842 4500							●	●	420
80	Two Peoples Bay N.R.	81	08 98464276				●	●	●▼	●	●▼	439
81	Valley of the Giants	76	08 98401826	●					●▼	●	●▼	433
82	Walpole - Nornalup N.P.	76	08 9840 1027		▼	●	●	●	●▼	●	●▼	423
83	Waychinicup N.P.	82	08 9842 4500		●		●	●	●	●	●	469
84	West Cape Howe N.P.	79	08 9842 4500		●		●	●	●	▼	●	384
85	William Bay N.P.	78	08 9840 9255						●	●	●	425
	WHEATBELT REGION											
86	Boyagin Rock N.R.	105	08 988 1144				●	●	●		●	145
87	Buckleys Breakaway	105	08 988 1144								●	139
88	Dryandra Woodland Reserve	98	08 9884 5231		▼	●	●	●	●		●	160
89	The Humps N.P.	107	08 988 1144								●	356
90	Wave Rock Reserve	107	08 988 1144	●		●	●	●	●		●	341
	GOLDFIELDS REGION											
91	Boorabbin N.P.	114	08 9021 2677				●	●	●			450
92	Burra Rock N.R.	112	08 9021 2677		●		●	●	●			609
93	Cave Hill N.R.	112	08 9021 2677				●	●	●		●	635
94	Dundas N.R.	–	08 9021 2677									750
95	Frank Hann N.P.	111	08 9071 3733									492
96	Goongarrie Station	115	08 9021 2677		●		●		●			720
97	Holland Track	116										390
98	Jaurdi Station	114	08 9021 2677		●		●		●			520
99	Kalgoorlie Arboretum	117	08 9021 2677					●	●		●	596
100	Peak Charles N.P.	113	08 9071 3733				●	●	●		●	655
101	Rowles Lagoon C.P.	115	08 9021 2677		●		●	●	●			627
102	Victoria Rock N.R.	113	08 9021 2677				●	●	●		●	597
	NULLABOR REGION											
103	Eucla N.P.	123										1489
104	Nuytsland N.R.	122	08 9071 3733									1215
	MID WEST REGION											
105	Abrolhos Islands	136	08 9921 5955									474
106	Alexander Morrison N.P.	132	08 9652 7043									251
107	Badgingarra N.P.	132	08 9652 7043								●	190
108	Coalseam C.P.	133	08 9921 5955		●		●	●	●▼			402
109	Coomaloo N.R.	132	08 9652 7043					●			●	227
110	Drovers Cave N.P.	129	08 9652 7043									261
111	Ellendale Pool Greenough Shire	133	08 9921 2533				●	●	●			418
112	Kalbarri N.P.	137	08 9937 1140	●			●	●	●	●	●▼	550
113	Lake Logue N.R. Carnamah Shire-Eneabba	133	08 9955 1058		●		●	●	●		●	282
114	Lesueur N.P.	131	08 9652 7043							●	●	250
115	Moganmoganing N.R.	127										114
116	Moore River N.P.	127	08 9561 1004								●	120
117	Nambung N.P.	128	08 9652 7043	●			●	●	●▼	●		245
118	Shark Bay World Heritage Area: Monkey Mia Reserve	138	08 9948 1366	●			●	●	●	●	●	853
119	Francois Peron N.P.	140	08 9948 1208	●	▼		●	●	●▼	●	●	841
120	Shell Beach C.P.	141	08 9948 1208						●			786
121	Hamelin Pool Marine N.R.	140	08 9948 1208								●	732
122	Stockyard Gully N.P.	129	08 9652 7043					●			●	295
123	Tathra N.P.	130	08 9652 7043									295
124	Watheroo N.P.	133	08 9652 7043					●	●			215
	PILBARA REGION											
125	Cape Range N.P.	146	08 9949 1676	●	▼	●	●	●	●▼	●	▼	1311
126	Collier Range N.P.	152	08 9143 1488									1034
127	Dampier Archipelago	148	08 9143 1488		●							1528
128	Karijini N.P.	150	08 9143 1488	●	▼	●	●	●	●▼	●	●▼	1378
129	Kennedy Range N.P.	159	08 9948 1208		●				●		●	1142
130	Millstream-Chichester N.P.	148	08 9143 1488	●	▼	●	●	●	●▼	●	●▼	1480
131	Mount Augustus N.P.	157	08 9948 1208					●	●	▼	●	1392
132	Ningaloo M.P.	145	08 9949 1676							●		1132
133	Rudall River N.P.	153	08 9143 1488									1544
	KIMBERLEY REGION											
134	Drysdale River N.P.	173	08 9168 4200	●								3021
135	Geikie Gorge N.P.	164	08 9191 5121				●	●	●▼	●	●	2658
136	Lennard Gorge	169	08 9191 1332									2591
137	Mitchell Plateau (Ngauwudu)	174	08 9168 4200	●						●		3034
138	Mirima N.P.	171	08 9168 4200	●				●	●	●	●	3329
139	Mount Hart	166	08 9191 4645						●			2641
140	Parry's Lagoon	171	08 9168 4200								●	3320
141	Prince Regent N.R.	173	08 9168 4200									–
142	Purnululu N.P.	175	08 9168 4200	●	▼		●	●	●	▼	●	3122
143	Rowley Shoals M.P.	115	08 9192 1036									2537
144	Silent Grove/Bell Gorge	169	08 9193 1411		▼	●	●	●	●	▼	●	2635
145	Tunnel Creek N.P.	164	08 9193 1411							●		2664
146	Windjana Gorge N.P.	165	08 9193 1411		▼	●	●	●	●	▼	●	2699
147	Wolfe Creek Crater	177	08 9168 4200									3067

▼ denotes in appropriate columns (**bold**) **Camping** fee; **Toilets** for Disabled; **Ranger** present seasonally; & **Walks/Trails** for Disabled.

Please note: phone numbers can change; also rangers may not be available. Contact CALM H.O. Perth 08 9334 0333 for further info.

Abbreviations: N.P. National Park; **R.P.** Regional Park; **N.R.** Nature Reserve; **M.P.** Marine Park; **C.P.** Conservation Park

References for Maps

- Freeways
- Proposed Freeways
- Highways
- Unsealed Highways
- Main Roads
- Sealed Roads
- Unsealed Roads
- Tracks
- Railways
- Rivers & Lakes
- National Parks & Reserves
- Marine Parks
- × Mountains
- × Hills
- ∘ Rock Formations

Diving	4WD Four wheel driving
Picnic tables	Parking
Shelter shed	Fishing
Toilets	Ranger station
Barbecues	Fuel
Drinking water	Accommodation
Caravaning	Swimming
Camping	Boating
Walking tracks	Telephone
Lookout	Wheel chair access
No camping	Gas barbecues
Caving	No caravaning
Climbing	Station stay
Meals	Farm stay
Information	Chalet stay
Town with all facilities	Telephone
Showers	

This concludes Section 1 as stated in the text.

These are suggestions only to assist you with your pre-travel planning. Seek further advice from Four Wheel drive clubs, the RAC and more in depth books than this. When you have finished the planning and preparation stage the following parks and reserves in Section 2 await your travels.

Longreach Bay, Rottnest Island

Perth
REGION

SECTION 2

Wandoo woodland with acacia understorey–Avon Valley National Park

Perth
REGION

Situated on the Swan Coastal Plain, Perth is one of the most isolated state capitals in the world, but its growth outstrips most other Australian cities having to date a population of 1.4 million people. Although the city is spreading fast and wide, there are still many wonderful parks that the visitor can retreat to and find peace and quiet away from the pressures of urban life.

Perth lies on the Swan Coastal Plain, a broad flat sandy region that runs alongside the western edge of the massive granite Yilgarn Shield. It stretches from the Whicher Range near Busselton in the south to beyond Gin Gin in the north. From the coastline to the edge of the Darling Range, the plain varies between only twenty to thirty kilometres wide with limestone and sand being the principal underlying soils.

Due to the expanding city, there are few parks adjacent to the city coastline with Woodman Point south of Fremantle being one of the few. There are however, still good beach reserves such as at City Beach. The larger areas of woodland on the coast are north and south of the city as in Yanchep and south of Rockingham.

There are a few parks on the coastal plain where one can walk and see few people. At the northern end of Thompson Lake for example are some areas that you can walk without seeing anybody and it is hard to imagine that one is walking close to a city centre.

Most of the larger parks are located in the hills. Some of them like Walyunga and John Forrest National Park have high numbers of visitors particularly in the spring months where as others like Avon Valley National Park or parts of Kalamunda National Park can be relatively quiet. If you seek out the smaller reserves mentioned in the book like Bickley Brook or bungendore Reserve, you will find some wonderful walking trails and some very secluded picnic sites where few people visit.

The vegetation on the coastal belt consists of heathlands and shrublands overlying rocky areas of limestone, supporting stands of Parrotbush (*Dryandra sessilis*), Honey Myrtle (*Melaleuca huegelii*), an array of spectacular spring wildflower heaths and some important mallees such as Fremantle Mallee (*Eucalyptus foecunda*), Limestone Mallee (*E. petrensis*) and the rare and restricted Yanchep Mallee (*E. argutifolia*).

Set immediately behind the Quindalup coastal limestone belt, is a set of wetlands that runs all the way from Yanchep down to Busselton. In the Perth region they lie on the Spearwood and Bassendean sands. These wetlands, particularly the Beeliar wetlands, are a very important feature of Perth and hold a great variety of wildlife, which will be discussed later in this section. These lowlands are dominated by Flooded Gum (*E. rudis*), Holly leaved Banksia (*Banksia ilicifolia*) and the Freshwater paperbark (*Melaleuca rhaphiophylla*).

Covering most of the undulating Swan Plain are mixed woodlands of eucalypts, predominantly Jarrah (*E. marginata*), Tuart (*E. gomphocephala*) and Marri (*E. calophylla*) and banksias such as Firewood Banksia (*B. menziesii*), Slender Banksia (*B. attenuata*) and Bull Banksia (*B. grandis*).

Above the Swan Coastal Plain rises a low range of hills known as the Darling Range, stretching 350 km from north to south and just 50 km wide near Perth. The range is the western edge of the ancient granite plateau, known as the Yilgarn Craton. The bedrocks represent some of the oldest rocks on earth consisting of granites, gneisses and quartzites and are over 2500 million years old.

Over a million years ago the granite bedrocks split away and the Darling Fault was created, lifting the eastern block 10,000 m above the western block and now the western block is covered by the coastal sands and oceans we see today.

Here ancient monsoonal climates produced a pebbly orange laterite crust formed some 10 million years ago. It is here that one of Australia's major forest regions occur and the two dominant trees are the Jarrah and Marri eucalypts.

The Darling Range has an annual rainfall of 1300 mm on the western edge near the scarp and drops right down to 700 mm on the eastern side.

Jarrah (*Eucalyptus marginata*) and Marri (*Eucalyptus calophylla*) are the predominant trees of the Darling Range with other trees like Bull Banksia (*B. grandis*) and Sheoak (*Allocasuarina fraseriana*) being also common.

On winter-wet sandy sites a low forest of paperbark (*Melaleuca rhaphiophylla*) and (*M. preissiana*), and Swamp Banksia (*B. littorea*) occur. On the damper loamy river sites Blackbutt (*E. patens*), and Flooded Gum (*E. rudis*) occur.

Where the Darling Range drops away on the east and rainfall is lower, the Jarrah/Marri forest converges with Wandoo (*E. wandoo*) and Powderbark Wandoo (*E. accedens*) on white and granite clays.

Where to go: The Perth region has been divided into three primary areas so that the reader can combine various destinations in one visit if need be. **1. Coastal Parks 2. Swan Coastal Plain Parks 3. Hills Parks**

Coastal parks
OF PERTH

Family looking at an Australian Sea-lion

Penguin Island
CONSERVATION PARK

Although Penguin Island is only a small island of 12.5 ha, it holds a wealth of wildlife and recreational opportunities for the visitor. Situated just 48 km from the centre of Perth, it lies 700 m from the Rockingham coastline in Shoalwater Bay. There is a regular ferry that transports people from Mersey Point (Rockingham) to the island, leaving on the hour from 9.00 am till 3.00 pm. The journey takes approx.15 min.

When you first disembark on the island, there is a general picnic site with tables located under the Rottnest Teatree *(Melaleuca lanceolata)*. There are no barbecue facilities or fires allowed on the island so bring foods that do not require fires to cook. Adjacent to the picnic area is the well-designed Penguin Experience – Island Discovery Centre and entry cost is included in your ferry ticket. Many people come to the island to try and see Little Penguins and it is not an easy task as they come on land at night. During the day, when not feeding, they live in burrows and under cave ledges away from strong sunlight. Scientists monitoring the population on the island became concerned about the increase in the number of people trying to find these marine birds and felt the best solution was to build an enclosure with a sea water pool and a viewing area. It has been a great success and is a credit to those involved in the project.

The island's population of Little Penguins *(Eudyptula minor)* is the largest colony in Western Australia. Penguins are members of an ancient group of birds that are found only in the Southern Hemisphere. There are 17 species in the world and they vary in size from the Little Penguin which is the smallest at 40 cm long to the 1m tall Emperor Penguin of the Antarctic.

Penguins are flightless birds but in water their well-developed wings make them masters of underwater flight.

Little Penguins are the only penguins that nest on the mainland of Australia and those on Penguin Island are mainly sedentary (stay in the local area) although immature birds will disperse to other colonies. After feeding on small fish and crustaceans during the day, they form small groups just off shore one or two hours after sunset, then together they walk up the various beaches to their respective breeding or roosting burrow. Breeding normally takes place between June and November. Little Penguins have very dense feathers, forming a watertight barrier above the skin. Unlike most birds that shed feathers throughout the year, Little Penguins come on land during December and January to moult. During this period they cannot return to the water to feed and must remain on land until they have developed a totally new coat.

Besides the penguins there are several other birds that nest on the island, the two major species being the Crested and Bridled Terns. The Crested Tern is all white with a black crest and the Bridled Tern has sooty black wings and back as well as a black cap with a black line running from the base of the beak to the eye — hence the name 'Bridled'.

Australian Sea-lions: There are three families of seals. The Ododbenidae or walrus, the Otariidae or eared seals and the Phocidae or true seals. Only two species of seal breed in Western Australia and they are both eared seals *(family Otariidae)*. The New Zealand Fur-seal *(Artocephalus foresteri)* breeds on islands off the south coast but here on Penguin Island you may see the Australian Sea-lion *(Neophoca cinerea)*. The Sea-lion is the larger of the two seals attaining lengths of over 3.5 m and weighing 1,100 kg.

Their common name is derived from the long shaggy mane that the bull seals have. Males will often fight for dominance over a group of females and while at rest they may seem docile, the sea-lions can be aggressive, so if they are basking on a beach or one of the many caves on the island, keep yourself at a safe distance. Do not land on breeding islands, as the females are highly protective of their young and will attack if people walk into a breeding colony. Also when swimming, contrary to belief, you should not swim too near seals as some may become aggressive.

Seals were hunted almost to extinction in some areas and the Australian Sea-lion is in fact one of the rarer seals of the world with a population size of approx. 10,000 individuals. This is not a large number when you consider that their distribution stretches from the Abrolhos Islands to Kangaroo Island in South Australia. About 1,000 of the Sea-lions live between the Abrolhos and Perth and about 2,000 on the south coast of Western Australia.

Seals, like us, are mammals. They are warm blooded, feed their young on milk and are quite intelligent. They are totally adapted to a marine life, being masterful swimmers and feed on squid, shellfish and fish. They can dive to great depths; around 300 m below the surface. At shallow depths they seek their prey using their good eyesight but when at very low depths they detect their prey by echolocation and are able to distinguish their prey from static rocks. They do this by sending out high pitched noises that reflect back to their ears and are able to chase and catch fish by using the hairs on their muzzle to feel the prey.

What can you do on the island: After possibly visiting the Little Penguin Discovery Centre, there are numerous walks that will lead you to various beaches. If you are exploring the caves you may come across a sleeping seal or in the deep rock crevices you may catch a glimpse of a Little Penguin. From October onwards, the Bridled Terns will be nesting in the limestone holes and under the Sea Spinach *(Tetragonia decumbens)*. There are a few lizards on the island and the largest, the King's Skink *(Egernia kingii)*, are quite numerous and you may see them on their search for unattended nesting chicks or eggs.

There is a lookout in the centre of the island which gives you 360 degree views.

The western side of the island is popular with young surfers. Beach fishing is allowed but people are asked to be careful with casting as many people visit the island.

There is a wonderful dive site at the southern point of the island and it is one of the best locations to dive in the metropolitan area; as there is no need for scuba gear so it is an ideal place for beginners to enjoy snorkelling, maybe combine it with a picnic on the island. There are seagrass meadows and underwater limestone caves (do not enter caves as this can be very dangerous with sea currents). There are several low reefs that form a chain from the island reef platform. There is quite a variety of fish to be seen as well as colourful invertebrates.

To get to the dive site, take the path to the left of the Discovery Centre (there are normally resident DCLM officers who will assist you with information) and head along the beach to the end of the island. You will however need protective booties, as you must first walk across the reef platform to the edge of the reef where a drop off to a depth of 2-3 m exists. This dive site is best in the morning on a calm day or with only mild easterly or northerly winds blowing.

Main picnic ground

Rottnest Island

Affectionately called "Rotto" by Western Australians, this would have to be one of the most relaxing places to visit close to Perth. The island lies just 18 km off the coast and is 11 km long by 4.5 km wide. Its coastline provides wonderful moorings for boats, alternating between rocky cliffs and sandy beaches. The central part of the island has undulating low hills with quite a few salt lakes in the north eastern part of the island.

Although the island is administered by the Rottnest Island Authority, most of the island is still an 'A' class reserve, protecting the well known marsupial the Quokka (Setonix brachyurus) and many plants typical of coastal islands. It is an important wintering area for migrating waders from the Far East and Siberia.

History: In geological terms, Rottnest has only been an island for 6,500 years. Prior to this, sea levels were lower and the island was just a higher set of hills on the ancient coastal plain, but sea levels rose even higher than now on two occasions, once 5,500 years ago and again only 2,500 years ago. This greatly affected the plant life of the island.

The first record of any European to set foot on Rottnest was Samuel Volkerson, commander of the vessel the "Waeckende Boey" in 1658. It was another 38 years before another Dutch vessel DeGeelvinck, commanded by Willem De Vlamingh visited the island. It was he who named the island Rottnest meaning 'Rats' Nest'. When Vlamingh saw the small Quokka, he thought it was a large rat.

Not until nearly 200 years later did Captain James Stirling anchor in these waters on his journey to establish the colonial settlement of Swan, named after the unique Australian Black Swan that once frequented the Swan Estuary not so long ago.

The first European family to live on the island was the Thomson family, Thomson Bay being named after them. They settled on the island in 1831 making a basic living by farming sheep and curing fish for sale in the Swan Settlement. It was to be a short stay as 7 years later, the government took back the lease to form a prison to house Aboriginal people and in 1838, the first prisoners arrived. Many of the old buildings one can see today were built by the hard labour of Aborigines.

There are now developments in progress to identify the locality of Aboriginal burial sites and pay respects that are now well overdue.

In 1903 the prison was closed and the island became a retreat for tourists and then finally in 1917, the island was declared a reserve and a board was established to administer the island as a reserve and centre for tourism.

Today, Rottnest has a multitude of venues for tourists with all levels of accommodation including campsites, very basic chalets, cottages, motel units and two hotels to cater for some of the 250,000 people who visit the island each year.

Quokka

Australian Shelduck

▲Ruddy Turnstone

▼Crested Terns

Some of the Island's original accommodation is still used today on Rottnest

What to do: There are no vehicles allowed on the island except those run by the island authorities. However, there are bicycles for hire or you can bring your own. There are walking trails and the Rottnest Island Authority organise nature walks. There are some wonderful beaches, ideal for swimming particularly at The Basin, Longreach Bay and Geordie Bay. For those who have the time and energy, cycling to the other end of the island gives great rewards and even more beaches with fewer people. To cycle around the island will take you approximately 3 hours.

There are bus tours that tour the island stopping en route to look at Quokkas and various historical sites. Fishing is popular particularly from boats.

Flora and Fauna: The Quokka was once found throughout the south west but is now restricted to a few islands and some dense swamp heaths and dense river creek systems in the deep south west. On Rottnest, without the predation of feral animals, the Quokka is quite common and readily seen.

The Quokka is a distinct marsupial being the only member of its genus –Setonix.

Birds: Bird watching on the island can be quite rewarding along the coastal edge, seeing Osprey, Reef Heron, Ruddy Turnstone, Pied Oyster Catcher and Caspian Tern. On Green Island there is a small colony of breeding Bridled Terns. On the small islands on the central lakes Crested and Fairy Terns nest.

The lakes are perhaps the best place to see birds and many of our migrating waders feed on the edge of these lakes, including Red-necked Stint, Eastern Golden Plover, Terek Sandpiper, Curlew Sandpiper, Sanderling, Grey tailed Tattler, Greenshank, Red-necked Avocet, Pied Stilt and Banded Stilt. Banded Stilt come regularly to Rottnest but their breeding grounds are inland salt lakes which are often more than a thousand kilometres away.

A rare bird that is often sighted in summer is the beautiful wader the Red-necked Phalarope, which migrates all the way from the Siberian tundra. The Siberian population mostly over-winters on the northern New Guinea coastline, but for some reason many keep travelling south 5,000 km further than normal, making their journey over 10,000 km. They will lose at least a third of their body weight after these monumental flights.

Around the edges of the lakes, one of the less common parrots of Western Australia, the Rock Parrot, can be seen feeding on Samphire *(Halosarcia indica subsp. bidens)* and Beaded Samphire *(Sarcocornia quinqueflora)*. These small, dull green, parrots slightly bigger than Budgerigars, nest on the small offshore islands.

Flora: Most of the plants are very hardy, having to withstand the buffeting of hot dry winds often laden with salty sea spray. Near the beach line, the spiky plant is Beach Spinifex *(Spinifex longifolius)*. Small blue flowers with succulent leaves are Thick-leaved Fanflower *(Scaevola crassifolia)*. Less common but very attractive is the Wild Rose *(Diplolaena dampieri)* with pendant red flowers.

Rottnest was once well covered with vegetation but with land clearing, cutting of timber for fire wood and general fire damage, the vegetation cover has decreased. There are four native trees on the island, Rottnest Tea-tree *(Melaleuca lanceolata)*, Rottnest Island Pine *(Callitris preissii)*, Weeping Pittosporum *(Pittosporum phylliraeoides)* and Summer-scented Wattle *(Acacia rostellifera)*.

The more dominant large trees are all introduced such as the old Moreton Bay Figs and Aleppo Pines planted in the early 1900's. The tallest eucalypts are the Tuart trees *(Eucalyptus gomphocephala)* but these too were planted. Also the oldest and largest olive trees in the Perth region are on Rottnest.

Marine Life: Due to Rottnest's location in the centre of the south flowing warm Leeuwin Current, the marine life is more diverse than on the adjacent mainland coast; for example there are 97 species of tropical fish compared with 11 species on the Perth coast. There are 360 species of fish and 20 species of coral.

The Leeuwin Current is an interesting phenomenon. While most coastlines in these latitudes have cold waters, especially in winter, the waters off the Perth coast receive a thin 50 km band of southerly flowing warm water, with low

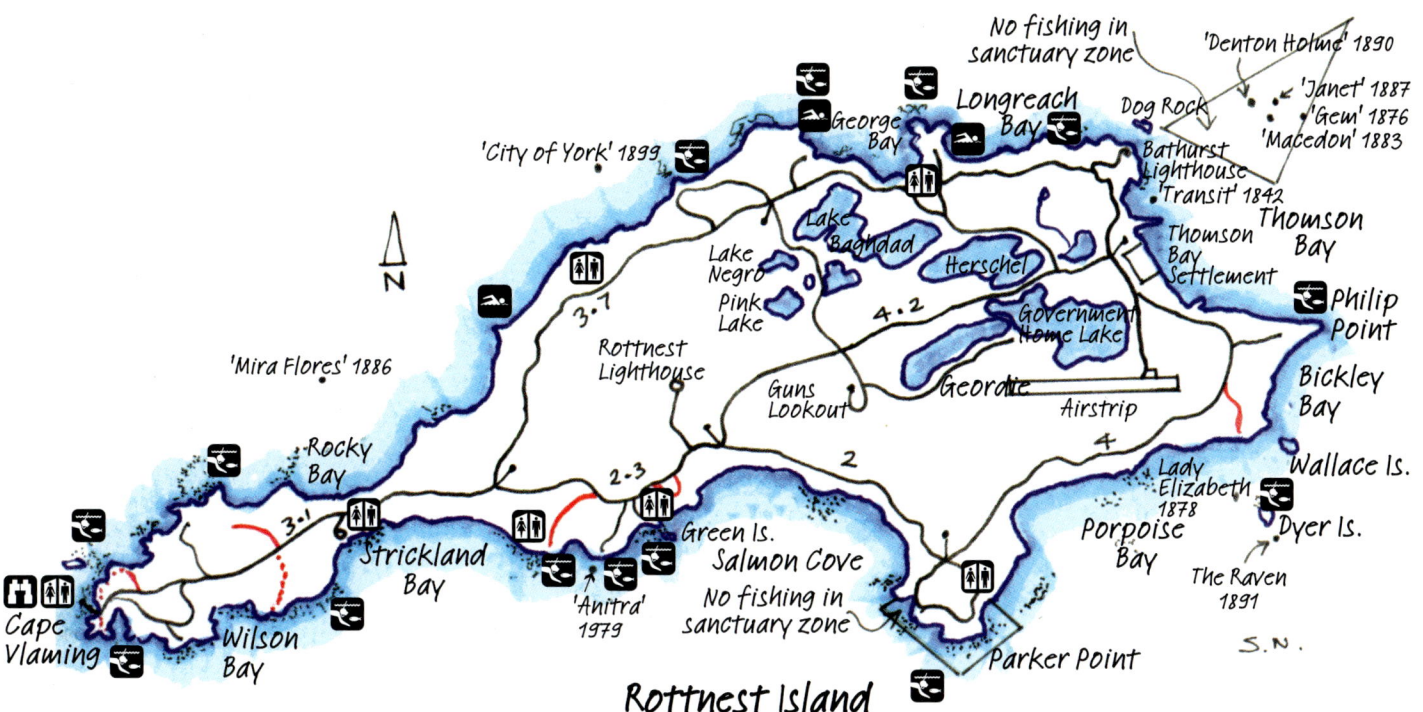

salinity, travelling between 2-4 knots. The current flows in autumn and winter, comes all the way down from Exmouth, past Cape Leeuwin and dissipates out past Esperance. The current brings with it a wealth of marine life that is food for many species and hence the high numbers of different fish that could not otherwise survive here.

The fishing is great and people are allowed to take the bag limit of crayfish in season by pot. There are two sanctuary zones where no fishing or collecting of any marine life is allowed. These areas are at Kingston Reef (Thompson Bay) and Parker Point/Little Salmon Bay. Spear guns and hand spears are not allowed on the island or in use on its coastal waters. Other than that, normal bag limits apply.

Diving: Rottnest is noted for its good dive sites. The Basin is one of the easiest dives and a good way to get used to snorkelling. Pocillopora Reef is a wonderful dive and can be done with just snorkel gear and is relatively easy. There are good dive sites at Little Parakeet Bay, Armstrong Point and Fish Hook Bay, Mary Cove, Celia Rocks, Little Salmon Bay and Geordie Bay.

There are dive companies that will take you to Rottnest and they know the area well, so it is well worth considering joining a group.

Remember lives have been lost doing SCUBA and snorkelling so do respect the sea, find out best weather conditions and local currents. Never use SCUBA gear without doing an accredited course. All divers using SCUBA on Rottnest must fly the international 'A' flag. This book should not be used as a guide for diving sites or diving technique. The diving localities are only discussed to let you know what opportunities there are in each area.

Marmion
MARINE PARK

Declared in 1987, this was the first Marine park in Western Australia. It covers an area of 10,500 hectares and extends from Trigg Island in the south to Burns Beach in the north.

Even though these waters are so close to urban development, they still hold much to enthral the visitor. The limestone reefs that run parallel with the coast contain underwater limestone platforms and caves with many temperate and tropical fish; in fact these waters hold 136 species of fish.

The warm Leeuwin current that flows down from the north allows these waters to hold, not only the temperate species of fish, but also some fish typical of waters further north in the tropics.

The park has extensive seagrass meadows that hold a wealth of marine life that make this a great spot for people to experience the wonders of diving both with snorkel and tanks.

Two species of mammal frequent these waters regularly, the Australian Sea-lion (*Neophoca cinerea*) and the Bottlenose Dolphin (*Hyperoondon planifrons*). In May the Humpback Whales (*Megaptera novaeangliae*) pass through these waters but are rarely seen on the journey north, as the adult whales are intent on getting to the breeding grounds in the tropics. When they return from breeding, however, between September to mid November, the adults, particularly the females with young, take their time passing through these waters. It is well worth taking one of the whale watching tours that depart from Hillarys to view these wonderful creatures.

There are three main zones that the visitor should be aware of when travelling in these waters.

1. Sanctuary Zones: The three sanctuary zones are Little Island, The Lumps and Boyinaboat Reef. A floating marker buoy in each corner of each sanctuary with the words "sanctuary zone" written down the vertical pipe easily identifies them. These are areas that you can visit and explore but there is no fishing or collecting of marine life allowed and penalties do apply. They are particularly good areas to dive.

2. Recreation Zones: In the southern area just south of Beach Road is the Watermans Observation Area adjacent to the fisheries research laboratory. This area is used by scientists to monitor the conditions of marine life and no form of fishing other than line fishing from the shore is allowed.

3. General Use Zone: This covers the majority of the park and allows general recreation with normal bag limits applying as well as some licensed fishing under permit. Remember collecting without a permit or license is an offense and these waters are regularly patrolled. Spear fishing within 1800 m of the shoreline is not allowed and divers using scuba or hookah are not allowed to spearfish anywhere in the Marine Park.

Little Island: This is a great place to visit and lies just 2 km from Hillarys Boat Harbour. Here Australian Sea-lion can often be seen. Close to the island there are extensive limestone reefs and seagrass meadows with colourful coral, anemones and fish.

Marmion Marine Park

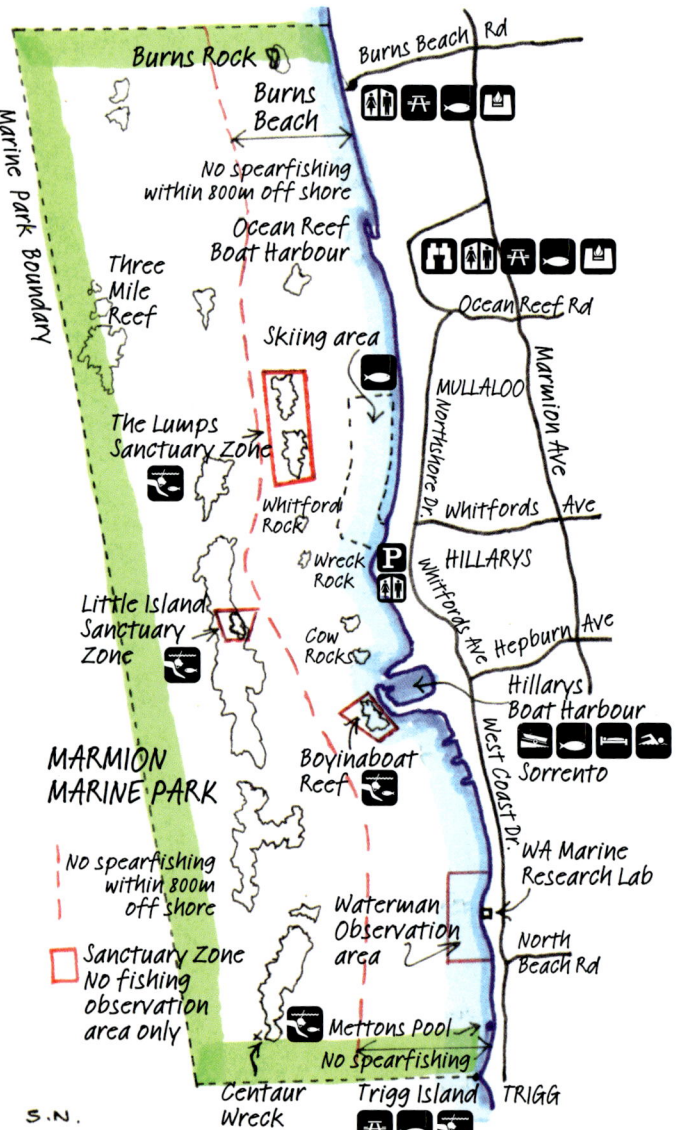

The beach within Hillarys Boat Harbour

DCLM have created an Underwater Nature Trail that explains details about the interesting marine lifeforms of this area. As you snorkel (or dive) along the trail there are 10 information plaques to search for and find. You may experience Sea-lions coming close to you under water as they are very inquisitive and simply want to check you out. To enjoy this encounter it is recommended that you swim slowly and take care to keep at a respectful distance from them.

There are several good dives in the park including Boyinaboat Reef just 75 m from the Hillarys sea wall, Cow Rocks 500 m west of Hillarys Boat Harbour, Wreck Rock 3 km north of Hillarys, North Lump 4.5 km north of Hillarys and Mettams Pool just 30 m off the shoreline near Lynn Street, North Beach.

It is worth purchasing DCLM's two books Dive and Snorkel Sites in WA and More Dive and Snorkel Sites in WA; they contain very good sketch maps of where to dive, including depths and degree of difficulty.

Remember, do dive with a friend and display a dive flag if you can. In summer, morning dives are best as the sea breeze comes in around midday making swimming tricky. In winter check forecasts beforehand and choose clear sunny days.

Underwater World: At Hillarys Boat Harbour is the Underwater World Oceanarium. It is a great place to take the family and introduce children to the wonders of the marine world. Included in the tanks are turtles, sharks, stingrays and countless species of fish. Twice a day, divers enter the tanks to feed the fish by hand; quite a sight to see for young and old.

From Hillarys Boat Harbour you can take a ferry to Rottnest.

Situated 8 km south of Fremantle, Woodman Point is an unusual reserve with an interesting history. In the 1890s the land was set aside for the quarantine and holding of stock prior to distribution. It was particularly needed when diseases broke out with cattle from the Kimberley.

In 1904, part of the land was set aside for the quarantine of people and was used intensely during and after the First World War between 1919 and 1924. The Quarantine facilities continued well into the 1950s, where people immigrating to Australia had their baggage and clothing fumigated as a precaution against foot and mouth disease.

From the early 1900s much of the reserve was used for the storage of explosives and if one walks through the 'preservation area' the old cemented sandbag bunkers can be seen with small gauge rail tracks that were used for the unloading of explosives.

The whole area has now developed into primarily recreational zones and is administered by DCLM.

John Graham Reserve located at the end of Nyerbup Road has a first class recreation area catering for large numbers of people, with extensive playing apparatus for children, electric barbecues, tables, shelters, toilets, showers and access to the beach. Much of the area is floodlit at night during most of the year. This is an excellent area for family groups.

Located in the 'preservation zone' accessed through a gate on Quarantine Road, is a small area of remnant Tuart and coastal heath that contains many of the plants of the Spearwood Dune system including some of the most extensive stands of Rottnest Pine in the Perth Metropolitan area. There are about 70 species of native plants found in the Woodman Point area and most can be found in this enclosed reserve.

Even though there are townships close by, this area is very peaceful and you can walk the few trails where some impressive large Tuart trees grow.

In the few patches of heath that occur, one can find Spider-net Grevillea (Grevillea thelemanniana), Panjang (Acacia lasiocarpa), Wild Rose (Diplolaena grandiflora) and Snakebush (Hemiandra pungens). Very few people know of this area so for the keen naturalist, it is well worth exploring.

There is a dive site located at the old "ammunitions" jetty where the old piers run about 100 m from the beach. There is a profusion of coloured invertebrate life growing off the old piers and quite a few fish frequent the deeper piers. Be careful of fishing lines.

At the southern end of the reserve is Woodman Spit and Woodman Point, accessed via Woodman Point View. People rock fish here and the spit itself on a quiet day holds many migrating waders in summer and occasionally Rock Parrots feed on the coastal succulents.

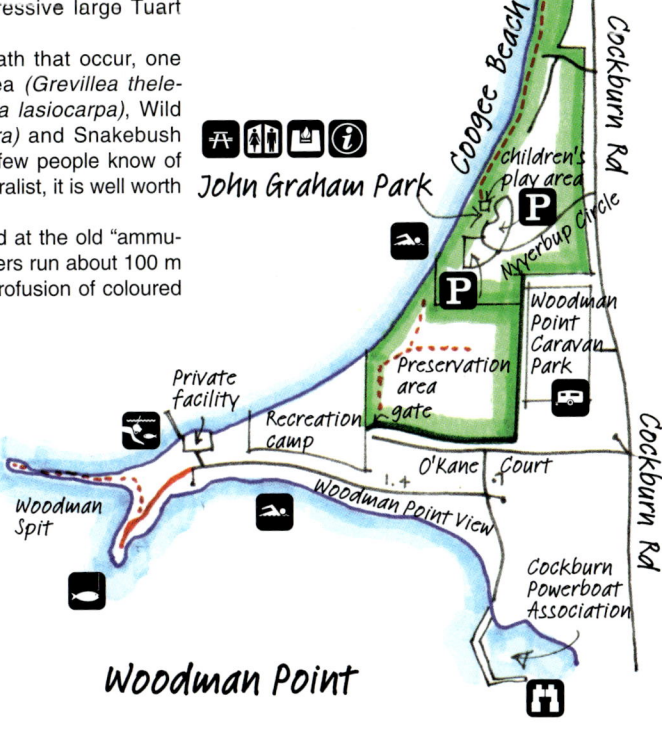

Shoalwater Islands
MARINE PARK

Looking out over Shoalwater Bay

The coastline of Western Australia stretches for 12,500 km; much of the adjacent coastal land is not protected under reserves or National Parks and it is vital that we conserve some of the coastal lands and marine waters that lie off them. It is not just for recreational reasons that we must protect much of our waters but simply that the state and health of these waters are what supports much of our amajor commercial fishing areas.

The Western Australian Government has recognised and set aside a few areas as marine parks and they include Ningaloo Marine Park, Shark Bay Marine Park, Hamelin Pool Marine Nature Reserve, Abrolhos Island Marine Park, Marmion Marine Park, the Swan Estuary Marine Park and, at Rockingham, the Shoalwater Islands Marine Park. As a rule, we tend to concentrate our interests and protection on land parks but there are also many areas that really should be set aside as marine parks. Luckily this is now being recognised as a very important environment, so we can protect all marine life for future generations. Australia is leading the way in many of these endeavours.

Shoalwater Islands Marine Park covers an area of 6540 ha, stretching from the northern end of Garden Island Causeway south to Becher Point. There are several small limestone islands located in the park, including Penguin and Seal Islands.

The area contains extensive seagrass meadows and limestone reefs and is one of the best locations to dive close to Perth. Besides the dive site mentioned south of Penguin Island there are a few other worthwhile dive sites including the south end of Seal Island. This is an ideal site for beginners but also has much to offer the experienced diver. The Sisters is a very good dive at the southern end of the park, 3 km north west of Becher Point. This is an easy to moderate dive depending on weather conditions.

Seal Island is used as a resting place for Australian Sea-lions after feeding in deeper waters. There is a 45 minute boat tour with commentary that visits close to Seal Island and returns people to Penguin Island so you can return from Penguin Island at your leisure.

Wetlands
OF PERTH

Southern Brown Bandicoot *(Isoodon obesulus)*
Photo by Michael Morcombe

Dragonfly *(Odonata coruliidae)* Photo by David Knowles

Baillons Crake

Spotless Crake

Buff-banded Rail

Australian Spotted Crake

Living in a city that has a Mediterranean climate with mild winters and hot dry summers, many people realise how precious water is. Long before Europeans settled on the Swan River, the coastal plain was always a major breeding ground for water birds. Many species that frequent the drier wetland lakes in the goldfields and wheatbelt in the winter months, would migrate to the Perth wetlands at the end of summer and autumn.

Things are, however, changing. Urbanisation is expanding at a phenomenal rate and many wetlands are being either filled in or degraded by removal of surrounding vegetation.

Often the lakes become over-enriched, or technically termed 'eutrophic' which means that waters are altered by higher levels of nutrients from many sources, including septic tanks that leach through the soil and fertilisers entering from cultivated and home gardens. This leads to a complex array of problems such as algal bloom or increased breeding numbers of midges that affect neighbouring properties.

When we remove or fill in our wetlands, it creates a chain reaction in the ecological balance of nature. However some species such as the rare migrating wader the Long-toed Stint require wet lush grasslands on the margins of wetlands, as well as mud to feed. The south west is the main destination in Australia for this bird to end its 12,000 km migration. When it gets here, areas that were once common feeding grounds are now gone and it must concentrate on the last remaining wetlands like Thompson and Forrestdale Lake to feed and survive.

Alas, there is a general lack of community awareness of the importance of wetlands and the complex ecosystem that exists around them. It is vital that if we are to have a balance between urban expansion and maintaining some degree of environmental balance, we must try to include wetlands into all major development schemes. Luckily there are some verygood wetland reserves that not only act as refuges for wildlife but are great recreational areas, having facilities for picnics, walking trails and playgrounds. There are 26 wetlands in the Beeliar chain of lakes alone.

Great Crested Grebe

Purple Swamphen

Black-fronted Dotterel

Nankeen Night Heron

White-faced Heron

Canning River Regional Park

Pacific Black Duck

Black Swan

Yellow-billed Spoonbill

Australian Wood Duck

Darter

Beeliar
WETLANDS

Running parallel with the coast are two chains of lakes and swamps in the south west part of Perth, known as the Beeliar Wetlands. They are named after the Aboriginal tribe that lived south of the Swan River and used these wetlands as a major hunting ground.

There are 26 lakes and numerous wetlands that occur in the Beeliar chain, covering an area of approximately 3400 hectares.

The first chain of wetlands lies on the Spearwood sand dune system about 1-3 km inland from the coast. The most northerly Lake is Manning Lake in Hamilton Hill and the southernmost is Madora Swamp north east of Mandurah.

The second chain lies about 6-8 km in from the coast. The northern-most is Blue Gum Lake in Mount Pleasant and the southern-most is Beenyup Pool in Baldivis.

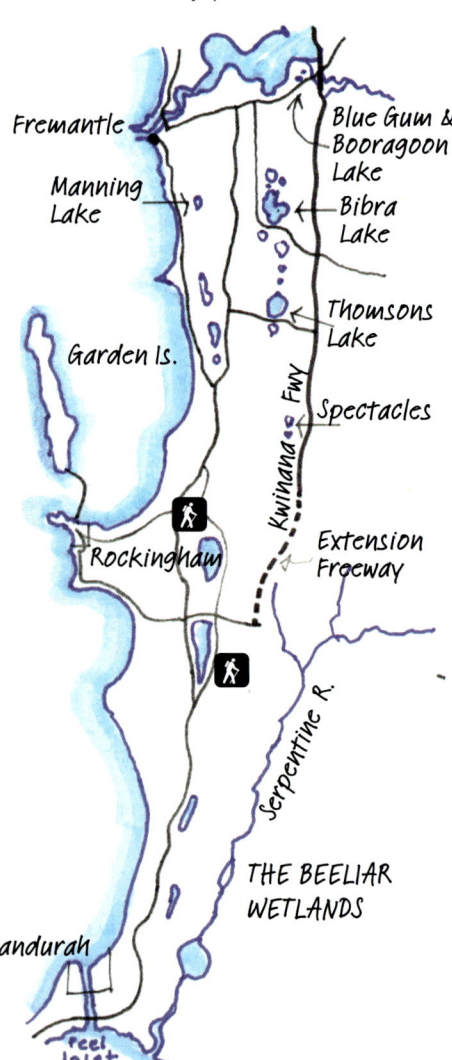

The Azelia Manning Homestead and Museum

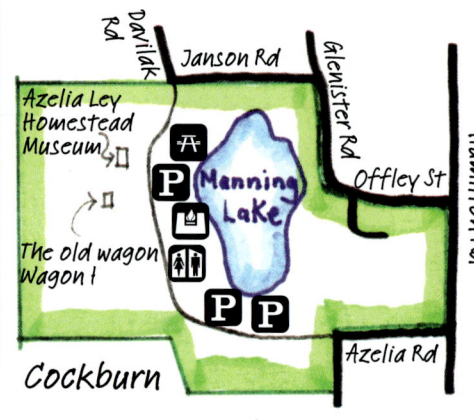

Manning
RESERVE

Named after the Manning family who were very prominent in the Cockburn area from 1859 onwards. Manning Reserve is a pleasant small park situated in the southern suburb of Hamilton Hill. Manning Lake is the most northerly of the western chain of the Beelair Wetlands. The small lake is surrounded by Swamp Paperbarks with White Ibis and Sacred Ibis common visitors to the water's edge.

In 1860, Charles Alexander Manning, a wealthy merchant bought 900 acres from George Robb, where the park is now located.

One of Charles' five sons, Lucius Manning, built a large house just south of the lake, Aborigines who lived in the area thought that bad spirits haunted the lake after dark and they called it "Davalak" – Devil's Lake. The name was given to the Manning's main homestead; years later the house was burnt to the ground.

Located in the grounds of the reserve is an old historical building now known as the Azelia Ley Homestead Museum. It was built by Lucius Manning for his daughter Azelia and her new husband Johnny Ley in 1905. After Azelia died the house was left in disrepair. It was only recently restored by the Cockburn Council in 1983, with help from a few prominent people who lived in the area. It now contains some fascinating historical artifacts and is well worth a visit as it is a great insight into early colonial life. The house and museum are open every Sunday from 1.30 to 4.30 pm. There are picnic tables, a gas barbecue, toilets and open grass areas for picnics adjacent to the lake.

The park is accessed either from the southern end of Davilak Avenue or Azelia Road off Hamilton Road, Hamilton Hill.

Boardwalk on east side of Bibra Lake

North Lake & Bibra Lake

Both these lakes provide opportunities to see a large number and variety of waterbirds, particularly during the summer months. There are picnic tables on the western side of North Lake and some walking tracks on the east side among extensive areas of banksia and Jarrah woodland as well as more open areas. North Lake provides a quieter more secluded area for walking than Bibra Lake. Bibra Lake, however, has more facilities. There is an extensive picnic ground on the west side near Progress Drive, with two children's playground facilities, barbecues, tables, toilets and normally a private caravan trailer with food and drink facilities. There is a 5.5 km cycle

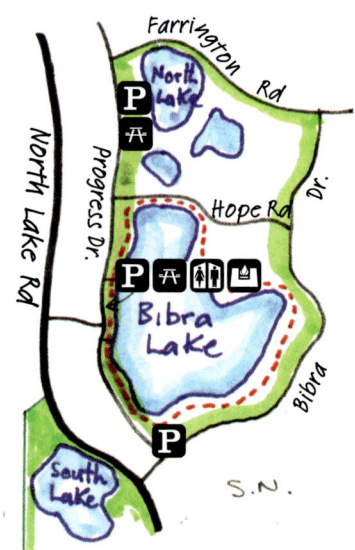

way that runs around the lake. On the eastern side there is a walkway leading out to the edge of the lake. The eastern side is quieter and more bush birds can be seen there. The city of Cockburn, in conjunction with a generous sponsor have developed Cockburn Wetlands Education Centre located on Hope Road, Bibra Lake here programs for community groups and schools are organised.

Booragoon Lake

This is an important breeding lake for Cormorants, primarily Little Cormorants but Pied, Black and Great Cormorant also breed here, although not in the same numbers as Little Cormorant. Other birds breed here such as Australian Darter, White Ibis and Yellow-billed Spoonbill. The reason why they still select this very urban location to breed, is that it is one of the few lakes that is still surrounded by paperbark trees. There is an excellent walkway out to the edge of the lake that is accessed from Alderidge Road between Shadbolt and Sicklemore Streets.

Boardwalk on north side of lake

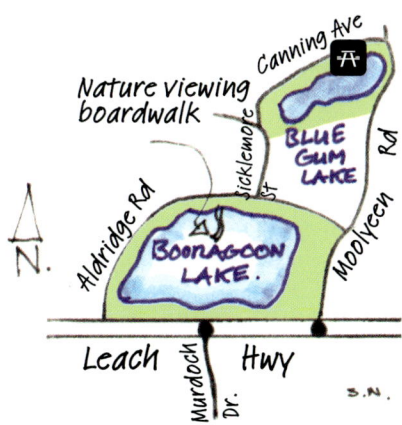

Thompson Lake

This is a very important wetland and is listed with RAMSAR as being of international importance for migratory birds that require wetlands. RAMSAR has listed wetlands throughout the world that play a major part in the preservation of feeding areas for migratory birds as well as sedentary birds.

Thompson Lake has had over 10,000 birds feeding in the shallow waters just prior to the lake drying out in early to mid summer. Most of these are Red-necked Stint as well as Greenshank, Sharp-tailed Sandpiper and the rare Long-toed Stint, Ruff and Pectoral Sandpiper have also been seen here.

The Swamp Harrier one of Australias raptors, can often be seen quartering just a few metres above the reed beds, while higher up the Little Eagle makes a spiralling flight over the wetlands. The lake will, however, invariably be dry by January and February. In the last few weeks when the mud is exposed on the perimeter of the lake hundreds of waders can be seen feeding in earnest before they make their 12,000 km flight to Russia and the far east.

For the keen bush walker, Thompson Lake is one of the few reserves in the metropolitan area where one can walk for the full 5.7 km around the

Jarrah forest at Thompson Lake

reserve (part of the walk is closed at present). There are four marked walking trails, three commence at Branch Circus entrance, leading off Hammond Road and the other starts at the Russell Road car park. There is another less used entrance at the end of Pearse Road that is closest to the reed beds.

The 2 m high vermin proof fence bordering the reserve has allowed the Southern Brown Bandicoot or Quenda *(Isoodon obesulus)* to increase in numbers. Both the Western Grey Kangaroo and Brush Wallaby exist in the park. On the early morning walks you will invariably see Western Grey Kangaroos.

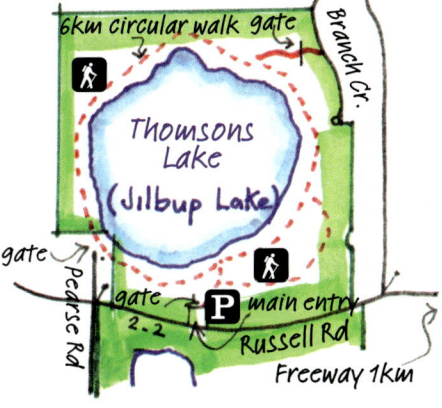

For those who are interested in plants the reserve supports a species list of over 200. In spring there are several species of orchids that can be found below the Jarrah and Tuart woodland.

When walking close to the reeds on the lake edge do be careful of Tiger Snakes; they are highly venomous but are rarely seen and will normally move away from you.

The main entry car park is off Russell Road just east of Pearse Road and this is the recommended entry point for those visiting the reserve for the first time.

The Spectacles

Mining companies often bear the brunt of conservationists' outcry but they often plough back thousands of dollars into community projects and the Spectacles is just one small example. Alcoa had the lease on mining this area for mineral sands, but due to the low yield they decided not to mine. Rather than just leave the land vacant, they worked in conjunction with Kwinana Town Council, DCLM and the Wetland Conservation Council to develop and protect the two wetlands located on their land, donating $250,000 towards the project in the process. The result is a series of walking trails and a very good boardwalk that passes through thick stands of paperbark trees to a bird hide. These paperbarks are the most extensive of any of the Beeliar Wetlands. You will not see hundreds of water birds here but there are several species that require these quite well wooded paperbark margins. The boardwalk through the Paperbark woodland gives the visitor one of the best locations for viewing this type of Swamp Paperbark habitat and if you are seeking a reserve

The boardwalk meanders through a thick stand of Paperbark woodland

that is very peaceful, then this reserve should please you. Between the 2 parking areas around the northern end of the reserve is an Aboriginal Heritage Trail. The interpretive trail tells stories of tradional life and aboriginal culture, as told by a Nyoongar elder.

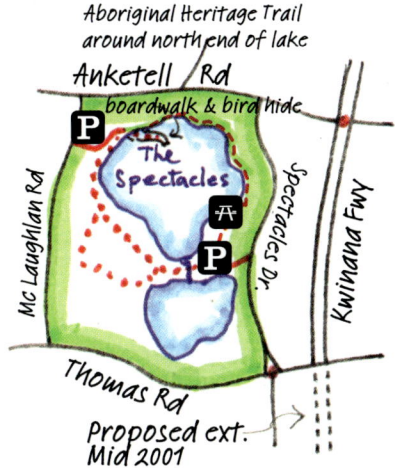

Access is off Spectacles Drive; there is a car park that leads to the wetlands and a nature walk. You can also park off McLaughlan Road that leads off Anketell Road. This is a shorter walk to the bird hide but walking the full length of the reserve is well worth it.

Other wetlands not in the Beeliar Wetland system

Paperbarks on the edge of Forrestdale Lake

Forrestdale Lake

The lake was originally known as Lake Jandakot, a Noongar word for Whistling Kite, but was changed to Forrestdale in 1915. Like Thompson Lake, the RAMSAR Convention also recognises Forrestdale Lake as being of great importance as a wetland environment and refuge for birds. In January 1983, 17,485 water birds were recorded on the lake. To date 72 species of waterbirds and 74 species of bush birds have been recorded for the entire nature reserve.

The number of birds reaches its peak just before the lake dries out in summer. As the waters recede, lots of marine life is exposed in the mud and waders take advantage of this situation. Some like the Red necked Stints take from the surface layer, the Greenshank and Wood Sandpiper feed deeper in the mud.

The lake, unlike those of the Beeliar system, lies on the older Bassendean dune system and is one of the largest lakes in the south west, covering an area of 192 ha.

There are a few access points to get to the lake. The main two lead to Skeet Memorial Park accessed off Armadale Road via Weld Street; there is a boardwalk and picnic table at the end of Moore Street. Weld Street leads to Commercial Road and if one drives around the perimeter of the lake you will come to the end of the road and you can park there.

The walk will take you past the extensive stands of Swamp Paperbark (*Melaleuca rhaphiophylla*), Flooded Gum (*Eucalyptus rudis*) and on the higher sandy soil there is banksia woodland consisting of Firewood Banksia (*Banksia menziesii*) and Slender Banksia (*Banksia attenuata*), as well as Sheoak (*Allocasuarina fraseriana*), Christmas Tree (*Nuytsia floribunda*) and Paperbark (*Melaleuca preissiana*).

Due to the many types of vegetation understorey the reserve supports 24 species of orchid, one of the largest numbers in the metropolitan area.

Forrestdale is one of the best places in the Perth region to try and see the elusive Southern Brown Bandicoot or Quenda (*Isoodon obesulus*). The best time is on the tracks just at dusk as they come out to feed.

For those interested in frogs, 7 species have been recorded including the Western Banjo Frog (*Limnodynastes dorsalis*), Western Green Tree Frog (*Litoria moorei*), Slender Tree Frog (*Litoria adelaidensis*), Moaning Frog (*Heleioporus eyrei*), Tiny Froglet (*Ranidella insignifera*), Red-thighed Froglet (*Crinia georgiana*) and Guenther's Toadlet (*Pseudophryne guentheri*).

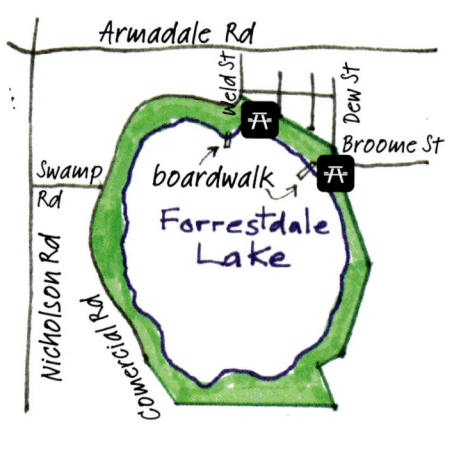

Picnic area off Lakeside Rd south west corner of Herdsman Lake

Herdsman Lake

Herdsman Lake Regional Park has had a varied and often controversial history. With the commencement of European settlement, it was first named 'Great Lake' by the surveyor J.S. Roe in 1837. Then, soon after, it got its current name 'Herdsman Lake'. At the turn of the century the Catholic Church owned the land. After the First World War part of the land was purchased from the Roman Catholic Church under the Soldier Settlement scheme. In 1921 they tried to drain the lake but with no real success, so it reverted back to a grazing and market garden growing area. In the 1960s pressure was mounting to have the marginal land developed for housing and that has continued until only the last few years.

Although only 6 km from the centre of the city, this is one of the best wetlands for viewing water birds in the Perth region. It has one of the greatest varieties of species, particularly ducks. There are also two very uncommon species that exist in the lake reed beds, the Australasian Bittern and the Little Bittern, but they are extremely hard to see and certainly present a challenge for the avid birdwatcher.

All the waterbirds illustrated in this section, can be seen at Herdsman Lake at most times of the year.

Turning off Pearson Street into Falcon Avenue will lead you to one of the best areas for viewing wildlife. There is a small play area and some tables under shade and a pleasant walkway. At the northern end of Lakeside Road is a path that will take you to a boardwalk leading into the reed beds but if the water is too high, the boardwalk will be covered.

At the northern side of the intersection of Selby Street and Fynn Street, there is a driveway that leads to the Herdsman Wildlife Centre run by the WA Gould League. Here schools and adult groups come to learn more about the natural world.

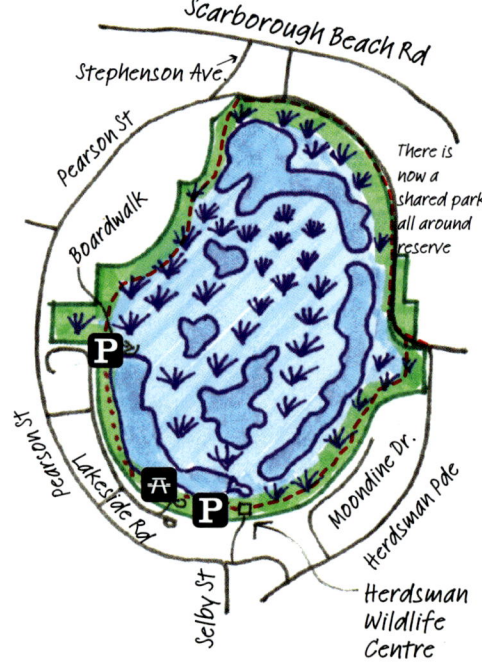

Paperbarks in the south west corner of Star Swamp

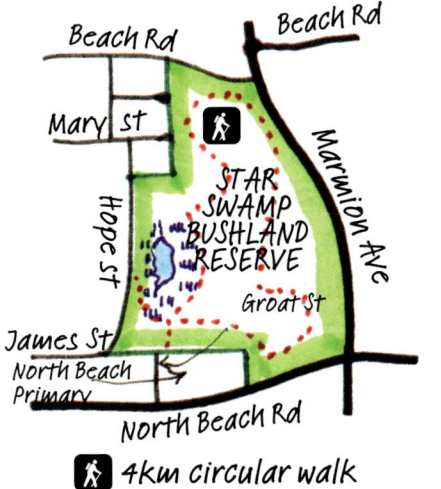

4km circular walk

Playing apparatus at Neil Hawkins Park

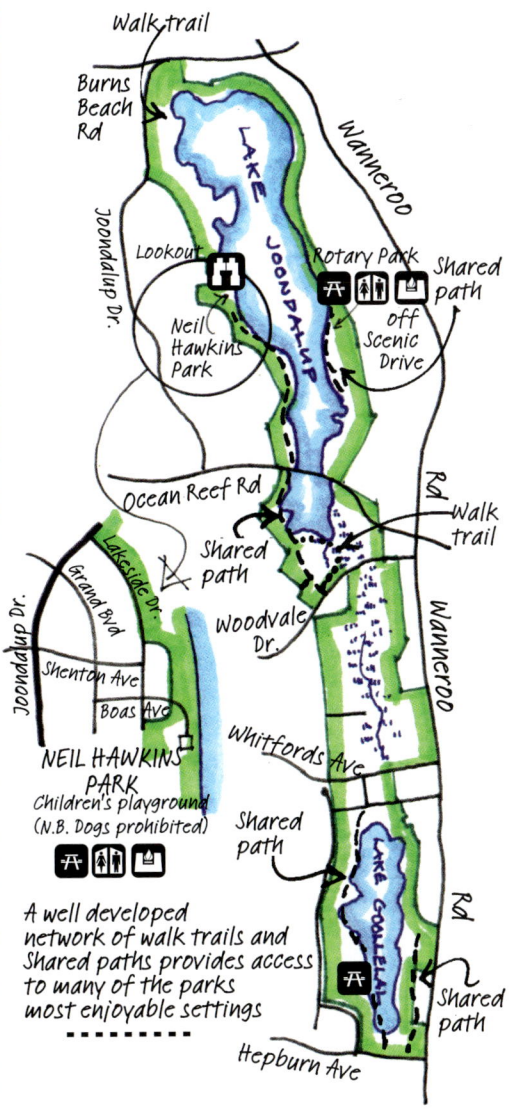

Star Swamp

Located in the northern suburb of North Beach, Star Swamp is a small one hundred hectare reserve, where one can take a walk on the Star Swamp Heritage Trail. This walk will take you through banksia woodland including Firewood Banksia, Slender Banksia, Acorn Banksia *(Banksia prionotes)* and Bull Banksia *(Banksia grandis)*, past Tuart trees and Swamp Paperbarks.

There are various points of interest along the trail such as an old Aboriginal camp and tree, plus a drovers camp, old orchards and pasture lands. There are good stands of the coastal limestone-frequenting tree, the Tuart. East of the Tuart forest is an area of heath and in spring this really comes to life. There are over 200 species of plant recorded for the Star Swamp reserve.

You can visit the wetland swamp from the car park at the end of Groat Street that leads off North Beach Road. You will see the Heritage walking trail sign and information board at the start of the 1.4 km walking trail. The walk is suitable for wheelchairs.

Local communities can do so much to protect the last remnant areas of bush that exist in this large city and groups such as the Waterman Community Association, the Friends of Star Swamp, Friends of Bold Park and the Friends of Forrestdale, as well as countless other community groups do so much to protect and nurture our last remaining remnant bushlands and wetlands. The individuals involved often go without any form of recognition and do not seek kudos but we have a lot to thank them for when we visit these areas.

Yellagonga
REGIONAL PARK

This is a fairly large regional park for a city environment, covering 1500 ha and includes two lakes, Lake Joondalup and Lake Goollelal running in a north-south direction between Joondalup Drive and Wanneroo Road. There are also two important swamplands, Walluburnup and Beenyup Swamps.

The park was named after the Aboriginal leader whose people lived in this area and the name of Joondalup also derives from an Aboriginal local word for the area.

The lakes are some of the largest freshwater lakes in the south west and their water quality compared with many other Perth wetland reserves is good, hence there are large numbers of waterbirds, especially ducks.

It is a good place to see Australasian Shoveler, Blue-billed Duck, Grey Teal, Pacific Black Duck and Musk Duck. It is also a good location for Yellow-billed Spoonbill, Australian White Ibis, White-necked Heron and White-faced Heron. Along the muddy margins of the lake you can see both Black-fronted Dotterel and Red-kneed Dotterel.

The southern part of Joondalup lake just south of the Ocean Reef Road causeway, often becomes dry in mid summer and it is one of the best localities to see many of the migratory waders.

For those who just want to come with the family or friends and have a picnic, the City of Joondalup has developed a very good picnic ground in Neil Hawkins Park, located at the bottom of Boas Avenue that leads off Lakeside Drive east of the Joondalup Shopping Centre. The park is equipped with barbecues, toilets, tables and a very good children's play facility.

Also on the eastern side of Lake Joondalup is a picnic area with barbecues in Rotary Park near the intersection of Scenic Drive and Church Street.

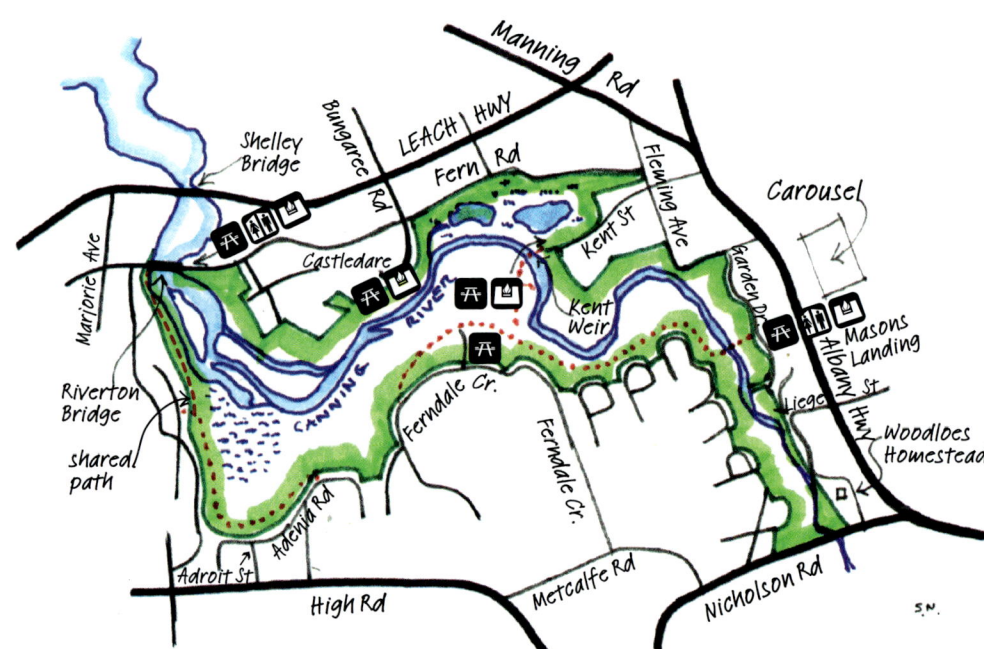

Quiet backwaters of Canning River

Canning River
REGIONAL PARK

This 266 ha reserve was set aside to protect the Canning River wetlands. Even though the park is surrounded by the busy suburbs of Wilson, Riverton, Ferndale and Cannington, it is surprisingly peaceful. The best area to launch a canoe and enjoy a quiet 10 km canoe trip between Riverton Bridge and Nicholson Bridge and back. The City of Canning have a canoe trail brochure, guiding paddlers down the river. At the Kent Street Weir there is a marked change between the brackish water towards the Swan River and fresh water upstream. It is a good place to see water birds.

There are several picnic site locations along the river. All of the picnic grounds are ideal for families but there are walks that take the visitor away to many quiet places along the riverside. There have to be some quiet areas in this park as two native animals still survive here, the Southern Brown Bandicoot or Quenda and the Water Rat, both of which require the thick vegetation that lines freshwater creeks and lakes.

Riverton Jetty Park: This park is situated on the Wilson side of Riverton Bridge. There are full barbecue facilities with toilets and playground and kiosk.

Adenia Park: Adenia Park is located off Adenia Road in Riverton. The park has open grass areas for picnics, no barbecues or toilets, but it does have a playground.

Masons Landing: This is the site of the old Masons timber loading area. It is located at the end of Liege Street in Cannington. There are barbecue facilities and toilets.

Wilson Park and Kent Street Weir: Located at the bottom of Kent Street, Cannington. There are barbecue facilities, playground and toilets. This is one of the most visited parts of the park.

Castledare Picnic Area: Located on the north shore of the river at the end of Castledare Place in Wilson. There are barbecue facilities and also adjacent to this, the Castledare Miniature Railway.

Woodloes Homestead: Located in Cannington, access is off Albany Highway. Turn off at Liege Street, turn right into Marriamup Street, then right into Woodloes Street. The homestead is on the right.

The homestead was designed and built by the architect Francis Bird in 1874 as his own residence. It is one of the few remaining houses in this area that dates back to the 19th century. It was restored by the City of Canning in the early 1970s and opened to the public in 1978. Open on Sunday 1 p.m. to 5 p.m. The house contains some wonderful old artifacts of the late 1800's and early 1900's.

Swan Estuary
MARINE PARKS

Not only do we need to protect the coastal marine areas but many of our estuarine environments need protection too, as urban development has encroached on many of our foreshore areas.

Three reserves have been selected for their environmental importance. All have intertidal sand beds that are very important for migratory waders and some sedentary species. The marine parks include Alfred Cove, Pelican Point and Milyu.

All are important but Alfred Cove has by far the highest diversity of bird species of these three areas.

Alfred Cove: Alfred Cove is located adjacent to Burke Drive in Attadale. The actual cove itself is enclosed on three sides; amongst the reed beds are uncommon species like Buff-banded Rail. In the small samphire pools at the western end of the cove, you can see Wood Sandpiper, Greenshank, Red-necked Avocet and Black-winged Stilt. When the tide is out the sandbanks in Lucky Bay hold a wealth of water birds that rest between feeding periods, particularly in summer, and include several terns such as Caspian Tern, Crested Tern and the uncommon Fairy Tern, the smallest tern in Western Australia. When the mudflats are exposed there can be hundreds of waders like Great Knot, Sharp tailed Sandpiper, Red necked Stint, Curlew Sandpiper, Grey Plover, Red-capped Plover, Eastern Curlew, Marsh Sandpiper and Bar-tailed Godwit. In amongst the many common Red-necked Stint, the keen bird watcher can sometimes see Broad-billed Sandpiper, a very rare wader throughout Australia.

The Alfred Cove Nature Reserve is not just for bird watchers, it is a place where you can walk for over 4 km one way from Alfred Cove all the way to East Fremantle Yacht Club, enjoying the beautiful foreshore that we are so lucky to have in this large city. Point Walter is one of the most

Looking across to the city centre from Alfred Cove

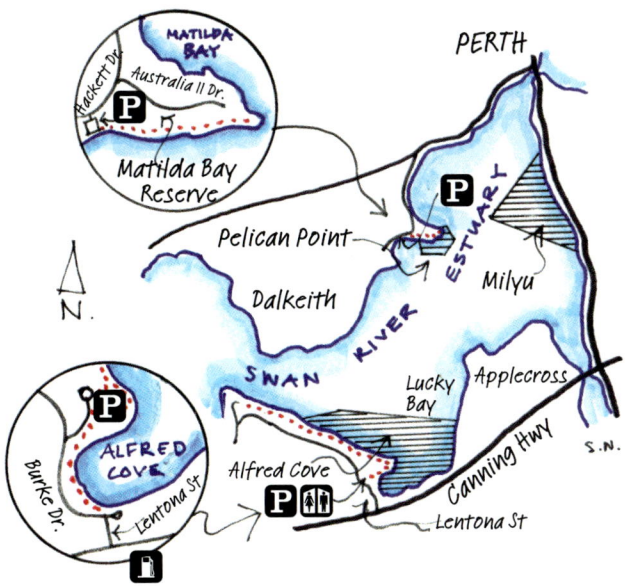

pleasant spots to have a picnic and there are tables and toilets here.

Also don't forget you can cycle entirely the full length from just west of East Fremantle Yacht Club near Blackwall Reach Parade, right around to the Kwinana Freeway and then all the way to the Narrows Bridge, then around to Nedlands and Dalkieth.

Diving: Many SCUBA divers go diving into Blackwall Reach, the channel that lies between Mosman Park and Bicton; you may ask why in a big city. Well, even though our waters are no longer in pristine condition, they are far better than most urban waterways in the world. The Swan is relatively clean and divers particularly on a night dive have the opportunity of collecting the odd prawn or Blue Manna crab. The best times for clarity are in summer and autumn. Please remember to take just what you need and adhere to the bag limits and always dive with dive flag and at night have a light connected to the buoy. Also please remember there is no fishing or the taking of any form of marine life allowed in these marine reserves areas but outside them there is no problem except that bag limits and season limits must be adhered to.

Pelican Point: Pelican Point is primarily good for birdwatchers and is accessed via the eastern end of Australia II Drive, in the suburb of Nedlands, just past the main entrance to the Royal Perth Yacht Club. It is only a small reserve.

Milyu: Milyu is the Noongar word for Samphire that grows along parts of the foreshore at Milyu. Again this was chosen as an area to protect the foreshore, due to the quantity of water birds that feed and roost on the sandbank here. Keep your eyes out for the raptor (bird of prey) the Osprey. It can be seen here looking for fish on the foreshore. The main spit and sand bar is opposite the northern end of the Royal Perth Golf Club.

Yanchep
NATIONAL PARK

This park has perhaps the most diverse range of recreational opportunities one could wish for; you can take long or short walks, picnic alongside Wagardu Lake, see Koalas in captivity, take a tour into the subterranean caves, hire a rowboat on Wagardu Lake, play golf, eat at the historic Yanchep Inn, view the beautiful wildflower gardens or visit the Gloucester Lodge Museum and learn about the early history of the area. So there is lots to see and do.

The park lies 50 km north of the city centre covering an area of 2,842 ha.

The name Yanchep comes from the Noongar word "Yandjip' the word for Bulrush *(Typha domingensis)* and Wagardu Lake was an important hunting area. The Bulrush that surrounds the lake was used as a food, the roots being crushed to make a type of flour which was baked on ashes.

Two Aboriginal groups overlapped in this area, the northern clans coming from as far as Moore River and the southern groups coming from the Swan River Estuary.

Europeans in the 1880s used to bring their cattle up from further south to graze on the lush grasses around the wetlands. They erected a stone hut, known as the hunting lodge, from which the original stones were used for the present McNess House.

The first European settler to live in the Yanchep area was Henry White and during the early 1900s he took a keen interest in the Yanchep limestone caves. In 1903 he was appointed honourary caretaker and guide to take people through the caves. You can see at the Gloucester Lodge Museum the original visitor's book that Henry kept.

In 1905 the government recognised the area's importance and an area of 5,640 acres was set aside. Not until the depression did any development of the park take place but, in 1930, Sir Charles McNess donated a large sum of money towards the park, and sustenance workers (people working for just food and a bed) helped with developing the park.

In 1932 McNess House was built and used as a guesthouse for people viewing the caves and in 1933 Gloucester Lodge was built. The Koala colony was established in 1935 and is still one of the main attractions in the park.

During world war II, the park was taken over as a radar base and a convalescent home for troops wounded in action with nurses being housed in McNess House. There were many developments over the next years and finally in 1985, when DCLM became responsible for the management of the park, many major projects were introduced. The park is still in the process of being improved.

Fauna and Flora: The vegetation of Yanchep lies on the narrow bands of the Spearwood, Quindalup and Bassendean Dune Systems, that run parallel with the coast for over a hundred kilometres.

The large eucalypts are typical of those of most of the Perth coastal parks, being Tuart, Jarrah and Marri. However, the northern heaths that cover much of the park have quite a diverse species list with beautiful Featherflowers *(Verticordia species)* blooming in early summer, underneath the Slender Banksia and Firewood

The Koala can be seen at Yanchep National Park, although it is only found in the wild in Eastern Australia

Banksia as well as Wild Wisteria *(Hardenbergia comptoniana)*, Yellow Buttercups *(Hibbertia hypericoides)* One-sided Bottlebrush *(Calothamnus quadrifidus)*, Yanchep Rose *(Diplolaena angustifolia)* and Lilac Hibiscus *(Alyogyne huegelii)*.

It is a great place to see the Red and Green Kangaroo Paw *(Anigozanthos manglesii)* and the shorter Common Catspaw *(Anigozanthos humilis subsp. humilis)*.

The Western Grey Kangaroo is very common in the park and quite often seen in the late evening, particularly on the golf course. The native Water Rat *(Hydromys chrysogaster)* can sometimes be seen by the keen eye swimming in

The Yanchep Inn

Looking across Loch McNess

the quieter corners of Wagardu Lake. Look for a large rat with a prominent white tip on the tail. It takes most of its food from the water in the reed beds and is often out in early and late daylight hours.

The bird species are quite well represented. The big black parrot with a languid flight is Short-billed Black Cockatoo and in summer large flocks can be seen and heard. They use the park to roost and drink at the lakeside. In the heath areas the Western Spinebill, White-cheeked Honeyeater, Little Wattlebird and Red Wattlebird are quite active feeding on the various flowers in spring.

Walks

There are many walks that one can take, starting from a simple one kilometre walk to a long back pack walk of 55 km to Melaleuca Conservation Park that will take 3.5 days.

Besides pleasant short walks to the edge of the lake and visiting the various old buildings, there are several walks including:

Woodlands Walk Trail: This is a one hour return walk that takes you through the coastal woodlands of marri, tuart, banksia and paperbark woodlands. It starts at McNess House Visitor Centre.

Dwerta Mia Walk Trail: This leads to a small pool at the base of the limestone ridge. It is a short 500 m walk and accessible for wheelchairs. It will take you past Doorda Cave where Aboriginal artifacts were found. The walk commences near Gloucester Lodge Museum.

Wetlands Walk Trail: This will take you around Loch McNess. It starts on the edge of the lake opposite McNess House and heads south. This is an easy walk and will give you a great appreciation for the wetland ecosystem. It will take you past head high reed beds, paperbark trees and some of the most northerly Tuart trees in the state. Keep an eye out for the native Water Rat and the Long-necked Turtle *(Chelodina oblonga)*. The trail finishes near Yanchep Inn.

Cockatoo Walk Trail: This is a long walk of 17.5 km and takes you into Gnangara Park. It traverses a variety of habitats. There is a campsite/shelter on route.

Yanchep Rose Walk Trail: Another long walk of 14 km that passes by the Second World War Radar bunkers. The walk will give you panaramic views of the sea and inland to the Darling Range scarp.

Ghost House Walk Trail: This is an 9.2 km moderate walk that will take roughly 4 hrs to complete. It follows part of the Yanjidi Trail and then on the western side of the lake it branches off to the left. Once you have left the lakeside path you will pass through Tuart trees and then enter heath country. This part of the walk in spring and early summer is most rewarding with the many flowers that bloom. At the northern end of the circuit route are the ruins of an old homestead. Returning via the eastern side of the wetlands, you will pass over some limestone outcrops typical of coastal belt. Then the final part of the walk takes you back to the main centre past the golf course.

The Caves: There are over 400 caves recorded for the park. The caves are quite fascinating and there is a daily tour of Crystal Cave and also Yonderup Cave is open to the public. Crystal Cave is still an active cave where water continually seeps from the roof. Yonderup has ceased to be active but is still well worth visiting. They contain the typical formations that are common to most large limestone caves that experience continual water seepage. The features include stalagmites, stalactites, flowstone, shawls, and helictites. Refer to Leeuwin Naturaliste Park in the South West Region section for how limestone caves are formed. The caves have produced some fascinating fossils over the years, including animals that now can only be found in Tasmania, such as the Tasmanian Devil and the now extinct Thylacine, proof again that this south west region once had a wetter climate. Fossiled bones of ancient animals have also been found such as a huge 2.5 metre tall kangaroos that grazed in this area.

It is recommended that you visit the visitor's centre and they will give you more detailed information on any specific area you wish to visit. There are plenty of good picnic spots in the park. Meals and snacks are available as well as accommodation at the old Yanchep Inn.

Caves Walk Trail: A short walk that takes you to Crystal Cave. It is a guided tour and can be booked at the visitors centre. You will learn about the history of the area and how limestone caves have been formed.

Yanchep National Park run various day tours and overnight tours which include enviromental and cultural activities. There are also interpretive activities for schools which are particularly useful in learning about Nyoongar cultural life.

Overnight Hikes

The Coastal Plain Walk Trail: This is a 55 km walk that takes normally 3.5 days (one way) and commences at the Ghost House in Yanchep Park. It is strongly suggested that you seek information first before commencing the long walk. The walk has four campsites on route, each with a hikers hut, water tank and bush toilet, based on a first come first serve basis.

The walk is particularly enjoyable in spring and autumn. This walk is not reccomended in the summer months when the temperature can be very high.

There are very good information sheets and maps available for the walks.

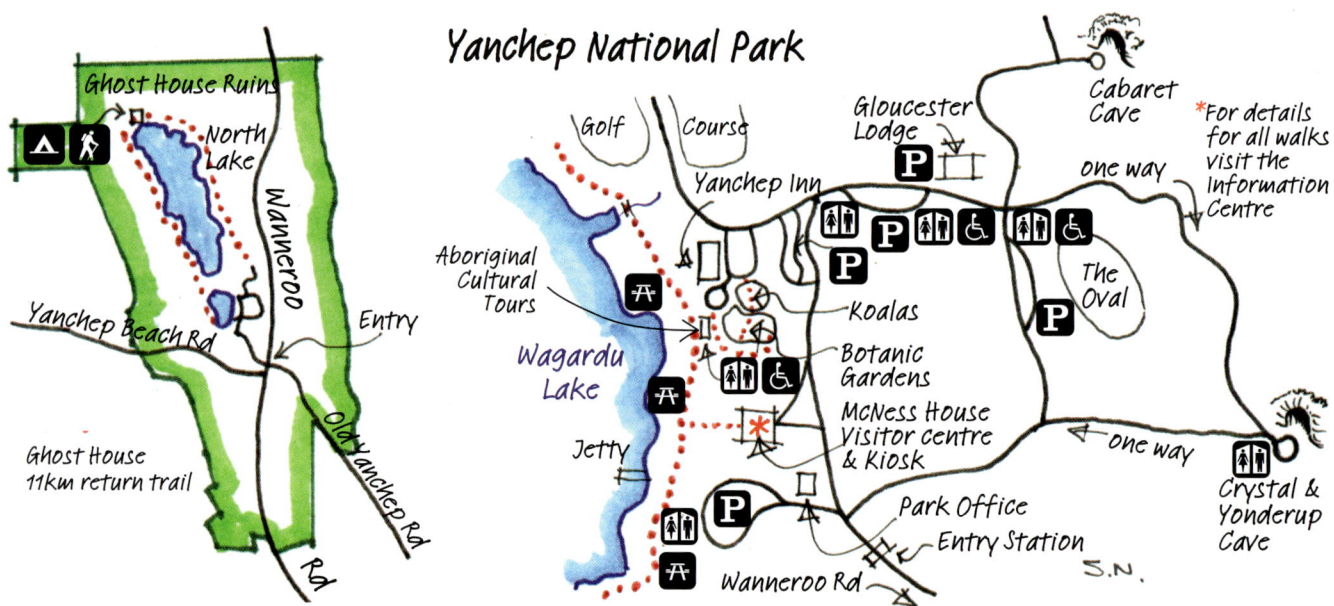

Kings Park

Western Australia is very fortunate to have such a large park, covering 404 ha, right in the centre of the city. In fact it is the largest area of natural bushland found near a city centre of any state capital. The park was founded in 1895, John Forrest planting a tree to commemorate the occasion. It is also the most visited park in the State due to its proximity to the city centre, giving superb views across the Swan River and the Darling Range in the distance.

Nearly two thirds of the park is natural woodland containing around 291 species of native plants. The balance of the park is made up of superb cultivated native gardens and open recreation areas.

Alongside the main entry along Fraser Avenue are tall white barked Lemon-scented Gums (Eucalyptus citriodora), which are not native to Western Australia but they certainly make a wonderful welcome to this large park. At the base of most trees are commemorative plaques in memory of soldiers who sacrificed their lives in the war years, so that we may enjoy the freedom of walking in such wonderful parks.

The main woodlands are dominated by Jarrah and Marri as well as 5 species of banksia; Firewood Banksia, Slender Banksia, Bull Banksia, Acorn Banksia and Holly-leaved Banksia (Banksia illicifolia).

Botanic Gardens: Perhaps the most impressive part of Kings Park is its wonderful cultivated native gardens covering an area of 17 ha. Over 2,000 species of flowering plants have been planted in various sections that emulate the regions where they originate, so plants from the northern mallee shrublands and heath or the Jarrah forest, are kept together. This is very useful for people who may be visiting a region and wish to know what typical plants they may find in that locality.

Located near the Tennis Courts off Kings Park Road in the Ivy Watson Playground, is a small garden set aside for plants with strong aromas such as the herbs etc. The flowerbed has been raised so that people in wheelchairs or with sight disabilities can enjoy the wonderful sensation of smell that is particularly heightened when one has lost one's sight.

In the same locality is the Metropolitan Garden; here are displays of plants that can be grown quite easily by people living in the Perth Region. You can park near the garden and the entrance is opposite Outram Street, West Perth.

Glasshouses: There are separate glass-houses that represent areas where special controlled climatic conditions are required. Some represent plants that exist in hotter and drier weather conditions, namely the Pilbara and the dry inland regions and the Kimberley Region. Some of the houses contain specific groups of plants like the Ferns, the Halophytes and Carnivorous Plants; Western Australia has a few carnivorous or partly carnivorous plants in the form of the Sundews (Drosera species) and the Albany Pitcher Plant (Cephalotus follicularis).

You can access these glasshouses off Fraser Avenue just 250 m from the main entrance. There is a small car park at the end of the driveway.

Picnic sites and playgrounds: There are numerous picnic sites and if you wish to avoid the main focal point for visitors around Fraser Avenue you can visit the following areas:

Arthur Fairall Playground: This is the largest playground and picnic site in the park with a small ornamental lake and a food kiosk. There are children's play apparatus and several picnic tables and toilets. The area is situated on May Drive on the south western side of the park.

Ernst Wittwer Recreation area: This location is quieter than many picnic areas and has several picnic tables, toilets and barbecues. Parking is on May Avenue at the junction of Saw Avenue in the northwestern part of the park.

Hale Recreation Area: This area has picnic tables, barbecue facilities, playground facilities, toilets and a good cafeteria. The Aromatic Gardens are located here as well as the Metropolitan Garden.

Botanic Gardens: Located on Forrest Drive at the Pioneer Women's Memorial is a large open area of cleared lawns between the cultivated botanic gardens, which is an ideal picnic spot for those who wish to be adjacent to the main native botanic gardens. The area is not geared to small children who require playground facilities and there are no picnic or barbecue facilities. It's really a pleasant spot to bring a packed lunch and be close to the wonderful native flowerbeds. There are toilet facilities.

Fraser Avenue facilities: Adjacent to the main war memorials off Fraser Avenue are the main car parks and restaurant, kiosk and gift shops.

A useful place to visit is the main Kings Park information centre located between the restaurant and food kiosk. Here the volunteer Kings Park guides can assist you with any enquires and they can also tell you about the botanical guided walks that are available in the park.

Wildflower Festival: This really is something that everyone in Perth should try and see at least once in their lifetime. The work and energies put into the wildflower displays by the staff of Kings Park are second to none.

The wonderful garden beds created by the staff of Kings Park for the Wildflower Festival

Many varieties are planted in close proximity and there are stalls with varying information on subjects related to the plant world. It runs normally in the last week in September.

Walks and cycle ways: There are literally kilometres of walking trails in the park too numerous to detail but the adjacent map should assist with localities.

Fauna: Although this is a very large park for a central city location, the very presence of thousands of visitors and years of habitation with all the pressures of domestic dogs, fires, traffic etc means the large native marsupials are gone. But the bird life is quite prolific particularly around the cultivated gardens with increased volumes of nectar and insects that abound around so many flowering plants. You can park off Forrest Drive at the parking area near the Roe Memorial, you can walk along many tracks that meander through the native wildflower beds that have been cultivated below the original vegetation of Jarrah and Marri trees.

It is a good place to look for two endemic birds, the Western Spinebill and Western Wattlebird: other birds including Red Wattlebird; New Holland, White-cheeked and Brown Honeyeaters. In the treetops are Ring-necked Parrot, Red-capped Parrot and Spotted Pardalote.

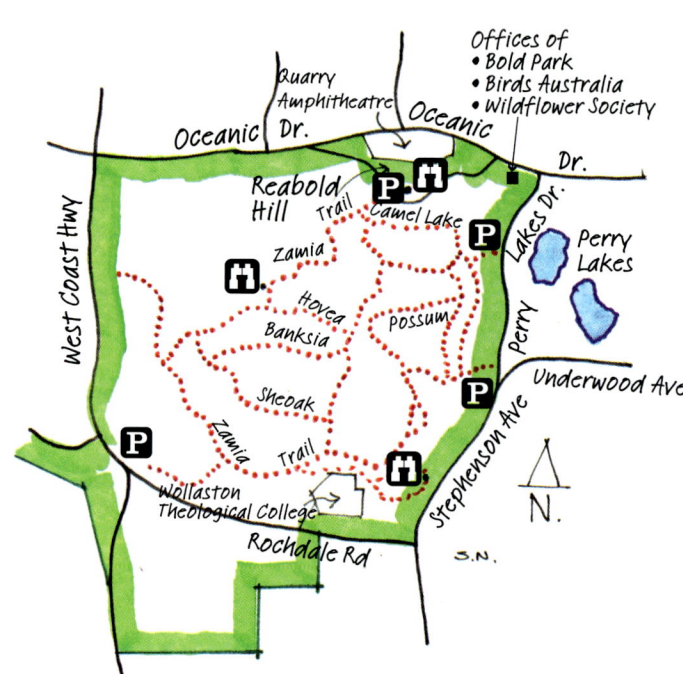

Looking west from Reabold Hill

Bold Park

Most people think that Kings Park is our largest reserve near the city but it is now Bold Park, much of it thanks to the hard work of many members of the Friends of Bold Park who played a major role in stopping a large area adjacent to the reserve from being cleared for a major urban development.

The Park covers an area of 437 ha and contains lots of natural remnant bushland now rare on the Swan Coastal Plain.

The park rises to 93 m at Reabold Hill and from the hill one can gain some very good views out to the coast and also back to the centre of the city.

There is a car park at the top of the hill and numerous paths that can give you a circuit route of as long as 4.5 km on the Zamia Palm Walk. Entry to Reabold Hill is via Scenic Drive, a narrow one way road (be careful of walkers coming down) leading left off Oceanic Drive. Entry must be made heading west.

Much of the vegetation is on Spearwood dunes and Quindalup Sands overlaying Tamala Limestone rock, although the limestone is exposed in many areas. On the sandier areas Firewood Banksia is very prolific, best seen in flower between mid March and May. In the valleys on the coastal side of the park are natural stands of Tuart.

Besides the Tuart, Jarrah and Marri trees, there are three uncommon eucalypt mallee species here: Fremantle Mallee (*Eucalyptus foecunda*) Limestone Marlock (*E. decipiens*) and Rock Mallee (*E. petrensis*).

Between Oceanic Drive and Underwood Avenue are the Perry Lakes. They are not high in variety of water birds but make a pleasant spot to picnic.

Possum Walk, which leads up the hill opposite from the junction of Perry Lakes Drive and Underwood Avenue, often has a good variety of bush birds and is one of the most natural bushland settings in the metropolitan area.

Whiteman Park

Boardwalk for Mussel Pool

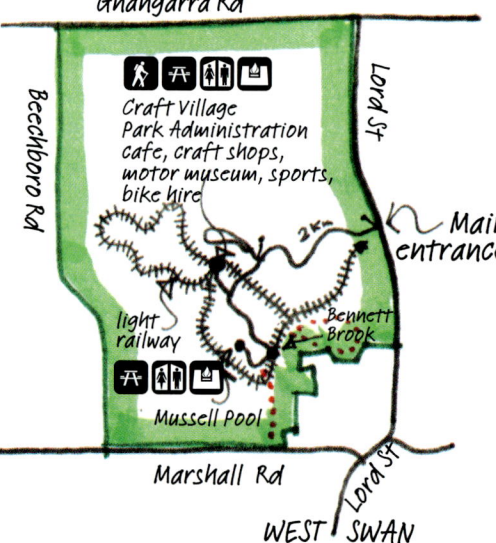

The park has been a popular recreation area since the early 1960s, when Lew Whiteman, who originally owned part of the park, developed an area for the local community, where people could come and picnic and pay no fees. The area was named Mussel Pool and this location is still the most popular part of the park. The land was sold eventually in 1978 to the Government to provide a recreational park for the people of Perth.

It is one of the largest parks in the metropolitan area, covering 2,600 ha consisting predominantly of pasture land, with Jarrah, Marri and banksia woodland and some small swamplands. The vegetation grows entirely on the narrow north/south band of Bassendean sands. There is also a small population of Western Brush Wallabies (*Macropus irma*).

Walks: Goo-loorto Walk Trail (red markers) leaves the main picnic area at Mussel Pool, crossing over the tram tracks and then through the first gate. The path then follows the west side of Bennett Brook, passing through another gate to the boundary fence of the park, from here retrace your steps back to Mussel Pool. It is an easy walk of 3 km return.

Werillyiup Walk Trail (blue markers) is an easy 2.5 km loop walk around Horse Swamp.

Wunanga Walk Trail (yellow markers) is an easy 4 km return walk.

Yonga Neandup Walk Trail (orange markers) is an easy 3 km return walk. There are brochures available from the main information centre on the walks and administration requests that only those walks marked should be undertaken.

Activities: Whiteman Park administration runs several activities during the year and you can contact them to check what future activities are being held. There are two main picnic locations, one at Mussel Pool and the other at the "Village"; there are barbecues, picnic tables and toilets at both locations and a playground facility at the "Village" picnic ground as well as a motor museum, cycle hire and restaurant. There is a small steam train that takes people through part of the park, which is very popular. The park is very much geared to family outings and is in no way a wilderness park although there are substantial areas of wild bushland. Access is via the main entrance on Lord Street, West Swan.

Looking across the Darling Range from Mt Dale

Hills
PARKS

Perth Hills
NATIONAL PARKS

The State Government in 1997 made a commitment to allow DCLM to manage the development of 16 regional parks within the Perth region. One of the most important outcomes was recognising the Darling Range as a significant region to conserve parklands and reserves and linking them into a continuous band of parks that would run from the Avon Valley all the way down to Serpentine. The combined area would cover over 38,000 ha of land set aside to protect the outstanding environmental, and recreational values of these parklands. It is proposed to connect trails and protect other very important natural bush areas particularly on the Darling Scarp, like Bickley Brook and Ellis Brook, where at present there is a complex number of government landholders ranging from crown lands, State Water Commission lands and private lands. The State Planning Commission is at present acquiring the land so that much of the Darling Scarp will become a protected area for the people of Western Australia. It is a farsighted vision that can only benefit the people of Perth and future generations.

In the hills there are a multitude of wonderful parks to visit; some are very popular and well frequented, some at times have few people and you can often be the only ones there. In an overcrowded world, we are so lucky that just 30-50 km from the city centre are such quiet places that the visitor can experience solitude and peace from the pressures of a big city.

1 Araluen Park
3 Bibbulmun Track
5 Bickley Brook
8 Boulder Rock **CLOSED**
9 Bungendore Reserve
11 Christmas Tree Well
12 Churchman Brook Dam
13 Ellis Brook
15 Fred Jacoby Park
16 Gleneagle
17 Gooseberry Hill
19 Hills Forest Discovery Centre
20 John Forest N.P.
21 Kalamunda N.P.
23 Karakamia Sanctuary
24 Langford Park
25 Lesmurdie N.P.
28 Mt Dale
29 North Ledge
30 Paruna Sanctuary
33 Serpentine N.P.
35 South Ledge
38 Sullivans Rock
41 Walyunga N.P.
44 Wungong Dam

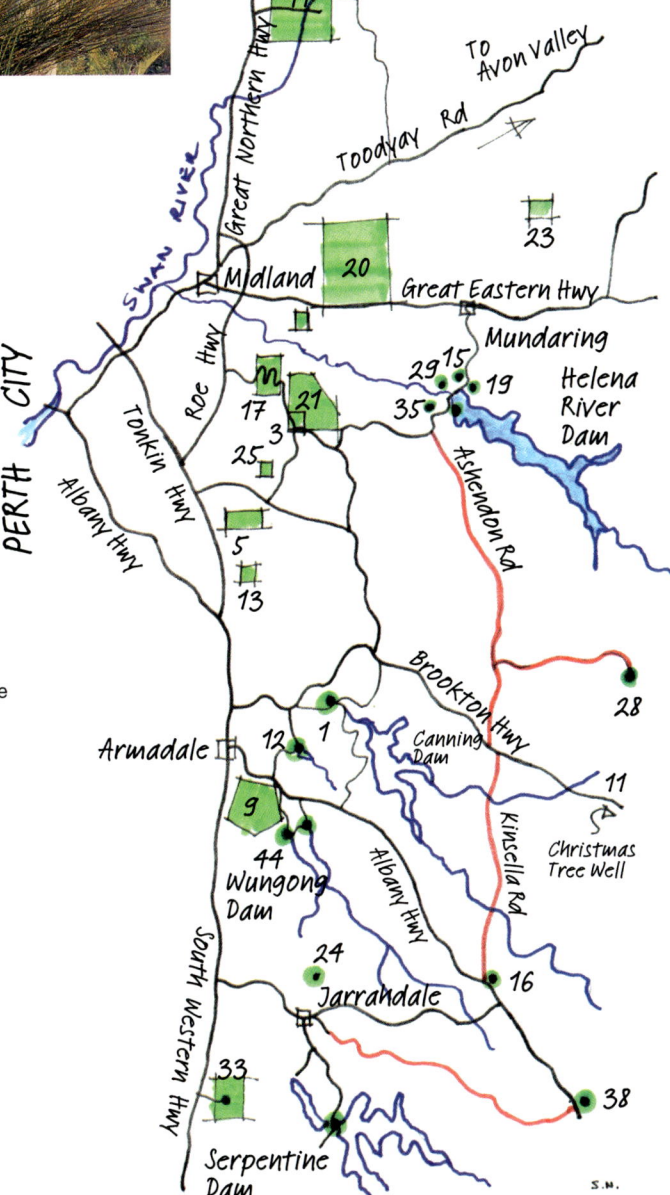

Avon Valley

Located 60 km from the city centre, Avon Valley is just that little bit further than the majority of the hills parks but the extra distance one has to take to visit it, makes it well worth it. If you want to avoid large crowds that often frequent the busier parks visit Avon Valley.

It is hard to imagine that one can drive for just one and a half hours from the city centre, pitch a tent under wonderful old Wandoo trees and wake in the early morning to the crisp fresh air of a healthy forest full of bird song. This wilderness experience is a privilege that few other capital cities can enjoy.

Here the Avon River, known as "Golguler" in Noongar language, cuts its way through the laterite and ancient granite rocks making its way across the Swan Coastal Plain to the sea. The 4,400 ha park straddles the river.

It was here that Joseph Bolitho Johns, later to be known as 'Moondyne Joe' spent many of his early years in the 1860s. His story as so-called bushranger and various successful escapes from Newcastle (now Toodyay) prison and Fremantle Gaol became the folklore that legends are certainly made of; he was a likeable, non-violent character but always walked a fine line between the law and crime. His exploits make excellent reading.

Flora and Fauna: The park lies on the transitional zone between the wetter western side of the Darling Range and the drier woodlands of the eastern range and the wheatbelt.

The Jarrah and Marri forest starts to become more of an open forest here. The shallow clay soil valleys support beautiful stands of Wandoo (*Eucalyptus wandoo*). The higher ridges particularly above the Avon River support stands of Powderbark Wandoo (*Eucalyptus accedens*).

The wildflowers that occur in the understorey of the open Jarrah woodland include Hairy Jugflower (*Adenanthos barbigerus*) and Milkwort (*Comesperma confertum*). Near the granite outcrops above the Avon, clumps of Fuchsia Grevillea (*Grevillea bipinnatifida*) and Lemon-scented Darwinia (*Darwinia citriodora*) grow.

In the Wandoo valleys the orchids appear in early September, such as the Blue China Orchid (*Cyanicula gemmata*), Cowslip Orchid (*Caladenia flava*), Zebra Orchid (*Caladenia cairnsiana*), Blood Spider Orchid (*Caladenia filifera*), and Splendid Spider Orchid (*Caladenia splendens*).

There are still reasonable populations of the larger marsupials in the park; besides the common Western Grey Kangaroo, it is a good place to catch a glimpse of the Euro or Common Wallaroo (*Macropus robustus*). This is a very stocky macropod; here it is at the most south western edge of its range which stretches right across Australia but avoids the wetter regions. It is well adapted to arid conditions. It is a smaller kangaroo than the Grey Kangaroo and at first is not easy to differentiate, but it has a shorter neck and rather shaggy hair, being much darker in colour than the Grey Kangaroo. It likes the rocky hillsides of the Avon Valley. The Chuditch or Western Quoll (*Dasyurus geoffroii*) still exists here but is very uncommon with an estimated population of around 6,000 animals in the entire south west region. However with fox baiting, it is increasing in areas of the Jarrah forest. It is a nocturnal marsupial and is carnivorous, eating large insects, small mammals and birds.

What to do, where to go: There are picnic sites on Bald Hill, Drummonds, Homestead Campsite and Valley Campsite.

Most people go down to Valley Campsite as canoes are often launched from here. If you want a quieter spot then visiting the other three areas should give you fewer visitors. The views from Bald Hill are wonderful over the Avon Valley and a walk around the granite outcrops should always be rewarding particularly in winter, spring and early summer.

The camping grounds have wood fires, picnic tables and pit toilets. There are obviously strong fire restrictions in summer. There is a self-registration entry station at the start of Quarry Road and small fees apply. All the roads within the park are unsealed and not recommended for caravans, as many of them are quite steep.

Looking down the Avon Valley from Bald Hill

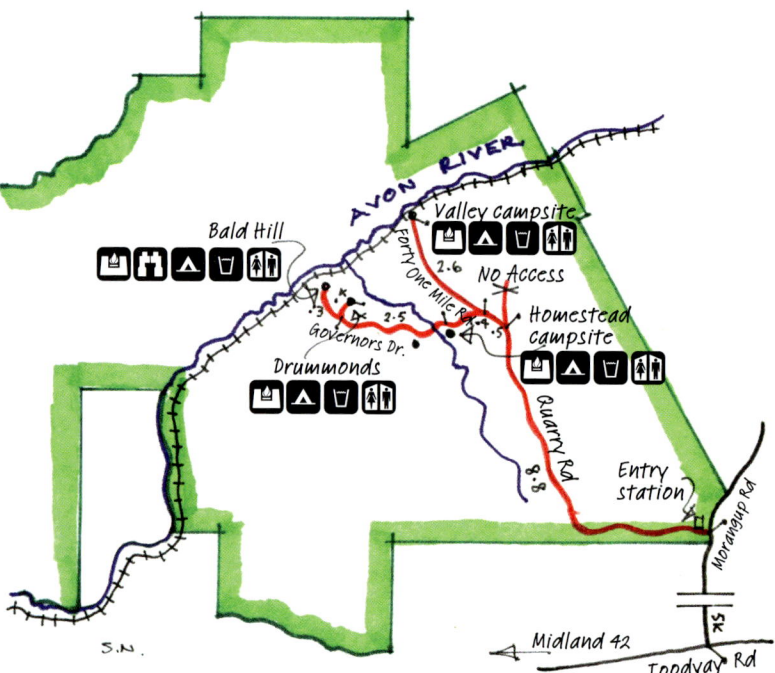

Looking across Syd's Rapids

Rafters getting prepared for their adventures down the Avon River

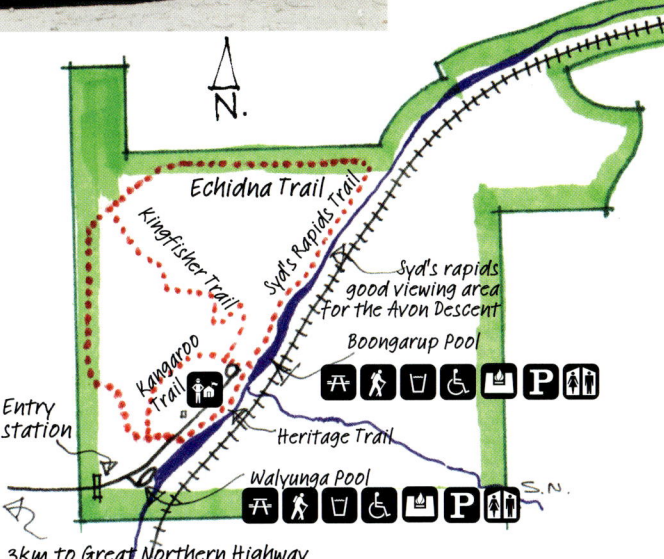

Walyunga
NATIONAL PARK

The park is situated 40 km north east of Perth City, covering an area of 1,800 ha. Within the park lies one of the most significant Noongar archeological sites near Perth and it is not surprising as here lie permanent fresh water pools that are replenished every winter from the rains that rush down from the Darling Range, originating in the Wheatbelt.

The main tribe was the Whadjuck but other tribes would meet for ceremonies from as far as Moore River. The country here had plenty of food and on the hillside there was chert and quartz rocks that could be chipped and the stones used for spears and basic knives.

Throughout Australia, wherever there was permanent water and plenty of available food, these were the main areas chosen and passed down for thousands of years as centres for important tribal business and ceremonies which would take a few weeks; Walyunga was such a place where hill tribes would meet coastal tribes.

The park, like John Forrest National Park and Serpentine National Park, lies on the western edge of the Darling Range, giving it similar vegetation communities of Jarrah and Marri woodland, Wandoo woodland, granite outcrops and heath. Along the river edge are large Flooded Gums *(Eucalyptus rudis)*.

A major feature of this park is the Avon River that flows through it. It is the largest free flowing river to enter the Perth region and when in full flood the rapids make a spectacular sight. In the first weekend in August, the Avon Descent takes place and many people flock to Walyunga to watch the various canoes and powerboats descend the rapids, particularly around Syd's Rapids.

Canoeing is great fun and after the main winter rains have finished, it makes an exciting river to canoe down but there are certain things you should know when canoeing to avoid serious accidents and it is best to travel with licensed tour operators who will take you down the Avon.

There are two main picnic sites, the first is at Walyunga Pool and most people go in here, however if you just go a little further (about 600 m), you come to Boongarup Pool. Fewer people seem to congregate here but there are toilets and picnic sites. It makes the walk to Syd's Rapids a little shorter.

Walks: There are several walks in the park ranging from a 1.2 km to a 10.6 km walk.

Aboriginal Heritage Trail: This takes you from Walyunga Pool to Boongarup Pool and back. It is 600m one way and gives you an insight into some of the Aboriginal mythology of the area.

Syd's Rapids: This is a most popular walk that takes you along the banks of the Avon River to where the water drops down at Syd's Rapids. It is an easy but long (5.2 km) return walk, allow 2 hrs. The flowers on the hillside and around the granite boulders are quite splendid in spring.

Kangaroo Trail: This is a 4 km circular route and takes about two hours. The start is at the eastern end of Walyunga Pool car park. Follow the yellow 'Kangaroo' markers. It will take you over the road and over a small creek, then at the junction of the Echidna Trail veer right. Cross the small creek again and slowly walk up the hill. Near the top you will come to granite outcrops. Keep following the markers till you come to the Kingfisher turn off, keep right and walk back down the hill, passing through the Boongarup picnic area and meeting up with the Heritage Trail which will take you back to where you started.

You should be in moderate health to walk this trail.

Kingfisher Trail: This is an 8.5 km walk, allow about four hours. The walking directions are the same as the Kangaroo Trail until you get to where the Kangaroo Trail turns to the right and you take the Echidna Trail to the left. You will pass through Wandoo woodland, and when you get to the junction where the Echidna Trail turns left, you take the track with the blue 'Kingfisher' markers to the right heading in a southerly direction. Around a dam you will soon join up with the yellow markers of the 'Kangaroo Trail' taking you through the Boongarup picnic area and along the river back to where you started.

You should be fit and well prepared for this walk and understand compass bearings.

Echidna Trail: This is an 11 km walk taking about 4-5 hrs. It too starts where the Kangaroo Trail starts. Keep following the yellow 'Kangaroo' markers, then take the blue 'Kingfisher' marked track until it joins the pink 'Echidna' markers. Follow the Echidna signs from here on and you will climb to the highest point in the park known as Woodsome Hill at 260 m. From here you will slowly drop down the hill, with the Avon Valley coming into view and you will meet the walking trail that leads to Syd's Rapids, turn right and walk downstream along the Heritage Trail back to the start of your walk.

You should be fit and well prepared for this walk and use a compass.

Gooseberry Hill
NATIONAL PARK

A small 33 ha reserve that lies just on the Darling Scarp. There are wonderful views of the city from most parts of the park. The park is accessed via Kalamunda, via Williams Street that leads into Lascelles Parade and finally Zig Zag Scenic Drive. This drive winds its way down through the park. It is hard to imagine that this was once the track of a railway line, where wagons loaded with timber from the hills, were shunted backwards and forwards at the end of each bend till they made it to the bottom; quite an engineering feat.

The species count of wildflowers per hectare on all the granite scarp slopes is higher than that of the Jarrah Forest and in spring, you will see a mass of flowers. You can see Granite Petrophile (*Petrophile biloba*), Spindly Grevillea (*Grevillea endlicheriana*), Lemon-scented Darwinia (*Darwinia citriodora*) and Fushsia Grevillea (*Grevillea bipinnatifida*).

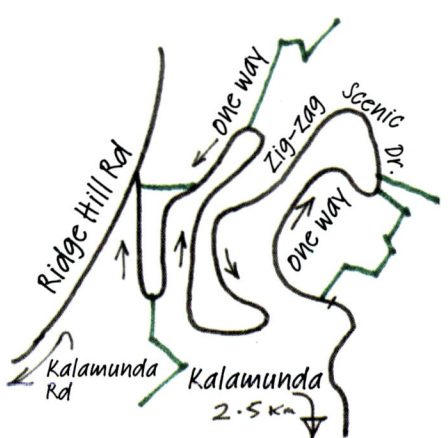

Wildflowers in full bloom on Gooseberry Hill

Kalamunda
NATIONAL PARK

One of the less frequented large parks of the Darling Scarp, Kalamunda National Park contains some beautiful walks among fine granite outcrops and Wandoo woodland. The park is particularly good for wildflowers and contains some very rare plants just restricted to the park.

The Bibbulmun Track commences in Kalamunda at the junction of Railway Road and Mundaring Weir Road near the roundabout. You can walk through part of the park on the Bibbulmun Track and have someone pick you up at Fern Road that leads off Mundaring Weir Road giving you some idea of what it is like.

The main access point to walks in the park are from the end of Schipp Road off Hummerston Road in the south part of the park. This will take you down Piesse Gully. There is also an entry point from Spring Road. At the end of Crescent Road off Mundaring Weir Road is a small reserve called Jorgensen Park that blends into Kalamunda National Park. It has picnic tables, barbecues and toilets.

There is an entry point into the northern part of the park coming from the suburb of Helena Valley via Helena Valley Road (a very narrow road, be careful) but the last 1 km is a dirt track and not really suitable for 2WD, as there are exposed granite rocks and pot holes, giving problems to low clearance vehicles. Park at the end of the bitumen if you think you will have problems. There is a car park at the end of the dirt track. The walk takes you up a bridle path with Wandoo and Flooded Gum trees and open heath.

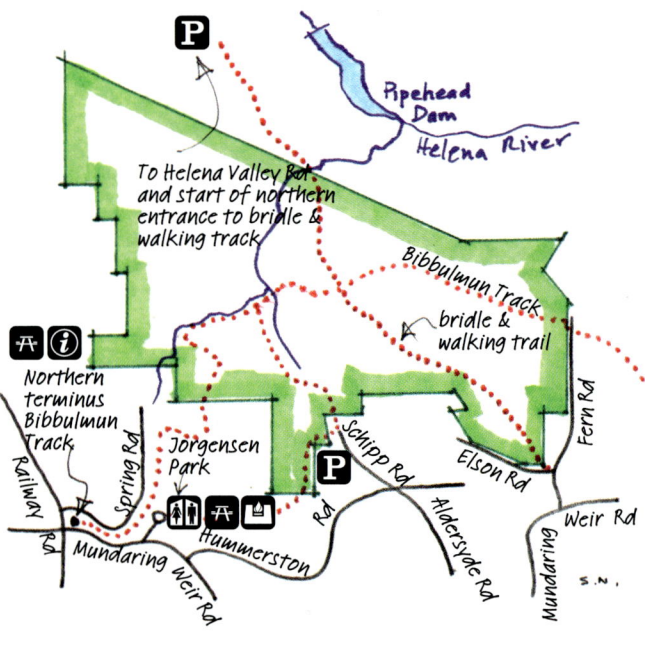

Bridal trail on the northern boundary of the park ▶

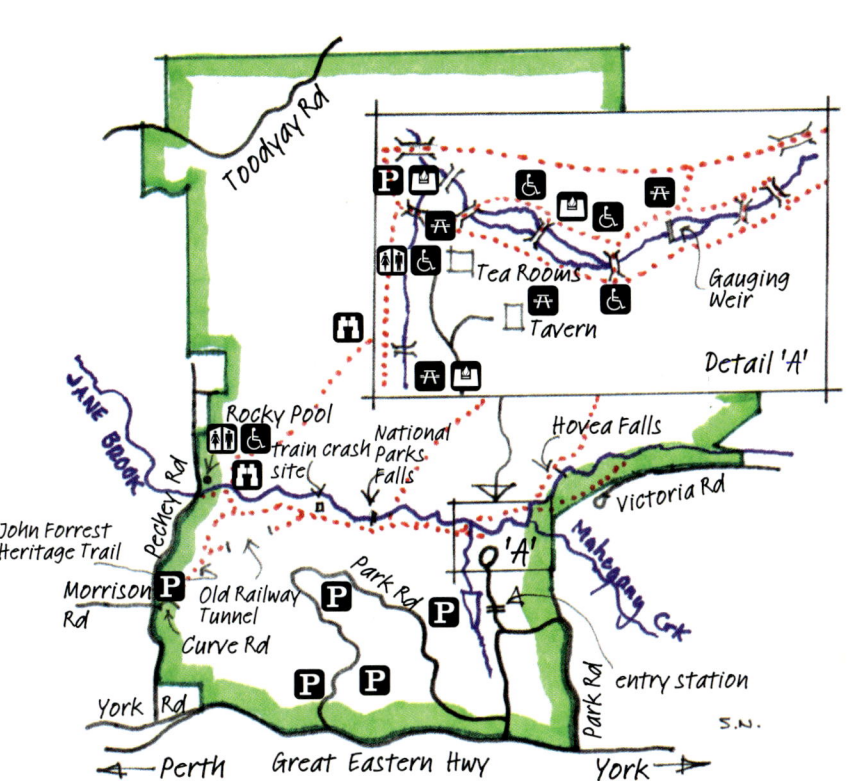

The main waterfall on the John Forrest Heritage Trail

John Forrest
NATIONAL PARK

This is Western Australia's first National Park and was set aside for conservation and recreation as early as 1898, being proposed by the Surveyor General Mr H.F. Johnston. Two years later it was named as Greenmount National Park and several years later it was changed to John Forrest National Park.

It was the second park to be named a national park in Australia, the first being Royal National Park in Sydney.

Before the park was established, a new railway line was surveyed and constructed through the park by the engineer C.Y. O'Connor who engineered and delivered the first piped water to the eastern Goldfields from Mundaring Weir. Sadly he committed suicide; a tragic end to a fine engineer.

The railway was also no mean feat, as it climbed its way through the Darling Range from Perth to Beverley and Northam, eventually going all the way to Coolgardie. A tunnel and many bridges were built passing through the central part of the park. The first trains ran on the new line in 1896. It remained in use for 70 years and was finally closed in February 1966.

Later the standard gauge railway line was built through the Avon valley to the north.

Much of the walkways and rock gardens near the tavern and tearooms were built in the depression years of the 1930s. Over 400 sustenance workers worked on the project of improving the park, just as they did at Yanchep National Park.

When the facilities were finally built in the mid 1930s, trains would take picnickers from Perth all the way to the park, proving a great success.

The park to this day is one of the most visited parks in the Perth region.

Walks: The park is located at the top of Greenmount Hill and the main entry is 26 km from Perth. You enter north of the Great Eastern Highway on Park Road and a further 3 km takes you to the main recreation area. There are numerous walks that one can take and much of the northern part of the park is little visited and would suit experienced bushwalkers.

Part of the John Forrest Trail: Most people who visit the park like to wander down past the tea rooms to Jane Brook, staying on the left side of the brook and walking alongside the path where the old railway line used to run. At the start of the walk is where the old railway station was. Try to imagine the hundreds of gents and ladies in their Sunday best in Victorian times disembarking from the train to walk to the gardens you have just left.

If you walk about 700 m from the main recreation area, you come to the 25 m drop National Park Falls; when the water is running well after the first winter rains, it is a very pretty sight and best seen from July to late September. Most people return from here; for those who are interested in the historical aspects of the early railway line, you can continue down the track all the way to Pechey Road a distance of 2.5 km.

You can carry on down the old railway path about another 200 m and find the site of a very bad rail crash. On the 30th June 1895, the Perth to Northam train was shunting backwards onto a siding line to let the main Perth passenger train pass. The train pulled 22 six ton wagons, consisting of general stores, seven horses and now just two passengers (two had just disembarked). A coupling between two of the carriages broke and 20 of the 22 wagons started to roll back down the hill. The guard applied the brake on the guard's van and then leapt off and tried to jump up and apply the brakes on the other wagons but they were travelling too fast.

The two remaining passengers remained in their seats; at the very point here just 4-500m west of the National Park Falls on a tight bend just before the railway tunnel, the carriages left the rails at a speed estimated to be in excess of 190 km per hour and tumbled down the embankment. One of the passengers survived, the other was killed along with all seven horses.

Past this point is the only railway tunnel ever built in Western Australia; it was, however, to give many problems particularly with excessive smoke that caused major inhalation problems and it was finally closed and a deviation built in 1945.

Glen Brook Dam Walk: Another short walk of just over 2 km will take you over the footbridge where Glen Brook meets Jane Brook. If you turn left and walk alongside Glen Brook, the track will take you up the hill alongside Glen Brook Dam. You can return around the southern end of the dam, crossing over the stream and walking back the other side of the dam to the main facility area. It is a good walk in spring when all the wildflowers are out.

Eagle's View Walk Trail: There is a long 15 km walk for keen bush walkers that will take 5-7 hrs depending on fitness. The Eagle View Trail was developed by the Perth Bush Walkers Club in conjunction with DCLM; the club is well worth joining if you are a keen bush walker. It goes to some of the more remote parts of the park and is simply a great walk. It's best to simply take your time with a backpack, taking plenty of water and food. This way, instead of hurtling through the bush as if it's just a race, you can stop, take your time and inspect the many wonderful plants and enjoy the spectacular views through the Wandoo woodland to the coastal plains en route. Maps are available from the main DCLM office in the park but you must register at the Main Office before you take this walk.

Rocky Pool Picnic Site: On the western boundary of the park opposite the junction of National Park Road and Pechey Road, is an entry to the picnic site. There is a car park just 200 m from Rocky Pool. Above the pool, a series of rapids run down Jane Brook. The surrounding bush has some lovely Wandoo trees, a great place to look for orchids in early spring. There are picnic facilities and a toilet.

Drive: For those interested in wildflowers, a slow drive along the full length of Park Road will show you many of the 500 odd species of wildflowers that have been recorded for this park. The reason for the fairly high species count is that the park is quite large, covering 2,676 ha and includes some good patches of heath, particularly on the scarp and near granite outcrops. The Wandoo woodland is a great place for orchids.

Facilities: Around the parking area past Glen Brook Dam are all the main facilities with barbecues, picnic tables, toilets, kiosk, cafeteria and a tavern.

The main ranger office is based here. Although on busy days you will have passed entry stations where entry fees are charged and they can give you most information you may require, long distance walkers should register at the main office.

Paruna & Karakamia
SANCTUARY

We hear so often how the wealthy add to their already vast accrued assets by purchasing additional luxury items that foster their innate desire to attain supposed wealth.

It is a rare individual though, that spends substantial sums of money on projects where the main objective is to restore an area of bushland and return fauna that once was prolific in that region.

Martin Copley is one such individual, spurred on by his good wife Lorraine Copley who was inspired by Dr John Wamsley's Warrawong Sanctuary in South Australia.

Karakamia: The first sanctuary to be established was Karakamia named after the Noongar word for 'home of the Red–tailed Black-Cockatoo' which frequents the area.

Karakamia is now a 280 ha sanctuary located near Chidlow. Even though this is not a vast area, it still contains the major habitat types that occur in the Darling Range, namely Jarrah and Marri woodland, Wandoo woodland, granite outcrops and riparian vegetation (creek lined vegetation systems).

Surrounding the sanctuary is a sophisticated electrified fencing system. After baiting and eradicating the vast majority of feral animals in the reserve, those animals that once were plentiful in the hills such as the Quenda (*Isoodon obesulus*), Brush-tailed Bettong or Woylie (*Bettongia penicillata*), Quokka (*Setonix brachyurus*), Ringtail Possum (*Pseudocheirus occidentalis*), Numbat (*Myrmecobius fasciatus*) and Tammar Wallaby (*Macropus eugenii*) have been reintroduced and numbers have increased for all species each year. Other marsupials that were present before in low numbers have now increased in numbers.

There are guided spotlighting walks available with group sizes of 8–20 people but bookings must be made prior to visiting the reserve. The spotlighting activities are most rewarding for everybody, particularly for children (minimum age 7). Fees do apply.

Paruna Sanctuary: This was the second major project to be undertaken by the Copley family. The sanctuary forms a link between Walyunga National Park and Avon Valley National Park and is federally listed as land vested with a 'not for profit' environmental organisation.

There are a series of well-defined walking trails, many of which have been created and laid out, with the aid of community groups and the Green Corps traineeship. Small cantilevered viewing platforms and hundreds of metres of timber steps have been neatly built into the hillsides to aid the visitor with their walk.

The public are welcome to visit the sanctuary but an entry fee is charged and a map of the particular walk chosen will be sent to visitors on request. It is essential that prior bookings are made. Allow minimum 2 days.

The sanctuaries are a credit to all involved and particularly to those who manage them and most of all to the Copleys who had the vision to create such beneficial environmental projects for all of us to enjoy.

Looking towards one of the few viewing platforms in Paruna Sanctuary

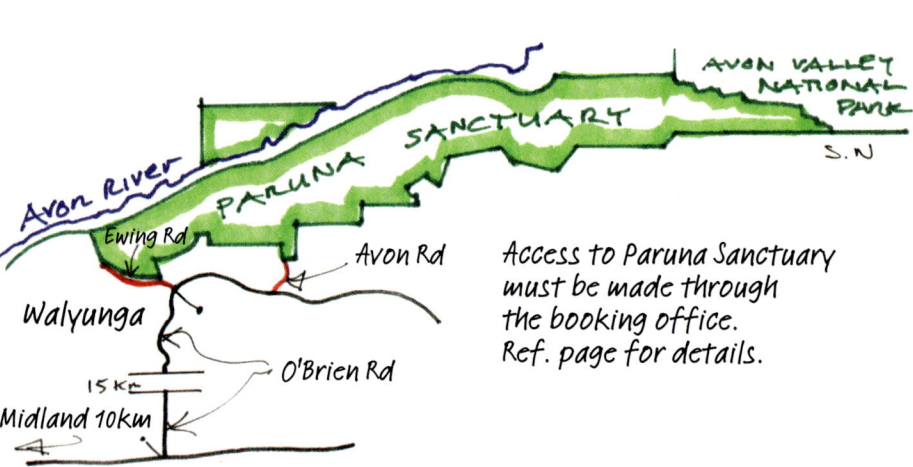

Access to Paruna Sanctuary must be made through the booking office. Ref. page for details.

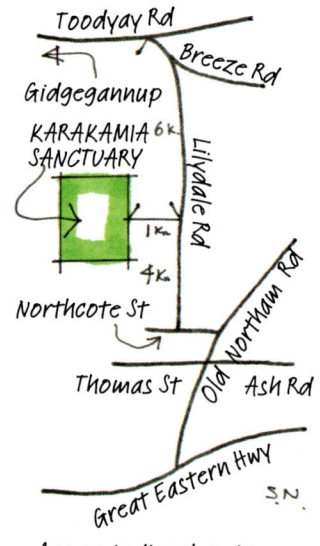

Access to Karakamia must be made through booking office ref. page for details

North Ledge picnic area   View from South Ledge

North Ledge

Not far from Mundaring Weir, this is a very pretty spot on the side of Helena Valley, giving views of Helena Reservoir. There are picnic tables and barbecues set amongst lovely Wandoo trees. There are many flowers around the granite rocks in spring. A short 15 minute loop trail gives views over Helena Reservoir. There are toilets available.

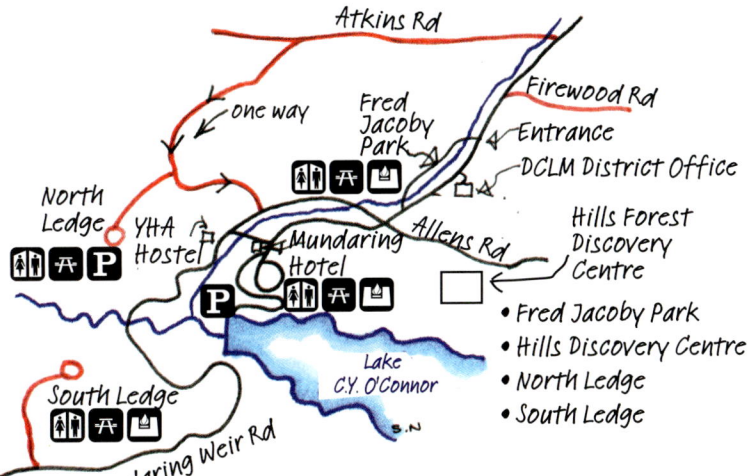

- Fred Jacoby Park
- Hills Discovery Centre
- North Ledge
- South Ledge

South Ledge

A small quiet picnic area located south of Mundaring Weir on Weir Road. The turn-off is 2 km south of Mundaring Weir, then a 1 km dirt road. There are several picnic tables, toilet and adjacent walks. There are Jarrah and Marri trees around the picnic area and quite a few flowers out in spring where the granite outcrops occur.

Hills Forest Discovery Centre

Hills Forest Discovery Centre

This centre was established in 1992 with the objective of assisting people with various programs that would enhance their understanding and interest in the Jarrah forest; it is the main focal point from which many activities are held or organised.

The various outdoor (and indoor in the case of the Hills Forest Centre) activities are centred on visiting parks and reserves in the Mundaring, Kalamunda and Karragullen region such as John Forrest, Gooseberry Hill, Kalamunda and Lesmurdie National Parks and Mt Dale Conservation Park.

In the early stages of the Hills "Go Bush" project, there were just a few activities available but now there are many and varied activities with over 20,000 visitors attending annually.

The program is vast and includes: night walks, bush art and crafts, Aboriginal cultural activities, bats in the bush, meet our marsupials, abseiling, Bibbulmun discovery, Noongar bush women's issues, Noongar bush men's issues, bush foods, discovering various parks, star gazing, bird watching walks and many other activities. There are facilities and programs for handicapped people and a strong school activity program. Camping facilities are provided at the centre including bush camping sites on the Bibbulmun Track and adjacent forest areas.

The fee is small to enter a program and it is great value. The centre is based on Weir Road, Mundaring. Phone 9295 2244 to find out what programs are available.

Lesmurdie Falls

Lesmurdie
NATIONAL PARK

Lesmurdie National Park is one of the many small parks that lie on the Darling Scarp. Lesmurdie Brook runs through the park, cascading over a 50 m waterfall in winter and spring. Above the falls is a raised platform that looks over the falls and gives views of the city below. There is a track that will take you down to the base of the falls. There are picnic tables, barbecues and toilets both at the top and bottom of the park. Access from the top of the hill is via Falls Road off Lesmurdie Road in Lesmurdie, or at the base of the park via Palm Terrace in Wattle Grove.

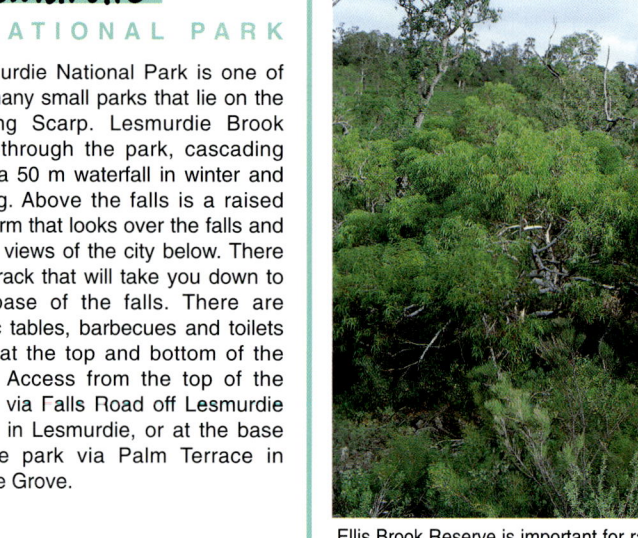

Ellis Brook Reserve is important for rare and restricted eucalypts

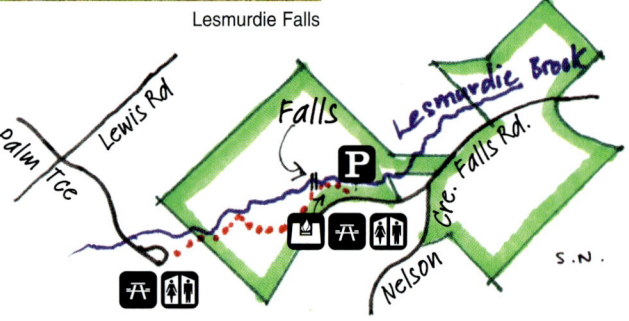

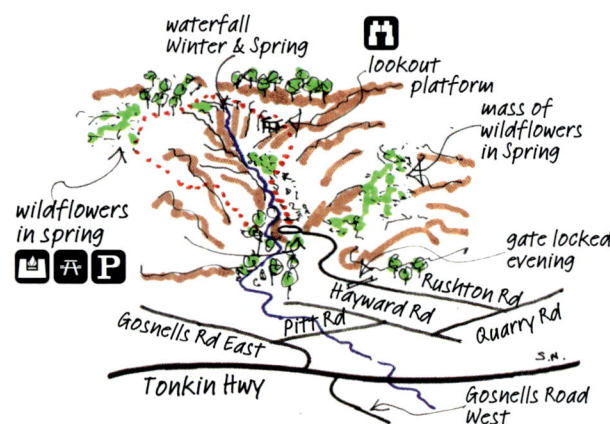

Fred Jacoby Park

The park is surrounded by state forest and consists of landscaped gardens and many trees planted from around the world. Fred Jacoby developed the gardens in the early 1900s. He was a tireless worker and organised the building of the Goldfields Weir Hotel (now the Mundaring Hotel). Mr Jacoby died in 1954 and his daughter Mrs Elfreda Devenish, donated the land around Jacoby Park to the people of Western Australia. It is now managed by DCLM and lies near their Hills Activity Centre. There are pleasant walks along Bending Gully and the 27 km long Kattamorda Heritage Trail passes through the park. There is a relatively short walk known as the Portagabra Trail, which is a 3 km loop trail leading from and returning to the park. There are picnic tables, barbecues, playground and toilet facilities. The park is on the north west side of Mundaring Weir Road, Mundaring.

Deciduous trees dropping their leaves in winter in Jacoby Park

Ellis Brook Valley Reserve

Like Bickley Brook Valley, this area is not as yet administered by a park authority but may later form part of the proposed Darling Range Regional Park. The valley is not as extensive as Bickley Brook but the wildflowers in this area are some of the most prolific in the metropolitan area. You can park at the end of Rushton Road and walk 15 minutes up the hill to Ellis Brook Falls, which runs in winter and spring. On the way there is a lookout platform below the falls. Above the falls are exposed granite rocks and near here are some uncommon Salmon White Gum *(Eucalyptus lanepoolei)*.

It is a great place to come in winter and spring. The heath on the hillside opposite the toilets (burnt down by vandals in 1999), in the lower valley has some of the highest concentrations of wildflower species in the Perth region.

It is not a simple route to the valley. The visitor must leave the Tonkin Highway at Gosnells Road East, turn right into Pitt Road, then right into Hayward Road, left into Quarry Road and finally left again into Rushton Road.

Bickley Brook Valley

This has to be one of the most pleasant valley walks near Perth and takes the walker past beautiful Wandoo woodland up the hill to granite rocks and Jarrah and Marri woodland. In spring the valley is full of wildflowers, particularly on the scarp heath just past the Bickley Brook Recreation Camp on Hardinge Road, Orange Grove and in the higher valley where Bickley Brook cuts through the granite and dolerite rock. Here, lots of Lemon-scented Darwinia (Darwinia citriodora) will be in bloom, as well as Fuchsia Grevillea (Grevillea bipinnatifida), Pindak (Calothamnus sanguineus) and the lovely Candle Cranberry (Astroloma foliosum).

There are many birds to be seen in the valley including Scarlet Robin, Western Yellow Robin, Red-eared Firetail, Splendid Fairy-wren, Red-winged Fairy-wren, Red-capped Parrot, White-naped Honeyeater, Golden Whistler, Rufous Whistler and Wedge-tailed Eagle. On the heath slopes near Bickley Reservoir is one of the few sites in the metropolitan area where you can find the diminutive Southern Emu-wren.

The valley does not come under the administration of any parks authority at present, so there are no facilities and much of the land is vested with the Water Authority, but in the future, there are plans in progress for the Darling Range Regional Park and this wonderful valley hopefully will come under that plan.

The valley forms part of the 27 km Kattamorda Heritage Trail that runs from the township of Mundaring, all the way past Mundaring Weir, Kalamunda and eventually down the Bickley Valley to Bickley Reservoir.

It was in the Bickley Valley in 1864 that Benjamin Mason established the first sawmill in the Darling Range employing over one hundred men, mostly ex-convicts. Timber was hauled by horse-drawn teams all the way down to Masons Landing on the Canning River.

From Bickley Brook Reservoir to Mason Mill Road is a 4 km walk one way.

There are barbecues, picnic tables and toilets at the base of the valley in Hardinge Park just below Bickley Brook Reservoir.

The valley can also be accessed from the car park on Mason Mill Road off Canning Road, Carmel. The car park is difficult to locate but drive down the Victoria Reservoir Road for 200 m and on the right is a dirt track. Turn here and drive down the hill to the clearing. The walking trail is quite clear then. There are no facilities.

Part of the Kattamorda Heritage Trail

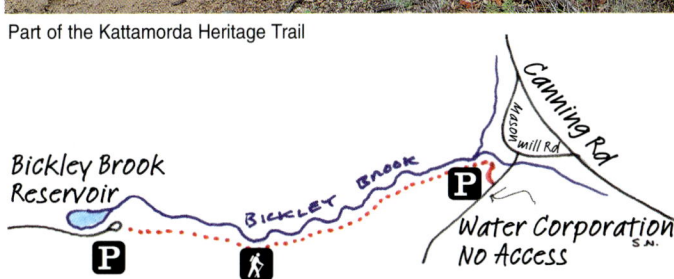

Bungendore Park

Bungendore is a wonderful woodland area to walk and is only 5 km from Armadale but it could be worlds away when you enter some of its quieter corners. It is an 'A' class reserve covering 500 ha not far from Wungong Dam. Its name comes from the Noongar for "place of blossom".

Most of the park is a lateritic plateau some 280 m high. Where the park falls away to Wungong valley on the western borders and the Darling Scarp, granite bedrock is often exposed.

Most of the park is Jarrah and Marri woodland, with Parrot Bush (Dryandra sessilis) and Bull Banksia with an understorey of many different flowering plants like Prickly Bitter-pea (Daviesia decurrens), Yellow Buttercups (Hibbertia hypericoides), White Cottonhead (Conostylis setosa), Drumstick Isopogon (Isopogon sphaerocephalus) and Woolly-flowered Grevillea (Grevillea pilulifera). Some of the terrestrial Orchids include Common Donkey Orchid (Diuris corymbosa), Red Beaks (Burnettia nigricans), Blue China Orchid (Cyanicula gemmata), Purple Enamel Orchid (Elythranthera brunonis) and Star Orchid (Thelymitra stellata).

As the scarp area is approached around Cooliaberra Spring, open areas of Wandoo appear with understorey wildflowers like White Myrtle (Hypocalymma angustifolium) and Prickly Moses (Acacia pulchella). On the southern side of the Cooliabarra Spring valley, is a lovely patch of heath near the granite slopes with Featherflower (Verticordia acerosa), Roadside Tea-tree (Leptospermum erubescens) and Spindly Grevillea (Grevillea endlicheriana). On the lower slopes near the Wungong valley, Blackbutt (Eucalyptus patens) grows.

For the birdwatcher, there is much to see. The park is a good area to see the Red-tailed Black-Cockatoo (Calyptorhynchus banksii subsp. naso), Rufous Treecreeper and Western Yellow Robin as well as all the regular birds like Golden Whistler, Rufous Whistler, Inland Thornbill, Western Thornbill, Western Gerygone, Red-capped Parrot and Long-billed Black-Cockatoo.

Access is off Admiral Road off the Albany Highway in Bedfordale. The parking area is just past the entrance to Emmaus Christian Primary School on the west side of Admiral Road.

At the entry point off Admiral Road

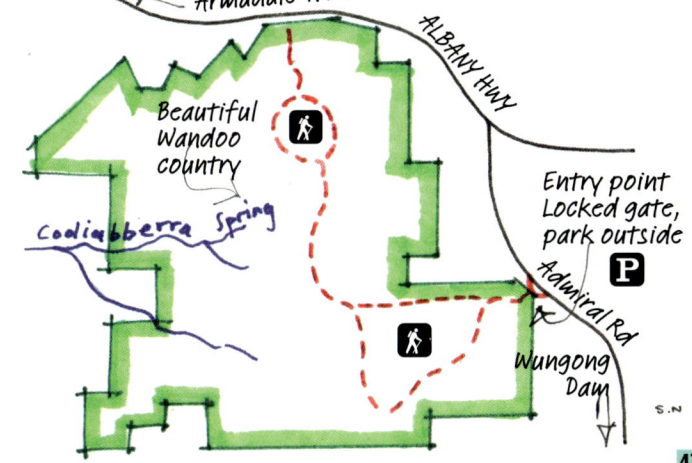

Araluen
BOTANIC PARK

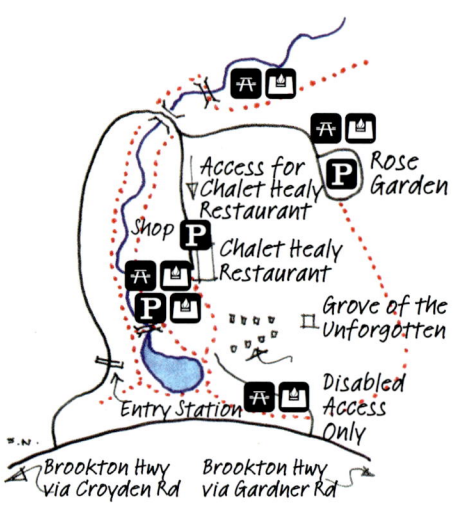

Located near the end of Croyden Road, Roleystone. J.J. Simons, set aside 60 ha in 1929 for the Youth Australia League. The League members and volunteers made pathways and terraces to form the foundation for this park. They are some of the best ornamental gardens in the hills. There are lovely picnic sites, toilets, kiosk and a very pleasant restaurant that has views over the gardens. If you like flowers at all times of the year and enjoy introduced plants set in well planned gardens, then this small park should please you. There is a small entry fee as the park is self-funded.

The Christmas Tree (*Nuytsia floribunda*) at Christmas Tree Well

Plenty of shady areas at Langford Park–great place for children

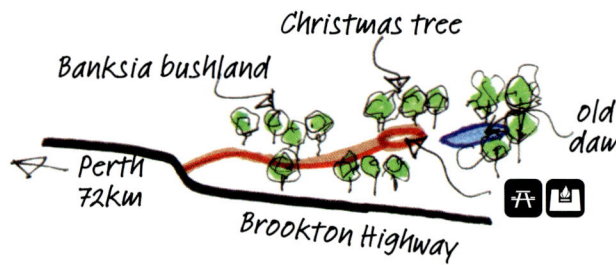
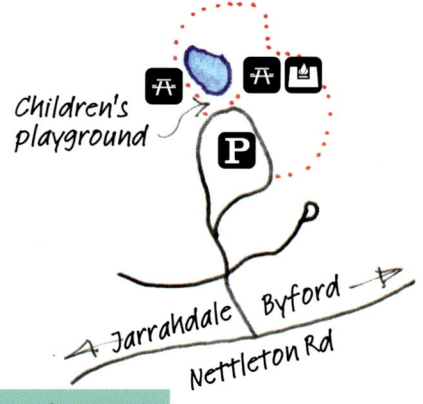

Christmas Tree Well

Situated 70 km from the city centre, this is a useful spot to pull off the Brookton Highway and see one of the old water holes that was used by early travellers through the Jarrah forest. Adjacent to the small pool are Swamp Paperbark trees and a fine group of Christmas Trees (*Nuytsia floribunda*). It is hard to imagine that these large trees are in fact members of the mistletoe family. They spread out large root systems that draw nourishment from surrounding plants, although this is only part of their nutrient source. There are some old log tables and an open fireplace. Be careful of snakes near the edge of forest water holes.

Langford Park

This was once one of the earliest bauxite mining sites. It has been well landscaped and the visitor would hardly know that mining operations were carried out here in the early 1970s. There is a small artificial lake. Surrounding it are well-kept lawns, picnic tables, barbecues, toilets and a good children's play area.

Located off the South Western Highway at Byford, take Nettleford Road, keep driving up through the hills for a few kilometres; on the right, is a sign to Langford Park and just 1 km in is a small roundabout; take the road straight on, not right, and you will come to the car park.

Sullivan Rock & Mt Vincent

If you wanted to experience and understand the nature of a large granite rock and the surrounding vegetation communities it creates, then Sullivan Rock is one of the best to visit near Perth.

Situated 65 km from Perth, the rock is accessed via the Sullivan picnic site on the west side of the Albany Highway, the site of the old "40 mile well" used when the first Perth to Albany Road was constructed.

To get to the rock first pull off the highway on the right hand side if you are travelling from Perth. There is a sign. Drive around the back of the picnic site and you will see a small track that leads into the picnic area. Park here and walk across the highway where the Bibbulmun Track sign is located. Be very careful with children crossing here, as cars from Perth are travelling down hill at high speeds.

The track will take you through a narrow band of Jarrah and Marri woodland. You will see quite a few species of wildflowers here, including Couch Honeypot *(Dryandra nivea)*, Honeybush *(Hakea lissocarpha)*, Crinkle-leaved Poison *(Gastrolobium villosum)*, Hairy Jugflower *(Adenanthos barbigerus)*, Ribbed Wattle *(Acacia nervosa)*, Broad-leaved Brown Pea *(Bossiaea ornata)*, Prickly Bitter-pea *(Daviesia horrida)*, Dwarf Sheoak *(Allocasuarina humilis)* and Wilson's Grevillea *(Grevillea wilsonii)*.

About 200 m through the woodland you will come to the base of Sullivan Rock. Here you can climb up to the top of the rock. In the gullies that gather additional vegetation litter, you will see many of the granite outcrop frequenting plants like Sea Urchin Hakea *(Hakea petiolaris)*.

If you want to make a real walk and enjoy great views, then a combined walk including Sullivan Rock and Mt Vincent is well recommended. It is a 7 km return walk but you must be fit as it leads up steep granite slopes at times. Be particularly careful when it is wet.

To walk to Mt Vincent, walk to the top of Sullivan Rock and then over the top into the Jarrah woodland. Be careful here as the track is not obvious until you enter the woodland. After about 200 m you will come to a 4WD track; the Bibbulmun Track with yellow markers will go to the left, keep going into the Jarrah woodland opposite where you entered and keep walking along the track. There are beautiful mature Sheoak *(Allocasuarina fraseriana)* trees in this area. Keep following the track until you come to another exposed granite outcrop. Continue walking up the hill. When you pass the granite rock, you will pass through a thick patch of dryandra bushes; at the fork take the lower track. As you climb Mt Vincent there is a side track to the right that leads to a lookout. Keep to the left and climb up to the summit of Mt Vincent with its stone cairn. There are great views from here across the vast Jarrah forest that we are so privileged to have so close to Perth. Return the way you came.

Walking in the mist towards Mt Vincent

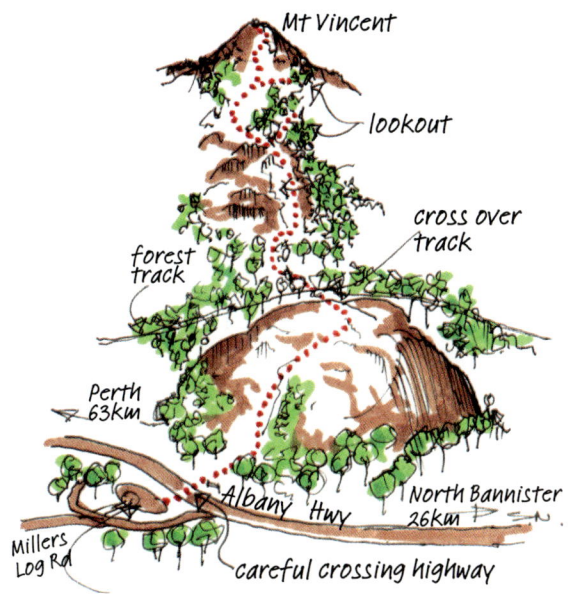

Wilson's Grevillea *(Grevillea wilsonii)* from below Sullivan Rock ▶

Serpentine
NATIONAL PARK

Europeans have been visiting Serpentine Falls for over one hundred years and the Whadjuk Tribe for probably thousands of years before that, to take fish, dig for succulent roots and hunt animals. Two of the streams above the falls still have the Aboriginal names of Carralong and Gooralong.

In the mid 1850s much of the land on the adjacent coastal plain was cleared for farming and also a water mill for grinding wheat was established on Gooralong Brook. Over the next forty years much of the mature Jarrah timber was cut, with the timber town of Jarrahdale not being that far away. In 1891, the Western Australian Natural History Society was founded. Very soon they realised that most of the Darling Scarp was losing much of its timber in recreational areas, so they recommended to the State Government that 160,000 acres be set aside in the Serpentine region and the state's first Reserve for Flora and Fauna was established. In 1911 the reserve was cancelled due to pressures by landholders to have orchards etc in the lower valleys. Serpentine Falls was, however, set aside as a reserve and a caretaker was housed near the falls, due to the quantity of people who still visited the area.

There are three main recreational areas within the park and include the following:

Serpentine Falls: The falls are located 49 km south east of Perth and are accessed off the South Western Highway. Turn off at Falls Road heading east and the falls parking area is 2 km along Falls Road.

There are barbecues, picnic tables and toilets. The falls are a short 15 minute walk and can be accessed by wheelchair. People still try to swim in the falls area but serious accidents have happened so it is not recommended. There is a timber viewing platform and when the water is in full flood, it is quite a sight. Around the grass lawns in the late afternoon, Western Grey Kangaroos come down to graze and are quite unconcerned about visitors. If you have children make sure they do not get too close as kangaroos, particularly males, can be unpredictable. There is always a temptation to feed them with bread but try not to, as it's very bad for them in the long term. It can also encourage aggressive behaviour.

Walks: Located to the left of the toilet block is the track to Baldwins Bluff, it is a 6 km walk and you should be reasonably fit as it climbs up gravel tracks to Baldwins Bluff. You will pass through Jarrah and Marri woodland, eventually coming to Wandoo woodland and then finally over exposed granite. There are great views in to the valley and across the Swan Coastal Plain. Allow 2 hours.

Kitty Gorge Walk Trail is an 11 km, 5 hr, marked walk that takes you up Serpentine Gorge to Gooralong Brook and then into Kittys Gorge. The track begins from the lower car park.

It is important to remember the gates close at 5.00 p.m. at Serpentine Falls.

Gooralong picnic and camping area: This area lies on the northern part of the park and is accessed via the township of Jarrahdale. Turn south off Jarrahdale Road in the town at Oak Way, which shortly leads to Atkins Street, turn right and follow the road west. It will turn sharply left and Gooralong Road will be on the right. There are barbecues, picnic tables, toilets and a camping ground. This is one of the closest bush camping sites to Perth and quite a number of people use it. If you want a more wilderness type experience then this is not for you but it is great if time is limited and you just want to get away for the weekend.

Walk: Kitty's Trail. This is shorter than the Kitty Gorge Walk, from Serpentine Falls, but links with it. It is a 4.5 km loop walk, starting from the Gooralong camping ground car park; cross over the bridge at Gooralong Brook and walk downstream and you will come to a granite outcrop area, then further you will pass the water gauging station building. Cross the brook below the building and walk along the weir access track. It will turn sharply east. Keep walking until markers point away from the track, follow them and it will take you over granite rocks and woodland, finally meeting another track. Turn left and head for the pine woods and where you started.

Pipehead Dam: This area is run by the Water Commission, and there is a dam and an overflow area that runs over granite boulders. It is a good location if you have a family, as there is a good

Serpentine Falls

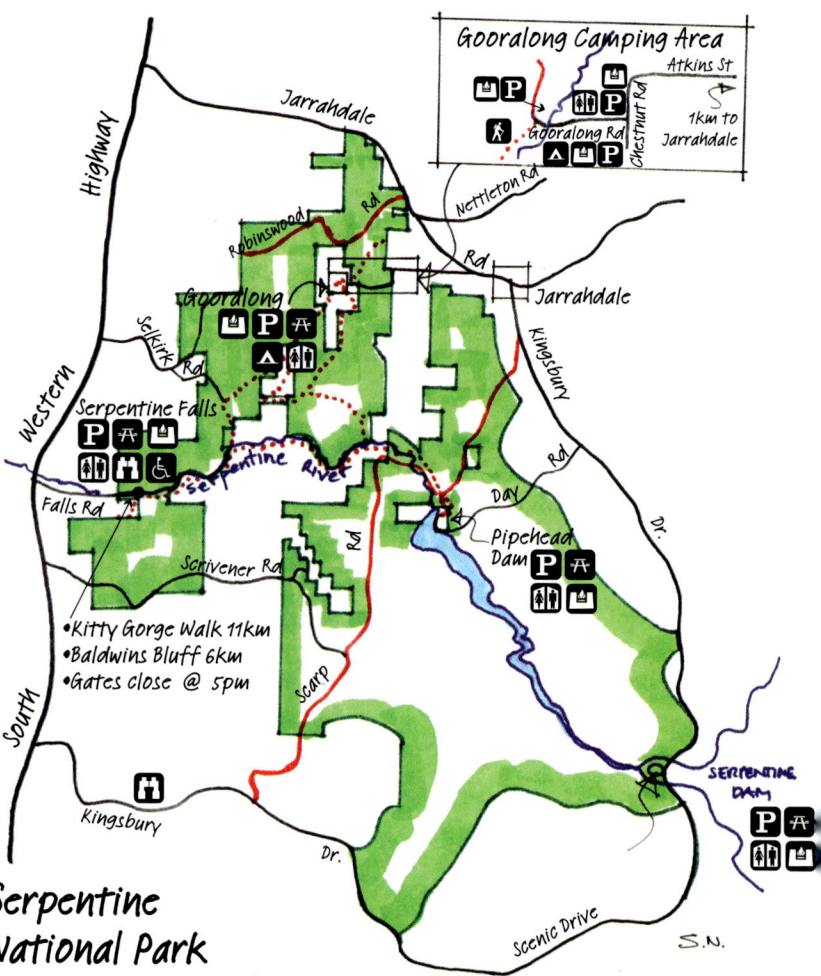

Serpentine National Park

playground facility and barbecue, tables and toilets. It does not have the high number of visitors that some dams do, so can be relatively peaceful. The picnic ground is accessed via Jarrahdale. As you are leaving the eastern side of Jarrahdale, take the right hand turn down Kingbury Drive and about 3 km on the right is Day Road. A further 2.5 km will bring you to the picnic grounds.

Flora and Fauna: The park has varied plant communities including Jarrah/Marri woodland, granite outcrop communities, heath and riverine habitat.

The park has two restricted and uncommon eucalypts namely Salmon White Gum *(Eucalyptus lanepoolei)* and Darling Range Ghost Gum *(E. laeliae)*; both are found on the scarp and can be seen on the walks leading above Serpentine Falls. In the heath country there are many wildflowers in season, including the rare Summer Pimelea *(Pimelea rara)* and the uncommon Prickly Wattle *(Acacia horridula)*, making it an important refuge for these plants.

The following marsupials have been recorded for the park: Mardo *(Antechinus flavipes)*, Brushtail Possum *(Trichosurus vulpecula)*, Southern Brown Bandicoot *(Isoodon obesulus)*, Western Brush Wallaby *(Macropus irma)* and Western Grey Kangaroo *(Macropus fuliginosus)* as well as the monotreme, the Short-beaked Echidna *(Tachyglossus aculeatus)*.

For the birdwatchers, the park is a great place to see some of the birds that are endemic to Western Australia and require riverine habitats, namely the Red-eared Firetail, White-breasted Robin and Red-winged Fairy-wren. The Wandoo woodlands are a good place to see the pretty Western Yellow Robin.

Boulder Rock

This is a good example of how the granite bedrock can be exposed through the laterite duricrust. On the top of the main rock are huge boulders, remnants of a layered granite that fractured along fault lines, formed cubic shapes and over thousands of years the corners were slowly weathered by winds to produce these spherical balls.

You can see the many plant colonisers that grow on all south west granite outcrops. The first basic plant life to colonise the rocks is the living algae, which produce the dark stains that follow the water run off courses. As the algae slowly breaks down the granite crust, small depressions are created, where the next larger coloniser takes hold, the mosses. Along with mosses, the lichens take hold and spread out from a central core. The lichens, mosses and algae all contribute by secreting acids that, over hundreds of years, slowly break down the granite, which in turn is washed away, forming small depressions in which wind blown debris and sands form small areas of soil within which plants like the Pincushion *(Borya sphaerocephala)* and small ferns can take hold.

There are always more of the Pincushions and ferns on the south facing slopes as, there, they can avoid the intense summer sun. Most of these plants survive the hot dry summers by literally closing down all growth systems waiting for the first autumn rains to bring everything back to life.

At the base of the rocks there are several plants found around granite outcrops making use of the additional water run off, such as trigger plants *(Stylidium species)* and Sundews *(Drosera species)* and larger plants like Mouse Ears *(Calothamnus rupestris)* and Sea Urchin Hakea *(Hakea petiolaris)*.

Look out for orchids, even on the south facing slopes amongst the mosses and deeper vegetation.

There are no facilities at Boulder Rock.

Huge ancient rocks weathered with time that lie on the summit of Boulder Rock

Mount Dale

Situated 64 km from Perth, Mount Dale is 542 m high. It has been a small picnic area for many years giving the visitor splendid views of the Darling Range and the expanse of forest from the coast to the edge of the wheatbelt. You can drive almost to the top, getting spectacular views.

One kilometre below the top car park is a pleasant picnic spot with a few picnic tables. Normally this is a very quiet location but a great place to just get away and wander around the granite outcrop. In spring there are many orchids in the area and several of the granite frequenting plants. The turnoff on the Brookton Highway is opposite the Lesley picnic ground. From the turn-off, go 5 km north and then 12 km east to reach Mt Dale. The road is dirt. Be careful of people driving fast on these quiet roads, as they often think they are the only ones on the track.

Looking across the Jarrah forest from Mt Dale

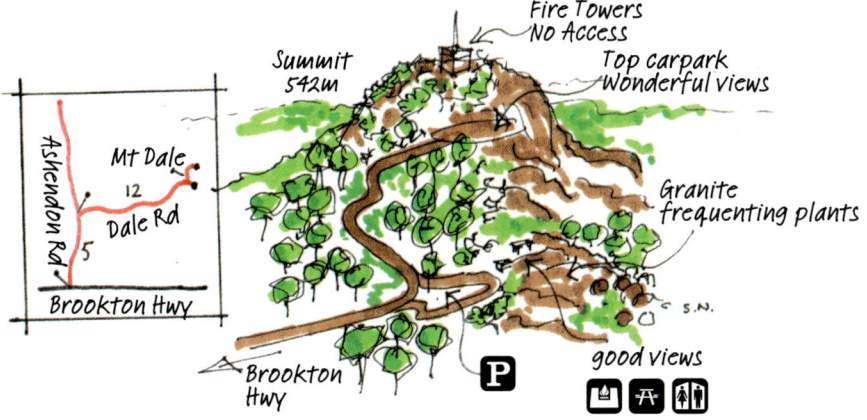

Hills
RESERVOIRS

Wungong Reservoir

Churchman's Brook Reservoir

Supplying enough water for the fast growing city of Perth is a great concern to many who understand the problems of limited water supplies in a city that has a Mediterranean climate. The reservoirs in the hills are the major supplier of Perth's water needs but each year the pressure to secure more water for the expanding urban area increases. If we could grow more native plants and fewer lawns we would be improving the environment in two ways. Firstly, the total surface area of grass lawns in the metropolitan area is vast and the water to keep these lawns alive in summer is also vast. If we grow native plants that occur naturally in the region, they are adapted to Perth's climate and will need far less water. Secondly, growing plants native to the region will attract the native species of birds and insects that feed on their flowers and fruit, and this will help to restore some of the natural balance of nature we have largely destroyed. Birds attracted to the native plants would include the Red Wattlebird, Little Wattlebird, New Holland Honeyeater, Brown Honeyeater, Singing Honeyeater and Silvereye. Think about it, your water bills will certainly be less.

There are five major reservoirs close to Perth:
- Helena Reservoir accessed via Mundaring Weir Road, Mundaring.
- Churchman's Brook Reservoir accessed via Churchman's Brook Road, Roleystone.
- Canning Reservoir accessed via Lady McNess Drive in Roleystone or Lady McNess Drive off Albany Highway in Bedfordale.
- Wungong Reservoir accessed via either Admiral Road or Springfield Road off Albany Highway, Bedfordale.
- Serpentine Reservoir accessed via Kingsbury Drive, south of Jarrahdale.

All are administered by the Water Authority and they maintain recreational facilities at each of the above reservoirs, including barbecues, picnic tables and toilets. Most have playground facilities so they are very suitable for families.

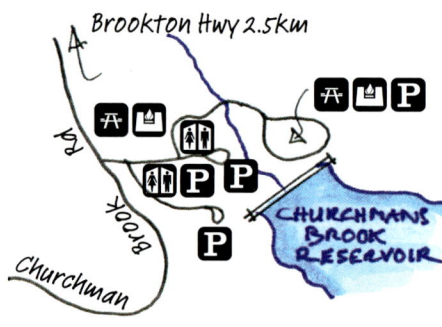
Churchmans Brook

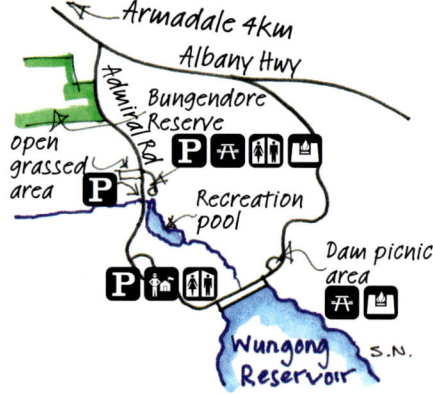
Wungong Reservoir

Munda Biddi Trail
FOREST CYCLING TRAIL

"Munda Biddi" comes from the Nyoongar language and means 'path through the forest'.

This is a new long distance cycling trail that starts in Mundaring in the hills east of Perth and eventually will finish in Albany.

The trail is being developed by DCLM and several other state government departments, local government departments, local governments, businesses and the community.

The first part of the trail from Mundaring to Collie, will be completed in 2003, then Collie to Pemberton in 2004 and finally, Pemberton to Albany in 2005. The trail has been designed for cyclists of all ages and passes throgh magnificient jarrah and karri forest.

There are overnight shelters along the trail. There is a Munda Biddi Trail Foundation that is is a not-for-profit organisation that assists with the development of the trail. You can become a member and assist in this worthwhile project. Contact DCLM or Munda Bidi Trail Foundation for more information.

Phone: 0422 11 3339
Email: foundation@mundabiddi.org.au Website: www.mundabiddi.org.au

Munda Biddi Trail

The Bibbulmun Track

When one person's dream becomes a reality, there is a great sense of achievement. The Bibbulmun Track was bush walker Geoff Schafer's dream and coming from the state of Victoria, he knew a lot about long walks, especially the Victorian Alpine trail. He thought that a similar track would benefit the people of Western Australia and most of all get them out to experience the bush.

In 1972 he presented his concept to the then Minister for Forests, Mr H.D. Evans and from there it was slowly developed over the years by the then Forests Department and afterwards by DCLM. Now, thanks to the hard work of many volunteers, prisoners, foresters and DCLM employees, the dream has been realised and we have a 960 km world class, long distance overland walking trail.

On the track there are 48 campsites, each with well constructed timber shelters, sleeping from 8-16 hikers. There are small fire places at most of the camp sites between Kalamunda and the Shannon River. Due to fire risk and scarcity of firewood, the use of portable fuel stores is encouraged and is is indeed essential between Shannon River and Albany. There are areas set aside for tents and pit or composting toilets, picnic tables and rain water tanks.

You can't book the shelters as sleeping space is taken up on a first come, first served basis. Groups of 8 or more are asked not to occupy shelters before nightfall. The campsites are set between 10 and 20 kms apart, based on a full days walk between campsites. There are gold triangular track markers depicting a snake symbol that represents the Waugal creation being of the Nyoongar people who occupy the south west of Australia. These markers guide walkers along the whole distance of the track.

There are many ways one can walk the track. Obviously to walk it all, takes several weeks and not everyone wants to do this. Most will tackle a shorter section and may then choose to stay at a range of lodgings located close to the track rather than at track campsites. There are also dropoff and pickup services at some of the towns along the way.

Plenty of vehicle access points enable you to walk shorter parts of the Bibbulmun Track from a range of locations between Kalamunda to Albany. Walking through the jarrah forest is a wonderful feeling and the coastal views from the walk between Walpole and Albany are simply breathtaking at times.

Very good, detailed maps and guide books published by DCLM are available and a map is an essential item for even shorter walks.

Remember that a full days walk on any section may be fairly demanding, so you will enjoy your walk better if you are reasonably fit. Good footwear is essential. Drink water before you start and carry at least 2 litres along with map or guide book, compass, adequate rain gear, warm clothes and a hat. Most important, let people know your intended route and when you plan to return. Don't be too ambitious, select a shorter section to get a feel for it and you will probably return and walk more of this magnificent track.

There are many points the Bibbulmun Track can be accessed from, but the principal parks and major recreation sites that the track passes through are: Kalamunda NP (new Helena and Mundaring NPs), Dale Conservation Park, Monadnocks CP, Lane Poole CP (soon to be NP), Harris River Dam, Noggerup, Preston and Dalgarup (Karri Gully) CPs, Golden Valley Tree Park, One Tree Bridge CP, Beedelup NP, Big Brook Dam, Gloucester NP, d'Entrecasteaux NP, Shannon NP, Walpole Nornalup NP, Valley of the Giants – Treetop Walk, William Bay NP, West Cape Howe NP and Torndirrup NP. (Some of these parks and localities are not listed in this book.)

The Bibbulmun track passes by huge Tingle trees in the Walpole Nornalup NP

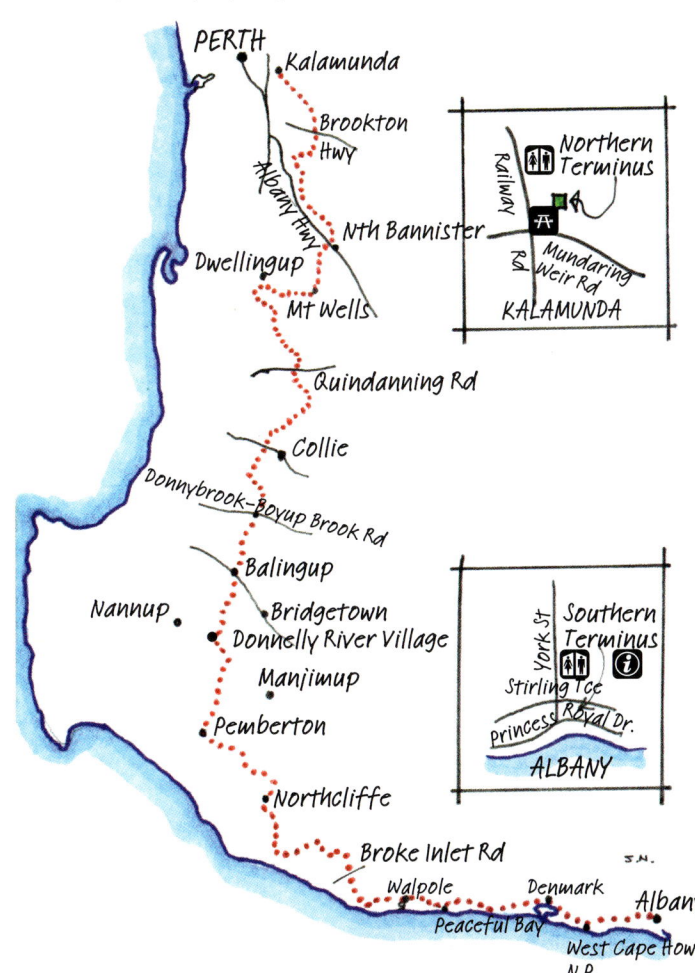

Gleneagle

This was an old timber mill town site; all that remains of the early days are several trees that are not endemic to Western Australia like the Jacarandas, pine trees, Blue Gums and some tall acacias. It is a pleasant stop if you need a break on the Albany Highway. There are several picnic tables and it is best to drive to the far side away from the highway noise under some large pines. There are tables, barbecues and toilets.

Located 55 km south of Perth, the turn-off is on the north east side of Albany Highway.

There are many exotic deciduous trees planted at Gleneagle, the site of the old town mill

Canal Rocks—Leeuwin Naturaliste National Park

South West
REGION

South West
R E G I O N

Travelling south of Perth most people travel down the coastal highway passing through Mandurah. This route leads to some interesting coastal parks with fishing, walking and camping and other recreational opportunities. Many people head for the Margaret River region, which gives ample opportunity to relax, with its beautiful coastal scenery and wineries, as well as a great variety of accommodation possibilities.

The South Western Highway, offers the option to visit many of the Jarrah forest parks. If you have a few days break, then Lane Poole Reserve is a great place to camp with family or friends. You can canoe down the Murray River, take walks into the Jarrah forest or relax around the campfire. It is also a great place to take larger groups camping and there are designated areas to do so. The great thing is that the park is only 2 hrs drive from Perth. Besides Lane Poole Reserve there are countless small picnic and camping places in the south west Jarrah forest, many included in this section.

For those who wish to experience the cool, tall Karri country, then travelling down to the Pemberton region will certainly offer one of the best areas of tall forests in the world. For the traveller who wants remote, wilderness areas where one can walk, fish and camp with few, if any people, then D'Entrecasteaux National Park is one place to visit, particularly if you have a 4WD. It is a wonderful feeling to know one can leave Perth in the early morning and be camped on a remote beach by mid-afternoon, having the camping spot all to oneself.

◀ Driving through the Karri and Tingle forest in the deep south west

Coastal parks
OF THE SOUTH WEST

Yalgorup
NATIONAL PARK

Yalgorup is located just south of Mandurah, and has a total area of around 12,000 ha. The park consists of some of the best preserved coastal vegetation of the Swan coastal plain, particularly its Tuart and Peppermint woodlands.

Yalgorup is the Noongar word for the 'place of lakes', which is not surprising as there is an important chain of 10 lakes, the largest being Lake Clifton and Lake Preston. These are major wetlands for migrating birds from Asia, plus at times it has large numbers of Black Swan, Australian Shelduck, Musk Duck and Banded Stilt. In 1986 there were 13,800 Australian Shelduck counted on Lake Clifton alone.

At the northern end of Lake Clifton there is a very good viewing platform that allows one to view stromatolites and thrombolites. These algae growth structures represent some of the oldest known examples of cellular life, pre-dating most life forms today, and are literally living fossil rocks. They can be seen most times of the year but are at their most exposed in March and April. The viewing causeway has two new access points signed off Old Coast Road, Lakeside Parkway coming from north and Clifton Downs if coming from the south. There is a small information bay describing the stromatolites and local fauna.

Further south in the park there is a camping area at Martins Tank. There is a walk to Lake Pollard that starts at the turn off to the camp ground passing through some lovely Tuart and Peppermint woodland. In spring and winter this is a lovely area to just get away from the big crowds that congregate at Mandurah and other places only a short journey away. All large groups wishing to camp should seek advise from the ranger. There are other picnic localities in the park. A good picnic stop at the site of the old Whittakers Mill on the Old Coastal Highway 4 km south of the entrance road to Preston Beach makes a welcome stop if you are on a long drive.

Only the lower third of Lake Preston is for boating and other water recreational sports. The rest is a set aside as a nature reserve and no boating acivities are allowed.

One of the park's landforms is coastal sand dunes of the Quindalup Dune System that comes inland as much as 2 km. The vegetation consists of coastal spinifex *(Spinifex longifolius)*, Thick-leaved Fanflower *(Scaevola crassifolia)* and Silky Scaevola *(Scaevola anchusifolia)*.

On the established older dunes Peppermint *(Agonis flexuosa)* and Coastal Wattle *(Acacia rostellifera)* grow and then behind that again, mixed eucalypt woodland comprising of Tuart *(Eucalyptus gomphocephala)*, Marri *(E. calophylla)*, Jarrah *(E. marginata)*, and Christmas Tree *(Nuytsia floribunda)*. Around the lakes the Saltwater Paperbark *(Melaleuca cuticularis)* and Swamp Paperbark *(Melaleuca rhaphiophylla)* grow. Between the dunes is a series of lakes which are part of the Vasse Lagoon System. Further inland is the Spearwood dune system with outcropping limestone.

On the limestone there is also Tuart, Jarrah and Marri with Slender Banksia *(Banksia attenuata)*, Swamp Banksia *(Banksia littoralis)*, Bull Banksia *(Banksia grandis)*, Sheoak *(Allocasuarina fraseriana)* and Narrow-leaved Red Mallee *(E. foecunda)*.

Looking at the ancient stromatolites on Lake Clifton

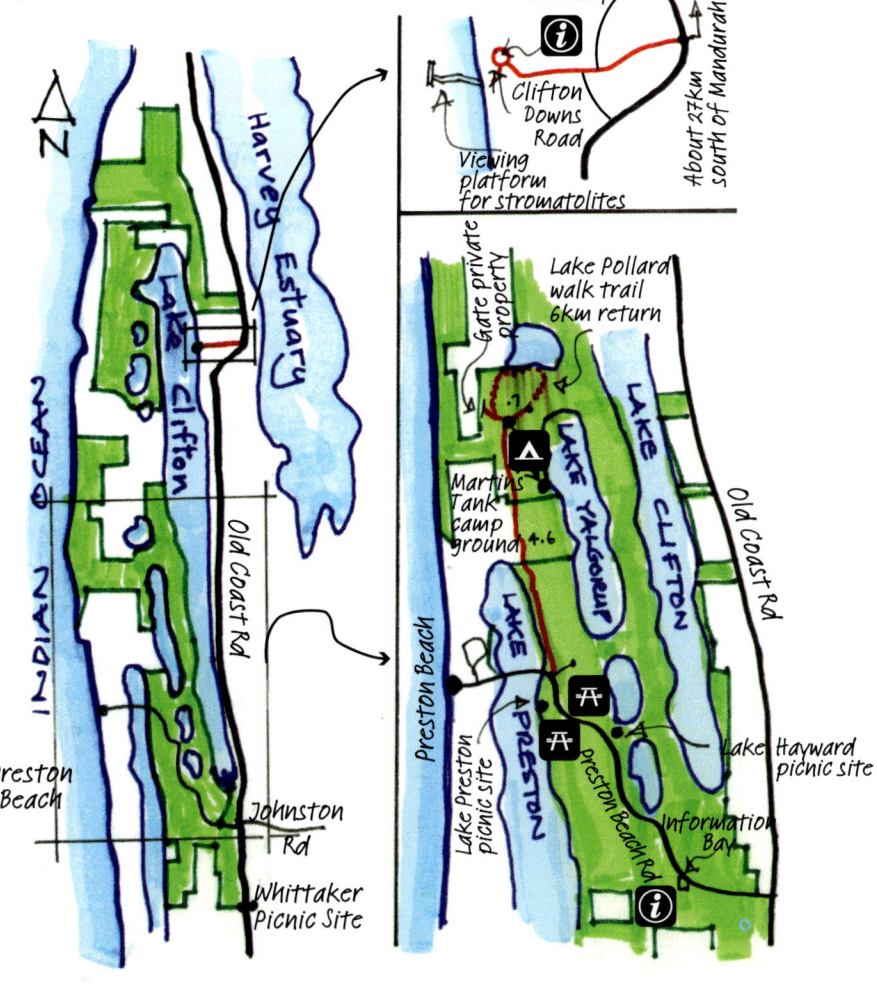

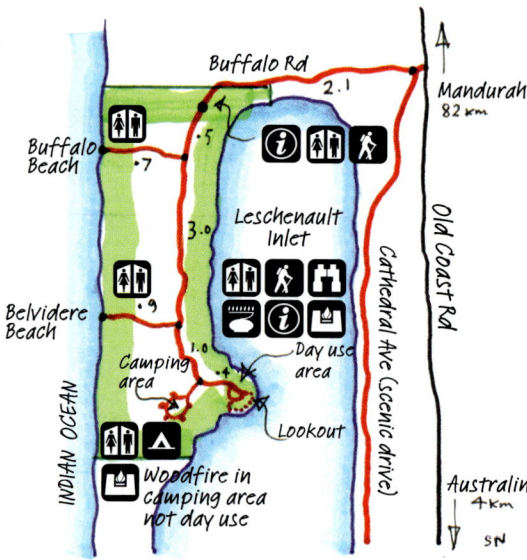

Belvidere Beach

Leschenault Peninsula
CONSERVATION PARK

This park is located on a thin peninsula that divides the Indian Ocean from the Leschenault Inlet. Entry is from the northern end and leads to two beaches, Buffalo and Belvidere Beach, and a camping ground at the historic site of Belvidere. There is also a camping ground and picnic location at the southern tip of the peninsula that can only be accessed by boat.

There is extensive peppermint and Tuart woodland behind the foreshore dunes, home to many Brushtail Possums, and now some Ringtail Possums have been released there and are doing quite well, as DCLM has a fox baiting program in this park.

There are long beaches with ample opportunity for beach fishing. The camping ground at Belvidere is set amongst beautiful Peppermint and Tuart woodland, with ample shade, good fireplaces and toilets. Just past the camping ground there is a day use area with gas barbecues and tables and a lookout over the inlet.

The locality of Belvidere has had an interesting history. The land was purchased by Thomas Little, who bought it on behalf of Charles Robert Prinsep who required horses for the Indian army. Over the subsequent years there were a few owners breeding and raising cattle and then in 1967 it was purchased by Wallace Greenham and Shirley Rodda to develop a small alternative community. The community had 14 houses at the height of its development, with its own school, but in 1984 the authorities closed it down, apparently on the basis of health standards.

There are warning signs about contracting Ross River Virus in the Leschenault region. It is wise to take insect repellent and obviously try to avoid being bitten by mosquitoes. It's not a major problem but people have contracted it, particularly in the Mandurah to Busselton region.

Leschenault Discovery Centre

If you're passing through Australind, on the estuary foreshore, near the junction of Paris Road and the Old Coast Road, is an information centre with the local history and information on the estuary. There are toilets, barbecues and tables here. It is very useful for a quick stop if you need a break.

Camping ground at Belvedere

Leschenault Discovery Centre

Capel Wetlands
CENTRE

Located just off Tuart Drive, the wetlands have been created from past mineral sands development with the foresight of the mineral mining company, RGC (now Iluka), and other environmental groups. An educational wetland centre has been developed to show the many benefits of restoring previously mined sandpits. It is ideal for school groups wishing to know more about wildlife and land reclamation. The Science Teachers Association had a lot to do with the wetlands development and Birds Australia.

There are picnic tables and a new barbecue.

Capel Wetlands

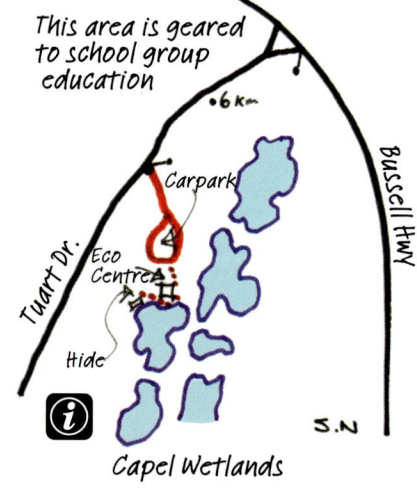

Tuart Forest
NATIONAL PARK

Even though this is a small park of only 1,786 ha, it protects the largest and tallest Tuart trees in the south west that only grow on the coastal limestone soils. There are two day-use picnic sites.

At Layman picnic site near Wonnerup House is a spotlighting walk, which is perhaps one of the best areas in the south west for looking at the now restricted Western Ringtail Possum (*Pseudocheirus occidentalis*). Although the Ringtail Possum has become quite rare in most parts of the south west, it can be found right in the township of Busselton, and also in Albany. The Common Brushtail Possum (*Trichosurus vulpecula*) has fared much better than its smaller relative, the Ringtail.

Opposite the picnic site is a walk to a bird hide on Malbup Creek.

The Vasse Estuary, adjacent to the Tuart Forest, is one of the best wetlands for water birds in the south west. In 1986 an organised bird count was made and 33,000 birds were counted at the Vasse Estuary and Wonnerup Estuary. This ranks as the third highest water bird count after Peel Inlet and Lake Dumbleyung (in the wheatbelt), both far larger in terms of surface area. So it can be seen that this area plays a very important part in bird movements, particularly those flying down from Asia to over-winter here. The estuaries are at their best for bird watching when many other wetlands are drying up, which is the summer and autumn months when breeding has also finished for the duck population.

One of the major problems is, however, that most of the lands surrounding this fantastic wetland are privately owned. However, in April 2003, the Busselton Wetlands Conservation Strategy was released that will provide a framework for the sustainable use and management of this significant wetland.

Wonnerup House: Regardless of whatever views we may have on the nature and actions of early settlement in Australia, it was certainly a hard, tough life to survive in those early days. The story of Wonnerup and the Layman family who pioneered this area is a classic testimony to this hardship.

It was George and John Layman who first immigrated to Australia, arriving in Hobart, Tasmania, in 1827. George was the younger brother, being only 17 years old. He was fortunate not to lose his life when a band of escaped convicts stole all his possessions. It may have been this encounter that prompted him to travel to Western Australia, where the Swan River Colony was developing. He left on the ship 'Orelia' and arrived in 1829 with just sixpence in his possession.

George first went to Augusta and subsequently married Mary Ann Bayliss. On a journey to Perth, a walk of over 300 km, he was speared in the hip by a group of Aborigines on the Murray River; it's recorded that he carried the spearhead all through his life. After several years in the Augusta region, George visited the Vasse area and was so impressed, he applied for and received land title to the area where Wonnerup House stands.

Wonnerup House

After bringing his family up from Augusta, he first settled on the coast, as there were still hostile Aborigines defending their land around Wonnerup. In 1837 he felt the time was right to settle in the Tuart forest and in 1838 Mary gave birth to her first child, George Layman II.

Sadly George senior was speared in 1841 when only 31 years of age. Mary Layman managed to run the property with her young children. A year later she married Robert Heppingstone. It was a marriage that was again to end in tragedy, as he was drowned when his fishing boat hit rocks and sank in 1858.

The running of Wonnerup now lay in the hands of the young 20 year-old son, George Layman II. It was some task to run the property plus the whaling business and assist his mother with the bringing up of seven children. The Layman family was to experience yet another tragedy when their house burnt down, but young George, in typical pioneering spirit, kept going. A year later in 1859, he married Amelia Harriet Curtis and in that same year built the main house one can see today.

The farm developed over the years into one of the best dairy properties in the area. George was a keen horseman and had a horse called Ben Bolt. It was to beat all contenders and become one of the best race horses of the late 1800s.

In 1916 Amelia passed away and then in 1921 George finally died. Over the years most of the family left Wonnerup, including the oldest son, George Layman III, and it was his son James who ran the property until his early death in 1912, aged 32, from a rare disease.

The property was left to George II's four daughters. They were hard working and well respected in the community. As the women aged, the property began to be difficult to run and the youngest sister Nina died, aged 59, in 1937. A nephew, Ivan Webster, assisted with the running of Wonnerup. Stella Layman died in 1962, being the last of the Laymans to live in Wonnerup. Ivan Webster then sold the property, but the buildings were no longer used by the new owners. In 1972 the National Trust purchased the homestead and surrounding grounds. The property was faithfully restored by local volunteers and was opened to the public in 1973. The tranquil setting of Wonnerup and its old buildings belie the hardship and toil that the Laymans, as early pioneers, must have endured.

The buildings are open daily from 12-4 p.m.

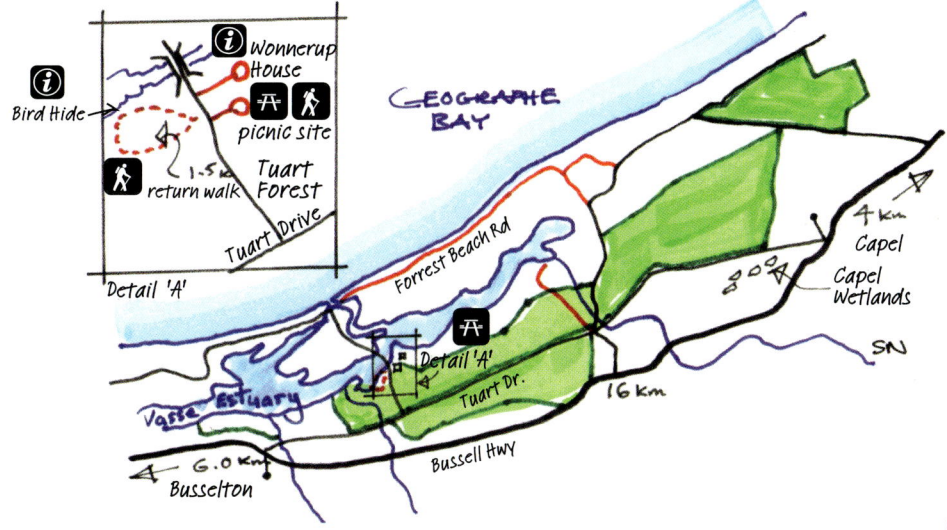

Forest Heritage Centre, Dwellingup

Forest Heritage Centre
DWELLINGUP

This is a unique project bringing together various organisations interested in timber and timber products. The creative plan of the Forest Centre building is based on the shape of three Jarrah leaves protruding from a central stem.

Each separate building houses three individual facilities. One is a gallery showing various wood products, many of which are for sale. Another building houses a museum displaying the various historical and natural aspects of the world of the forest, including its flora and fauna. Finally the largest building contains a school of fine wood crafting.

Outside the building there are walking trails with information boards and a small tree-top walk amongst the Jarrah and Marri.

There is even a low cost accommodation and small conference facility at Jarrah Forest Lodge, just 5 minutes away, and you can book to attend a fine woodworking workshop held at the centre.

The centre is open every day of the week from 10 a.m. to 5 p.m. There is a small entrance fee.

The whole project is well worth the visit if you are coming this way. The nearby town of Dwellingup is a typical timber workers' town with a good tourist information centre. Not far from here is Lane Poole National Park, so a combined trip could include these two locations and it is only 1.5 hrs from Perth.

Baden Powell Water Spout

Lane Poole
CONSERVATION RESERVE

Lane Poole Reserve is the largest park in the northern Jarrah forests, covering 54,000 ha. The great thing is, it is only just over 100 km from Perth, so it's not a long journey, to enjoy the outdoors and camp under the stars, for those that are visiting or live in Perth.

Through its centre flows the longest permanent river in the Jarrah forest and one of the major rivers not to be dammed. In the summer and autumn it is normally a slow moving, tranquil stream, but after the big winter rains it becomes quite rapid. It is a great place for a family to visit, with many camping locations along the river. There are some individual camping areas and some for groups. The river is ideal to canoe on when conditions are favourable, ideally in spring. Remember, canoeing can be dangerous, particularly when rivers are in flood but even when these forest rivers are moving slowly they can still have their hazards. The main problem is when trying to pass under fallen tree trunks that are just above the surface, the force of the water can wedge a person under the log. Do gain information from more experienced canoeists before tackling any forest river system, and better still join a canoeing club and learn the many handy tricks to help negotiate rapids and other dangers (refer page 197 for canoeing information). There are launching points at Baden Powell, Stringers, Scarp Pool, Island Pool and Yarragil.

All the tracks within the reserve are dirt so drive carefully. There are many side bush tracks so it is best to stick to the main wide tracks as it is easy to get lost.

There are many camping areas for groups or individuals. There is also a camping ground at Icy Creek near the old Nanga Mill site set aside for educational groups, and teachers should contact the rangers and ideally visit the area prior to the main visit.

There is fishing available with appropriate recreational licenses. The main fish to catch here is the introduced trout. There are also freshwater marron. Get the Recreational Fishing Guide from the Fisheries Department to help you know sizes, limits and seasons.

There are short walks marked at some of the campsites and the long 18 km King Jarrah Track starts from Nanga Mill Campsite; part of it follows the Murray River, the other passing through Jarrah and banksia woodland.

Flora and Fauna Spring and early summer are the best times here with all the wildflowers out. There are a few eucalypts along the river, including Jarrah, Bullich (*Eucalyptus megacarpa*), Blackbutt (*E. patens*) and Flooded Gum (*E. rudis*) in the southern part of the park. Where the country flattens out, some open Wandoo forest occurs.

It is worth trying to spotlight for native animals in the park as you may see Brushtail Possums, Tawny Frogmouth and Southern Boobook Owl and with luck the Chuditch or Western Quoll and Quokka (yes, they are here in the Jarrah forest as well as on Rottnest Island).

Lane Poole was named after C.E. Lane-Poole, the second Conservator of Forests to advise on the management of the forests. We have a lot to thank this man for, as for over 70 years prior to his appointment there were little or no restrictions on woodcutting. It was literally a free-for-all situation. He had the foresight to see disastrous consequences if some form of control was not implemented. He subsequently set in motion government policies on how and where timber could be taken. He had strong opposition from the timber merchants, but in 1918 he assisted in the establishment of the Forest Act and the first controls on random felling were set in place.

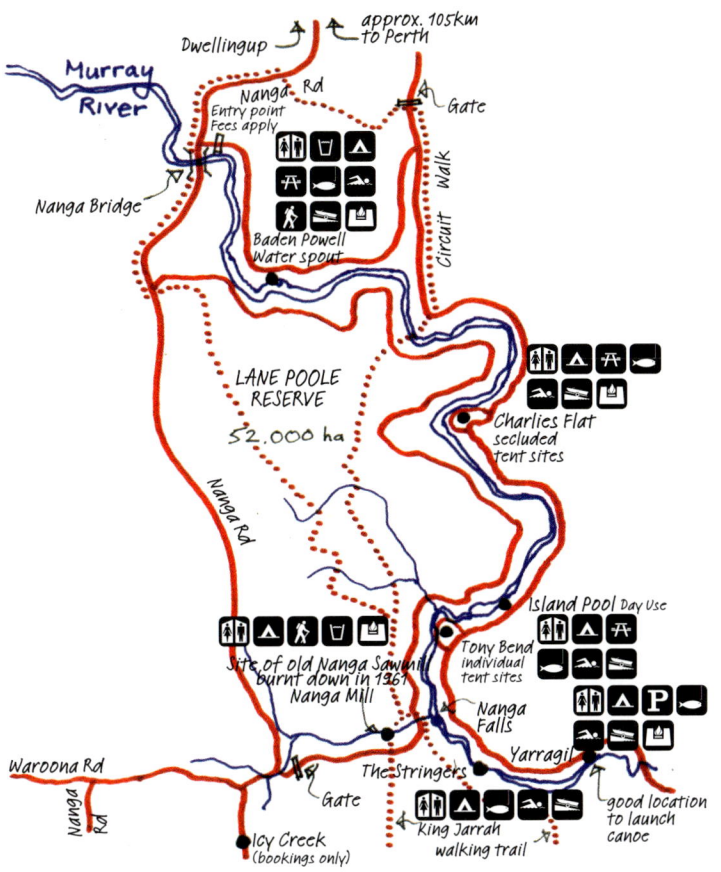

South West Dams

There are many dams in the south west. Some allow power boats and water skiing, some have commercial camping/caravan grounds like Waroona Dam and Lake Brockman adjacent to Logue Brook Dam, and some allow just fishing and have picnic facilities.

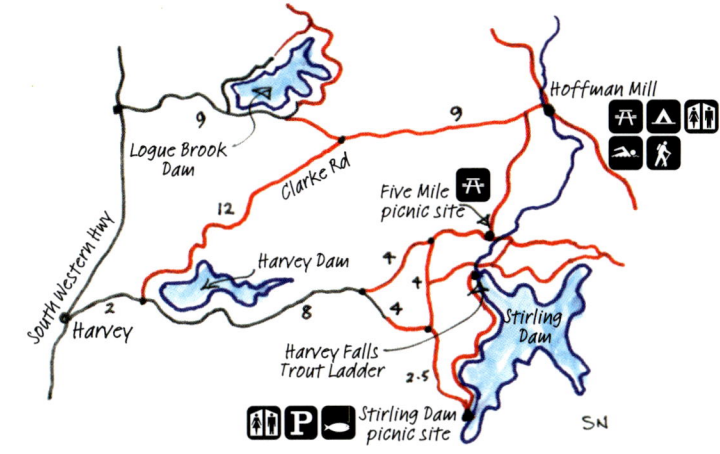

South West
RECREATION AREAS

In the south west there are many recreation areas and camping grounds that do not get mentioned in many publications. They are often very attractive and have the added bonus of being quieter in the busy times, while still having much to offer.

Hoffman Mill

The Millars Timber and Trading Company built a foresters' township, known as Old Hoffman, in 1919, located 12 km north of the present recreation area.

Alas, it was burnt down, so a new mill was built, called 'New Hoffman'. You can still see parts of the logging ramps and old rusty remnants of some of the early machinery; most, however, was removed when the mill was relocated in 1961. At the height of its production, Hoffman had 35 houses, a school, general store, post office and community hall.

After devastating wildfires burned down the old mill at Nanga Brook, Millars decided to rationalise a few of its small townships set in the Jarrah forest and closed New Hoffman down in 1961.

The eastern states traveller may recognise some of the trees, as some eastern state species were grown as trial experiments to check suitability for plantation use.

The camping grounds and day-use areas are located on the banks of the Harvey River and it is a very pleasant spot, with BBQ facilities, toilets and ample shade. There is a wonderful pool for swimming, but even though it is small in area it is deep for children, so they should swim with supervision. There are picnic tables right next to the pool.

There are two walks at Hoffman: the Formation Trail, a short informative track around the settlement, and the 3 km Bridges Trail that starts at the recreation site and crosses the Harvey River into the Jarrah forest and back.

Barbecues at day use area–Hoffman Mill

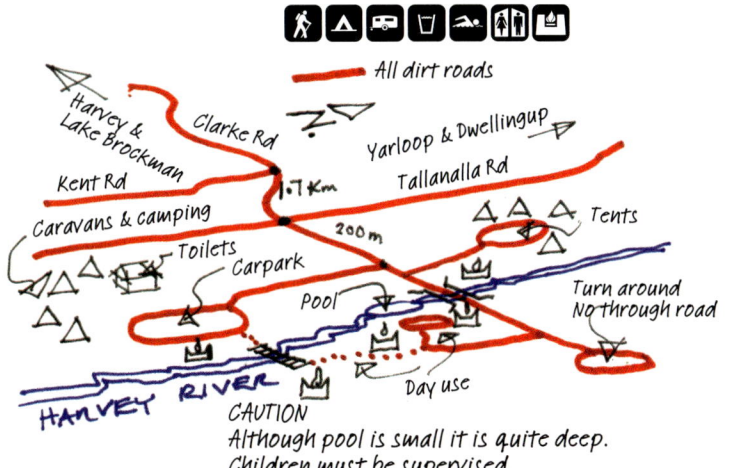

Canebrake Pool

The recreation area and camping ground is located in Rapids Conservation Park, one of the many small conservation parks set in the south west forest region. The camping ground and day-use area is set on the banks of the upper reaches of the Margaret River. There is a large pool, ideal for swimming, but the water is always cool here in the deep south west. The recreation area can be accessed by 2WD but tracks may be closed due to flooding or dieback control.

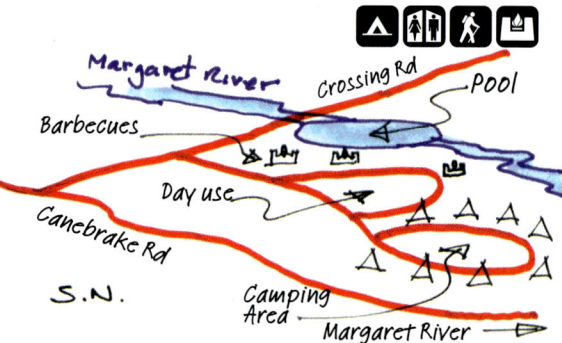

◀ Canoeing entry point on the main Canebrake Pool

BLACKWOOD RIVER CAMPING GROUNDS

The Blackwood is one of the longest and best rivers to canoe on and is relatively safe downstream from Sues Bridge, particularly good for those who are just starting canoeing. It's a lovely river, great for trying your hand at marron fishing (remember you need a license and also to know the season when you can take them). Large marron are now hard to get but if you do canoe to those parts of the Blackwood away from vehicle access, then your chances are greater. It is a peaceful river no matter what time of year unless after heavy rains have fallen, when it will certainly be flowing well, and canoeing should only be done by those who are well experienced.

Sues Bridge

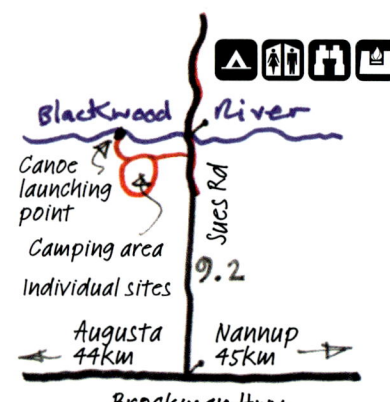

The Blackwood River

As mentioned this is a good place to start canoeing from, with little interference from fallen logs. The camping ground is located near the bridge and is 9.2 km north of the Brockman Highway on Sues Road; it is another pleasant camping ground with individual camping bays set amongst the Jarrah. There is a launching ramp near the camp ground.

Hut Pool

Cleaning up after canoeists have left at Hut Pool Crossing

Located further down the Blackwood River, there is a pool and a launching ramp just adjacent to the concrete causeway. The Great North Road south of the river can be a little rough so 2WD drivers should drive with care.

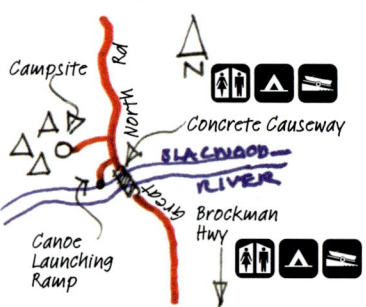

Chapman Pool

Located near Warners Bridge on the Blackwood River, it has individual camping areas, with a day-use area not far away and a launching area for canoes.

Camping area at Chapman Pool

Leeuwin–Naturaliste
NATIONAL PARK

This park stretches 120 km from Cape Naturaliste in the north to Cape Leeuwin in the south. It covers an area of roughly 20,000 ha, mostly as a narrow coastal belt being no more than 10 km wide at any point. The region is often called the 'Cape to Cape' coast and it has some of the most beautiful and finest surfing beaches in Australia. Just behind the coast the Margaret River region also has some of the premier vineyards in Australia.

There are spectacular walking trails that hug the coast, scenic drives through Karri trees in the Boranup Forest, countless caves, many open to the public, showing beautiful stalactites of all shapes and sizes, and some great dive sites, particularly in the Augusta/Hamelin Bay area. There are many types of accommodation as well as some top camping locations. Combine all of this and you have one of the best places to visit in Western Australia. You will, at certain times of the year, see many people travelling this small corner of this vast state but if you plan your trip well, there are some magic locations that can be very peaceful, with few visitors.

History: The Dutch were the first to discover this coast on their way to the East Indies, naming it the "Land van de Leeuwin", meaning the "Land of the Lioness", but it was also the name of the Dutch East India Company's ship, the "Leeuwin". Many explorers followed, including Matthew Flinders in 1801, who named Cape Leeuwin. Later the French captain and explorer Nicholas Baudin named Cape Naturaliste and Geographe Bay after his two ships of the same names.

Governor Stirling of Perth set up a new settlement around the existing township of Augusta in the early 1830s; alas it failed and many of the settlers opened up land around Busselton, which was easier land to work in those days.

In 1880, a South Australian businessman named Maurice Coleman Davies developed a timber-cutting and export business based around Karridale near Augusta. He initially required timber for a large contract to build the Melbourne to Adelaide railway. The company eventually became a huge enterprise, so much so that Davies had his own company bank notes printed, that could be cashed in Karridale or in Perth at the Union Bank.

The company built its own log-hauling railway and built the original 600 m jetty at Hamelin Bay that could load several ships at one time. The export earnings almost rivalled those of wool at one stage. The last mill to operate there was in 1930. Over 800 people were employed at one stage, having their own church, hospital and doctor, town hall etc. The downside was that this massive enterprise existed before the days when timber felling controls were in place and much of the land was totally clear-felled and taken over for agriculture.

Near Black Rocks Beach ▲

Cape Naturaliste Lighthouse ▼   One of the many spectacular beaches on the Leeuwin Naturaliste coast ▼

Cape to Cape

The lighthouse at Cape Naturaliste can be visited daily from 9.30 a.m.–4 p.m. The lighthouse was made from local limestone and still is used as a warning light to sea vessels. It has a small museum and there is a guided tour available.

From the top of the lighthouse there are fine views across to Sugarloaf Rock and the sheltered waters of Bunker Bay. Several walks lead from the lighthouse. There is a track to Naturaliste Lookout, and you can walk around the head of the cape to the whale lookout platform. This is a great place to view Humpback Whales as they migrate south between October and December. The Southern Right Whales may sometimes be seen as they come this far north to calve, best when they are returning to the sub Antarctic, as they spend longer with their calves. There is a longer walk of 3.5 km return that passes Willanup Springs and goes to Sugarloaf Rock. This takes you on part of the 'Cape to Cape Walk' and crosses over the West Coast Track.

The Cape to Cape Walk is one of the finest walks in Western Australia. It commences at the lighthouse car park. The bonus is that this walk can be done at any time of the year, although obviously in summer walking in the morning is best. It takes about 5–7 days for a moderately fit person to walk and covers a total of 130 km to Augusta. It is primarily a ridge walking track with spectacular views along many beaches and cliff faces as it meanders through the Peppermint and Karri forest of this dramatic coastline. Even though it basically takes the walker along the ridge that runs as a spine from cape to cape, there are numerous side detours that can be taken to the coastal beaches. There is an excellent book covering the walk and natural history of the region .

About 1.5 km on the bitumen road before the lighthouse, is Bunker Bay Road, which goes to a pleasant sheltered picnic site at Shelley Beach, ideal when there are strong westerly winds blowing.

It is well worth the drive down Sugarloaf Rock Road to the car park above the beach and rocky lookout opposite Sugarloaf Rock. This is one of the three known breeding sites in Western Australia of the uncommon Red-tailed Tropicbird, which is bigger than the Silver Gull and has two beautiful thin red trailing tail feathers. It flies all the way down from the tropical seas north to breed here from October through until January. This is a great place to come on a stormy day and see the might of the Indian Ocean swells hitting the hard granite rocks, creating huge breakers.

Yallingup: This area has been popular for years, with the old Caves House Hotel and the beach town of Yallingup. Some of the best board riding and windsurfing can be had here.

There is a pleasant drive down Canal Rocks Road to the coast, only 3 km off Caves Road, just south of Yallingup. There are many forms of accommodation around Yallingup and Dunsborough.

Just before the turn-off to Caves Road on Yallingup Beach Road is Ngilgi Cave (formerly Yallingup Cave). It is well worth exploring at least one of the five main caves on this coast. Ngilgi Cave is open daily but opening times vary with the season, so do check.

There are over 300 caves between the capes and there are five major viewable caves that have guided tours: Ngilgi near Yallingup, Lake and Mammoth near Margaret River, and Jewel and Moondyne Cave near Augusta. There are a few caves like Giants and Calgardup Cave where you can enter on your own; both caves are well signposted with information boards inside but no lighting, so you have to take torches and wear sturdy footwear. It is a great experience to venture into caves on your own and the caves recommended are relatively safe. Contact the local tourist centre for information on what caves you can enter.

People have been visiting these caves on a regular basis since the early 1900s. The origins of these caves go way back to the time when the great ocean seabeds covered much of the planet. When the seas receded they left great piles of shells and marine life that were washed up on the coastlines. They formed huge ridges that overlaid the ancient bedrocks of granite. Over thousands of years these marine sands were cemented together into the soft rock we all know as limestone. Slowly the rains that fell passed easily through the porous limestone and made its way to the hard bed rock of granite. On the granite there were often depressions and water would literally form underground streams. These would slowly erode the limestone and with time the ceiling of these river

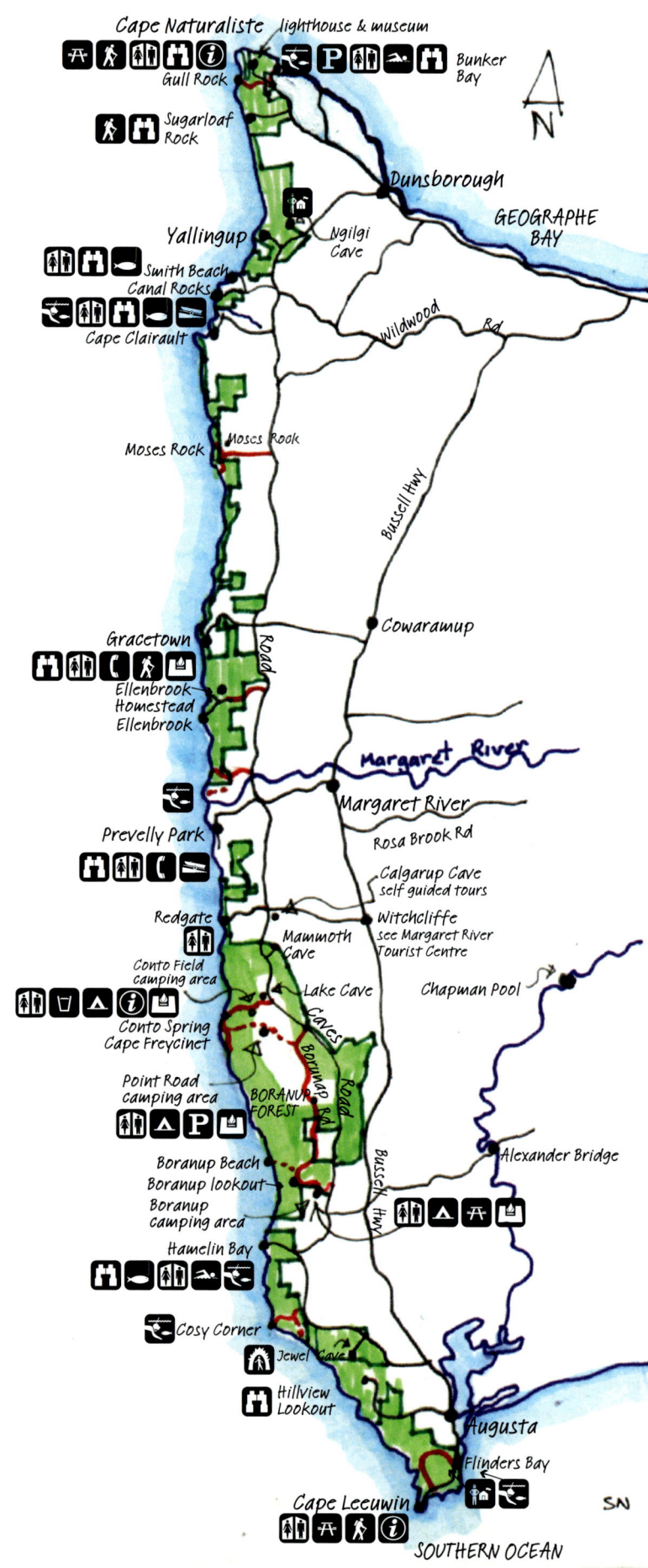

Ngilgi Caves

tunnels would collapse and the fallen rubble would slowly be washed away, forming even larger caverns. This form of erosion is known as 'mechanical erosion'.

The wonderful stalactites, stalagmites, helictites and shawls that one can see in these caves are created by a complex chemical process, involving the pure rainwater mixing with the acidic soils of the rotting vegetation on the surface. This produces a solution of carbonic acid which in turn dissolves the limestone, forming a solution of calcium bicarbonate. When the solution enters the ceiling of a cave the carbon dioxide component is released into the air. With the pull of gravity the solution drips down leaving small amounts of 'calcite' which forms the stalactites and shawls we can see. The stalagmites are created when more calcite drips onto the floor of the cave.

Margaret River: This is the main central town of the Leeuwin coast, with many restaurants and lots of accommodation nearby. It has a very good tourist bureau that can book accommodation and give you all the information you need.

Gracetown and Prevelly are popular coastal townships that have shops, with good beaches for surfing and fishing. They are, however, very busy places to be in school holidays and the summer vacation period.

There are many side roads off Caves Road that lead to the various beaches along this coastline, too numerous to mention in this book, but if you have a 4WD it can take you to some very quiet locations. The drive down Redgate Road to Black Rocks is a pleasant drive. Just off this coast Sam Isaacs and Grace Bussell helped some of the survivors of the "Georgette", wrecked on this coastline in 1876.

Past Lake Cave on the Conto Road is an excellent bush camp created by DCLM inland from the coast, with some good camping bays under the Peppermint trees. Conto Road will take you further down to the coast where there are several turn-offs to various beaches and rocky lookouts, including Round Rocks and South Beach. Rock fisherman love this spot but be very careful of freak waves and wear a harness whenever possible.

Back from South Beach is the turn-off to Point Road. This could be traversed in a 2WD but it is very bumpy and passes through some wet patches in the Karri forest. Nevertheless, it is a lovely drive and not many people use it. It also

Point Road camping ground

leads to a bush camp set in amongst the Peppermint trees with good fireplaces and if you enjoy quieter camping then you should enjoy this spot. Contact the ranger first to check if there is room as there are only a few camping bays.

Point Road is 6 km long and will take you through to 2WD Boranup Drive, which meanders through the Karri, and it is hard to believe that this forest is mostly regrowth forest now in its 120th year of growth. It is also the furthest west that any Karri grows, the nearest being 100 km east. At the southern end of Boranup Drive is the Boranup Lookout and Boranup camping ground. A dirt track takes you past the camping ground to Boranup Beach, one of the longest and most beautiful beaches that is often favoured by the experienced surfers.

Bush camping in the national park is available at Conto Field, Point Road and Boranup, and fees are applicable. There are rangers based at Yallingup, Cowaramup, Boranup and Augusta.

Augusta: Augusta lies at the southern tip of the Cape to Cape coast and is one of Western Australia's oldest settled towns. It is still a small town with a few restaurants and shops and overlooks the Hardy Inlet and Flinders Bay. South of Augusta is the most southerly point of the Leeuwin coastline, where the Cape Leeuwin lighthouse is situated. It was built in 1895, and before it was built there were 16 wrecks around this headland alone. It is open to the public every day. There are boat trips that go out to Flinders Bay to view both the Southern Right Whales and the Humpback Whales, and Seal Island to view the New Zealand Fur-seals.

Protected from the strong westerlies by Hamelin Island, lies Hamelin Bay. It is a top fishing spot and has good camping and caravan facilities. There is a boat ramp and from here not only can you go out and fish but there are also some great diving spots for those who are experienced in scuba and snorkel diving.

Fishing: This coastline is noted for its great beach and boat fishing, particularly when the salmon are running from May to June. The warm Leeuwin Current makes it a great place to catch snapper, dhufish, skippy, flathead and whiting.

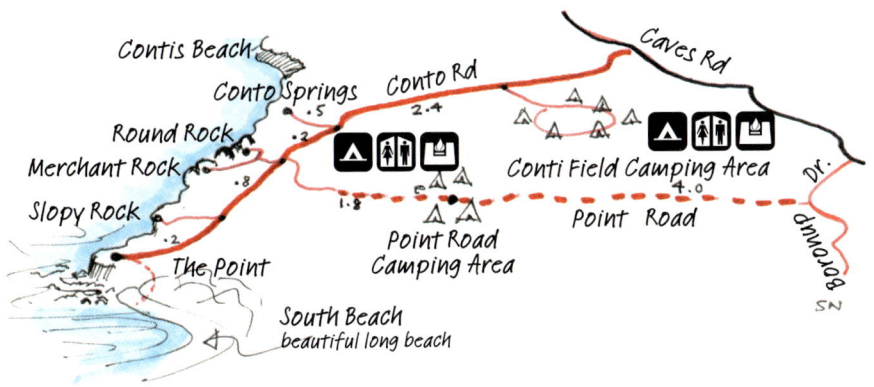

The Pemberton
KARRI FORESTS

Pemberton is a small timber town, with a good tourist information centre and museum, and a few restaurants and shops. It is situated right in the heart of the tallest Karri country with trees exceeding heights of over 80 m. There is a steam train that runs most of the year through the Karri forest which is a novel way to see these ancient forests. There are many types of accommodation in the area, most of them having a rustic feel about them. When the summers are hot in Perth, it can be much cooler down here, making a welcome change from the big city.

One pastime that is growing is that of trout fishing and for the few that master the art of fly fishing, there is nothing more challenging and rewarding than to catch a fish by the art of dropping a fly lure right over a feeding trout.

There are many walks in the Pemberton region and the tourist centre should be able to help on this point Some of the walks include Big Brook Dam walk, 3.5 km grade-easy, and Big Brook Arboretum, 1.2 km grade-easy.

Warren
NATIONAL PARK

Dave Evans Bicentennial Tree
Only a 15 minute drive out of Pemberton, on a 2WD, dirt road circuit track. This has to be one of the most pleasant short drives in the south west, passing through tall old growth Karri trees with understoreys of Karri Hazel *(Trymalium spatulatum)* and Karri Sheoak *(Allocasuarina decussata).* The drive, however, has some steep winding parts on the Heartbreak/Maidenbush Trail section, caravans and buses are not allowed. There are some lovely picnic stops along the side of the Warren River, four in all having barbecues and tables and one, toilets and a camping bay.

If you are passing through the park on the Old Vasse Road you can tow caravans through here and it will still give you great views of the tall Karri. Along this road is the Dave Evans Bicentennial Tree which can be climbed to a lookout tower. The lookout tower is 75 m high, and the first rest platform is 25 m up. When there is a fairly strong breeze, the tree will sway 1.5 m at the lookout level. The tree was named after Dave Evans who was a local politician and who had a special interest in the south west's tree towers. It has far fewer visitors than the Gloucester Tree and is set amongst some of the best tall Karri in the south west. There are toilets, barbecues and tables. There is also a large shelter with tables which is a great place to come if it is raining in the area or to seek shade on a hot day. There is also a 2.5 km walking trail; grade – easy.

Dave Evans Bicentennial Tree

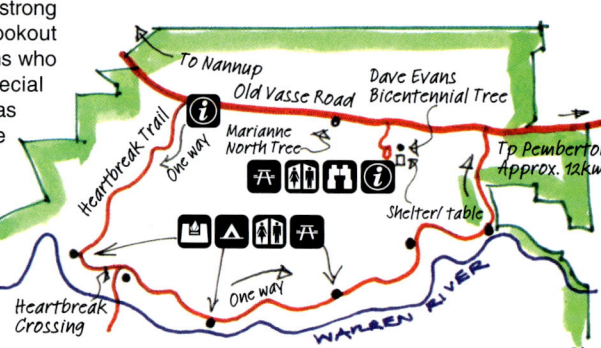

The Gloucester Tree

A fire lookout tree, built in 1947. It is one of eight fire lookout trees built in the 1940s. The Gloucester Tree is 60 m high and 7.3 m around the girth. It was a monumental task to climb the trunk, removing the various branches, and then to hammer steel pegs into the trunk itself. While the fire lookout was being constructed, the Duke of Gloucester from England happened to be travelling in the south west and it was included in his itinerary. The tree and the park take their name from the Duke.

It is hard to imagine, but by 1990 approx. 220,000 people had visited this tree, and of these, 44,000 had climbed to the top; such is the popularity of this natural feature. There are picnic tables, barbecues and toilets near the base of the tree, which make it a good place to take time out while the energetic climb to the top.

There are a few walking trails from the Gloucester Tree: The Duke's Walk, a short 400 m walk; Karri Views Walk, just 800 m; grade – easy, which takes you to the edge of the valley over looking East Brook, and there is a long walk, the Gloucester Walk, 10 km, grade – moderate, which leaves from the picnic grounds, crossing small creeks and up and down a few valleys through the Karri and Marri forest. You can walk half way along the Gloucester Walk and be picked up at the car park along the scenic drive.

Access to the Gloucester Tree is from Pemberton, just 3 km east of town. There are two other lookout tree towers that can be climbed and they are the Diamond Tree just south of Manjimup and the Dave Evans Bicentennial Tree in the Warren National Park.

◄ Gloucester Tree

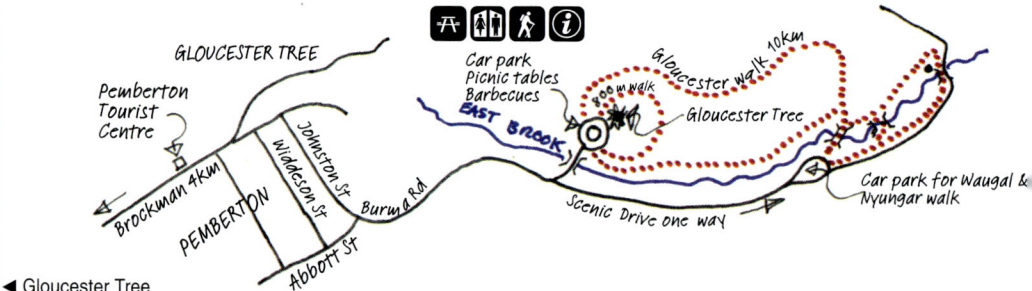

The Karri & Jarrah Forests
OF THE SOUTH WEST

The main body of the south west forests starts just north east of Perth and stretches 350 km to the south coast. It broadens out in the deep south to a width of 150 km, the Jarrah forest covering the largest section, with the Karri forest dominating in the central southern region. There are two major factors that dictate why and where they are located and that basically applies to most plant growth of the world. That is simply soil type and rainfall.

Jarrah requires an annual rainfall of between 700-1,000 mm and Karri, 1,200-1,400 mm. Jarrah requires nutrient deficient soils and grows primarily on laterite soil. Karri requires higher nutrient soils which can vary in type but primarily consist of red sandy loam soil. In a few locations they grow on granitic or limestone soils but the topsoil still holds enough acidic loam for them to survive.

There are several other eucalypts that grow in the south west, mostly in riverine locations, except the Marri *(Eucalyptus calophylla)* which grows alongside both Karri and Jarrah at certain locations.

Jarrah *(Eucalyptus marginata)*: A long lived Jarrah tree would live to roughly 350 years old, not as old as many people think. There are older trees in the south west like the Wandoo *(E. wandoo)* that lives to 420 years, and the Salmon Gum *(E. salmonophloia)* of the wheatbelt that lives to around 450 years.

Jarrah when cut, produces a beautiful deep red timber, hence its common name, in the early years, of Swan River Mahogany. The timber has been well known both in Australia and Europe for years as a fine woodworking timber. In some ways it is sad that so much was cut just to make railway sleepers, not only in the west but also thousands of tonnes were shipped over east, and in the early years thousands of tonnes went to Europe.

Most trees around the world grow in close proximity to many other species, but Jarrah often grows as a pure stand. With such nutrient deficient and stony soils, one would not expect trees of the size of Jarrah to grow so well but they have adapted by having two types of root system. The first layer is almost horizontal and sends roots out up to four times the height of the tree. The other root system reaches way down to the water table.

Karri *(Eucalyptus diversicolor)*: Karri is the tallest tree in the south west, attaining heights of 90 m and girths of 7 m. It is a true 'gum' tree having a smooth trunk. Pure stands of Karri require very fertile soil (Karri loam) but coexist with other trees like Jarrah and Marri in less fertile areas.

Wildfires can kill Karri, unlike Jarrah which can survive the most intense fire. These fires, however, allow young Karri trees to develop as the fallen seeds germinate in the soil, and within a year the saplings can attain a height of 2 m.

Of all national parks, the Shannon and Mount Frankland National Parks have the greatest stands of Karri. There are small forest pockets as far west as The Leeuwin-Naturaliste National Park and as far east as Mount Manypeaks National Park, due east of Albany.

A walk through the Karri forests

Splendid Fairy-wren

Purple-crowned Lorikeet

Red-tailed Black-Cockatoo

Custard Orchid
(*Thelymitra villosa*)

One of the many beautiful Hoveas
(*Hovea stricta*)

Red-thighed Froglet (*Crinia georgiana*)
Photo by Brad Maryan

Green-bellied Froglet (*Geocrina leai*)
Photo by Brad Maryan

The internal timber of Karri is very similar in colour to Jarrah and the old test was to burn a splinter of each. Karri left pure white ash and Jarrah left a grey/black ash. Although Karri does not make a fine furniture timber, it certainly makes a very strong structural timber, particularly over long lengths for trusses and roof beams.

Wildlife of the south west forest: To be honest the south west forest is not the richest habitat zone for birds and wildflowers. However, even though marsupial numbers are never high in any zone in Western Australia, they are well represented in these south west forests.

Wildflowers: The richest flora areas are to be found in the Kwongan heath of the open sandplain country. However, in spring the wildflowers throughout the Jarrah and Karri forest are one of the highlights of any walk. To see the yellow wattles set against the bright purples of the hoveas in the Karri forest is a real delight. Much of the understorey of the Jarrah forest was saved from grazing due to the presence of the highly toxic pea family, mainly the genus *Gastrolobium*. Native fauna had evolved a tolerance for these plants but not those introduced, such as sheep and cattle. In the wheatbelt where there was better grazing, they literally had to clear every single *Gastrolobium* plant out if the sheep were to survive.

Birds: The only bird that is restricted to the Jarrah and Karri forest is the sub species of the Red-tailed Black-Cockatoo (*Calyptorhynchus banksii subsp. naso*). There are birds, however, that have their highest concentrations in the south west forest; they include the Long–billed Black-Cockatoo, Purple-crowned Lorikeet, Red-capped Parrot, Western Rosella, White-breasted Robin, Scarlet Robin, White-naped Honeyeater, Western Thornbill, Red-winged Fairy-wren and the introduced Laughing Kookaburra. Yes, hundreds of Laughing Kookaburras were released from the Perth Zoo between the years 1897 and 1912. Even though we may love their call many of the endemic birds like the Western Yellow Robin have not fared well in the Jarrah forest thanks to this patient but efficient killer of small nestlings.

If you walk, for example, in Warren National Park, you may get glimpses of the White-breasted Robin endemic to the south west. Or on the tree trunks of the Karri, working its way up the bark, could be a rusty coloured bird—that's a Rufous Treecreeper. Then another bird may appear on the tree trunk getting under the loose bark, gleaning small beetles. At first its bright yellow and black markings make it look like the more common Golden Whistler but no, this is one of our rarer forest birds, the western form of the Crested Shrike-tit. Birding can be rewarding for the patient viewer, made even more rewarding with the aid of binoculars, bringing out all the details and colours.

Marsupials: There are several marsupials that live in the Jarrah and Karri forests—most are nocturnal and to see them one has to go spotlighting. It is, however, extremely rewarding when you can get to see some of the little critters that roam around at night. Australia sadly has lost forever quite a few marsupials since European settlement and the feral cat and the fox have been the primary culprits. DCLM, through a thorough baiting program, has turned the declining population around in quite a few areas and this book will discuss this in greater depth under the Wheatbelt section. Two animals that are faring better in the forest region through aerial baiting and other means are the Chuditch (*Dasyurus geoffroyii*) and the Wambenger or Brush-tailed Phascogale (*Phascogale tapoatafa*).

Chuditch: This white-spotted little marsupial is about the size of a rabbit. It is entirely nocturnal and feeds on lizards, large insects, spiders and small animals and birds. Even though it is a carnivore and kills its prey in a quick and efficient manner, it is no match for the feral cat and fox. Over the last few decades its population has declined substantially which is sad as its range once spread as far as the desert regions.

Chuditch can move swiftly both on the ground and along branches of trees. They require a large territory of up to 2-3 square km. They live in tree hollows, hollow termite mounds, under rocks and occasionally in burrows. The female weighs about 1 kg and produces a litter of up to 6 young between May and September. A Chuditch has a life expectancy of 3-4 years.

Brush-tailed Phascogale: A squirrel-like marsupial, the male weighs 250 g (female smaller) with a body length almost 400 mm long although the conspicuous brush tail takes up half that length. It feeds mostly on small insects and will take nectar from flowers but on occasions it will tackle larger prey such as small birds.

It is almost entirely restricted to the tree canopy, being a fast and efficient climber of trees, with recorded jumping spans between trees of over 2 m. The female gives birth to as many as 7-8 young. Some of the young normally die through the lactation period, nature's way of making sure the breeding stock is strong. They forage in a restricted area of between 30 and 80 ha, though will cover longer distances of up to 5 km if the feeding area is not prolific with food.

They build substantial nests for their size in hollow trunks, sleeping through the day except on very cold winter days, when they may forage early or late evening. If you see a Brush-tailed Phascogale, you are very lucky as they are in low densities and being small and arboreal, are hard to spot.

Western Quoll (*Dasyurus geoffroii*) and Brush-tailed Phacogale (*Phascogale tapoatafa*)
Photos by Michael Morcombe

Western Grey Kangaroo
(*Macropus fuliginosus*)

Brushtail Possum (*Trichosurus vulpecula*)
Photo by Greg Barron

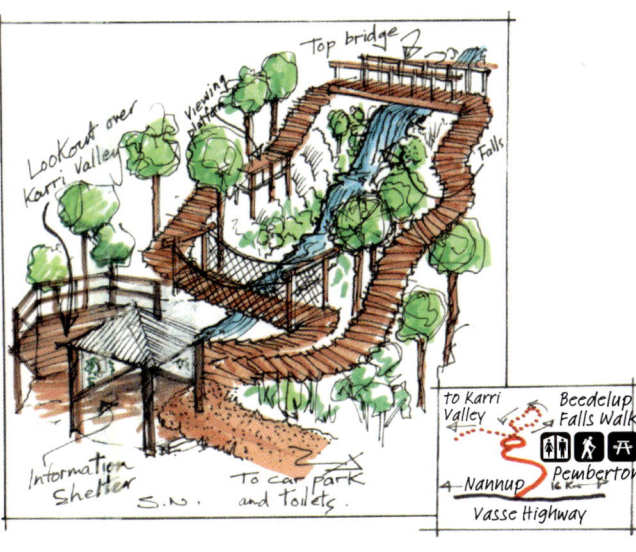

Beedelup
NATIONAL PARK

A 20 minute drive out of Pemberton on the Vasse Highway, this is a small national park. Its main feature is a small waterfall where the Beedelup Creek cuts its way over the edge of some resistant granite rock. It is not a spectacular waterfall but it is certainly a very pleasant walk around the boardwalk, that takes you to the top of the falls and back along the other side of the creek. Total distance is 600 m, grade-easy, although there are some steep steps to climb.

A new lookout provides spectacular views over the falls in winter.

Beedelup Falls

Mandalay Beach

The turn-off to Mandalay Beach Road is off the South Western Highway only 12 km west of Walpole.

Just off the highway on Mandalay Beach Road is Crystal Springs camping ground, where there is a resident ranger. This is normally a very quiet camping ground and one of the few DCLM managed campsites in the Walpole region.

The drive to Mandalay Beach is about 8 km on a graded track. From the car park there is a short walk over the sand dunes and then down a boardwalk to an elevated timber platform. It is a wonderful view from this point looking east along Mandalay Beach to Long Point.

Mandalay Beach gets its name from the Norwegian ship the "Mandalay". The ship was travelling from Albany to South Africa, when it was caught in a violent storm on the 15th May 1911. The Captain, Emile Tonnessens, managed to avoid Chatham Island but when he rounded the corner and saw Long Point he knew he would never make it with his three masted sailing ship. There was only one solution and that was to turn directly to the sandy beach and run the ship aground. This he succeeded in doing and miraculously no lives were lost.

Even though there was a violent storm, he and his crew managed to get all major provisions and cargo on shore. The crew spent the next 5 days on the beach, then on the sixth day they were sighted by members of the Thompson family, who lived 13 km away at Tinglewood Lodge, and subsequently were rescued.

The figurehead that stands on the timber platform at Mandalay Beach is a cast replica of the original figurehead taken from the Mandalay. These stories remind us of how travelling at sea in those days was a very hazardous affair.

Mandalay Beach

D'Entrecasteaux
NATIONAL PARK

Of the 114,566 ha of this large national park, most of it could be classed as a wilderness area. In many ways, we have to thank the foresters of the Pemberton, Northcliffe and Manjimup region for instigating proposals to have this region set aside as a protected region, to stop development of the coastline. The 'Institute of Foresters' put the first major proposal to the government and then later the Environmental Protection Authority also recommended that land be set aside for a national park. It has not been an easy process for DCLM to handle, trying to please all interested parties. There are, however, locations set aside as wilderness areas that can only be accessed by hiking. There are restrictions on where 4WDs can go as there have been too many tracks throughout this coastal belt.

For 2WD vehicles the only access points are at Windy Harbour, Broke Inlet and Mandalay Beach.

The park stretches all the way from Black Point in the west to the border of Walpole National Park in the east, being 130 km long by 20 km at its widest point. There are rugged cliffs with basalt columns, lots of low-lying swamp heath, huge mobile landlocked sand dunes and patches of Karri forest, as well as more extensive Jarrah and Marri forest at the east and west ends. The largest freshwater lake in the south west, Lake Jasper, is confined to this park. Some relatively large rivers flow through the park to the coast, namely the Donnelly, Warren and Gardner. The Shannon River flows into Broke Inlet. Most of these rivers are good canoeing rivers and take the canoeist to some rarely visited areas.

On the way to Windy Harbour there is a small picnic area at the base of Mount Chudalup, 15 km south of Northcliffe; walk up to the top of the 180 m high granite rock if possible - it's a moderate climb. It gives one a great appreciation of the vast wilderness region that surrounds this rock. Take time to look at the flora on the granite. The Plumed Featherflower (Verticordia plumosa) may be out between November and early December.

At Windy Harbour there are fishermen's huts and houses that have been there since long before the national park was gazetted. The actual land around the buildings is under the jurisdiction of the local shire and is not part of the park. Just before Windy Harbour, there is a dirt road to the right. A 3 km drive leads firstly to a lookout with superb views of Salmon Beach (shown above), and it is a great place to hang glide from. Dropping down the hill, there is a car park behind the foreshore with picnic tables with shade cover and toilets. It is a beautiful long beach, particularly when the tide is out. The north western end of the beach stops at high cliffs and to the south are the cliffs of Point D'Entrecasteaux.

South of Northcliffe there is the turn-off to Chesapeake Road; 2WD can normally be driven on this road but when there has been excessive rains the road can become flooded. Check in Northcliffe for the state of the road as this area receives some of the highest rainfall in the south west, averaging nearly 1,400 mm a year. The road passes through heathland, Karri and Jarrah forest and is a relatively little used road but worth cutting through if you are going to Walpole from Northcliffe. Chesapeake Road enters Broke Inlet Road at the eastern end. To the north is the South Western Highway and to the south, Broke Inlet. There are fishermen's huts on the shoreline of Broke Inlet and this small area again is vested in the shire. There are no tourist facilities but you are able to launch a boat from here.

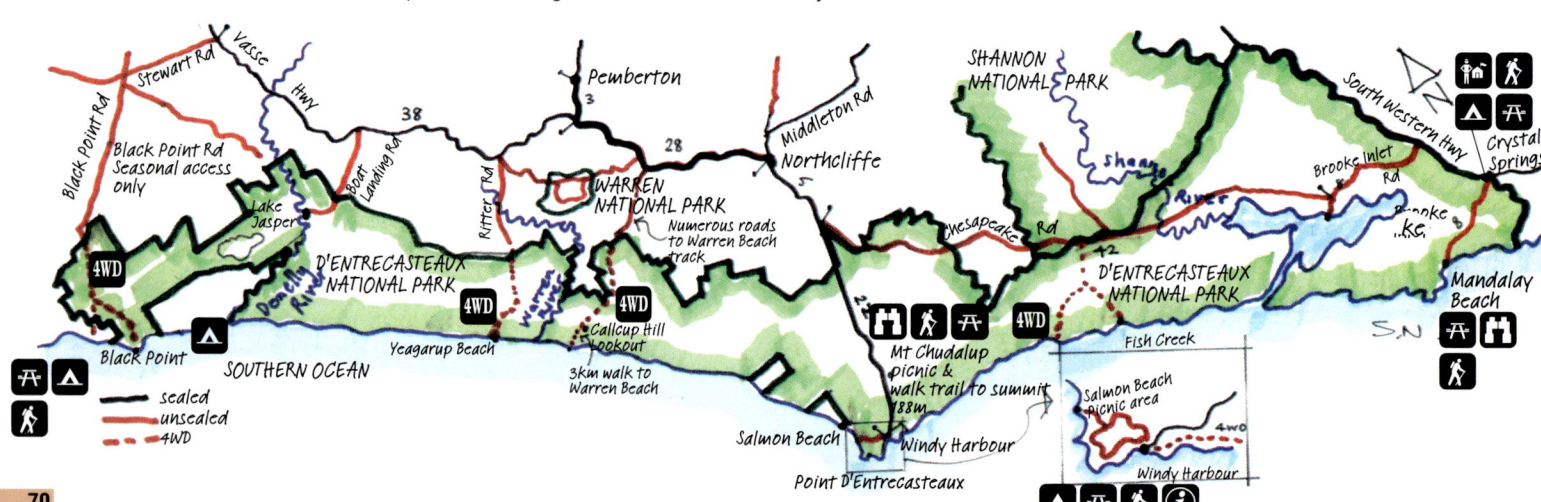

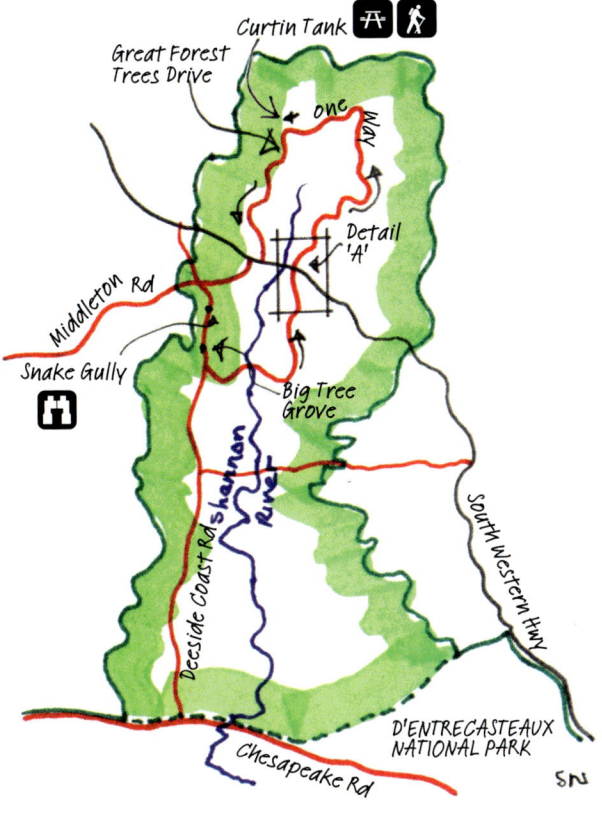

Snake Gully Boardwalk on Deeside Coast Road

Shannon
NATIONAL PARK

If one wanted to spend a few days just relaxing and getting to know the Karri forest in peace and quiet, then this park would certainly fit that specification. There are lovely walks, with the Bibbulmun track passing through this location. There is a 48 km self-guided drive with information radio stops at certain sections. There are also lots of camping areas and small timber cabins with their own wood fires that can be hired.

Shannon National Park is a big forest park covering 53,500 ha and it is some comfort to know that of the Karri that grows in state forests nearly half lies within national parks. It is also the only major park in the south west with an entire catchment area as a boundary of a park, making it relatively pristine in terms of its ecosystem.

During the mid 1900s the Shannon Basin was one of the last areas to be logged, due to its remote location. The first timber felling commenced in the early 1940s and the Shannon Mill was established in 1948. At the height of production the mill employed 162 men and for a while was the largest mill in the state.

The mill was eventually closed down in 1968, which was just as well, because in 1969 there was one of the worst wildfires ever experienced in the south west, created by a landowner blasting away tree stumps. It must have been a frightening experience, as on the third day there were sparks sent flying up to 8 km away and the fire was burning through the forest at a rate of 3.5 km an hour.

Logging was still carried out until 1983. The Environmental Protection Authority and conservation groups pressured government to keep the Shannon as a conservation area and it was gazetted a national park in 1988.

Walks: There are several walks. The Shannon Dam walk is an easy 3.5 km walk. It starts from the information shelter. The first 600 m of the track has been sealed to allow access for disabled people. Along the walk you will see the remnants of the old steam railway track. The dam was important for the community, particularly through the summer months when the creek would almost dry up. It's a good place to swim or catch marron (license required). You can extend the walk, making it a 5.5 km walk, but this takes you up over steep granite rocks so you must be reasonably fit. You start by crossing the river below the dam wall. From here the track takes you up a valley and onto two granite rock areas; after the first you will climb up the hill through Jarrah country and then climb Mokare's Rock.

There are great views across the Shannon Basin from here. Then climb down the rock and walk through sheoaks and Karri back to the information shelter.

The Great Forest Trees Drive: The 48 km return drive commences at the information shelter, just north of the South Western Highway, at the old Shannon townsite. It is a one way 2WD track. In the remote possibility of a fallen log blocking your way, return with extreme caution with lights on be very careful on bends, and let DCLM know. There are 6 picnic sites en route and a short walk to platform lookouts in the southern part of the drive. The first part of the drive goes for 23 km before returning to the highway. Here turn right and then left off the highway, travelling for another 25 km. The route is well marked so you should not get lost. Tune in to the FM radio channel 100 at the start of the drive and you will get lots of information on the history and wildlife of the area. The drive finally passes through the camping ground to the highway. DCLM produce a very good booklet on the drive and various other interesting information about forests and their ecology.

The nearest town from the caravan and camping ground is Northcliffe, just 32 km away.

Looking across canola fields to Bluff Knoll

South Coast
REGION

South Coast
REGION

If you have plenty of time, then a journey travelling via Walpole along the coast all the way to Esperance will give by far the best opportunity to see this southern region. If your time is limited and you want to concentrate on just a few localities, then drive down from Perth via the Albany Highway, deviate through Cranbrook, take the centre road through the Stirling Range via Red Gum Pass Road, then drive down to the Porongurups and finally to Albany. It is a full day's trip, not the ideal way to travel as there is so much to see in the Stirlings and the Porongurups alone, but it will get you to the south coast in one day

Albany is certainly a good base to radiate out from, if time is limited. The road between Albany and Walpole is well worth the drive, particularly if you can take the Lower Denmark Road, which will give access to West Cape Howe National Park.

Walpole is a green, lush area most times of the year, with spectacular Karri and Tingle Forests, including the Great Tree Walk and the Tree Top Walk. There are beautiful beaches and lots of rustic accommodation as well as good camping and caravan localities. Beaches like those at William Bay are some of the safest for children on this exposed southerly coastline.

A short distance from Albany is Torndirrup National Park; which is certainly worth a visit to see how rugged the south coastline can be.

North of Albany are two mountain ranges, the Stirling Range and the Porongurup Range, both totally different. Porongurup National Park is covered in Karri forest and can be cooler and wetter than the Stirlings. The Stirling Range National Park has some of Western Australia's highest mountains. Its vegetation is predominantly heath and stunted Jarrah and Marri woodland. The wildflowers in spring have to be seen to be believed with 1580 species of which 85 are endemic to the Stirling Range area.

Travelling due east of Albany, to Esperance, takes you to drier areas. The first major park on the coast is the 80 km long Fitzgerald River National Park, where there are more flowering species than in any other park in Australia (around 1900 species). Much of the park is a wilderness region with wonderful long walks.

In the Esperance region there is lots to do, great diving, very good fishing, tours to offshore islands, and an excellent coastal drive. Even further east is Cape Le Grand and Cape Arid, similar, having beautiful beaches interspersed with rugged headlands and low hills. There are remote beaches for fishing and secluded camping spots. Your only problem in this south coast region is having enough time to see it all.

Centre Road
RECREATION AREA

On the east side of Deep River, is a small day use area with a fireplace and table. The causeway crossing is only passable in summer. On the west side of the Deep River near the crossing is a small wooden chalet that can be used for an overnight stay.

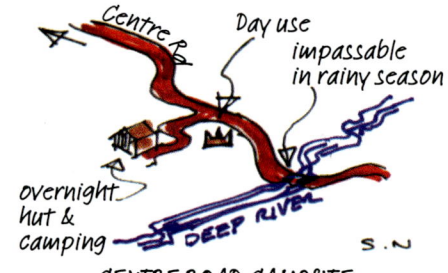

CENTRE ROAD CAMPSITE

View looking south towards the coast from the top of Mt Frankland

Mt Frankland
NATIONAL PARK

Both Mt Frankland and Shannon National Park contain the largest stands of virgin Karri forests in the state and much of the forest remains little visited. Most people choose to visit Mt Frankland itself. The distance from Walpole is 48 km and the latter part of the drive is on dirt roads but 2WDs can get to the Mt Frankland car park. It certainly is a pleasant drive as one climbs up and up to the mountain car park. Not only is there a small camping area with fireplaces and tables, there is also an overnight timber hut that can be used by hikers or travelling tourists, ideal for those cool southern nights that can occur even in the middle of summer. It really is a lovely spot and as yet not too frequented to spoil the atmosphere.

The walk to the top of the granite dome is a little tiring and should only be done by those who are fit. It begins with a slow walk up the track to the base of the rock (which is relatively easy), but then one has to negotiate a very steep steel ladder that requires fairly strong arms to pull ones body weight up. There is then a steep walk over the granite rock to the top. The outlook, though, is absolutely superb, giving a total 360 degree view over the entire Mount Frankland Park.

Fernhook Falls
RECREATION AREA

Between the South Western Highway and Mt Frankland on the Beardmore Road is Fernhook Falls, just 6 km off the highway. If you want to camp before Walpole this is one of the best spots in the area. The falls are not high but relatively wide and flow under the Beardmore Bridge and cascade down to a wide pool, where there is a launching point for canoeists who wish to canoe down the Deep River. It is a great canoe trip. At the camping ground are secluded and pleasant individual camping bays, each with a fireplace. DCLM has done an excellent job in creating this out-of-the-way camping spot. There is a day use area that has picnic tables and a barbecue area with a short walk to the pool and falls.

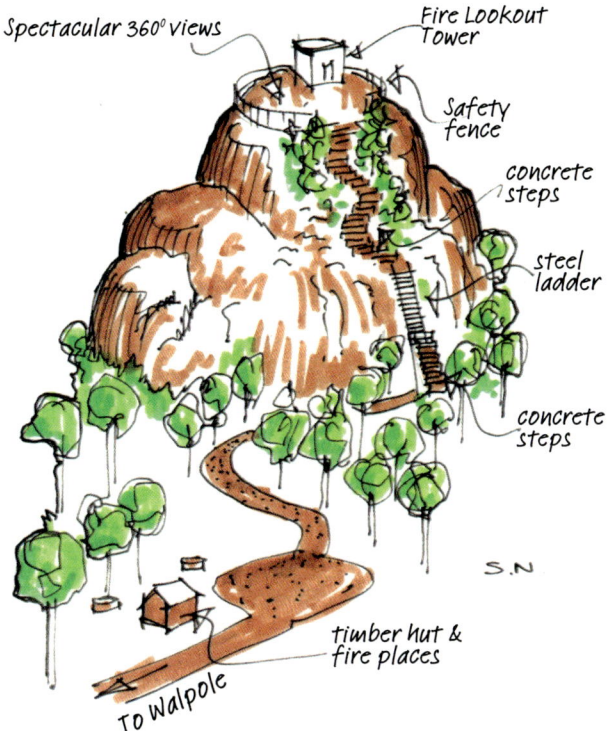

Fernhook Falls

John Rate
LOOKOUT

About 6 km west of Walpole is John Rate Lookout with picnic tables and toilets. A short walk takes you to a timber platform lookout which provides a view of Nornalup Inlet. It is certainly worth a stop, if you need a break from driving on the highway. John Rate was a forestry officer who did much to protect the forest areas of Walpole. He was also an honorary ranger in the early 1950s and convinced botanists of the existence of the third Tingle tree, the Rates Tingle (*E. brevistylis*).

◄ View through the Karri to the Walpole coast

Walpole–Nornalup
NATIONAL PARK

This park covers an area of 21,500 ha and is one of Western Australia's earliest national parks, being founded in 1910 and then extended over many years. The park basically surrounds two very large inlets, Nornalup and Irwin Inlets. Located near these inlets are the townships of Walpole, Nornalup and the small seaside village of Peaceful Bay. Most of the year the Walpole region looks very green, for it is the wettest location in Western Australia. That does not mean to say it rains most of the time, far from it. Its annual rainfall averages 1,400 mm compared with Perth's average of 800 mm. Without the drastic changes of seasonal weather that are experienced in the drier north, this relatively wet zone has many plants that are relicts of wetter times. There are 698 plant species recorded for this area, many of them being found only here. The largest group to be found here is the terrestrial orchids, with 104 species, an incredibly high concentration of orchids for just one locality.

Nuyts Wilderness Area: At the western end of Walpole National Park are 5,000 ha set aside just simply as a wilderness area. It is not far from Walpole and is accessed from the west on foot via Crystal Springs camping ground, Mandalay Beach or Long Point. The main entry is off Tinglewood Drive and the track leads to Thompson Cove. It is a wonderful area but alas dieback is spreading and there are controls on numbers entering this area, so do check with the local rangers.

Circular Pool

Hill Top Drive & Circular Pool

For vehicles not towing caravans there is another drive beginning just 3 km out of Walpole, called the Hilltop Road. It has fewer vehicles on it and allows you to see even more ancient forest, but it is, however, a one way circuit road. There is a hilltop lookout and picnic table at 2 km and then at the 5 km mark there is the car park that leads to the wonderful Hilltop Giant Tingle Tree Walk. This is an 800 m return walk, which meanders through Karri Sheoak (*Allocasuarina decussata*) and massive Red Tingle. Further along the Hilltop drive is the picnic spot of Circular Pool with small rapids on the Frankland River. The drive then returns via Walpole.

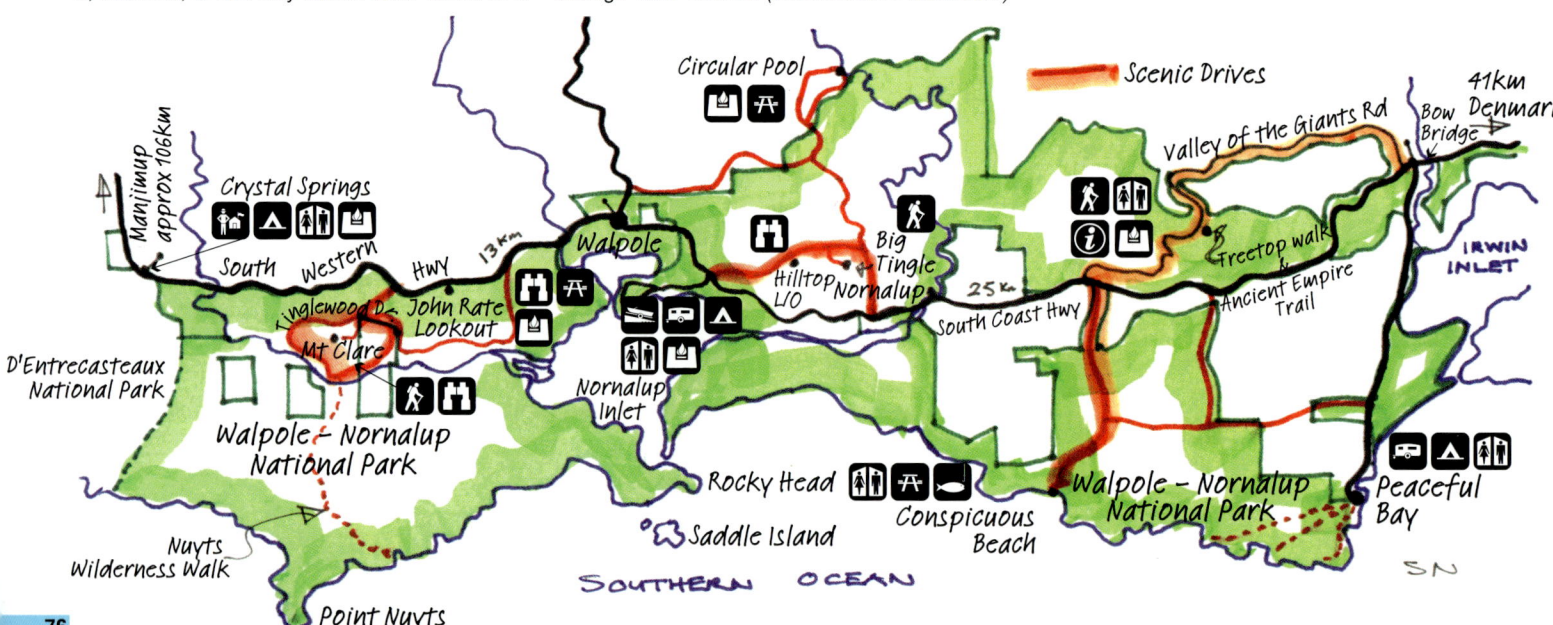

Tree Top Walk

The Walpole and Nornalup area not only has tall Karri trees, but is the location for one particular species of tree that is restricted to this area, the huge Red Tingle *(Eucalyptus jacksonii)*. Although not as tall as Karri, they certainly are massive, attaining girths of 20 m. The buttress roots stretch out over several metres. They are best seen on the Great Forest Drive, which is 14 km east of Walpole. Here you can also experience walking high amongst the tree tops on the now well known 'Tree Top Walk'. This walk was conceived by the past director of DCLM, Dr Syd Shea.

After you have walked high up in the canopy, it is well worth doing the 'Ancient Empire Trail' adjacent to the entrance to the canopy walk. It's called 'ancient' as these beautiful Red Tingle trees are over 400 years old, relics of a far wetter continent several thousands years ago. The board walk is well designed and allows the root systems of the trees to survive without the pressure of thousands of visitors annually.

Tree Top Walk

The wonderful walk on the Ancient Empire Trail

Conspicuous Bay

Conspicuous Bay lies south of the South Coast Highway on Beach Road or can be reached from Peaceful Bay via Ficifolia Road. Ficifolia Road is named after the beautiful Red Flowering Gum *(Eucalyptus ficifolia)*, which is one of the four eucalypts restricted to the Walpole area, the others being Red Tingle *(E. jacksonii)*, Yellow Tingle *(E. guilfoylei)*, and Rates Tingle *(E. brevistylis)*. Conspicuous Beach is one of the many wonderful beaches that one can see from here all the way to Cape Arid. There are picnic tables at this location, an information board, toilets and two walks. One will take you down the boardwalk to the beach area. Eighty metres down the track is a picnic shelter; ideal if it is raining or too hot. There is also a viewing platform above the beach for those who don't want to walk down to the beach which gives you wonderful 360 degrees views.

◀ Conspicuous Beach

Elephant Rocks

William Bay
NATIONAL PARK

Green's Pool has an absolutely beautiful beach, which is ideal for the family. The granite boulders off the beach act as a barrier to the rough seas and create, on most days, a dclm board-flat lagoon where parent supervision from the beach or rocks is easy. There is another small beach location called Elephant Rocks just over the hill. It is just east of Green Pool accessed up a timber boardwalk. Not as many people get to see it, but it too is a lovely spot with gigantic granite boulders and a small sandy beach.

There is a dirt track that passes the Elephant Rocks parking area and leads to Madfish Bay; a good fishing spot. On the way you pass by Tower Hill with its unusual granite boulders and a small patch of Karri trees.

William Bay National Park is accessed via the South Coast Highway. Turn-off the highway 14 km west of Denmark and travel 5 km south along William Bay Road to the beach car park. No camping is allowed but there is a camping ground at Parry Beach.

Peaceful Bay

This small township resort on the coast is a good caravan spot and ideal for fishing. There are 4WD tracks leading into the eastern end of Walpole National Park that take the keen fisherman to some great localities. Be careful though, as these are single lane sandy tracks and don't forget to let the tyres down to 16 lbs.

Green Pool, a relatively safe swimming beach for children with supervision

Albany
REGION

Even though Albany is still a growing town, it retains an old world feel, particularly near the foreshore, where there are some magnificent old colonial buildings. The views across the harbour from Mt Clarence and also along Marine Drive are quite impressive and show how this is one of the most protected harbours of any on the Australian coastline, allowing ocean going vessels to enter and dock right alongside the city foreshore. It was Captain Vancouver who named the harbour Princess Royal Harbour in 1791.

In 1826, Major Edmund Lockyer established a garrison here, as reports of a possible French colonisation of the west coast had been rumoured to the authorities in New South Wales. Lockyer was sent on the brig the 'Amity' with soldiers and a number of convicts. A replica of the Amity stands on the foreshore off Princess Royal Drive. There is also an excellent museum and buildings of the old gaol which was built by the convicts in 1850 as a hiring post, and was subsequently used as a gaol from 1872 to 1931.

An interesting fact is that settlement of Albany occurred before the larger Swan River Colony (Perth) was established.

Albany is a great place to radiate out from or to visit first and then stay in the areas of your choice. There are many parks to visit in the area. To the west along the coast, are West Cape Howe, William Bay and the parks around Walpole. To the south on the other side of the harbour is Torndirrup National Park with its rugged coastline. To the north are the magnificent parks of the Stirling Range and Porongurup Range. To the east there are Two Peoples Bay and Waychinicup.

This whole region has just so much to offer that you will not be able to do everything even on the longest of holidays, but if you plan well you can at least see most of the parks. There are hundreds of walking trails, some of the finest dive sites in Western Australia (even though these are cold waters), some of the best rock fishing and definitely some of the finest wildflower viewing areas, so all in all there is much to see.

Looking down to Shelley Beach from the hang glider ramp

West Cape Howe
NATIONAL PARK

Here the coast reaches its most southerly point at Torbay Head named by the Englishman George Vancouver as he sailed these seas in 1791. Although the park is relatively small, covering an area of 3,517 ha, there are some interesting features. The park is noted for being one of the best areas in Western Australia for the adventure activities, hang gliding and rock climbing.

You enter this park off the Lower Denmark Road either via Cosy Corner Road or Horton Road. As you enter the park there is a small but lovely regenerated woodland of Karri. The road passes down the hill and there is the option of turning up the hill to the hang-gliding launching car park.

The view from here is one of the finest on the south coast, looking out over Torbay. The hang-gliders can stay aloft for several hours working the on shore winds. Always watch the ocean and stay well clear of the sea and cliff edges. Below the car park is Shelley Beach, a small area used for camping. At present this is not a formal camping area and unfortunately it becomes overcrowded in the high tourist season, but this should not stop you visiting this lovely park. Camping fees apply. Not dogs or open camp fires allowed.

There are 4WD tracks that lead to several lookouts and beaches. These include Dunsky Beach and Golden Gates Beach which is one of the best surfing spots on the south coast, and Bornholm Beach, you can rock fish and the area is one of the best salmon fishing locations on the south coast. You must access these areas from the Lower Denmark Road via Lagoon Road which is a 4WD track on the western part of the park.

There are numerous tracks and work is being done to control the pressure on the sand tracks. Again remember to deflate your tyres to 15-20 lbs and be ready for oncoming vehicles over the crests of the dunes. Don't forget to reinflate your tyres when you leave the park.

The rock climbers have cliffs that reach 80 m from the sea; scary stuff but the experienced rock climbers love it, so just remember your safety is your responsibility no one else's, and only attempt the climb if you are appropriately equipped and experienced.

The Bibbulmun Track crosses the Shelley Beach Road but is best accessed from the Shelley Beach lookout. From this access point you can experience a section of this long walk—it will take you to Lowlands Beach, and on to Denmark.

Torndirrup
NATIONAL PARK

This park lies 10 km south of Albany on Frenchman Bay Road and consists of nearly 4,000 ha of a rugged peninsula that protects Albany from the unpredictable Southern Ocean. On the south side of the peninsula are some of the most impressive cliffs and rugged coastline that the south coast has to offer. It is here that the park has some of its most important scenic localities.

The Gap and the Natural Bridge: An easy short walk takes you first to the Gap on the left hand side of the entrance path. Here you can see the power of the southern seas forcing their way up the narrow gap in the massive gneissic (type of granite) rocks. Further to the right is the Natural Bridge consisting of a huge rock that spans a large gap forming a massive bridge. Just a word of warning: people have fallen or been washed over the edge here, so do be very careful and use the steel platforms provided to see the two locations.

The Blowholes: Further along Frenchman Bay Road is the turn-off to the Blowholes which are reached by a pleasant 1.5 km return walk. Here air is forced under pressure through a fault in the rocks and with rough seas a good deal of spray may come through.

Jimmy Newells Harbour: A short detour off Frenchman Bay Road takes you to the car park and only 100 m to a lookout that gives you views into Jimmy Newells inlet where you can look down to the clear shallow water of the small inlet.

Stony Hill: Stony Hill Road climbs steeply up to the top car park at Stony Hill. The 500 m heritage trail circuit walk is well worth it, as you get a 360° view, particularly along the coast to the east and west. Climbing onto the first the big granite rocks will give you the best views. The area was badly burnt in early 1999 but is regenerating well. At the northern side of the circuit walk there are great views of Princess Royal Harbour and Albany.

Salmon Holes: A right turn off Frenchman Bay Road takes you down to Salmon Holes car park from where you walk down about 60 m to the lookout. You can go on further down the steep steps to the beach itself. It's a lovely beach and you can look across to the tip of the peninsula at Bald Head.

Isthmus Hill to Bald Head: This is a long but very invigorating 10 km return walk (6–8 hrs) and you need to be fit as the path climbs steeply up to the headland, but it gives fabulous views in all directions. The start of the walk is accessed from a dirt track which turns off to the right from Murray Road.

Whale World: There is a museum located on the site of the Cheyne Beach Whaling Station, the last whaling station in Australia closing in 1978.

No one likes bad news, but two points should be mentioned regarding this park. Do lock vehicles and check who is around. Although not of a common occurrence, thefts have occurred while people have taken the longer walks. Secondly, the rock edges are quite dangerous and freak waves can come well above the rocks that are normally well out of the water. These waves can even occur on dclm days and originate often hundreds of kilometres away, so do stand high above the waterline near rocky areas.

There is no camping allowed within the park, but there are several commercial sites in and around Albany.

Two Peoples Bay
NATURE RESERVE

Access to this nature reserve is via the Lower King or Nannarup Road. The turn-off to Two Peoples Bay is on the left, 3 km before Nannarup. Although only 35 km east of Albany, this reserve contains some of Australia's rarest fauna and is the site of two discoveries of species that were thought to be extinct. One was the Noisy Scrub-bird *(Atrichornis clamosus)* and the other was Gilbert's Potoroo *(Potorous gilbertii)*.

It was the powerful territorial song of the male Noisy Scrub-bird that first drew the attention of the naturalist John Gilbert who discovered it in 1842. John Gould, who described and named the bird found this species particularly interesting as, unlike all other passerines (perching birds), it had no wishbone. It was known in the Margaret River area and around Waroona in the mid 1800s, and was reasonably common around Albany but by the turn of the century, no Scrub-birds could be found and it was presumed extinct, until a schoolteacher and keen amateur naturalist Harley Webster heard the bird at Two Peoples Bay. He wondered what bird it could be. When he saw it, he realised he had never seen the species before. It was of course the Noisy Scrub-bird.

The bird exists in very dense, almost impenetrable vegetation and makes a nest of the same type of sedge as its close relative the Rufous Scrub-bird which lives over 5,000 km away in the mountains of northern NSW and southern Queensland. Both birds are relicts of when Australia was a far wetter continent.

At the time there were plans to re-develop the whole area of Two Peoples Bay however concern was expressed about the loss of the last remaining habitat for this bird. What greatly assisted the situation was a visit by the Duke of Edinburgh, who supported the conservationists thus swaying the balance. Luckily the Noisy Scrub-bird has been brought back from the brink of extinction from an estimated population of just 80 to a population of about 1,900 in 2001, thanks to the dedicated work of several DCLM staff and numerous volunteers.

Gilbert's Potoroo was only rediscovered in 1994, when Elizabeth Sinclair, a research worker, was setting cage traps to search for mainland Quokkas and caught a Potoroo. The animal had been presumed extinct for the last 100 years but plans are now in place to increase the population and eventually translocate some individuals to other suitable habitat to increase the chances of its survival.

There is a very good visitors centre with lots of information about the rare fauna and flora of the area, particularly on the Noisy Scrub-bird and the Potoroo. The centre is located adjacent to the main entry car park.

Two Peoples Bay gets its name from an interesting chance encounter between two different nationalities. In 1802, the French ship the Geographe, captained by Nicholas Baudin, was laying up in Frenchman Bay in Albany. Baudin sent his midshipman Ransonnet to explore the coast due east. As he sailed into the bay, much to his surprise he saw an American whaling brig,

Looking across Little Beach

the Union, captained by Pendleton, laying up in the bay. These nations shared a common interest. The French were having trouble with the English in Europe and the Americans were having trouble with the naval authorities over in NSW, about fishing in Australian waters. The French commemorated the meeting by calling it "Baie de Deux Peuples" meaning "Bay of two nations". This was subsequently changed to its present-day name, Two Peoples Bay.

Regardless of its natural history and historical background, the reserve is a delightful spot and on a sunny day the turquoise waters set against the white sands of the bay are most attractive. One small area that should be visited is Little Beach. The turning is on the right off the entry road just past the main car park. Here you can walk down to a smooth sandy white beach or climb up onto the huge granite rocks that surround the beach and take a walk towards Two Peoples Bay itself.

Starting from the picnic ground is a 700 m return walk which will take about an hour and terminates at the top of the ridge overlooking Two Peoples Bay. The track passes through Peppermint woodland and some Bullich *(Eucalyptus megacarpa)* with its smooth bark and yellow flowers in spring. Near the top of the ridge the banksia is Slender Banksia *(Banksia attenuata)* and the sheoak trees are *Allocasuarina fraseriana*. There are picnic tables and gas barbecues, toilets and a boat launching area at the beach, so lots to do here. There is no camping or open fires in the reserve, no dogs allowed, and many areas are restricted, due to this being a particularly vulnerable area for rare animals.

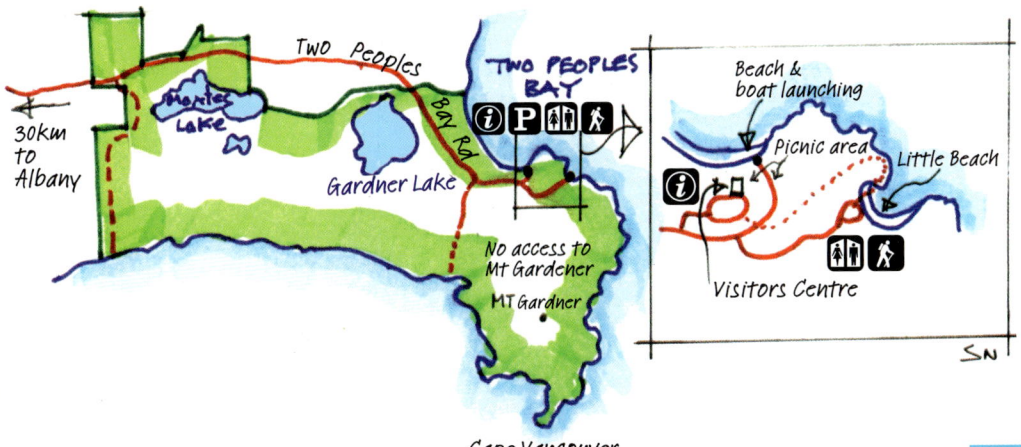

Waychinicup Inlet

Waychinicup
NATIONAL PARK

This park lies 70 km east of Albany, south of the South Coast Highway. Most people pass through the park on their way to Cheyne Beach, which is a small fishing village; the land around the township and the beaches north of the town come under the City of Albany's jurisdiction. The area is not geared to heavy tourist traffic. Cheyne Beach is a good fishing area and there are some 4WD tracks that lead to fishing beaches at the eastern end of Waychinicup National Park.

There are spectacular views of Bald Island off the headland near Mermaid Point.

A dirt road 5 km before Cheyne Beach leads to Waychinicup Inlet. The track can become flooded and ideally should be traversed in 4WD. The area is not suitable for caravans and there is limited parking space at the camping area. The inlet is exceptionally beautiful and is the location of 3 of our rarest birds. The re-located Noisy Scrub-bird, the Western Whipbird and Western Bristlebird all secretive species and rarely seen.

In the evening at the various camping bays, the Quenda or Southern Brown Bandicoot may come around foraging for food; they are about the size of a large rabbit, with a long pointed snout and very short tail. They are quite confident and will come close, but please don't feed them. Mainland Quokkas and the rare and endemic Dibbler also occur in Waychinicup National Park.

Porongurup
NATIONAL PARK

This range of hills is the result of the massive forces that pushed granite rocks high above the surrounding plains and 50 million years ago the Porongurup Range was in fact an island set high above the southern seas that covered much of inland Australia. With time, the granite has weathered to form massive round boulders that lie on top of the range in several locations.

The park is relatively small (2,511 ha) with the hills running 12 km in an east-west direction and rising to a height of 670 m.

People have been coming to the park since the early 1920s to holiday in the area, staying at 'Karribank Lodge', one of the oldest guest houses in Australia and still in use today. The travellers would take the steam train down to Mount Barker and then be transferred by horse drawn carriage for the final 21 km to the lodge. The area was always noted for its cool, mild weather. Even in summer, when Perth has some extremely hot days, down here the evenings can get quite cool.

Walks: The park is noted for its wonderful walks amongst the tall Karri trees. From the 'Tree in the Rock' parking area at the end of Bolganup Road, there are a few options. From the car park, you can take the short walk to the 'Tree in the Rock' just 100 m on the Nancy Peak circuit track. There is an easy 800 m walk, on the Bolganup Heritage Trail, that branches off the Wansbrough Walk, just 50 m up on the right. It takes you through Karri and Marri forest returning to the car park.

On the Wansbrough Walk, you can walk up the hill to the pass; it is a moderate climb of 1 km. From the head of the pass you can turn right and walk up over granite rocks and walkway bridges for a further kilometre to Devil's Slide. This section of the walk becomes more arduous and should not be attempted when rocks are wet. For the experienced walker you can carry on another 500 m to Marmabup Rock.

Alternatively, from the head of the pass turn left and walk to Nancy Peak and Haywood Peak, which is a 4 km hard climb that will return you to the car park. Whether you climb to Devils Slide, or Nancy Peak, you will have tremendous views across the farming country, with Albany to the south and the Stirling Range to the north.

At the eastern end of the park is the entry road to Castle Rock and Balancing Rock. It is a moderate 4 km return walk through moss-covered forests and rocks. The last part past Balancing Rock is a little tricky and some agility is needed to manoeuvre through the rocks to gain access to the steel ladder, which takes you to the top of Castle Rock, giving you spectacular views south. Be careful here on extremely windy days.

At the 'Tree in the Rock' picnic ground at the end of Bolganup Road there are gas barbecues, tables, toilets and an information board showing the various walks. Park entry fees apply. No dogs open fires or camping allowed.

Fauna and Flora: This is a great place to bird

Balancing Rock

The tall Karri trees on the Wansbrough Walk

watch; on the Wansborough Walk from the car park you may have already seen the rusty coloured bird on the tree trunks, a Rufous Treecreeper. The small green backed honeyeaters are White-naped Honeyeaters. In the canopy, the high pitched screech of birds flying like darts through the tops of the trees will reveal Purple-crowned Lorikeets. As you quietly stroll up the hill, a white and grey dumpy little bird may fly down to take an insect; this is an endemic bird to the west, a White-breasted Robin. The small wren that may be moving through the undergrowth with rust coloured wings and a dark blue breast and blue ear coverts (cheek feathers on birds) will be a Red-winged Fairy-wren. (The name is a misnomer as the feathers are a rust brown and quite dull); it is the multi-coloured blue head that is the most attractive feature. It too is endemic to the west. The beautiful bright red parrot with the bright yellow cheek is a Western Rosella, the smallest of Australia's eight rosellas. Keep walking and you may hear two soft extended whistles. This is the call of another endemic bird, the Red-eared Firetail. Even if bird watching is not your thing, the bright red cheek and the white spots set on the black belly of this bird will certainly catch your eye.

The floral smells are very strong in the wet forests of the Karri and in spring the Karri Hazel (*Trymalium floribundum*), Net-leaved Wattle (*Acacia urophylla*) and Tree Hovea (*Hovea elliptica*) will be in full bloom, and on the ground the lovely bright red flowers of the Running Postman (*Kennedia prostrata*) are sure to catch one's eye.

The park has a relatively high species count for its size with over 700 species being recorded. Alas nearly 150 of these are weeds. This is another great location for orchids with over 70 species recorded but you must look down amongst the base of trees, creek edges or underneath bushes to get these floral jewels.

There is no camping allowed in the park but there is camping opposite the entry road to the park, with very good 'A' frame chalets for hire and a lovely old fashioned tea room and shop on the main road.

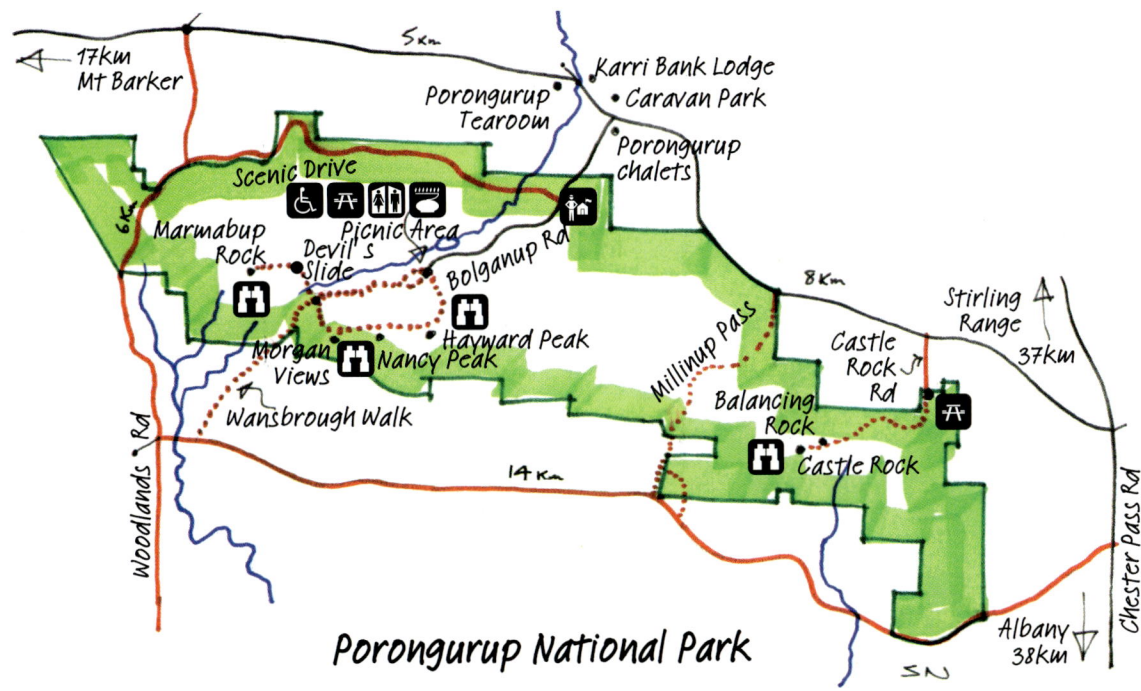

Porongurup National Park

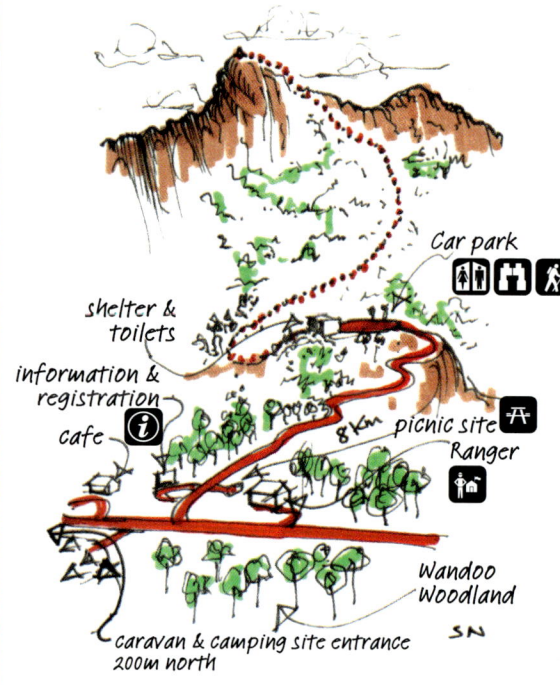

BLUFF KNOLL SUMMIT CLIMB
5km return 3-4 hours
Do not attempt to climb in hot or windy or very wet conditions. Do not attempt to climb with less than 3hrs of daylight remaining.

Bluff Knoll

Stirling Range (Koikyennurururff)
NATIONAL PARK

This park lies 76 km north of Albany and 30 km north of Porongurup Range. Although the two ranges are quite close, they are in fact different geologically. The Porongurups were formed from much older granitic rock, whereas the Stirling Range, although higher, is actually much younger.

The mountains were once ancient seabeds that have since been uplifted into the jagged conical ranges that are quite typical of younger mountain ranges, like the Andes in South America. The rocks consist of sandstone, quartzite (altered sandstone) and shales laid down in these early oceans and the ripples of the receding waters on the ancient sands, and examples of fossils found in them, can be found high in the mountain range.

Bluff Knoll (or Pualaar Miial to the Noongar people) at 1,093 m high, is not, contrary to belief, the highest point in Western Australia. Mount Meharry in the Pilbara region takes that title at 1,245 m. However it certainly looks higher, as it soars up from the almost flat farming country below.

The first European records of the range were in the journals of Matthew Flinders, who sailed the waters south of here in 1802, naming one of the eastern peaks Mt Rugged. The Stirling Range was named in 1832 after Captain James Stirling, the first Governor of the Swan River Colony, by the intrepid surveyor John Septimus Roe.

It was noted by Alexander Collie, in 1831, that the Noongar people had their own word for the range of mountains which described the mist that often circles the high peaks. Bluff Knoll was described as "the many faced hill". There is evidence in the park of their presence here, mainly in the form of stone tools. Such mountains with their changing weather moods must have given them lots to talk about, particularly with the belief that 'Noatch', who was the spirit of the dead, lived in the twirling mists and mountain tops of the range.

Flora: It was the botanist James Drummond who first really explored this region and collected many specimens that were to impress the various botanists around the world.

If the park had to be noted for one thing, it would have to be its incredible diversity of plant life. There are over 1,500 species within the park, with a staggering 384 genera and 82 species restricted to the park (Keighery 1993). To have so much diversity contained in an area just 65 km long by 20 km wide is quite remarkable. There are several reasons for this, the major factor being that there are many types of plant communities with differing habitat conditions. Here in the Stirlings there are mallee, mallee–heath, thicket (the dense vegetation on the mountain slopes), swampland and woodland communities. Some plants are common to several communities and some are just found in one community.

The increased rain brought on by the mountains' altitude, has enabled plants to grow where they would not have otherwise.

One group of plants that has fascinated the botanists are the mountain bells of the genus Darwinia. These magnificent bell-like flowers are found on different peaks and some valley locations, although all grow above the 200 m altitude level. To find them, one has to climb to the tops of mountains. Alas, with the spread of dieback, there is great pressure on these rare plants and several areas have had to be closed to the public and only the most popular walks left open.

This book has discussed the quantity of orchid species in several of the south coast parks, but here they reach an exceptionally high number with 123 species being found to date. The best time to view plants in flower is between mid-August and mid-October. In early November, if the summer heat arrives early, the displays on the lower slopes will soon drop off.

Fauna: Mammals have not fared so well, with 11 species of mammal becoming extinct over the last 100 years. Many required the open Wandoo and mallee country, and to a large extent these have been removed from the plains surrounding the mountains, and the feral animals would probably have taken the remaining few animals. Those marsupials that still remain common in the park are the diminutive Honey Possum (Tarsipes rostratus), Western Pygmy-possum (Cercartetus concinnus), Western Brush Wallaby (Macropus irma) and Western Grey Kangaroo (Macropus fuliginosus). Over recent years the numbat has been reintroduced to the park.

What to do: Running across the narrow part of the ranges is Chester Pass Road which will take you into the centre of the park. On the northern entry to the park is the access road to Bluff Knoll where there is an information bay (just off Chester Pass Road) giving you details of the park plus entry fees required. You can drive up to the main car park below Bluff Knoll. There are wonderful views from here as you will already be nearly 700 m up. There is a shelter with tables and access to these for disabled visitors.

Walks: The walk to the summit of Bluff Knoll starts from the car park. It is a 5 km return walk, and will take 3–4 hrs for a relatively fit person. The walk should not be done when the weather is very hot or very wet. There is a clear track but it is a strenuous walk and one should be in a fit state of health, have good walking shoes and plenty of water. Try also to drink a reasonable amount before you commence your walk. Take warm clothes in case the weather suddenly turns cold, which it does quite often.

The track first drops down to a creek and then goes across up the mountainside to a saddle, where there is a swampy area. Here you can look over the ridge to the south coast. From here you start walking to the left on the ridge to the summit. Be very careful near the cliff edges particularly if there are high winds and if thick cloud sets in.

Toolbrunup Peak (called Tualypaaranap by local Aborigines meaning 'drizzle carrier'), is the third highest peak; the main difference between it and Bluff Knoll is that it gives you a full 360 degree views when you are on the summit,

Looking east across the Stirling Ranges from Baby Barnett Hill

Gillam Bell *(Darwinia oxylepis)*

Mountain Pea *(Nemcia rubra)*

Queen of Sheba Orchid *(Thelymitra variegata)*

Wandoo woodland alongside Red Gum Pass Road

As you climb up from the Chester Pass Road you will pass by stunted Jarrah trees and in spring the Scallop flower (Hakea cucullata) and Stirling Range Bottlebrush (Beaufortia heterophylla) will be out. On the higher passes, some of the plants that grow only at high altitude, such as the Giant Andersonia (Andersonia echinocephala), Stirling Range Banksia (Banksia solandri) and Coneflower (Isopogon cuneatus), can be seen alongside the dirt road. At the car park at the top of the pass between Baby Barnett Hill and Mount Magog, in the height of the wildflower season, the surrounding area is ablaze with colour. Here you can see Gravel Bottlebrush (Beaufortia decussata), Corky Honeymyrtle (Melaleuca suberosa), Lambertia (Lambertia uniflora), and Mountain Pea (Nemecia rubra).

There are several good picnic sites on the Stirling Range Drive, mostly set under open woodlands of Wandoo. You can enter the park from the Albany Highway, passing through the small town of Cranbrook, then east along Salt River Road. Turn-off right onto Red Gum Pass Road and the left into Stirling Range Drive.

Camping: There is a bush camp site at Moingup Springs camping ground run by DCLM. Set amongst Jarrah and Marri trees and it is a lovely quiet spot. At the northern end of the park there is a very good private camping/caravan/chalet ground called Stirling Range Retreat. It is very well run and there are walking tours at very low cost for guests to find out more about the flora and fauna, especially the wonderful orchids.

There is a very good café opposite the camping ground.

The Wandoo woodland opposite the Stirling Range Retreat is ideal for orchids and birds, alas there was a control burn there which certainly killed many of the 200+ year old Wandoo trees (Eucalyptus wandoo). Wandoo forests do not need control burns in them as they are low fuel zones with little or no understorey and now that the native grasses have been burnt, many introduced weeds will proliferate and dominate.

however fewer people climb it. The walk is a little more difficult than the Bluff Knoll, mainly near the summit due to the rocky terrain. It will take 3-4 hrs return. Just over half way up you will experience rocky country so make sure you follow the markers to the top. It is very important you concentrate on your way down at the start from the summit, as a slight wrong angle will take you down areas you have not walked and off the main track.

There are other mountain peak walks that can be climbed; these are Mount Talyuberlup, a 3 km return walk (taking roughly 2.5 hrs), Mount Hassell, a 2 km return walk, (about 1.5 hrs) and Mount Trio, a 2 km return walk (2 hrs).

There are some long extended walks that take a few days but you should check all walks out with the ranger. Rangers must be notified of an extended overnight walk. Some walks may be closed due to dieback control.

Drives: The Stirling Range Drive that runs through the length of the range is well worth the drive and can be done in 2WD. It is not recommended for caravans, as there are some steep creek crossings.

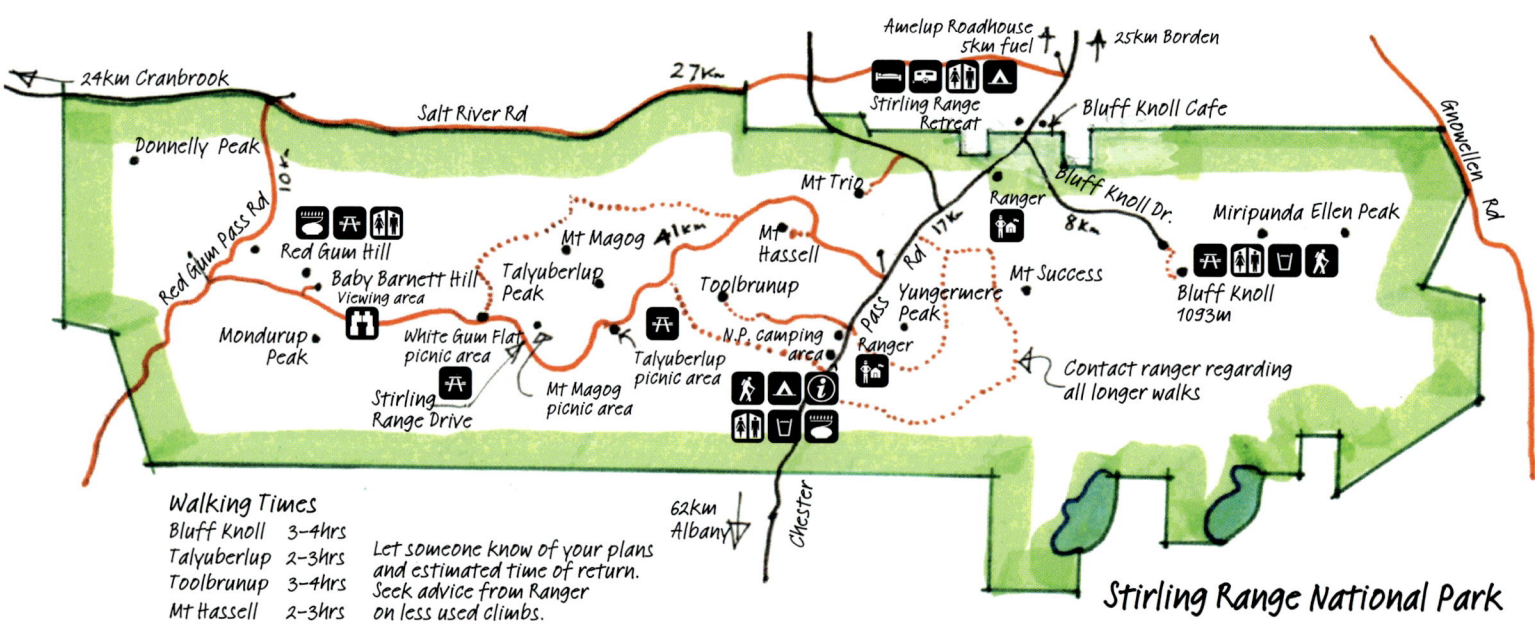

Stirling Range National Park

Quoin Head (accessed by 4WD only)

Fitzgerald River
NATIONAL PARK

The Fitzgerald River National Park is one of the true success stories for those who strive to protect and conserve wilderness areas. It was the diligent government botanist Charles Gardner who recognised the worth of the region and had it re-zoned to a 'C' class reserve to protect the immense variety of flora that exists in the park. This, however, gives little protection when mining rights or major pressures for land clearing are sought, without recall to parliament. Much of the land to the west and north of the park has been drastically cleared as late as the mid-1960s, then in the early 1970s, land within the present park was pegged for mining and applications were made to the Mines Department for the removal of quartz for glass and spongelite for building materials.

With a few local conservation-minded farmers and amateur botanists, who did care about the loss and damage to this pristine reserve, the mining development was halted temporarily. With the new Labor government coming into office, contested claims would be taken out of the hands of the Mines Department and dealt with by the newly appointed Environmental Protection Authority (EPA). Both the Mines Department and the EPA inspected the reserve. It was subsequently gazetted an 'A' class reserve and placed under the management of the then National Parks Authority. We must thank those dedicated people, like the late Ken Newbey and some of the locals, who formed the Fitzgerald River National Park Association, for saving what is one of Western Australia's most important National Parks and one of the world's most important reserves for flora.

To understand how significant that protection was, the whole park was later listed with UNESCO as an international biosphere reserve.

"A biosphere reserve is a protected area of land and coast large enough to be an effective conservation unit, and to accommodate different uses without conflict. It should have special value as a baseline for measuring long-term changes in the biosphere as a whole".

When Matthew Flinders sailed along the southern shoreline of the Fitzgerald in 1802, he named three of the main peaks West, Mid and East Mt Barren. He would never have called them barren had he explored them on foot, as their slopes hold a great variety of plant life and have a large number of restricted and rare species; more than any of the park's other landforms.

The park covers 329,589 ha of mostly wilderness, from the undulating uplands in the north, to the southern part of the huge gneissic Yilgarn Craton. The soil types are shallow loamy granitic sands with occasional exposed granite outcrops. These are mainly covered in mallee heath and contain numerous eucalypt species. In the middle of the park stretching from east to west are undulating plains consisting of marine plain soils with areas of spongelite siltstone. The vegetation consists of more open mallee and open low heath. One of he predominant eucalypts is Redheart (*Eucalyptus decipiens*).

Two major rivers, the Fitzgerald and Hamersley, dissect the plains. The gorges and river basins created by these rivers contain sedimentary soils with spongelite sands. The vegetation consists of open shrub mallee. Running parallel with the coast are several ranges of hills consisting of meta-sedimentary rocks made up of quartzite, dolomite and conglomerate rocks. The vegetation is banksia shrubland and heath with open mallee. The highest number of endemic plants of the park, including some of the rarest are located here on these quartzite systems.

Between the ranges on the coast are large sand dune systems consisting of calcareous sands laid over spongelite and quartzite. The vegetation consists of open mallee giving way to coastal dune vegetation.

Flora: The park contains the most plant species of any park in Western Australia with at least 1,893 species recognised and more being found as work continues. Seventy-five species can be found nowhere else. Newbey and Chapman identified 250 species as being of high conservation value, being either locally restricted or low in numbers. The range of banksias alone is enough to attract most flower enthusiasts.

If you are visiting the park between the months of August and November some of the various wildflowers you may encounter are described in the following.

Entering the park via the north east entry 20 km east of Jerramungup, you will pass through thick mallee country with the occasional open low heath. One of the first plants that will catch your eye is the Royal Hakea (*Hakea victoria*), named by Drummond in honour of Queen Victoria and collected by Baxter. At various levels, the leaves change colour from deep purple, red, right through the spectrum to bright yellow. The multi-columned plant is one of the most striking plants of Australia. People have tried to grow it in various parts of the world but it never develops such varied colours as here in the Fitzgerald, showing how subtle are the changes in nutrients that a plant requires from the soil.

Banksias adorn the drive into the park. One is large, round and fluffy and close to the ground, this is the is Woolly Banksia (*Banksia baueri*), and alongside it may be another smaller rust coloured pendulous banksia, Nodding Banksia (*Banksia nutans*). Further along Pabelup Drive there are numerous bright yellow banksias at eye level.

Looking at Southern Right Whales Point Ann

Chittick (*Lambertia inermis*)

Four-winged Mallee (*Eucalyptus tetraptera*)

Quaalup Bell (*Pimelia physodes—red form*)

Royal Hakea (*Hakea victoria*)

These are Baxter's Banksia (*Banksia baxteri*). The road then twists sharply around a double bend and drops down steeply to the lower heath plains. On the descent is a medium size banksia tree with bright yellow pendulous flower heads, Lemann's Banksia (*Banksia lemanniana*).

You may wish to visit or stay at the old Quaalup homestead on the edge of the Fitzgerald River National Park, which is a good base from which to explore this vast park. As you drive down Quaalup Road off Pabelup Drive, Royal Hakeas are everywhere, as well as the vivid Scarlet Banksia (*Banksia coccinea*). One flower that stands out amongst the many, is the Quaalup Bell (*Pimelia physodes*) with its long pendulous bell-shaped flowers.

Most of the mountain peaks have very restricted flowers. Climb either West or East Mt Barren and you will pass by the Dense Clawflower (*Calothamnus pinifolius*). Also half way up the hillside are Western Mountain Banksia (*Banksia oreophila*). This small dark mauve flower occurs on the Fitzgerald peaks and then 100 km west on the Stirling Range peaks.

On the eastern end of the park is Hamersley Drive. The drive twists its way through the upland and lower heath plains. In the height of the flower season, it seems to take so long passing through this area particularly if you are interested in wildflowers, as you will be forever getting in and out of the car to check the different species. Along the drive you pass by the endemic Weeping Gum (*Eucalyptus sepulcralis*). Also, the beautiful bright red flowers of Four-winged Mallee (*E. tetraptera*) may be out just opposite to the entry walk up East Mt Barren. If you are travelling the South West Region outside the flowering season, a visit to East Mt Barren should give you many species still in flower.

Fauna: The park has the most vertebrates (animals possessing a backbone made up of vertebrae) of any south west park; 22 mammals are recorded of which 5 are declared rare—the Southern Dibbler (*Parantechinus apicalis*), Red-tailed Phascogale (*Phascogale calura*), Western Mouse (*Pseudomys occidentalis*), Heath Rat (*Pseudomys shortridgei*) and Tammar Wallaby (*Macropus eugenii*).

These small creatures are hard to see as all of them are nocturnal. One tiny little creature that can be seen on a cool day feeding on the banksias is the diminutive Honey Possum (*Tarsipes rostratus*), or Noolbenger to the Noongar people. Even though it was known to the early naturalists in 1842, little about this mammal was known until recent years. It is unrelated to other possums and is one of the few mammals that exist almost entirely on nectar. Weighing on average only 9 g, it is about the size of a mouse. It runs at incredible speeds through the foliage of the shrubs, as it feeds from one flower head to another. Just like the honeyeaters of the bird world, it has a brush tip to its tongue; it does not make a nest but uses hollows or just rests in the foliage and often on a very cold night it becomes torpid and cannot move until temperatures increase.

The Honey Possum is restricted to the south west where the concentration of nectar-producing Proteacea, namely the banksias, dryandras and grevilleas is high. It is fairly common but if dieback takes more of a hold on the nectar-producing plants then it certainly will be threatened.

The Southern Dibbler on the other hand, is rare; even for those who study the animal it can be highly elusive. One research worker trapped a Dibbler and then just half an hour later, the same animal was caught in another trap 600 m away. For a creature with a body length of only 140 mm, that's a long way to go in less than an hour, so they can cover a large territory. Research has found that the Dibbler needs vegetation that is fairly well established and has not been burnt within a 20 year period. That restricts its range drastically and its population has been estimated to be as low as 1,000 individuals.

The name dibbler was recorded by the early naturalist John Gilbert, in 1843. It was collected by various people but it became rather elusive in later years, until the well-known photographer Michael Morcombe, who was trying to catch Honey Possums, captured an animal that did not look familiar; it was of course a Dibbler. Michael's photograph on this page, shows the teeth of this little carnivore quite well.

Scientists were becoming concerned for the survival of this small marsupial, that is obviously predated by the master hunter, the feral cat, but another surprise finding was made by Phil Fuller, a man of immense experience, particularly pertaining to desert fauna. He noticed on Boullanger Island (just off the coast near Jurien, north of Perth) the tracks of a creature he did not know. It was the elusive Southern Dibbler. This was a great find, as islands are very good areas to protect rare fauna, particularly from the attack of feral animals. Since that discovery the Perth Zoo has bred quite a few of these marsupials in captivity and hopefully more will be known about their ecology, survival and possible future translocation.

The Southern Right Whales (*Eubalaena australis*): Human beings can have a devastating effect on this planet, as we all know. In the early 1800s the Southern Right Whale was so numerous around the south coast that it was a hazard to the early sailors travelling the Australian Bight. By the late 1890s, the animal had almost been hunted out of existence. Between the years 1900 and 1960 there were only a few records of sightings of this species and it was presumed to be almost extinct by the mid-1950s. Since 1960, the whales have slowly started to increase. You can experience the privilege of seeing them between early August and late September at the whale lookout platform erected at Point Ann. They are in these warmer waters for only 4-5 weeks. Here, the mothers with their calves come to feed the young in the early stages of their development before heading out to the open seas.

These whales are classed as baleen whales, having not teeth but horny plates that hang down from the upper jaw. They feed entirely on plankton, which they sieve through these bony plates that have hairs that help filter out the small plankton.

Some of the most reliable bays to see these wonderful creatures are Flinders Bay near Augusta, Point Ann in the Fitzgerald River National Park and Tagon Bay in Cape Arid National Park.

The whales were called the Right Whale because the early hunters, in their open boats with hand harpoons, saw them as the right whale to catch because they were slow, floated to the surface when dead and yielded copious amounts of oil and fat.

Humpback Whales (*Megaptera novaeangliae*): The Humpback has always been in larger numbers than the Southern Right Whale. After World War II, over a 1,000 whales were taken off the Western Australian coast each year but by 1963 Humpback numbers were getting low and the whaling stations were closed down. You can visit the site of an old whaling station near Torndirrup National Park. Since the closure of the station, there has been a slow but progressive increase in the number of whales in this area.

Humpbacks are also baleen whales and make the more spectacular displays when diving out of water that we associate with our migrating whales. The Humpback gets its name from the distinct 'hump' as it turns to dive. They can be seen off Perth regularly and all the way up the coast as far as the remote Kimberley. In early May they can be seen moving north along the west coast, but do not make dramatic displays as much as on their return in September through to early November, with the peak period around mid-October. They travel huge distances from the

Pygmy Possum
(Cercartetus concinnus)
Photo by Greg Barron

New Holland Honeyeater on Round Fruit Banksia

Western Bristlebird

Hooded Dotterel

Honey Possum (Tarsipes rostratus)
Photo by Michael Morcombe

Southern Dibbler (Parantechinus apicalis)
Photo by Michael Morcombe

Huntsman Spider (top)
Badge Huntsman (below)
Photos by David Knowles

Fitzgerald River National Park

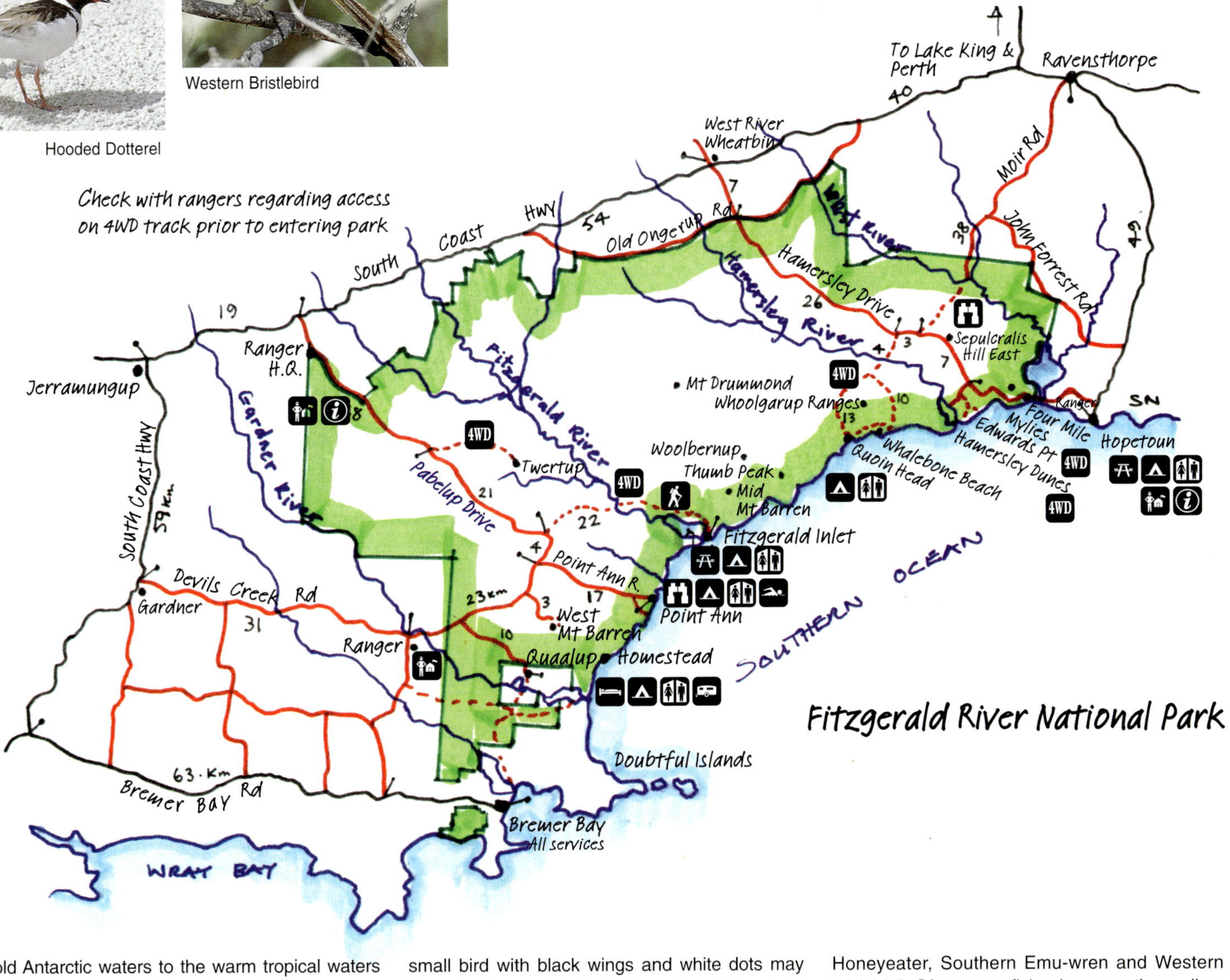

cold Antarctic waters to the warm tropical waters south of the Equator to breed.

There are also many other whales that enter our waters such as the various sperm and the bottlenose whales.

Birds: The bird list for Fitzgerald stands at 184 species. That is the highest for any south west park and is primarily due to the large size of the park and the many different vegetation communities.

As you drive through the mallee woodland, a few birds will be relatively common. One very small bird with black wings and white dots may fly out of a nest hole in the side of the sand tracks as you drive past. This is the Spotted Pardalote. If a bird with a constant repeated bell-like call is seen perched up on top of a mallee bush it will be the Crested Bellbird, with its white throat and black surrounding throat band.

Keen bird watchers come here to see some of the more uncommon species such as the Shy Heathwren, found in the thicker patches of vegetation in the mallee, along with the Southern Scrub-robin, Malleefowl, Purple-gaped Honeyeater, Southern Emu-wren and Western Whipbird. Often seen flying low over the mallee, the Square-tailed Kite is always a beautiful sight.

Two birds that are particularly rare here are the Western Bristlebird and the Western Ground Parrot. The latter is extremely rare and the Fitzgerald River National Park holds the main population of this species which is in a very precarious situation.

If you walk along some of the beaches, like Point Ann, two uncommon birds may be seen. They are the Hooded Plover on the beach sand, and the

Rock Parrot in the fringing beach vegetation; the latter should not be confused with its close relative the Elegant Parrot that exists in the Wheatbelt.

In the various inlets one can see an attractive duck, the Chestnut Teal, common in the eastern states but uncommon here. Among the Yate trees and thickets along the Gairdner River are the best places to look for the beautiful Red-eared Firetail.

The Invertebrates: All life forms that do not possess a vertebral column, are known as invertebrates. The arthropods, including among others the insects and spiders, are the most numerous and successful group of living creatures on earth, taking up 80% of all life forms on earth. That's a lot of species. The sad thing is, arthropods are the least studied and least known of all the animal kingdom. In the United Kingdom an entomologist (one who studies insects) would be lucky to find one or two insects new to science each decade. In Australia, at this stage, it is possible a keen entomologist could find many new species each year! In the Fitzgerald there are some fascinating insects, no more so than the spiders. These creatures are not always popular with people.

Drives: From the western end, you can enter the park off the South Coast Highway either via Devils Creek Road north Boxwood Hill or Quiss Road east of Jerramungup. There is an information bay at both entries to the park. Both roads are accessible by 2WD. The entry to Twertup and the Fitzgerald Inlet are both for 4WD only and may often be closed due to rain.

The drives to Quaalup homestead, West Mt Barren car park and Point Ann Beach are all accessible to 2WD.

At the eastern end of the park, you can enter via Hamersley Drive, at the northern entrance off South Coast Highway or from Hopetoun via East Mt Barren. The tracks to Edwards, West and Whalebone Beach are 4WD only, as is the track to Quoin Head. The access road via Moir Road from Ravensthorpe is 4WD and is not a recommended entry point. This track may often be closed due to rain. Always check with the rangers.

All roads mentioned are very good drives for wildflowers in season.

Walks: There is a multitude of walks available in the park and this book will identify just some of them.

West Mt Barren (The Queelup Walk) Queelup is the Aboriginal name of West Mt Barren. The walk starts at the car park and ascends via a stony track to the summit and there are marker pegs on the route. You should be fairly fit as this is a moderate to hard climb so wear walking boots.

Botanically this is a very interesting walk as it takes you past some very restricted plants. On the lower slopes there is Lemann's Banksia (*Banksia lemanniana*), Bell-fruited Mallee (*Eucalyptus preissiana*), Tallerack (*E. pleurocarpa*) and Oak-leaved Dryandra (*Dryandra quercifolia*).

As you climb higher there is an endemic prickly acacia (*Acacia cedroides*) and near the summit the Barrens Clawflower (*Calothamnus validus*).

Point Ann Heritage Trail This is an easy walk of just 1.5 km. It starts from near the car park where the trail sign is located and takes you up onto the ridge of the headland where the famous Rabbit Proof Fence terminated its long length here at Point Ann. From the headland there are magnificent views across the bay to Mid Mt Barren and Thumb Peak. See how the banksias and eucalypts that would normally grow quite high, like the Four-winged Mallee (*Eucalyptus tetraptera*), are stunted with the winds that blow off these southern seas.

Twertup Access to Twertup is 4WD entry only and it's best to notify the ranger of your intent to visit Twertup. There are a few walks that lead from the old homestead and spongelite quarry. Most take you from the top of the spongelite cliffs down to the lower flood plain. It is easy to get lost in this mallee so stay on the marked tracks that hug the cliff face. Here there are many eucalypt species, including Hidden Mallet (*Eucalyptus practermissa*), Moort (*E. platypus*) and Redwood (*E. aff. flocktoniae*). Please respect the privacy of people staying at the homestead by using the visitor's car park. There are great views from the car park across the Fitzgerald River Basin.

Sepulcralis Hill A short walk takes you to the lookout with views across the Hamersley River basin and the Whoogarup Range, to the right way out on the horizon is the lone peak of Mt Drummond. The beautiful weeping gums that you can see below you are the rare and very restricted Weeping Gum (*Eucalyptus sepulcralis*) from which the lookout gets its name.

East Mt Barren This is a fairly strenuous climb and you must be fit to climb the mountain. Walking boots are essential. It is a 3 km return walk taking between 2 and 3 hrs. If you are here in spring through to early summer, you may see the beautiful endemic Barrens Regelia (*Regelia velutina*). It looks like a bottlebrush with its bright red flowers. The views from the summit are spectacular and you can see almost right through the 65 km length of this wilderness park. Along the drive and at the car park on the Hopetoun side of the mountain (not where you start the walk from) there are several very rare plants and two rare eucalypts *E. coronata* and *E. burdettiana* which show the importance of these quartzite island mountains.

Before visiting the park it is wise to check road conditions in the park to avoid a wasted trip if many of the areas you planned to visit are closed.

Stokes
NATIONAL PARK

The park lies 106 km east of Ravensthorpe and 80 km west of Esperance covering an area of 9,726 ha. The country consists of mallee woodland and heath. Around the Stokes Inlet are salt water paperbarks and sedges. This park is a long way from Perth and many of its visitors are from Esperance. It has some great fishing areas particularly for salmon, mullet and King George whiting. There are two camping areas on the western side of the inlet with gas barbecues, toilets, and individual camping bays, with easy launching areas for small boats.

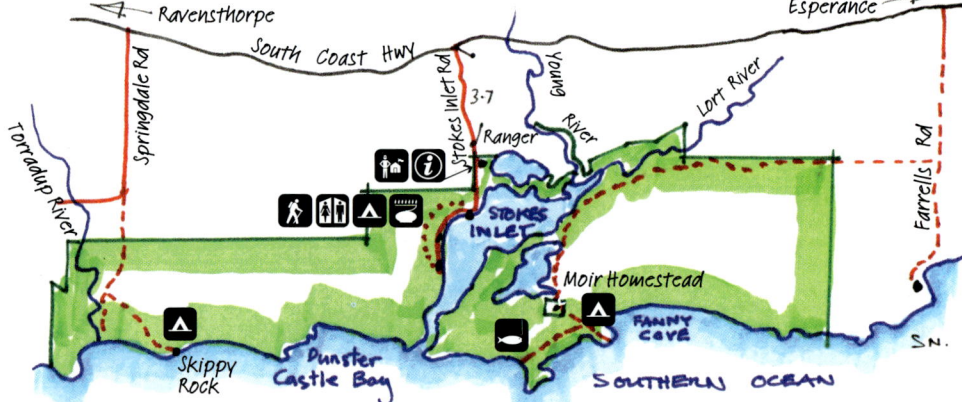

◀ Stokes Inlet

There are access tracks to Skippy Rock on the western side of the park. Entry is via Springdale Road but you will need 4WD and you must take your rubbish out. At the other end of the park is a track leading off Farrells Road that will take you to the old ruins of Moir Homestead built in 1877, but you will need a 4WD. South of the homestead the 4WD track takes you down to the coast near Fanny Cove and Shoal Cape. There is good fishing in these areas and few people go here.

Stokes Heritage Trail: There is an easy 2 km walk that takes you from the car park before Stokes Inlet on the western side of the road and climbs up to the limestone ridge. Take the first track to the left about 20 m from the start of the walk. This will take you to the first lookout overlooking the inlet. Then after a few hundred metres, the track turns back from the ridge along an old 4WD track and then returns to the starting point. You will pass through mallee and thick shrub lands of Showy Banksia (*Banksia speciosa*).

Esperance & the Bay of Isles

The Archipelago of the Recherché
'THE BAY OF ISLES'

Visitor facilities on Woody Island

The town of Esperance and the archipelago were named after the two ships that were sailing under the command of Rear Admiral Bruny d'Entrecasteaux in 1792, namely the Esperance and Recherché. They anchored in Esperance Bay for a few days after being laid up in a bad storm but they had to depart a few days later as no fresh water was found.

The town of Esperance has certainly grown over the years and in fact in the mid-1950s there were only 36 farms in the area where now there are about 630. Here there are some of the most successful cattle and crop farms in the State.

There are 105 islands large and small in the Archipelago of the Recherché, known more locally as the 'The Bay of Isles'. It is a wonderful sight, on a clear day driving along Twilight Beach Road looking out across the turquoise blue waters, with the many islands dotting the skyline.

You can visit a few of the islands from Esperance on a large offshore boat run by a local tour operator. These half day or full day cruises leave from the Taylor Street jetty. They will take you past Charlie, Rabbit and Cull Islands looking at the Australian Sea-lions and New Zealand Fur-seals. Sea-lions have external ears like the Fur-seal but have no thick fur on the underbelly.

Some of the small rocky islands are breeding grounds for the Black-faced Cormorant. The Archipelago is the most westerly this species comes. It differs from its close relative, the more common Pied Cormorant, in that it has a black instead of a yellow facial patch between the eye and the beak.

Another uncommon bird that is at its most westerly distribution is the western subspecies of the Cape Barren Goose (*Cereopsis novaehollandiae grisea*). The Cape Barren Goose was noted in the diary of Matthew Flinders in 1802. His crew brought 28 geese back to the sloop the Investigator. The geese would have supplemented the sailors' meagre rations on these long voyages. The Cape Barren Goose has been killed for the last two hundred years by whalers and sealers but is now protected. There are estimated to be at the very most 700 birds in the population of the Western Australian subspecies. There are more of the nominate race in South Australia and Tasmania. If you are keen to see Cape Barren Geese, they can be seen on the grasslands around the edge of town, for example at the Esperance Golf Course.

Those wishing to experience an overnight stay on one of the islands, can be taken to Woody Island, which lies just 15 km south of Esperance. There are permanent safari style tents available as accommodation. You can take walks around the island and walk to the top of the island, a height of 130 m. There are dense thickets of mallee consisting of Moort (*Eucalyptus platypus*), Bushy Yate (*E. lehmannii*), Ridge-fruited Mallee (*E. angulosa*) and Yate (*E. cornuta*), and a surprising number of birds may be observed including Brush Bronzewing, Golden Whistler, Spotted Pardalote, Silvereye, Red-eared Firetail, Sooty Oystercatcher, Rock Parrot, Black-faced Cormorant, Pacific Gull and Kelp Gull. Other sea birds include Flesh-footed Shearwater and Little Penguin.

There are various facilities and activities such as a playground area for children, glass bottom boat cruises, hiring of snorkel gear from the kiosk and a few walking trails. There is good snorkelling in the sheltered bay near the landing jetty, with two small wooden wrecks to explore.

Sunset over Woody Island

Esperance Lakes
NATURE RESERVES

These are a group of very important wetlands for birds, with an area of 3,383 ha. The main lakes include Pink, Warden, Windabout, Woody, Station, Mullet and Wheatfield Lakes.

Pink Lake gets its pink colour from the aquatic flora, the algae *Dunaliella salina*. As it develops and grows, it absorbs red hydrocarbons that exist in many of the plants on the fringe of the lake, giving the lake a pinkish colour when conditions are right.

Many species of birds utilise this lake system including Australian Shelduck, Black Swan's, Chestnut Teal, Musk Duck and, on the less saline lakes, Blue-billed Duck, Australasian Shoveler and Great Crested Grebe.

Some of the largest numbers of Hooded Plovers in Australia congregate on the edges of the lakes, particularly Lake Warden, which is estimated to contain 10% of the whole Australian population of this species. There are also large quantities of waders, all the way from the Arctic Circle, that descend on these lakes in the summer months. These include the Red-necked Stint, Sharp-tailed Sandpiper, and sometimes the rare Pectoral Sandpiper.

The 3.5 km long Kepwari Wetland Trail, containing interpretive material and two bird hides, provides an enjoyable outing through a tranquil landscape. Twelve kilometres west of Esperance is Monjingup Lake. This is a very good place for birds and has a bird hide and picnic area.

One thing that everyone who visits Esperance should do is take the circuit drive along Twilight Beach Road. The views out over the ocean are tremendous and you can return via the shores of Pink Lake on Eleven Mile Beach Road.

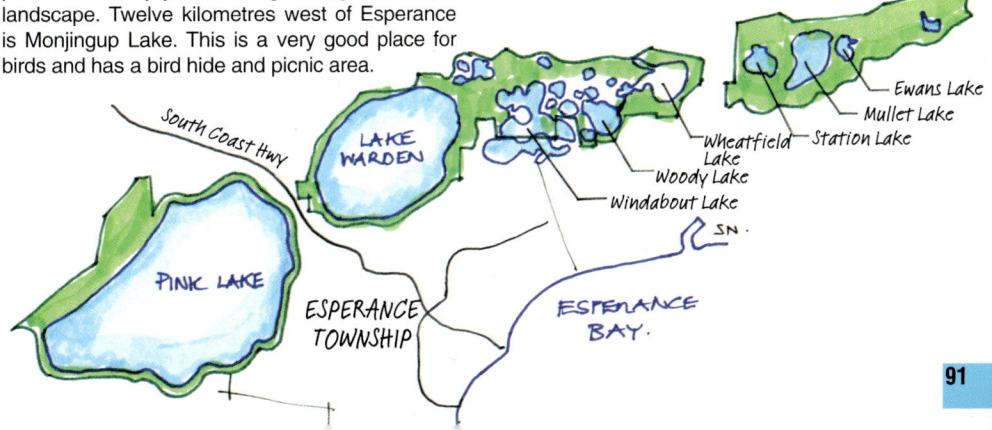

Cape Le Grand
NATIONAL PARK

The naturalist Labillardiere, sailing in 1792 under the command of Rear Admiral Bruny D'Entrecasteaux on the two ships the L'Esperance and Le Recherché, wrote in his diary after they anchored past Cape Le Grand during a bad storm. *"The Esperance was driving toward the land so rapidly that she was on the point of being stranded when citizen Le Grand went to the mast head in the very midst of the tempest and almost immediately came down, explaining with enthusiasm that the ship was out of danger, He then pointed out the anchoring place. The discovery saved both ships…We gave it (the cape) the name of citizen Le Grand."*

Many of the French names in this region given by this expedition are still used to this day, such as Rossiter Bay, Le Grand, Esperance and Recherché.

Cape Le Grand is certainly a grand park, with magnificent beaches like Le Grand Beach, Hellfire Beach, Lucky Bay and Rossiter Bay. Most people drive along Lucky Bay Road to the main camping and caravan ground at Lucky Bay. It is a beautiful bay. It is the best bay to launch small craft. The Lucky Bay camping ground is very small and can be quite overcrowded. The camping ground at the end of Le Grand Beach, accessed via Cape Le Grand Road, can be quieter, with individual camping bays set behind the dune and it too has a boat launching area. Both Lucky Bay and Le Grand Beach camping areas have toilets, solar hot water showers, fresh drinking water, gas barbeques and camp kitchen.

It was near Lucky Bay that the explorer John Eyre and his faithful Aboriginal companion Wylie stumbled on the French whaling ship the 'Mississippi' under the command of Captain Rossiter. It was just as well, as Eyre and Wylie were at a very low point on their gruelling journey from South Australia to Albany.

Walks: There are some magnificent walks available in the park. The longest is the Coastal Trail

Rocky outcrops at Thistle Cove

of 15 km. The scenery is superb. The walk comprises 3 sections and the first part from Lucky Bay to Thistle Cove is a relatively easy walk and well worth doing. It is a 1 hr return walk and normal shoes will do. The second part goes from Thistle Cove to Hellfire Bay and is a 2.5 hr return walk of moderate difficulty and requires walking boots. The longest walk is from Hellfire Beach to Le Grand Beach and is 3 hrs one way. It is a difficult walk and for experienced walkers only. Always drink prior to your walk and carry water.

There is a walk to the top of Frenchman's Peak, named by the surveyor Alexander Forrest in 1870 in reference to the outline shape of the hat worn by the French troops in the 1800s. The aboriginal name is 'Mandoorbureup'. It is a relatively hard climb and it is best to wear walking boots. It is a 2 hr return walk from the car park below the peak.

The whole park is a great location for fishing and holidaying. The wildflowers, like in so many southern coastal parks, are quite prolific in spring and early summer. There are some restricted species like the Silver Teatree (*Leptospermum sericeum*) seen below Frenchman's Peak on the main road and a lovely eucalypt called Bushy Yate (*E. lehmannii*). Other eucalypts include Hook-leaved Mallee (*E. uncinata*), Tallerack (*E. plurocarpa*) and Lerp Mallee (*E. incrassata*). The most prevalent banksia is Showy Banksia (*Banksia speciosa*). As you drive into the Thistle Bay car park there is the lovely orange form of grevillea (*Grevillea baxteri*) near the entrance to the rock picnic table. Captain Matthew Flinders named this bay after one of his sailors who discovered it.

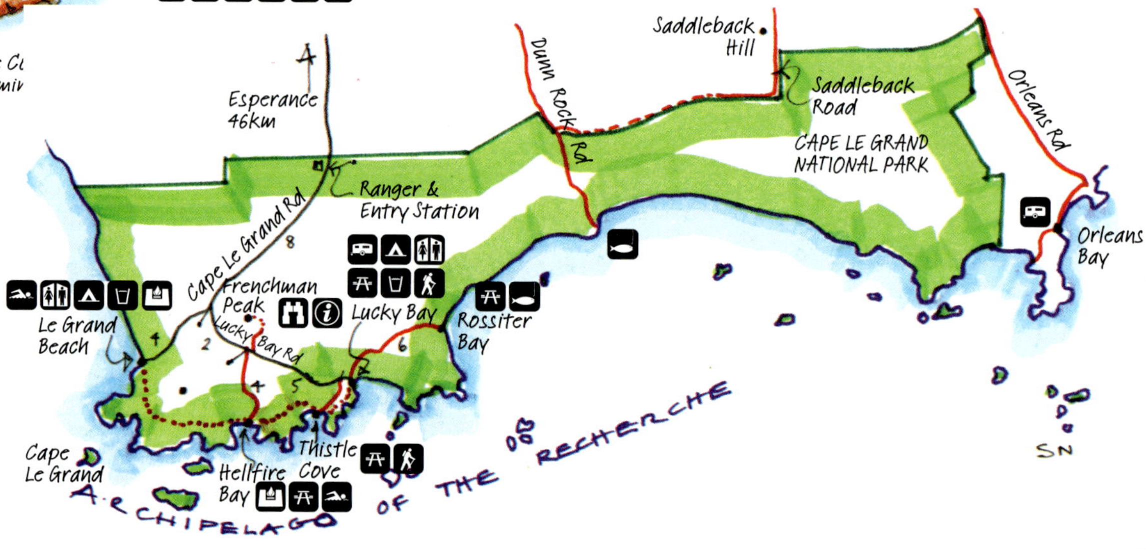

Cape Arid
NATIONAL PARK

Further east from Cape Le Grand National Park is Cape Arid National Park, some 120 km from Esperance. It was originally called Cape Arid by Admiral D'Entrecasteaux in 1792 as he sailed off this coastline.

It is a larger park of 280,000 ha; over eight times the size of Le Grand and much of it, especially in the north and east, is wilderness country.

The camping grounds are very good and often you will be the only people at some of the sites. For the keen fisherman, this is a top location, with beaches renowned for their length and beauty. There are 5 camping grounds in the park; they include Thomas River, Thomas Fisheries, Seal Creek and Jorndee Creek, all on the coast and one site inland at the remote location of Mt Ragged. There are gas barbecues at Thomas River and Seal Creek and the ranger is based up on the hill above Tagon Bay.

Thomas River and Seal Creek are the only campsites that are accessible by 2WD vehicles. Seal Creek must be approached via Baring Road. Driving from Esperance, the best way is to approach the park via Fisheries Road and Baring Road as the Merivale Road is dirt east of Thomas River and Tagon Roads, and often has water in the dips after wet weather.

Again the flowers are stunning and even in autumn and summer, there are flowers out, particularly the banksias such as Showy Banksia and Southern Plains Banksia (*Banksia media*). In spring the lovely pendulous Teasel Banksia (*Banksia pulchella*), only 60 cm tall, covers much of the heath country.

Mount Ragged: The first European to climb the peak, was the Surveyor–General John Septimus Roe in 1848.

The track that leads to Mt Ragged is definitely a 4WD track and really this area should only be visited by experienced bush travellers, as few people enter this region and the four wheel driving is rather tricky at times. The first few kilometres are on a gravel road which suddenly stops and leads into a very sandy and often wet track. Deflate your tyres here, but not too much as you may have to pass through deep water in places which remains long after the winter rains.

The track is about 50 km long from the junction of Fisheries Road to the base of Mt Ragged. The mountain is the highest peak in the whole region, rising to 585 m. The whole area is botanically very rich as this ancient uplifted quartzite mountain has different soils to the surrounding plains and has the same origins as the Barren Mountains in the Fitzgerald National Park. There is a small campsite at the southern end of the mountain. The walk to the top of Tower Peak takes 3 hrs return. Let someone know of your intentions to visit this area and when you plan to return. It is also wise to check the track conditions with the local ranger at Tagon Bay.

Walks: In the Thomas River area there are 3 main walks:

The Len Otte Walk This walk is named in memory of Cape Arid's first ranger who did much to make this park a memorable place. The walk is about 1 hr return. The walk starts in the car park below Belinup Hill, and the turn-off is before you get to the Thomas River Camping Ground. The start of the walk takes you through a dense coastal thicket of Flat-topped Yate (*Eucalyptus occidentalis*) and then up onto Belinup Hill with its open granite rocks and beautiful views across Yokinup Bay with its 10 km long white beach.

On your return on the edge of the granite you may pass by the lovely red flowers of Scarlet Honeymyrtle (*Melaleuca fulgens*). It is an easy walk but walking boots will make it easier.

Boolenup Walk Trail This is a 4 km return walk and relatively easy. The walk leads you to the edge of the shore of Lake Boolenup. You will first walk through banksia woodland, where there are

Fishing at Tagon Bay

4 species, including the prostrate Creeping Banksia (*Banksia repens*). The walk then drops down towards the lake and onto a granite outcrop. Another eucalypt that you may not have seen is found here; the Hook-leaved Mallee (*E. uncinata*). This is a very good walk for bird watchers, particularly for the elusive Southern Emu-wren.

Tagon Coastal Walk This is a long 7 km walk taking about 4 hrs. As the name implies, the walk takes you around the coast, starting at the end of the track to the beach entrance to Thomas River. It starts in a south westerly direction and takes you to Dolphin Cove, Little Tagon Bay and finally to Tagon Bay. Then you return up the 4WD part of Tagon Road to where the gravel starts and turn left back past the ranger's house and then right to Thomas River. If by the time you reach little Tagon Bay you have had enough, you can walk up to the car park above the bay and return on the 2WD gravel track.

Sunrise across Yokinup Bay

Looking across the paddocks from Contine Hill

Wheatbelt
REGION

Wheatbelt
REGION

Salmon Gum trees on typical wheatbelt dirt road

The region stretches from the eastern side of the Darling Range to the Vermin Barrier Fence east of Hyden and from the Murchison River in the north to Esperance in the south east. It is a vast area from which most native vegetation has been cleared for agriculture. Only 10% of the original vegetation remains and much of that is on private land and often degraded by grazing stock.

The percentage of remnant vegetation that remains varies from shire to shire; for instance, those shires that were cleared first, like Cunderdin, only possess 3% of uncleared land, whereas shires like Lake Grace that were cleared in the 1950s and 1960s hold far larger areas of uncleared land—around 31%. With greater understanding of the consequences that can occur from drastic land clearing, some shires left large roadside verges. These act not only as reserves for some rare flora but also as corridors through which the last remaining fauna can move from one area to another.

Even though such a vast amount of land was cleared, the Wheatbelt still possesses the largest numbers of species of flora in Western Australia, which also makes it one of the world's botanical "hot spots", with over 8,000 species being recorded for this region. These rich plant communities occur on the yellow and laterite sandplains called Kwongan, from the Noongar word for 'sandy plain'. They can be found in many reserves such as Tarrin Rock, Dragon Rock, Boyagin Rock, Dryandra and Tutanning, as well as on roadside verges and alongside railway lines.

In the early 1900s the first settlers moved through the Darling Range with its thick Jarrah forest and dense undergrowth, to the undulating plains, where York Gum *(Eucalyptus loxophleba)* and Jam *(Acacia acuminata)* dominated the landscape. These two trees were indicators of good grazing country and this was the first type of habitat to be cleared. Settlers often chose locations with natural springs or water catchment areas below granite rocks to establish their homesteads, each new settler taking land further east each year. As well as York Gum there were beautiful open woodlands of Wandoo *(E. wandoo)* trees and on the laterite ridges grew the Powderbark Wandoo *(E. accedens)* and Brown Mallet *(E. astrigens)*. As the settlers moved further east, they came to the country where Salmon Gum *(E. salmonophloia)*, Morrel *(E. longicornis)* and Gimlet *(E. salubris)* dominated. These trees, like the York Gum, were indicators of good soils to the settler, being classed as 'heavy soils', often occurring on the broad alluvial flood plains. Past the open woodlands of Wandoo and Salmon Gum, the country gave way to vast areas of mallee. Initially where mallees grew the soils were considered poor and the rainfall was lower, so land clearing diminished the further east one travelled.

From 1900 to 1940, clearing of land was slow. With the advent of heavy machinery after the second World War, land clearing took on a monumental pace; in fact over 50% of all land cleared in the wheatbelt took place after 1945. In the 1960s the environmentally disastrous government ruling of "conditional purchase" was in place, where farmers by law had to clear all useable land and fence the allotted area, only rugged ridge tops and swamplands often remaining.

By 1980, 90% of the Wheatbelt had been cleared and to this day there is still land being cleared. Luckily it is no longer an easy matter to blatantly clear land without government approval, although sadly it still does occur. We are now seeing the massive ramifications of salination problems due to over clearing in certain areas, costing billions of dollars to try to resolve, but this text is not the forum for these issues.

Where to go
IN THE WHEATBELT

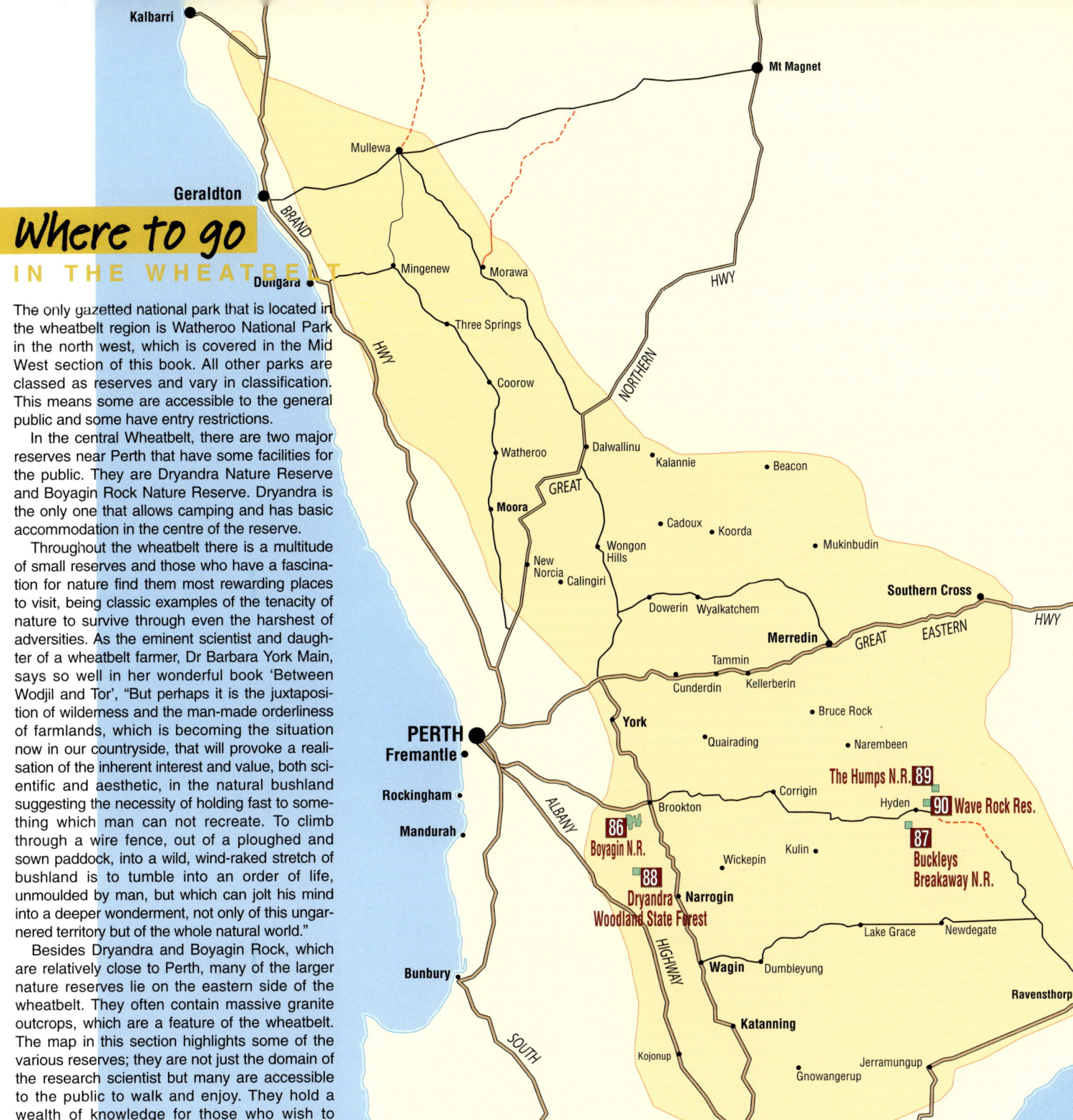

The only gazetted national park that is located in the wheatbelt region is Watheroo National Park in the north west, which is covered in the Mid West section of this book. All other parks are classed as reserves and vary in classification. This means some are accessible to the general public and some have entry restrictions.

In the central Wheatbelt, there are two major reserves near Perth that have some facilities for the public. They are Dryandra Nature Reserve and Boyagin Rock Nature Reserve. Dryandra is the only one that allows camping and has basic accommodation in the centre of the reserve.

Throughout the wheatbelt there is a multitude of small reserves and those who have a fascination for nature find them most rewarding places to visit, being classic examples of the tenacity of nature to survive through even the harshest of adversities. As the eminent scientist and daughter of a wheatbelt farmer, Dr Barbara York Main, says so well in her wonderful book 'Between Wodjil and Tor', "But perhaps it is the juxtaposition of wilderness and the man-made orderliness of farmlands, which is becoming the situation now in our countryside, that will provoke a realisation of the inherent interest and value, both scientific and aesthetic, in the natural bushland suggesting the necessity of holding fast to something which man can not recreate. To climb through a wire fence, out of a ploughed and sown paddock, into a wild, wind-raked stretch of bushland is to tumble into an order of life, unmoulded by man, but which can jolt his mind into a deeper wonderment, not only of this ungarnered territory but of the whole natural world."

Besides Dryandra and Boyagin Rock, which are relatively close to Perth, many of the larger nature reserves lie on the eastern side of the wheatbelt. They often contain massive granite outcrops, which are a feature of the wheatbelt. The map in this section highlights some of the various reserves; they are not just the domain of the research scientist but many are accessible to the public to walk and enjoy. They hold a wealth of knowledge for those who wish to study various aspects of nature. In each shire there are some reserves that may be accessed and DCLM or the local shires should know where and how you may enter.

The main thing is to be careful of spreading dieback, particularly in heath country when it is wet under foot—try and walk the firebreaks or cleared tracks. The big problem, though, is fire. Do not light fires unless there is a barbecue location already there and never in the hot summer months. These small wheatbelt reserves are extremely fragile and one fire will destroy the last remaining fauna as there is literally nowhere for them to escape and survive. (NB Open fires are not permitted in nature reserves.)

Powderbark Wandoo trees line the edge of a laterite breakaway in the Dryandra State Forest

Dryandra
WOODLAND STATE FOREST

Dryandra is one of the most important remnant reserves in the whole of the wheatbelt, made up of 17 separate vegetation blocks varying from just 87 ha to 12,283 ha, with an accumulative total of 28,066 ha.

Here one can see marsupials that, by the late 1970s, were on the brink of extinction. With hard work by some dedicated scientists and co-workers, their demise was halted by the use of poison baits that eradicated most of the European Red Foxes *(Vulpes vulpes)*. The results have been so successful that the Numbat *(Myrmecobius fasciatus)* and Brush-tailed Bettong or Woylie *(Bettongia penicillata)* populations are now reasonably well established in the reserve and both species are spreading out to adjacent island reserves.

Dryandra woodland has long been a hunting ground for the aboriginal Wilman Clan and an ochre pit, circular stones on a granite outcrop, a marked tree and some tool scatterings are all evidence of their use of this, their ancestral home.

In terms of European settlement, Dryandra survived the massive land clearing program of the early 1900s for one major reason, the existence of large stands of the eucalypt Brown Mallet *(Eucalyptus astringens)*.

The early farmers who established themselves in the western wheatbelt were keen to supplement their meagre incomes by harvesting the Brown Mallet. The tree's bark contained up to 40% tannin. This was used in the tanning process of leather and Europe required large quantities of this product. By 1905 the trade peaked at 20,700 tons giving revenue of £154,087. By 1925 nearly 130,000 tons had been shipped out of the country. Fortunately, Germany was the largest importer of tannin and during the war years, exports dropped dramatically.

Brown Mallet was still being cleared and the timber cutters were desperate for new timber, as most of the western wheatbelt was cleared of its virgin Brown Mallet. The Forest Department set about establishing Brown Mallet plantations within the Dryandra area. The first plantation was set aside in 1924, subsequently more areas being planted.

The beneficial side effect of this planting program was that much of the pristine open Wandoo woodland adjacent to the Brown Mallet, remained intact, much of it as water catchment areas for dams that supplied water for the 50-odd locomotives in the Narrogin area.

The water required to supply the needs of each steam driven locomotive, was so high that 15 of the locomotives were used for carting water, as each locomotive used 7,000 gallons a day. By the late 1950s the steam trains were replaced by diesel driven locomotives and the water problems literally evaporated.

In the early 1930s the foresters were housed in the Dryandra settlement which remained in use until 1962 when synthetic tannins became the chosen product for tanning leather.

So, indirectly, the need for Brown Mallet saved Dryandra woodland from being clear felled and subsequently it has become one of the major conservation reserves within Western Australia.

The Brown Mallet plantations are still utilised to this day, supporting a few small timber enterprises consisting of a tool handle manufacturer, a small amount of fence post products and a couple of licensed firewood and fence post cutters.

Dryandra woodland is approximately 180 km south east of Perth–roughly 2 hrs drive. The main entrance is 29 km north west of Narrogin on the Wandering/Narrogin Road

Flora

One of the major long term objectives of DCLM is to conserve the various representative species of flora and fauna that exist in the central wheatbelt by providing and maintaining suitable habitat for them on a long term basis. There are also plans to reintroduce fauna that was once prolific in these areas but is now extinct. Dryandra supports one of the highest flora specieslists for the wheatbelt with 816 species being identified including 1 species of declared rare flora and 21 species on the priority list. Part of the reason for this high species count is that the reserve is on the boundary between two botanic zones, that of the wetter Darling Botanical Province and the drier Avon Botanical Province.

Even though Jarrah and Marri exist in the reserve, the dominance of Powderbark Wandoo *(Eucalyptus accedens)* and Brown Mallet *(E. astringens)* over Marri *(E. calophylla)* on the laterite hillsides is typical of this transition zone.

To many who travel through the reserve it may appear that the area consists predominantly of open Wandoo woodland with the occasional sheoak woodland, dense heath and Jarrah/Marri woodland, but botanists like to be specific when they identify flora systems. When you really start looking closely at the various plant communities there is great variation. Here in Dryandra there are 12 distinct vegetation communities within the reserve: Laterite Plateau Woodlands, Dryandra/Petrophile Shrubland, Low Kwongan, Brown Mallet Forest, Powderbark Wandoo Woodland, Wandoo Sheoak Forest, Marri Woodland, Sheoak Low Forest, Lithic Complex (granite outcrops), York Gum Woodland and Jam Low Forest (D. Coates 1993).

The areas in which to find the greatest array of wildflowers are on the Kwongan heaths and lateritic plateaux. Even though these communities are small in size, they hold the greatest variety of plants.

In mid September, if you walk up from the settlement on the one way part of the exit road to Narrogin, you will climb a small rise, where suddenly the Brown Mallet forest with little or no flowering understorey gives way to a wealth of flowering plants. Here there is a small eucalypt, which at first glance looks like a small wandoo tree. It is, however, a different eucalypt that only grows amongst the flora-rich Kwongan Drummond's Gum *(E. drummondii)*.

The bright golden yellow flowers of the tall column dryandra are those of Golden Dryandra *(Dryandra nobilis)*. There is also the beautiful Blue Smokebush *(Conospermum amoenum)*. If you spend time here you can see over 40 flowering species, including small triggerplant, honeypot, poison pea flowers, isopogon, petrophiles, astroloma and stackhousia. If you come in November the featherflowers will be out and the beautiful prostrate Tangled Grevillea *(Grevillea leptobotrya, Dryandra form)* can be seen below the taller plants. There is simply so much to find in these flora-rich hot spots.

The alluvial clay valleys underlay much of the Dryandra woodland. It is here that the Wandoo tree dominates. The open understorey makes it easy to walk through; occasionally patches of Sandplain Poison *(Gastrolobium microcarpum)* form dense clusters, awash with colour in late September with their orange and yellow flowers in full bloom and there are at least eight species of Gastrolobium in the reserve. If you walk slowly through the open woodland, see how many orchids there are. The genus Caladenia is prolific, with the bright yellow flowers of the common Cowslip Orchid *(Caladenia flava)* being the easiest to see, but keep looking, as the Green Spider Orchid *(Caladenia falcata)* and Crimson Spider Orchid *(Caladenia footeana)* may not be far away.

The clay valley floor gives way to the rusty coloured soft gravel of the laterite slopes, where a different wandoo like tree appears. This is the Powderbark Wandoo *(E. accedens)*; touch the bark, you will see a white powder deposit on your hands. If there is a Wandoo tree nearby with its greyer mottled bark, check it out, and you will find no powder deposits on your hand.

Further up the steeper hillsides may be the Brown Mallet, then on the very top, where the laterite has formed a flat capping bed, many different flowers can be found, particularly of the Proteaceae family, like the dryandras, isopogons and petrophiles.

Kwongan heath on the Tomingley Road–the flowers in full bloom mid September

One of the many *Caladenia* orchids

Common Donkey Orchid *(Diurus corymbosa)*

Fringed Mantis Orchid *(Caladenia dillatata var. falcata)*

Tangled Grevillea *(Grevillea leptobotrya)* Dryandra form ▶

Fauna

If Dryandra is to be noted for anything, it would have to be its wonderful collection of marsupials, several of them extremely rare outside this unique reserve.

The Numbat is the animal most people would associate with Dryandra. Even though the population is fairly well established now, it is not always easy to see this diurnal animal (out during the daylight hours), particularly while walking, as it has very good hearing and smell and is constantly checking what's around, particularly overhead. If you are driving slowly (all driving in the reserve should be no more than 40 km per hour even on the main through road), there is a good chance you may catch one by surprise. It will go to its nearest bolt hole, normally a hollow fallen log, and it knows each one in its territory. If you tory and another cycle in the lives of these beautiful marsupials continues.

Numbats were first studied in depth as early as 1954 and then later in the 1970s. Up to 1974 there were a reasonable number of sightings in Dryandra but with the combination of extreme droughts in 1979 and predation by the European Red Fox (*Vulpes vulpes*), the population crashed and extreme concerns for the status of this rare animal reached new heights. Studies were set in place and the earlier work of the scientist Dr Jack Kinnear on the Black-footed Rock-wallaby (*Petrogale lateralis*) showed that removal of the Fox was a major factor in taking the pressure off threatened small to medium sized marsupials. After trials in the early 1980s proved that Fox baiting had a marked effect on the correct form of spotlight, you can see many nocturnal creatures.

They include the Brush-tailed Bettong, the Common Brushtail Possum (*Trichosurus vulpecula*) and Western Grey Kangaroo (*Macropus fuliginosus*). Less common are the Tammar Wallaby (*Macropus eugenii*), often found around sheoak habitat, and the Western Brush Wallaby (*Macropus irma*), preferring the denser shrublands. On most nights the Tawny Frogmouth can be seen and less frequently, the Southern Boobook Owl. On the edge of the paddock country a Barn Owl may be seen on a fence post or tree.

Other small marsupials exist in the reserve but you are unlikely to see them. These are the Honey Possum (*Tarsipes rostratus*), Western Pygmy-possum (*Cercartetus concinnus*), Mardo

Short beaked Echidna (*Tachyglossus aculeatus*)

Southern Carpet Python (*Morella spilota imbricata*)

Thorny Devil (*Moloch horridus*)

Brush-tail Bettong or Woylie (*Betongia penicillata*)

go up wind, say a good 30-40 m away, and sit patiently and quietly, it may come out after 10-15 min. It is an absolute pleasure to watch this very attractive small marsupial go about its daily life.

The Numbat has the most specialised diet of any marsupial, living almost entirely on termites and ants. It is not able to tackle the hard outer shells of the termite mounds but instead seeks out the subterranean termite runs. It does this by smell, breaking the earth's surface and placing its very long tongue down the various termite galleries.

Mating takes place around January, the mother feeding normally four young, one from each teat. She will carry them on her underbelly for the next 5–6 months and they become quite a load near the end. They are then left in a nursery burrow. By September they emerge for a few hours outside the nursery hole, then over the next few months they venture out further with their mother. In late October, they are weaned and by December they have left the home terri- the Numbat population, baiting commenced in full swing by 1987. Since then, in that brief period to the year 2000, the population has multiplied significantly.

One of the other small marsupials that have increased in numbers is the nocturnal Brush-tailed Bettong or Woylie (*Bettongia penicillata*). This rabbit sized marsupial lives predominantly on fungi with the addition of plant tubers, seeds and bulbs, and occasional insects. Often when walking in some quiet spot in the reserve, suddenly a small creature will tear out from under a low bush. It will most probably be a Woylie (the Aboriginal name). It builds a compact nest underneath a low bush, lining it with soft grasses that it gathers with its tail. Here it will rest until nightfall, coming out to feed at dusk.

Australian fauna, particularly the nocturnal marsupials, are not always easy to see and many people give up looking for these magnificent and unique animals. Well, Dryandra is one place in Australia where, if you are patient with (*Antechinus flavipes*), Gilbert's Dunnart (*Sminthopsis gilberti*) and the elusive Red-tailed Phascogale (*Phascogale calura*).

The reptiles are well represented here. The Thick-tailed Gecko (*Underwoodisaurus milii*) hides under the granite rocks. The Bungarra monitor lizard (*Varanus gouldii*) is occasionally seen as well as the beautifully marked Southern Carpet Python (*Morelia spilota imbricata*), which is basically harmless; although it can inflict a painful bite leaving puncture marks, it is non-poisonous, killing its prey by constricting them so they cannot breathe. You can see the Southern Carpet Python basking in the sun on a winter's day, particularly when digesting a recent kill. Most people associate the little Thorny Devil (*Moloch horridus*) with dry desert environments. They live in Dryandra too, feeding almost exclusively on a certain genus of ant. Their wonderful camouflage markings make them difficult to see unless they are crossing an open patch of ground, like a bush track.

Birds

Because Dryandra lies on the transitional boundaries of the wetter Jarrah forest in the west and the drier wandoo and mallee country to the east, it shares species of birds that exist in both regions. Here, the Red-capped Robin lives close to a similar species, the Scarlet Robin, both requiring subtle differences in habitat. The Scarlet Robin lives in the open Wandoo woodland and the Red-capped Robin in the denser stands of Jam *(Acacia acuminata)*. Two of the parasitic cuckoos overlap here, the Shining Bronze-Cuckoo and Horsefield's Bronze-Cuckoo, both needing to parasitise different bird species. The Shining Bronze-Cuckoo tends to occur in the wetter zones and the Horsefield's Bronze-Cuckoo in the drier regions of the state.

Dryandra, however, contains mostly birds typical of the wheatbelt woodlands, like the Rufous Treecreeper, Dusky Woodswallow, Yellow-plumed Honeyeater, White-eared Honeyeater, Western Yellow Robin, Hooded Robin, Elegant Parrot, Regent Parrot (not common here), Brush Bronzewing, Rufous Songlark, Restless Flycatcher, Square-tailed Kite and, until 1998, the Crested Bellbird.

If you stroll through the open Wandoo, the predominant honeyeater will be the Yellow-plumed Honeyeater and it is here all year round along with the Rufous Treecreeper, Painted Button-quail, Restless Flycatcher, Western Yellow Robin and Blue-breasted Fairy-wren. If you walk into some of the small patches of heath containing Drummond's Gum and dryandras, a bird with a strong "chop, chop" call may attract your attention. It will be a White-eared Honeyeater. They are sedentary in Dryandra, surviving in the few remaining patches of heath.

The movement of birds is always fascinating, be it migratory or nomadic movements. With the coming of spring, the Rufous Songlark, White-winged Triller, and all the cuckoos, (Horsefield's Bronze-, Shining Bronze-, Pallid and Fantail), descend on the reserve to lay their eggs in some unsuspecting bird's nest, the young cuckoo chick subsequently removing the eggs or chicks of the host species.

Sometimes birds that are at home in our desert country, such as the Black Honeyeater, fly deep into the south west in harsh, dry years,.

One of the birds that was once common throughout the wheatbelt before European settlement was the Malleefowl *(Leipoa ocellata)*. Dryandra still has a few Malleefowl remaining, although the quantity of active mounds is on the decline. In 1978, the author knew of 3 active mounds, but now it is hard to find one. We know that Foxes certainly kill Malleefowl, but the Fox numbers are now contrilled to a low level in the reserve, so something else is apparently affecting them; whether the gene pool is weakening, it is hard to say, although Malleefowl survive in remnant wheatbelt reserves far smaller than Dryandra.

Blue breasted Fairy-wren

Red-capped Robin

Dusky Woodswallow

Malleefowl

The ecology of the Malleefowl is a fascinating story. It is a member of the Megapode family ('mound builders') and that is precisely what the male does – he builds a huge earth mound. The male bird digs a nest chamber about 40 cm deep and 1.2 m wide in the ground. This is filled with leaves, retrieved from the surrounding leaf litter, to create a mulch. Earth is then piled on top of the leaves to a height of about 70 cm with a diameter of about 2.4 m (mounds, however, can be far wider and higher in some cases). The mound is opened up to get the first winter rains of May and over the next few months more leaves are scraped into the mound. By late August, the Malleefowl has covered the vegetation with dry earth. In mid September, the female inspects the work of her partner, checking the temperature with a special heat sensitive gland. She calls to the male uttering deep grunts when she is ready to lay and immediately he responds by returning to the mound and opening it up and checking that the temperature is correct.

The temperature through decomposition should be just right - about 34 C. The male creates a nest chamber deep in the mound. She inspects the situation and if happy, lays her first egg. The male immediately covers the egg with leaf litter, then earth. The complex cycle now commences in earnest. Initially the decomposing vegetation creates enough heat to aid the incubation process, and the male has to adjust the opening of the mound very little, but as the early summer months arrive, the vegetation has dried out and the external temperatures start to climb. The female lays between 12 and 29 eggs, normally at a rate of one every five days so that a constant temperature around 34 C can be maintained. The male must now control the heat. Overnight, while the temperatures are cool, the mound is well covered. In the morning the first warm rays fall on the mound and the male opens up the mound almost to the top of the nest chamber. The sun heats the foliage and he checks the temperature. As the midday heat rises the mound is covered up. By late afternoon the mound is opened up to let out heat if it has been exceptionally hot and later the mound is covered to its full height, ready for the cool to cold night.

The male moves up to two tonnes of earth a year in the incubation process. The adult birds play no role in the development of the young birds. The hatchlings, on breaking through the egg shell, claw their way to the surface. They have extremely well developed wings. Within 24 hrs they have the capacity to fly short distances and soon learn to fly up in to the lower branches of trees as soon as night falls, as all megapodes roost in trees. By midsummer the female has stopped laying and takes a well earned rest, but the male keeps checking the mound until the last chicks have gone, which may be as late as January. He then starts his mound building routine again in May.

Walks

A. Woylie walk: 5.5 km return, medium grade. The walk starts from the Old Mill Dam, crosses Tomingley Road and enters a Brown Mallet plantation. You will slowly climb up through Powderbark Wandoo, Kwongan heath and Jarrah and Marri woodland. Crossing Gura Road you enter Rock Sheoak (Allocasuarina huegeliana) habitat before returning to cross Guru Road again and slowly drop down through Brown Mallet to Tomingley Road again and finally back to the dam.

B. Ochre Trail: 5 km return. This is a moderate walk, starting just west of the Dryandra Arboretum. From the car park you pass through Wandoo woodland, slowly climbing up through Marri woodland and dryandra to the fire lookout tower. From here the track follows the edge of the laterite breakaway, passing through Powderbark Wandoo and dryandra bush. Half-way down the hill you come to an Aboriginal ochre pit - wet your finger and check the colour of the red soil. At the bottom of the hill, you pass close to an open paddock that leads to Tomingley Road. Turn left and return to the car park.

C. Wandoo Walk: 1 km return. This is a short walk and takes you through old established open Wandoo woodland. It is a great walk for birdwatchers. Those who are keen, can listen out for the mournful call of the Western Shrike-tit, one of the less common birds in this woodland; it will most probably be quite high up in the tall Wandoo.

F. Lol Gray Trail: 12.5 km medium grade, but a long 4 hr walk that begins opposite the tennis court at the settlement, just east of the settlement track. It passes through varied country. At the half-way point at the top of the hill is the Lol Gray Picnic site.

G. Lol Gray Loop: 3.2 km return, medium grade. It starts and finishes at the Lol Gray Picnic Site, passing through Powderbark Wandoo and Kwongan heath.

H. Kawana Road Walk: 3.2 km return. This is now a sign-posted walk but an easy walk from the Lol Gray Picnic site down towards Kawana Road (refer to sketch map of reserve). This is an ideal walk for those who have a particular interest in wildflowers, as you will see many species between early September and early November, although there is still a fair amount in bloom earlier, in August or later, in mid-December. You will pass through some of the most prolific Kwongan in the reserve. Keep going down the track to the cleared fire break and then return the way you came.

J. Congelin: This is a short 1 km one way linking Congelin Dam picnic site and camping ground. Interpretative signs explain the early history of the railway.

Drives: DCLM has introduced a very novel series of radio information drives. Tune to 100FM to receive the various stories at the marked points within the reserve.

Camping and chalet accommodation: There are basic old timber woodcutters' cottages, quite well fitted out at the main Dryandra Settlement. Camping is allowed only at the Congelin Dam at the south west corner of the reserve. There are very good camping bays, toilets, gas barbecue and firewood is supplied for the open ring fires provided. Do not light fires between the dates stated at the campsite. Dryandra Woodland is far too small and precious an area to withstand an out of control summer burn. The camping ground is a great place to see marsupials—try not to feed them, however tempting it is.

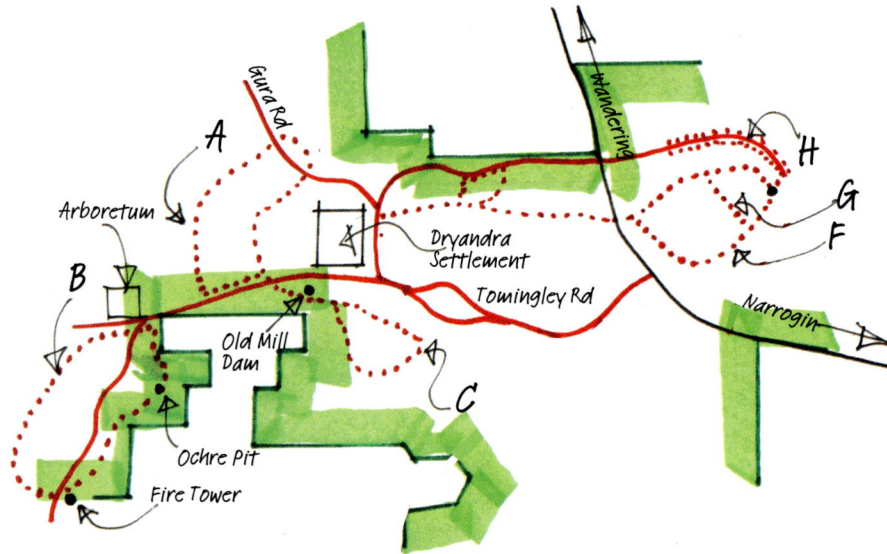

Looking at the Ochre Pit on the Ochre Trail

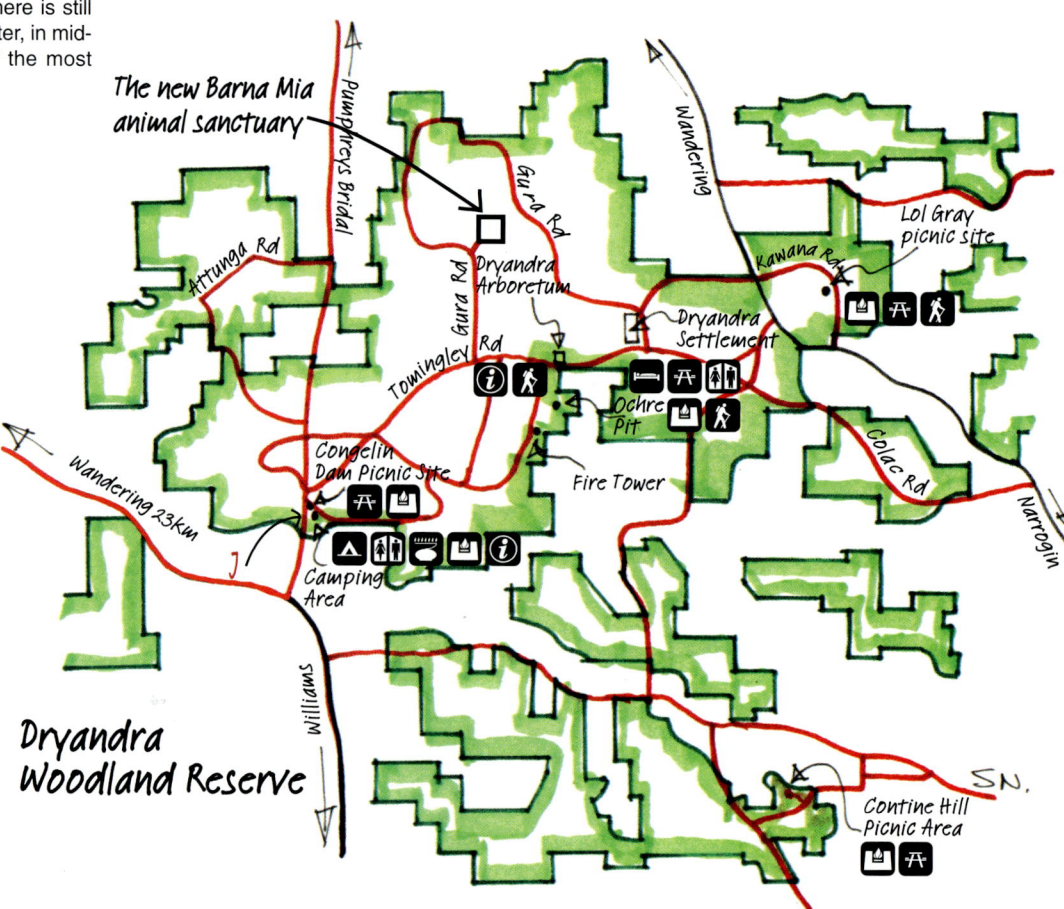

Dryandra Woodland Reserve

Close encounters with a numbat

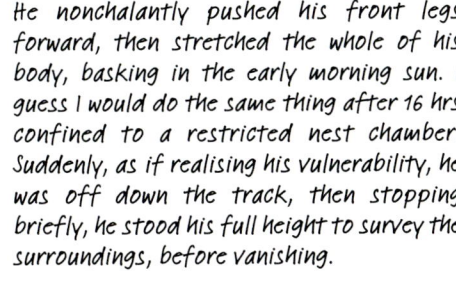

"I glanced at my watch; I had been in the hide for over an hour with my eyes fixed on the Numbat's entrance hole in the side of an embankment. Just as I thought he would never show, out popped a head, checking all was safe. The temptation to press the shutter release was immense, but I knew if I did, he may not show again for several hours.

He ventured out onto the track. I fired a few frames; standing up on his back legs he stared at the hide. I let him relax and then fired a few more. This time he just glanced my way as if the buzz of the motor drive, outside one's bush home, was an every-day occurrence.

He nonchalantly pushed his front legs forward, then stretched the whole of his body, basking in the early morning sun. I guess I would do the same thing after 16 hrs confined to a restricted nest chamber. Suddenly, as if realising his vulnerability, he was off down the track, then stopping briefly, he stood his full height to survey the surroundings, before vanishing.

After the tension, combined with the euphoria of the moment, I recorded the time—8.27 a.m. It may just have been no more than 2 minutes from the first to the last frame in the camera, but to me, it seemed like precious hours, another privileged experience in this special place—Dryandra".

Open Wandoo woodland

Barna Mia Sanctuary

The DCLM has recently constructed a 4 ha animal viewing enclosure, in the centre of Dryandra woodland. Within the enclosure, visitors have the opportunity to view some of our rarest threatened animals, They include Banded hare-wallaby (mernine), Bilby (dalgyte), Rufus hare-wallaby (wurrup), Borrowing Betong (boodie) and Western barred Bandicoot (marl). In the display building, visitors get an overview of the breeding and translocation program based in Dryandra woodland. The nocturnal tour, has a guide who will show and explain various aspects of these rare animals. There is a cost involved but the rewards of seeing such wonderful animals far outways such a small expense to view them.

There are disabled toilets and access.

For more information, contact DCLM's Narrogin District office on 9881 9200.

RETURNING ANIMALS BACK FROM THE BRINK OF EXTINCTION

Numbat *(Myrmecobius fasciatus)*

Information sign regarding 1080 Poison being laid as bait for feral animals

Australia does not have a good record when it comes to the extinction of our mammals. We have lost 18 species of mammals since Europeans set foot on this island continent some of them include the Lesser Bilby, Desert Rat-kangaroo, Crescent Nailtail Wallaby, Eastern Hare-wallaby, Toolache Wallaby, Thylacine, Desert Bandicoot, Pig-footed Bandicoot, Broad-faced Potoroo, Lesser Stick-nest Rat, White-footed Rabbit-rat, Big-eared Hopping Mouse, Short-tailed Hopping Mouse and Long-tailed Hopping Mouse. These marsupials listed are not figments of some scientist's imagination, the skins of these extinct animals remain to this day in various museums. Some, like the Thylacine, were photographed before the last individuals were shot out of existence.

The mammals that are not extinct, but are endangered or vulnerable in Western Australia, are the Bilby, Red-tailed Phascogale, Chuditch, Sandhill Dunnart, Dibbler, Gilbert's Potoroo, Quenda, Black-footed Rock Wallaby, Tammar Wallaby, Mulgara, Numbat, Western Ringtail Possum, Heath Rat, Western Mouse, Rufous and Banded Hare-Wallaby, Brush-tailed Bettong and Western Barred Bandicoot.

There have been several reasons for the demise of many of these animals, the main factors being the removal of much of their original habitat, the introduction of alien grazing animals that competed for food, the introduction and subsequent predation by feral animals such as the Fox and feral cat and the changes to feeding habits of some marsupials, making them more vulnerable to predation.

The European Red Fox *(Vulpes vulpes)* was introduced into Victoria in the 1870s and was used as quarry for the 'hunt', the pastime of the landed gentry. The Foxes soon adapted to local conditions, being assisted by the introduction and subsequent plague proportions of the European Rabbit *(Oryctolagus cuniculus)*.

Between 1910 and 1920 the Fox started to be seen in the eastern parts of Western Australia and by 1934 they had moved into the deep south west forests. In the mid 1930s, the populations of most of our small marsupials took a massive reduction in numbers and the Fox was one of the major contributors to that reduction.

A few of the most threatened species occur on a few remote islands, which feral predators have never reached, saving them from extinction.

DCLM has embarked on a massive project to turn this situation around and it is proving to be highly successful. The project is known as "Western Shield" and involves not only DCLM but other government departments and community groups. Much of it is administered by WATSCU, the Western Australian Threatened Species and Communities Unit founded in 1992.

When the first European shepherds grazed their sheep on the Swan Coastal Plain, they wondered why many of their sheep would suddenly and inexplicably die from grazing on the native vegetation, when the native animals obviously were having no problems. The cause of these deaths can be attributed to one group of plants of the pea family, which has been given the genus name of Gastrolobium. Over thousands of years, this genus has developed a highly toxic poison. It may have been a natural defence to protect it from over grazing from the native fauna. With time, however, the native animals developed a resistance to this toxin, including animals further up the food chain, such as birds of prey.

Scientists at the Agricultural Department found that the chemical make-up of the plant toxin was almost identical to the commercial poison used for eradicating rabbits, namely 1080 poison or sodium monofluroacetate.

By chance it was discovered that Foxes were not tolerant to this poison as they had never before in their European environment been exposed to it.

Trials were set in place where large areas were baited for Foxes using 1080 poison (meat injected with 1080) and compared with unbaited areas to see what effect there was on the native fauna. Dramatic results came into effect within a year or two with large increases in some of the native mammal populations. Tests done on the soils for 1080 poison contamination, showed that the 1080 poison dissolved and bacteria broke it down very quickly, DCLM set about funding and implementing the huge project, Western Shield. The areas chosen were areas that could be monitored to check changes in the marsupial population.

The three primary objectives of the project are to bait for Foxes on a massive scale, to drastically reduce their population; to increase research on the feral cat that does not take baits easily and is proving to be as big a threat to native fauna, particularly now that Fox numbers are being reduced; and finally, when specific areas have had the bulk of Foxes removed, to return those species that once existed there from other captive or wild populations.

Since the initial major baiting program commenced in 1994 there has been a marked increase in the populations of most marsupials. The Numbat population in Dryandra Reserve has increased dramatically. The Black-footed Rock-wallaby on some south west granite rocks has also increased in numbers. The populations of several endangered marsupials at Perup, Dongolocking and Batalling Reserves have increased markedly.

Perhaps one of the most adventurous and challenging projects is Project Eden, involving the region of Peron Peninsula in Shark Bay. Here a narrow neck of land at the base of the peninsula has been fenced from one side to the other, some 3.4 km long, with a 2.4 m high sophisticated electric fence.

All land to the north has been baited for Foxes and cats, with very good results, so much so that species that once existed there have now been re-introduced and plans are in place to introduce more.

This turning back the tide of extinction of various species is not just restricted to fauna and large projects are in place with local communities, particularly concerned farmers, in the protection of our rare flora. There are far more plant species threatened through loss of habitat than marsupials and as the areas involved are so immense, local shires and their communities are recording and protecting known populations of wildflower plants that are threatened. This form of government and community co-operation gives hope and inspires people in times when so much talk is of gloom and doom. These are the people who are embracing the problem and getting on with it and it is a credit to them all, as everyone can become the protector rather than destroyer of life on this small planet of ours.

Boyagin Nature Reserve

Another small reserve on the eastern side of the Darling Range is Boyagin Nature Reserve. It is not as extensive as Dryandra but is well worth a day's visit from Perth; it has two of the highest granite outcrops in the south west. Brush-tailed Bettongs, Numbats and Quendas have been reintroduced into Boyagin Nature Reserve.

The vegetation is similar to Dryandra, with Wandoo and Powderbark Wandoo woodland, sheoak thickets and some very rich Kwongan heath. The heaths are mostly on tracks rarely visited, but for the enthusiastic botanist, they are most rewarding.

Perhaps the most interesting part for the new visitor to this reserve, is the two huge granite outcrops mentioned. The access from the Brookton Highway sign posted to the reserve.

At the picnic site (administered by the shire), there is a walk that takes you through the sheoak woodland and up on to the rock itself; head slowly up the hillside. It is manageable by most reasonably fit people. There is an interpretive shelter.

You will pass granite plant species such as Granite Kunzea *(Kunzea pulchella)* and Mouse Ears *(Calothamnus rupestris)*, both having lovely red flowers in spring and early summer. As you walk up the rock, the Pincushions *(Borya species)* with their prickly foliage. The view from the top is well worth the climb. The large rock opposite contains some of the few populations of the mallee that is now widely grown in Perth, Caesia *(Eucalyptus caesia subsp. caesia)*, with its beautiful red pendulous flowers. It grows in the narrow rock crevices on a few wheatbelt granite outcrops. On the walk up to that rock from the car park in April and May, the Sea Urchin Hakea *(Hakea petiolaris)* will be in full flower.

Look under the Sheoak *(Allocasuarina huegeliana)* woodland in early spring and see how many species of orchid you can find.

Boyagin Rock

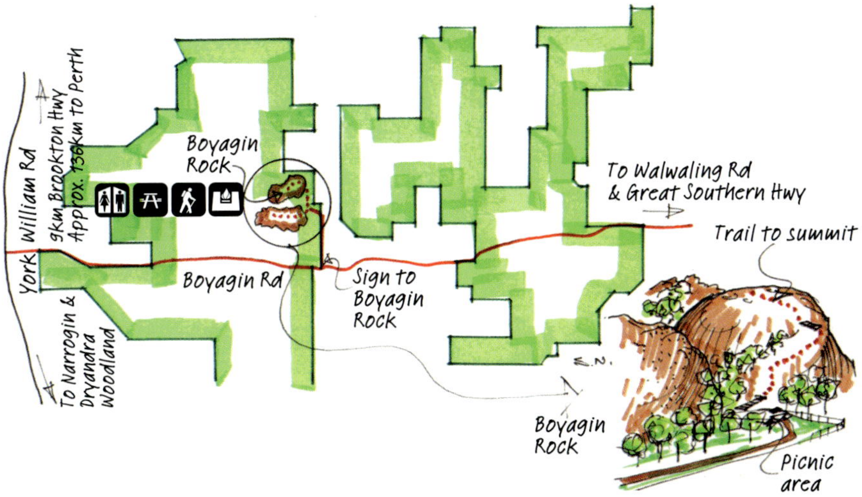

Buckley's Breakaway

This is not an exceptionally dramatic or highly scenic location but if you are travelling in this region, there is an interesting 'breakaway', a term to describe land that drops away suddenly from the surrounding plain. Here the rain has washed away top soils to expose the white subsoil making dramatic colour changes in the topography. The turn-off is about 15 km due west of Hyden. Turn south on to Karlgarin Road South, travel 17.8 km south and there is a small track to the left on a left turning bend; enter here and the breakaway is only 100 m off the road. There is a parking area with interpretive signs.

Buckley's Breakaway ▶

Small pool on a granite outcrop in the Fitzgerald River National Park

A granite rock garden of Pincushions (Borya constricta) and lichens on Victoria Rock

Ornate dragon (Ctenophorus ornatus)
Photo by David Knowles

Baxter's Kunzea (Kunzea baxteri)

Granite Outcrops

Below most of the south west region, particularly the wheatbelt, lies one of the most ancient bedrock landforms in the world, called the Yilgarn Craton.

2.5 million years ago this was a solid molten mass of magma that with time cooled near the surface of the earth, forming primarily the rocks we know as granite.

Younger mountain ranges, like the Himalayas or the Andes in South America, attain great heights, typified by a jagged topography. Here in the south west of Australia, the land is so old that over millions of years it has been weathered down by ancient rivers and rains to form a relatively flat undulating land surface.

Occasionally some of the magma reached close to the earth's surface, being pushed up by massive pressures. With time the surrounding softer soils were eroded away, leaving the classic features we call granite outcrops.

They are a major feature of the wheatbelt and the Aborigines have always used them to procure water from the surrounding rock pools and gnamma holes. The early settlers based their homesteads near them, knowing they could dam part of the rock for water run off. Sadly many of the large rocks have been spoiled visually by these rock wall features, even in the most remote locations like Cave Hill and Burra Rock in the Goldfields. One cannot blame the early settlers who desperately needed water, but it has affected the surrounding ecology of some of the granite rock areas.

The huge round boulders that often are seen on these outcrops, have been formed by a slow complex process. Initially the molten magma cooled and with this cooling process the rock would contract and at the weaker fault lines would split, forming both vertical and horizontal cracks. With time and weathering exposure the rocks would split and form square blocks that slowly weathered down; first to go would be the sharp corners and then bit by bit these rounded rocks would remain above the granite layer below.

You will often see quartz-type rock running as veins through the granite. This has been caused by the fault cracks being filled with harder conglomerate molten rock that will erode more slowly than the main granite rock.

Not only wind and rain has slowly weathered these ancient rocks but lichens, algae and mosses have played their part in recent times. The lichens, for example, produce weak acids that slowly eat away at the small granite particles. The lichens form the lovely rich orange colours that form patchwork patterns on the rock. The small granules of rock are slowly washed away down to where depressions have formed on the outcrops. Here, with increased soil depth, the prickly Pincushion Plant (Borya constricta) and Blind Grass (Stypandra glauca), grow. Where small cracks appear in the rock, plants like the Granite Kunzea (Kunzea pulchella) grow. In the larger cracks, Caesia (Eucalyptus caesia subsp. caesia), Silver Mallee (E. crucis), Sea Urchin Hakea (Hakea petiolaris) and Mouse ears (Calothamnus rupestris) grow all of which have beautiful flowers.

At the base of the larger granite outcrops, the tall Rock Sheoaks (Allocasuarina huegeliana) grow, while further out in the deeper soils, are the larger eucalypts such as Wandoo, Salmon Gum and York Gum.

The small lizard that often runs across your path when walking these rocks will most probably be the Ornate Dragon (Ctenophorus ornatus). There is only one marsupial restricted to granite outcrops in the south west and that is the extremely rare Black-footed Rock-wallaby; the south west subspecies was nearly extinct but now with Fox baiting the small populations are literally bouncing back.

There are no birds solely restricted to these rocks but the increased water run off at the base of the larger rocks makes excellent shrubland habitat for Redthroats and in the sheoak woodlands the Red-capped Robin is very much at home. Also if you have really sharp eyes, it is a favourite roosting locality for Tawny Frogmouths.

Yes, visit these rocks, take a picnic lunch and see how much life there is, especially in winter and spring. Take the children as they just love granite outcrops and that's the time to educate them in the wonders of the natural world; if you sow the seed of knowledge early enough, they will become the protectors of these fragile environments.

Wave Rock Reserve

Located 338 km from Perth, this granite outcrop is one of the most visited tourist localities in the state. It is basically a granite wall some 60 m long and about 15 m high. It is part of the exposed rock of the ancient 3000 million year old Yilgarn Craton that underlies most of the wheatbelt rocks and soils.

The dark stains that alternate along the rock face are forms of algae that grow on the rock face; the dark areas are living algae and the light brown areas are where the algae has died and is no longer present.

There are many fascinating granite outcrops near Hyden, such as Emu Rock and Graham Rock.

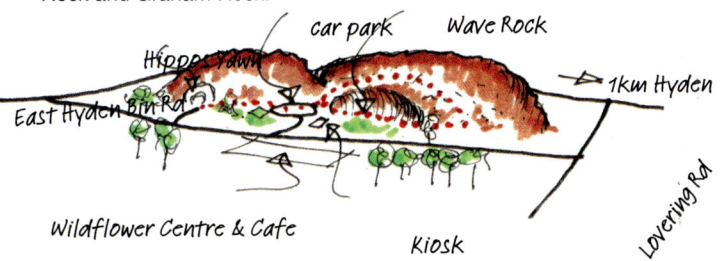

The Humps & Mulka's Cave

There is another interesting granite outcrop called "The Humps" only 20 km from Wave Rock. For those who can find the extra time to visit this area, I feel it is well worth it, as it gives you a good idea of the many features that granite rocks possess. Mulka's Cave has some faint Aboriginal hand stencils inside.

To visit Mulka's Cave, you enter part of the Lake Gounter Reserve, passing a sign to the dam; keep going and you come to the base of the rock. Turn left into the car park to Mulka's Cave. It is a short 5 minute walk. When you have seen the small cave, take your vehicle to the base of the main granite rock as marked on the sketch map. You will see a gnamma hole. Aborigines would use these deep holes for survival water in the very hot months, and normally a large flat stone would cover the hole to stop evaporation. Gnamma holes can be seen throughout the south west region and Aborigines knew the country well, knowing where each rock was on their journeys across the land.

If you back-track 150 m, as the map shows, you can park the car and walk up the main rock. Few people get to this spot but it really is a pleasant walk. You will pass another population of Eucalyptus caesia subsp. caesia just below the hill top at the base of the rock and in early summer the bright yellow flowers in bloom will be one of the Featherflowers *(Verticordia acerosa var. preissii)*

▲Wave Rock

▲Mulka's Cave

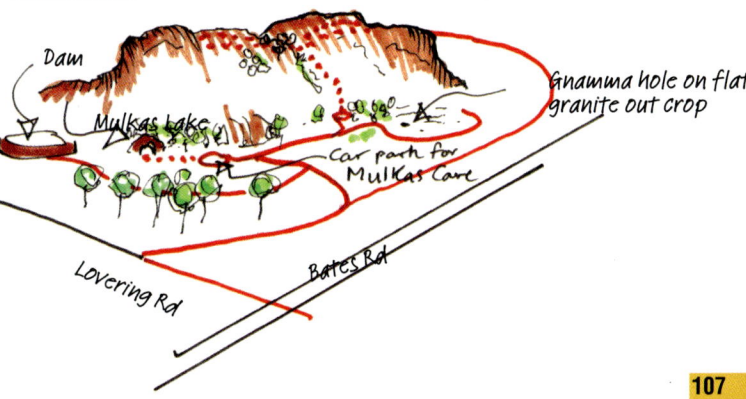
◀ The Humps with Caesia trees *(Eucalyptus caesia sub sp caesia)* in foreground

Bluebush country in the Goldfields

Goldfields
REGION

Goldfields
REGION

Names like Coolgardie, Kalgoorlie, Boulder, Leonora and Norseman conjure in the mind for most people the goldrush days. Well, there has certainly been a lot of gold taken from this region, over $1,000,000,000 worth to be precise.

When, in 1892 Arthur Bailey and Bill Ford rode into Southern Cross from where Coolgardie now stands, with 555 oz of gold, the 'Gold Rush' was on.

The population of Western Australia increased over 300% in just ten years.

Coolgardie had 25,000 people under canvas before the turn of the century and by 1900 the town had 15,000 people housed, the others having left for new localities. In 1893, gold was discovered near Mt. Charlotte, then gold was found south at the present location of the "Golden Mile" and the town of Kalgoorlie was developed. Railways, hotels and civic buildings, were all built around 1905 but in the short space of just 13 years the boom days were over, the First World War had commenced and the goldfield towns changed drastically, However, even in the depression between 1930 and 1933, with rising gold prices, the towns still remained buoyant.

Kalgoorlie developed into the largest town in the Goldfields and is still a busy prosperous town with a population of 28,000 people, steeped in history, as too are the other gold mining towns.

There is another rich treasure in the Goldfields and it is not a mineral, it is the eucalypt woodlands. Although if we had kept cutting timber at the rate they did at the turn of the century, we would have no woodlands left.

Over 30 million tonnes of timber had been cut for the mining industry. In the first few years all timber had been cut down within a 20 km radius of Kalgoorlie, and it was too big a task for horse and cart to haul timber from the outer areas.

One company that became quite large was the WA Goldfields Firewood Supply Company formed in 1903. They developed a series of railway lines that radiated out in all directions from Kalgoorlie. These narrow gauge rail roads became known as the "wood lines". There were several companies formed to haul timber by rail, employing about 1,500 men and supplying 500,000 tonnes of firewood. The overheads to run the rails and pay such large staff numbers created high costs and all the major woodline companies amalgamated.

In 1953 the coal fired engines were introduced and not long after, the diesel powered engine trains took over; both of which saved the forest regions around Kalgoorlie. The last timber was hauled by trains in 1965, and by 1967 all the railway lines were pulled up and sold as scrap. If you drive on the 4WD track from Burra Rock to Cave Hill, at times the track follows the old railway line and you find yourself several metres off the valley floor.

Luckily, over the last 100 years, the country has regenerated very well and little evidence of those early days shows in most of the Goldfields.

In this region is one of the richest concentration of eucalypts in Australia with around 80 species. Of these, many occur nowhere else, many of them being extremely rare and localised. Some of the main eucalypts include Goldfield's Blackbutt (Eucalyptus lesouefii), Gimlet (E. salubris), Coral Gum (E. torquata), Ribbon Bark Mallee (E. sheathiana), Red Morrel (E. longicornis), Merrit (E. flocktoniae), Rib-fruited Mallee (E. corrugata), Square fruited Mallee (E. calycogona), Snap and Rattle (E. celastroides), Cleland's Blackbutt (E. clelandii), Salmon Gum (E. salmonophlia) and Silver Gimlet (E. ravida).

Where to travel
IN THE GOLDFIELDS

Travelling in the southern Goldfields region via Lake King in the eastern wheatbelt, there are two National Parks, Frank Hann and Peak Charles.

The road that leads from Lake King to just north of Salmon Gums has very little traffic and can be driven in 2WD although often the track can have water on it and it is really ideal to have a 4WD, as it is a long way from any township.

Driving from Perth on the Great Eastern Highway, there is Boorabbin National Park, set aside primarily for its rich Kwongan heath and eucalypt woodland. At the eastern end of Boorabbin National Park is a turn-off to Jaurdi Homestead and it is a great place to experience the Goldfields eucalypt woodland.

South of Coolgardie are two interesting granite outcrops, reserves, namely Burra Rock Nature Reserve and Cave Hill Nature Reserve. You can take a 2WD to Burra Rock but between Burra Rock and Cave Hill it is definitely 4WD country and not always easy to follow the track. From Norseman, travelling to Cave Hill again, you are better off with a 4WD, but it is easier than the Cave Hill/Burra Rock track. North of Coolgardie there is the road to the old hotel of Ora Banda, and before this is the turn-off to Rowles Lagoon. This reserve is particularly good for those interested in wetland birds. The drive there also takes you through some magnificent Goldfields woodlands with a great variety of eucalypt species.

In Kalgoorlie there is an arboretum, an interesting spot to find out more about the many eucalypts of the Goldfields.

Travelling north towards Menzies is the turn-off to Goongarrie National Park and again it's best to have a 4WD to enter this park. Few people go there, so often you will have parts of the park to yourself. Very interesting vegetation here, being a transition area between the Goldfields and the desert. There are also granite outcrops.

The desert parks north and east of Laverton are not covered in this book as these entail real 4WD country and very remote areas which require a lot of planning to travel through.

A word of warning: Some of the parks listed in the Goldfields region are in areas where few people visit and the woodlands stretch for miles. Do not venture into country you are unsure of and do use that compass when you just walk off the track for a short distance. Take your bearings from where you enter the woodland.

Frank Hann
NATIONAL PARK

This park covers an area of 67,550 ha and the western boundary is 32 km east of Lake King and the bulk of the park straddles the Lake King–Norseman Road.

It is an interesting story that, in 1970, this area was set aside as a National Park by the Labour Government in response to the strong pleas and letters written by a traveller who was so impressed with this area of Kwongan heath and its fantastic wildflower displays.

There are no facilities in the park and people must be self sufficient. Most of the park is covered in mallee, interspersed with very rich Kwongan heath growing on the infertile yellow sands. One banksia, that only grows in the Goldfields, is found here, the Swordfish Banksia (*Banksia elderiana*) with its pendulous round yellow flowers. This is not to be confused with Tennis Ball (*Banksia laergata*) that also grows here, as it does not have the much longer and very narrow leaves of the Swordfish Banksia.

Access for viewing the park is primarily from the road, but just about 1 km past the turn-off to the small township of Cascade, east along the Lake King Road is a narrow 1.2 km track left (direction north). This leads to a lovely area of exposed granite named Lillian Stokes Rock. There is a gnamma hole here and lovely Sheoak country. It is a good bush camping spot but please do the right thing in all aspects, particularly taking your litter with you as there are no facilities.

There are lovely patches of Granite Bottlebrush (*Melaleuca elliptica*). A very peaceful spot and well worth a visit.

Lillian Stoke's Rocks

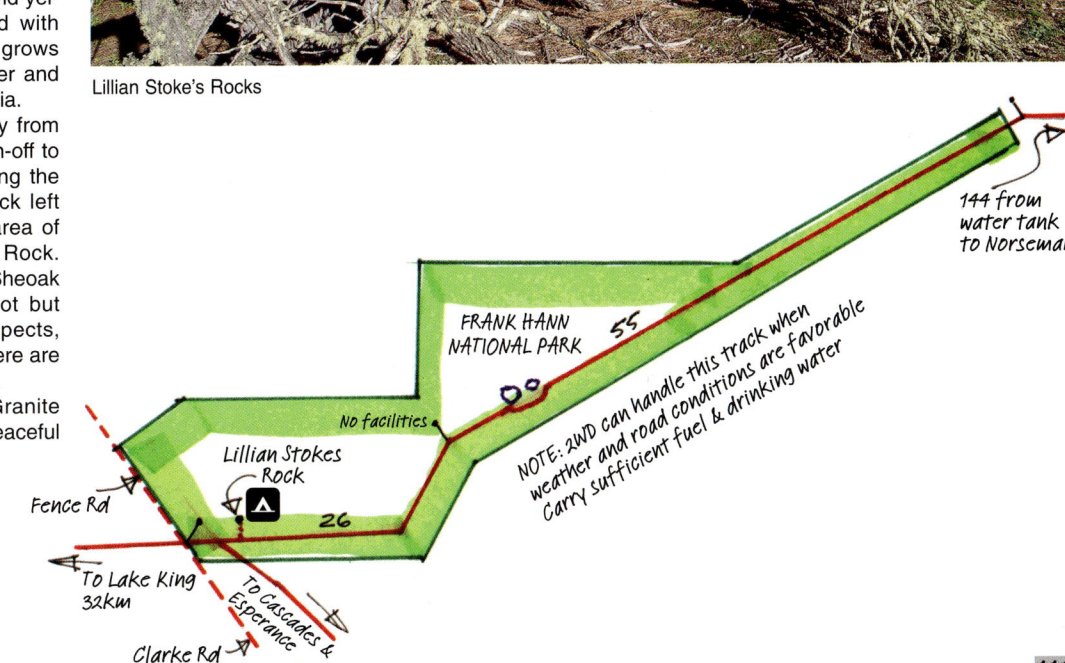

Burra Rock
NATURE RESERVE

The two granite outcrops south of Coolgardie really are worth visiting. Burra Rock is accessible by 2WD and is 57.2 km south of Coolgardie. The last 1 km in is a little sandy but if you keep the revs up and a reasonable speed you should negotiate the soft small patches of sand quite well.

Burra Rock is a large granite outcrop, with a large dam at the base having a capacity of 11 million gallons. It should have water in it all year round in most years. These dams were built to supply water to the timber cutters and supply the steam locomotives with water. The trains used thousands of gallons through the year but also filled up from the Coolgardie depot from the Perth–Kalgoorlie water pipeline after dropping off their timber load.

There is an information board on entry to the rock area. There are two small camping areas set amongst the lovely Rock Sheoak trees with a picnic table at each spot and a toilet. There is a walking trail from the furthest camping spot. There is also a day use area with picnic table, fire place, toilet and table with a short walk to the edge of the dam and from here you can walk up the rock.

This is a magnificent example of granite outcrops and a great place for travellers to stop.

Dam at Burra Rock

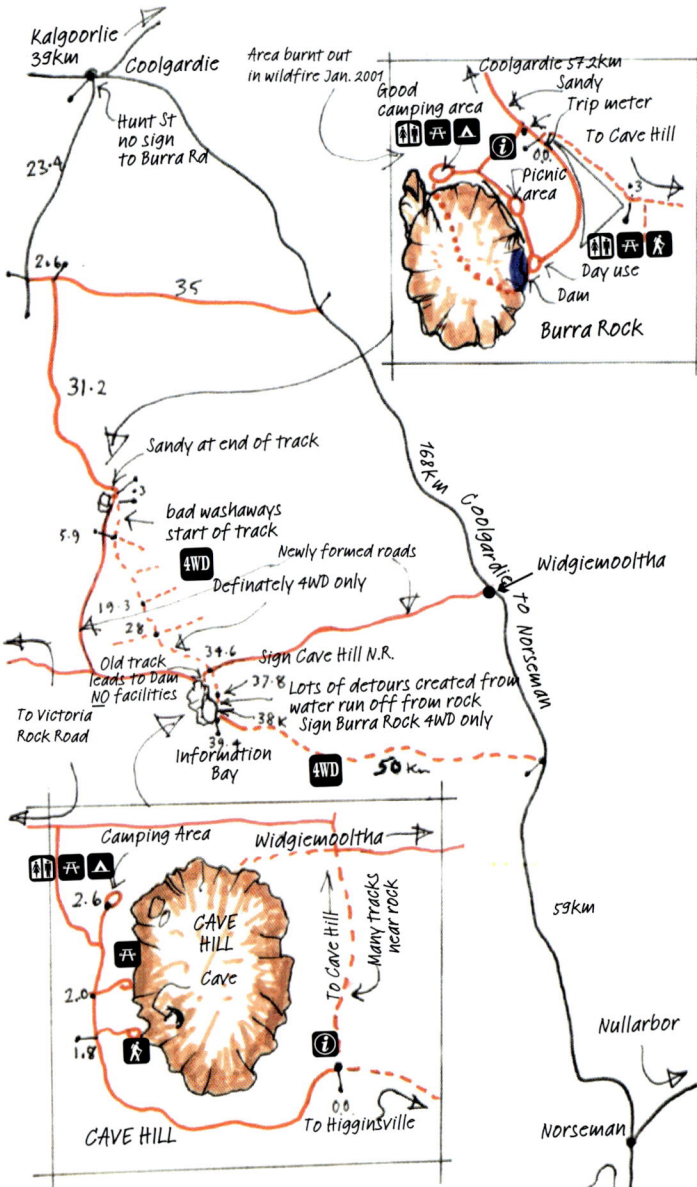

The main cave on the western side of Cave Hill

Cave Hill
NATURE RESERVE

Cave Hill like Burra Rock is certainly worth a visit. It is one of the most extensive granite outcrops in the south west of Australia being at least 1.5 km long. It has a dam on the north side of the rock. There are numerous old tracks around the rock area so do make sure you take note of where you entered. Even though this is a long way south of Kalgoorlie, it was still a major area for the supply of wood for the Goldfields and between 1925 and 1938 Cave Hill was used as a main base, being the southernmost point on the Kurrawang Woodline run by the Goldfields Firewood Supply Company.

There are two camping sites on the western side of the rock. The southern camping area has a walk that leads to a large cave. There is the lovely granite restricted grevillea, (*Grevillea magnifica* subsp. *remota*), a lovely wax flower (*Chamelaucium sp*) and Granite Kunzea (*Kunzea pulchella*), all just below the cave entrance.

The track leading from Norseman to Cave Hill is pretty straightforward and from the turn-off at the Coolgardie-Norseman Road to Cave Hill it is 49.7 km.

The track via many of the old woodlines from Burra Rock to Cave Hill is not always easy to follow so refer to the sketch map for details. It is particularly tricky leaving Cave Hill as the extra water run off from the rock has created wet areas and people have taken tracks all over the place to try and avoid them, but if you stay with your compass bearings and read the sketch map you should be all right.

If you can ignore some local graffiti in the caves, the rock area has much to offer the visitor.

Peak Charles
NATIONAL PARK

The Peak Charles National Park covers an area of 39,959 ha. There are two high peaks in the park; Peak Charles at 651 m high and Peak Eleanora at 501 m high. Entry is 21 km south of the Lake King–Norseman Road. After heavy rains there can be water in the low lying areas. It really is recommended to take 4WD here. There is a camping ground at the base of the granite rock, with only basic facilities and one toilet. There was an extensive fire in the park, about 1996, but the country was looking far better in 1999, with considerable regeneration. The walk to the summit and back will take at least 1.5 hrs and is a hard climb near the last massive rock face below the peak. Take care here as it is a real rock scrambling climb and you need to be quite agile. If you do not make the top, however, there are still fantastic views across the mallee and huge salt lakes to the east. It gives you a greater understanding of how the mallee and salt lake systems looked before the land was cleared.

On the walk up to the peak in spring there are some beautiful small plants with small red flowers. The plant is Peak Charles Drummondita *(Drummondita hasselli var longifolia)*, and is restricted to the granite rocks near Peak Charles. In the surrounding mallee near the camping ground, a bird about the size of a small dove with a rich chestnut colour will be the Chestnut Quail-thrush. It walks very slowly, often giving a high pitched but soft call and it is quite common in these Goldfields woodlands. When the eucalypts are in flower, small parrots that dart around like bullets in the sky are the Purple-crowned Lorikeets. They feed in the taller eucalypts. A smaller leathery leaved eucalypt, just as you start the drive off Lake King Road, with masses of bright yellow flowers, is the Coarse-leaved Mallee *(E. grossa)*, which flowers in spring.

Looking east from the summit of Peak Charles

Victoria Rock
NATURE RESERVE

Victoria Rock was named by John Holland while he was trying to find the best route for the 'Holland Track' from Albany to the Goldfields. It eventually ran from Broomehill to Gnarlbine Rock south of Coolgardie.

Victoria Rock is 45 km south of Coolgardie on the Victoria Rock Road that connects with the Norseman–Hyden Road. It is another of these large Goldfield granite rocks. On the eastern side is a camping area with toilets, barbecue pit and picnic table. There are also two day-use barbecue areas with tables and toilets.

The main eucalypts that surround the rock are Salmon Gum *(Eucalyptus salmonophloia)*, Gimlet *(Eucalyptus salubris)* and Redwood *(Eucalyptus transcontinentalis)* and some of the large Salmon Gum stumps can still be seen around the rock where the woodline timber cutters felled them in the 1920s.

On the rock, the red flowers of the Granite Bottlebrush *(Melaleuca elliptica)* will be in flower between August and October. The tall acacia bushes with long fine leaves, growing where the soil is deeper on the rock, are Silver Wattle *(Acacia lasiocalyx)* alongside the Roadside Tea-tree *(Leptospermum erubescens)*.

There is a gnamma hole at the southern end of the rock.

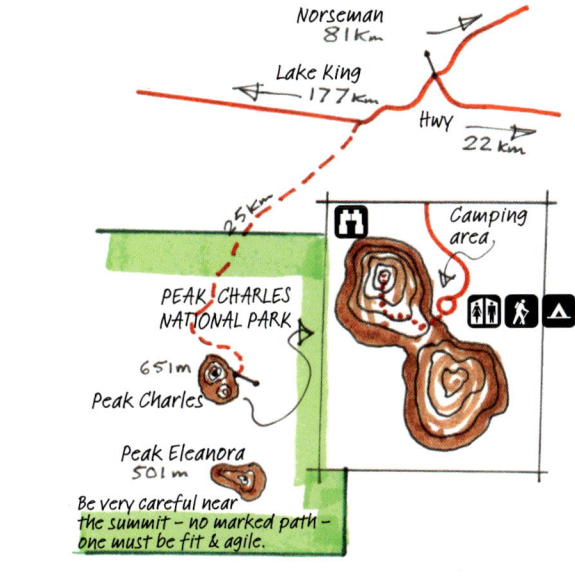

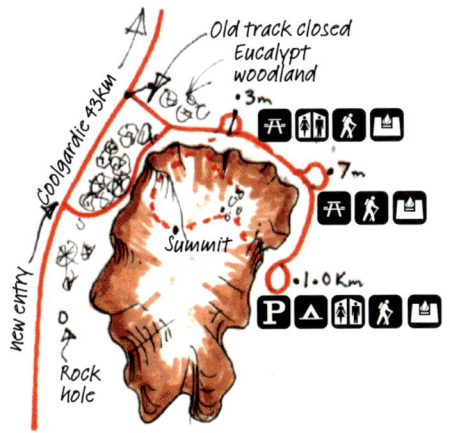

◄ Victoria Rock

Boorabbin
NATIONAL PARK

The Boorabbin National Park covers an area of 26,000 ha. It straddles the Great Eastern Highway for 28·5 km. The western boundary is 67 km from Southern Cross and the eastern boundary 98 km from Southern Cross. It is primarily Kwongan heath and throughout the year there is always something in bloom, but from August to the beginning of October it is at its best. There are many wildflowers including the tall Flame Grevillea (Grevillea excelsior) with its bright orange flowers. One of the many species of red flowering Toothbrush Grevilleas (Grevillea cagiana) is here; see if you can find one with black flowers, this will be the Toothbrush Grevillea (Grevillea hookeriana subsp. apiciloba). The bright red flowers of a plant that looks like a bottlebrush, is Emu Tree (Hakea francisiana).

A banksia restricted to the eastern Goldfields is found here, Banksia audax, which flowers in January like so many banksias and thus helps to keep the many species of honeyeaters, like the Black Honeyeater and White-fronted Honeyeater alive through the drought months.

Just before the western boundary of the park about 67 km east of Southern Cross, there is a MRDWA picnic ground with toilets and concrete fireplaces. The turn-off into the picnic area is north of the highway. It has some good examples of the various eucalypts that grow in this region. Stands of Gimlet (Eucalyptus salubris), with its lovely twisted copper coloured trunks devoid of any bark, and Goldfields York Gum (E. loxophleba subsp. lissophloia) are here, and unlike those in the central Wheatbelt have a smooth brown bark.

There are no DCLM facilities in Boorabbin National Park.

Early morning mist covers Boorabbin National Park

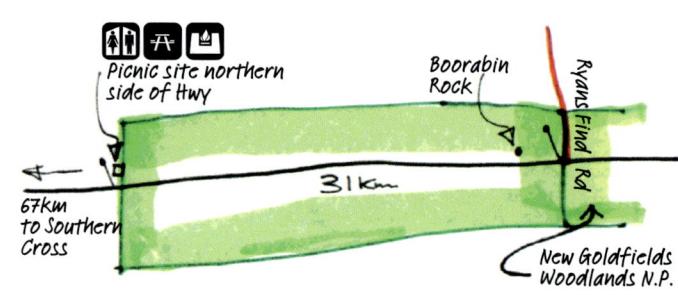

Jaurdi
STATION

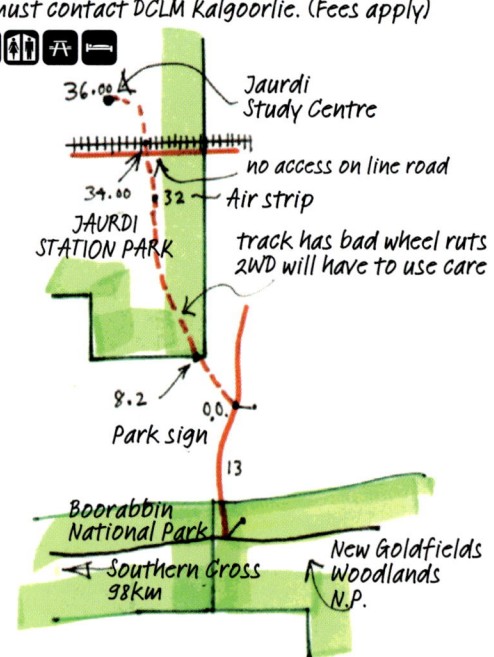

The accommodation shed of Jaurdi Station

Beautiful eucalypt woodlands as you enter the southern boundary

This reserve was once a pastoral station but DCLM is taking back some uneconomical pastoral leases and de-stocking the area.

Jaurdi is a lovely peaceful place to visit, but at this stage, notification should be made to the DCLM district office in Kalgoorlie to seek approval to visit the station. You can stay at the simple homestead, which has toilet, pot belly stove and running water from the rainwater tank (don't waste water, it's like gold out here). There are outside picnic tables and an open fire place. You get your own wood from the fallen timbers in the adjacent woodlands. You must book, as people who have booked take priority in staying at the accommodation. DCLM charges a very small fee per adult and it is just a great spot to get away from the big cities.

Access is off the Great Eastern Highway 98 km east of Southern Cross and just after the Boorabbin National Park boundary. The road leads initially due north over the water pipeline. You can take the graded Mt Walton Road for 14.6 km then turn-off to the left at the sign post to Jaurdi Station. The track although once graded has deep wheel ruts from winter wet driving and really is best taken in a 4WD vehicle. The reserve boundary is crossed at 8.2 km and then it is 25.8 km to the railway line and the homestead is across the open plains north of the line just a further 2 km.

There are wonderful eucalypt woodlands just as you enter the reserve and for the keen birdwatchers, you will see Gilbert's Whistler, Western Yellow Robin and White-fronted Honeyeater.

Around the homestead to the north is breakaway country and the most eastern stands of the Wheatbelt Wandoo (Eucalyptus capillosa) are near here.

There are old mine shafts north and east of the homestead so please be careful and there are mining rights still in place for a few areas.

All in all, a visit to Jaurdi woodlands is a great way to get to know some of the Goldfields woodlands.

Rowles Lagoon
CONSERVATION PARK

Rowles Lagoon

Fresh water lake systems are few and far between in the Goldfields but here, provided enough rains have fallen over the years, is a haven for waterfowl. As it is a conservation park, no shooting or dogs are allowed within the park. There are several lakes in the reserve including Rowles Lagoon, Carnage Lake, Muddy Lake and Clear Lake, but the main lake where there are facilities in place is Rowles Lagoon. There are picnic tables and camping areas with toilets. In 1999 much of the entry track was under water due to heavy rains and there is a wet weather detour across the open plain (refer to map).

There is a track around the edge of the lake and water skiing is allowed on the lake. It is a long way to drive here and is best visited as a side trip to the historic outback mining towns of Ora Banda and Broad Arrow.

Rowles Lagoon however, is a good spot for keen birdwatchers who wish to look out for waterbirds.

Access is from the township of Coolgardie—trip your meter here if using the map. The turn-off is on Moran Road where signs will say Bonnievale Railway Station 14 km and Ora Banda Inn 80 km. The road is a 2WD graded road, be careful of mining trucks entering the road. You will pass the old stone ruins of the derelict Kunanalling Hotel on the west side of the road at the 33·4 km mark. It is hard to imagine this building is all that remains of a small township of 800 people in the early 1900s, typical of many in the historic region. The turn-off at 58 km to Credo Homestead is where you leave the Ora Banda Road and at 67.6 km you turn right on a small track with a sign to Rowles Lagoon 6 km. A 2WD can get you to Rowles Lagoon when the tracks are dry but it is best in a vehicle with reasonable clearance.

If you intend to camp get firewood well before the lagoon or use portable stoves. Some idiots have cut into live trees adjacent to the picnic grounds, simply because they could not be bothered to collect firewood elsewhere. Luckily people who tend to buy this kind of book are not in that league.

The drive from Coolgardie is a revelation in terms of how many different Goldfields eucalypts there are, just check the many types of bark and colours. This region has some of the greatest variety of Eucalypt species in Australia.

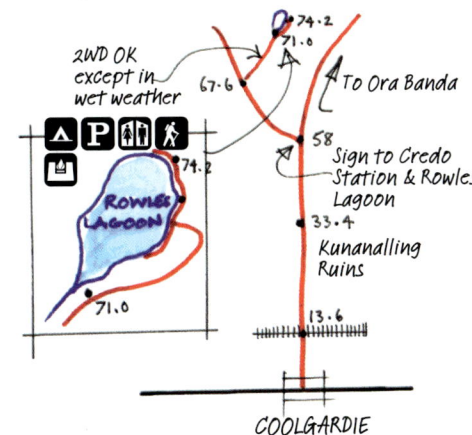

Goongarrie
NATIONAL PARK

This is a very large park and has now been extended further west and east, encompassing the old homestead. The main park on the east of the highway is approx. 140 km, travelling north then east, from Kalgoorlie to the western boundary of the park. From the highway you travel east along Pianto Road. The turn-off to Pianto Road is about 108 km from Kalgoorlie. Travel east along this dirt road for a further 35 km until you come to the park sign. There is a bush track near the sign on the right, that heads due south, which will lead you to one of several granite outcrops in the park. There are no facilities at this rock but there are lots of areas at the base of the rock where you can camp. This is basically a remote park and you should be totally self-sufficient and take rubbish back with you. The vegetation is totally different to the eucalypt woodlands around Kalgoorlie. Here there are mulga woodlands and cypress pines with some of the northern Goldfields mallees. Inform people if you are going to visit this park and contact them on your return.

There is some basic accommodation in the park, but this is located in the new extension to the park, at the site of the old Goongarrie Homestead. Entry to the property is south of Pianto Road, 90 km north of Kalgoorlie where the old township of Goongarrie used to be. There is a sign to the property 14 km. Turn west and enter the double gate. About 8 km further, there is a road left that leads to the abandoned township of Davyhurst; take the right turn to the main homestead. The accommodation consists of a homestead with beds for a maximum of 10 people in 4 separate bedrooms. There is a cottage with 4 separate bedrooms, all with showers and toilets but bring your own drinking water. You must contact DCLM Kalgoorlie and there is a fee involved.

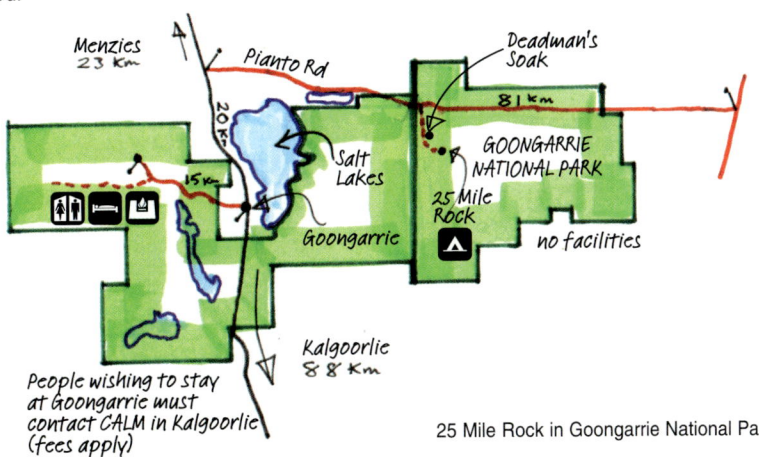

25 Mile Rock in Goongarrie National Park ▶

The Holland TRACK

When the word spread of Arthur Bayley and Bill Ford's gold find at "Bayley's Reward", where Coolgardie now stands, people started to descend on the Goldfields in droves. Besides those who travelled from Perth, many came from the eastern states by ship and disembarked at Albany and then made the train journey to York. The bush track from York was just under 500 km. It was a long hard journey and people travelled by horse and cart or walked pushing all their belongings on simple wheelbarrows.

Local people around Broomehill realised it would be beneficial to them to start a direct route to Coolgardie from their home town, as all the prospectors needed to purchase provisions and equipment to make such a long journey and they now were coming in their thousands.

Some people had tried to find a route but failed. John Holland approached local business people to finance an exploration team to open up a track. He was an experienced bushmen, being a Kangaroo shooter and sandlewood cutter, so he knew the country well.

Holland's expedition left Broomehill in mid-April 1893. He was accompanied by David and Rudolph Krakouer and John Carmody. They were well prepared, having a horse drawn cart carrying 100 gallons of water. As the journey progressed they relied on water holes near the various granite outcrops that they passed en route. Holland would ride ahead of the party and try and find the best route, plus water.

Eucalypt woodland at the northern end of the Holland Track

Old well near Mt Holland

State Barrier Spur Fence

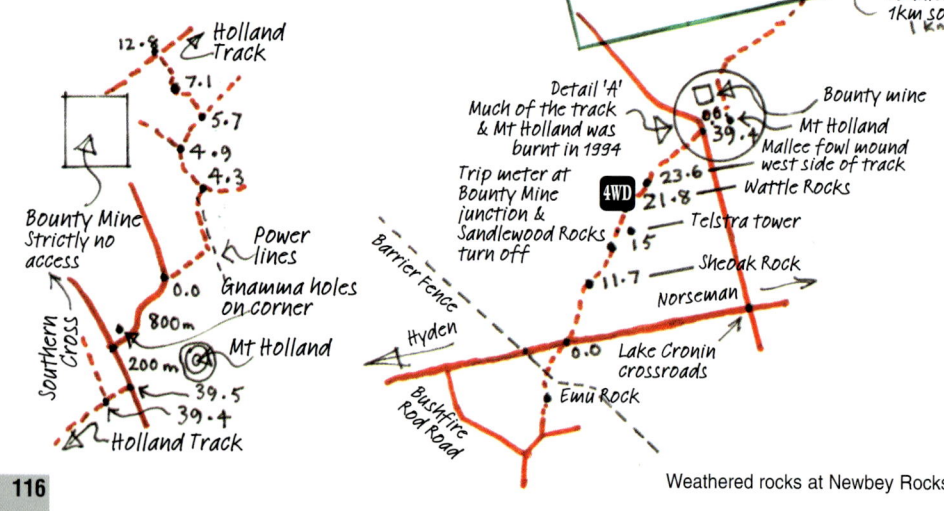

Weathered rocks at Newbey Rocks

EUCALYPTS ALONG THE HOLLAND TRACK

Yorrell *(Eucalyptus yilgarnensis)*

Gimlet *(Eucalyptus salubris* var. *salubris)*

Capped Mallee *(Eucalyptus pileata)*

They covered the country in good time and entered the town of Coolgardie on the 18 June 1893, completing their phenomenal trail-blazing feat in just over two months.

From then on many hundreds of prospectors used the route but it was to be short lived as three years later, a railway line was extended all the way to Coolgardie and the track was then little used.

Most of the original track that traversed from Broomehill to just east of Hyden has basically disappeared as land was cleared for farming, but from Emu Rock just west of the Vermin fence all the way to just south of Victoria Rock south of Coolgardie, one can follow much of the original route thanks to the hard work and dedication of several enthusiastic people who were interested in Holland's exploits. Adrian Malloy and Graeme Newbey, in particular followed much of the track between Broomehill and Mount Holland in 1984. Over the next few years they were to travel more of the old track and in 1992 Graeme's own tractor with an improvised rake was used to blaze much of the track that was overgrown. Finally in May 1993, Graeme led a six vehicle expedition that traversed the whole route from Emu Rocks to Victoria Rock. For those who have the privilege to traverse this wonderful part of the Goldfields, we can thank the many people who spent weeks opening up the old track for us. There is a useful booklet on the Holland Track available.

Driving on the outback Goldfields roads

Most of the rains fall in winter and that is when many people often decide to drive in this region. Remember tracks will become very boggy within a short period of time and even 4WDs will have problems. Also the shires will close roads without notice when rains have fallen. The damage done by vehicles travelling in mud cannot be removed without graders in the dry season so check weather conditions first. June and July can be very cold both in the day and especially at night, so consider this before you come in to the Goldfields—end of August into early October is better.

Kalgoorlie
ARBORETUM

If you wanted to know about any of the Goldfields eucalypts before heading off into the bush, then this is a great place to come. It is also a good place to have a picnic if you are visiting Kalgoorlie. It consists of a 26 ha park that was established in 1954 by the Forest Department. The trees were planted as a reference to the multitude of eucalypts that grow in the Goldfields. There are 60 species of eucalypt planted with interpretive walking trails. There are picnic tables and shade areas as well as a small dam. The area has been upgraded with the assistance of Kanowna Belle Goldmines, North Limited, DCLM and Landcare Australia—another great team community effort.

The entrance to the Arboretum is located off Hawkins Street, between Addis and Memorial Street on the north west side of Kalgoorlie.

Picnic area at Arboretum

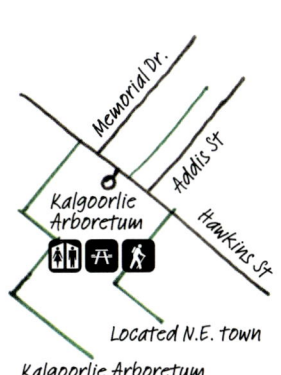

Located N.E. town
Kalgoorlie Arboretum

A typical fence line on the Nullarbor Plain

Nullarbor
REGION

Nullarbor
REGION

The treeless plains of the Nullarbor

Open woodland on the western edge of the Nullarbor

One of the many Nullarbor limestone sink holes

The Nullarbor Plain is the world's largest limestone Karst plateau covering a staggering 250,000 sq km. In the centre, it is almost featureless; devoid of trees and water on the surface, although below the surface are countless underground caves, one of them being one of the longest in the world. One diver went as far as he could before the cave became too narrow; that was at 6 km.

This vast limestone plain was below the seabed some 20 million years ago. This ancient seabed became a barrier between the higher lands of the west coast and those of the east coast. It was this division that still separates many of the plant communities that we see today.

Underlying the thinner limestone capping that covers the Nullarbor is an even deeper limestone bed some 200 m thick, known as the Wilson Bluff Limestone, named after the bluff in Eucla National Park. This ancient seabed was formed about 45 million years ago; when the Antarctic and Australian continental plates separated. The massive pressures created uplift and tilted the plateau towards the sea. With the subsequent rising oceans the Nullarbor became covered with sea water and marine life colonised the new lands. About 25 million years ago an ice age occurred, lowering the earth's oceans and the land became dry again. Five million years later, with the warming of the oceans, the sea level rose yet again, covering the old limestone. Over time the new marine deposits created the thinner crust of overlaying limestone, up to 30 m thick.

If you stop at one of the lookouts crossing the Nullarbor, you can see the darker grey-brown limestone above the clay coloured limestone of the older base rock limestone.

Most people only get to feel the vastness of the clear treeless horizons near the Nullarbor Roadhouse in South Australia but if you venture north of the central Nullarbor in Western Australia, the treeless plains soon come into view.

Even though the name Nullarbor has Aboriginal quality about it, the name is derived from the Latin "nullus bor" meaning "no tree". The Mirning people of the region called it "Gondiri".

Travelling from the west on the Eyre Highway, the traveller often expects to see wide open plains just past Norseman, but you will first pass one of Australia's great eucalypt wilderness woodlands. The first area of open country occurs near the old ruins of the Balladonia Telegraph Station, 220 km east of Norseman, and even then the country is dotted with the odd eucalypt and Western Myall (*Acacia papyrocarpa*). From here on the grass plains open up but there will always be the odd tree on the horizon all the way on the highway until Nullarbor National Park in South Australia.

Past Cocklebiddy, the highway drops down from the Nullarbor Plain to Madura, where the inland cliffs give way to a flat coastal plain that stretches 180 km from Madura to Eucla. At the Eucla end the road rises steeply off the coastal plain to the small township of Eucla on the Nullarbor Plain itself. From here it is just 12 km to the South Australian border.

Chocolate Wattled Bat
(*Chalindobus morio*)
Photo by Greg Barron

Southern Freetail-bat
(*Mormopterus planiceps*)
Photo by Greg Barron

White-striped Freetail-bat
(*Nyctinomus australis*)
Photo by Greg Barron

Red Kangaroo
(*Macropus rufus*)

Flora & Fauna
OF THE NULLARBOR PLAIN

Mammals: The vast treeless plains may look devoid of life, but there are several animals that exist in these arid areas. One is the only member of the family Vombatidae found in Western Australia. It is the Southern Hairy-nosed Wombat (*Lasiorhinus latifrons*). Alas this lovely animal is becoming rare in WA, as we have no major reserves set aside to protect this animal, so it has to compete with sheep, rabbits and predation from the largest feral cats found anywhere in Australia.

Its stronghold now is in South Australia where there are national parks large enough and free from the grazing of sheep, which has stripped much of the western parts of the Nullarbor of Blue Bush and perennial grasses.

It is a very sedentary animal, requiring little surface water. It derives its moisture from the plants it eats, being entirely herbivorous. The animal has developed many techniques to combat the loss of water. Firstly it is nocturnal, only venturing out in daylight on very cold winter days. When resting, its metabolic rate is two thirds that of most other marsupials. It also takes up to 8 days for digesting vegetation to pass through the gut, thus absorbing all water content and expending very little energy. It lives in a warren system having between 5 and 10 animals in a group.

One group of animals that many people feel uneasy with are the bats and there are about 70 species of bat in Australia ranging from diminutive cave bats with a head and body length of only 40 mm, to the large fruit-eating Flying Foxes at 300 mm long. The Nullarbor with its extensive cave system is one of the most important regions for protecting these animals as their habitat in many parts of Australia has gone.

There are some myths about bats that really have no foundation. The only vampire (blood sucking) bats are in Central and South America, and they are only 70 mm long. The only carnivorous bat in Australia is the Ghost Bat (*Macroderma gigas*) of the Pilbara and the Tropical North that kills small lizards, birds, small mammals and other bats.

Bats are placental mammals like ourselves and are the only mammals that are capable of true flight, like birds. They are thought to have evolved from primitive shrew like mammals. There are two basic groups or sub-orders of bat. The microbats, mostly insectivorous, which catch their prey at night and navigate through trees and other obstacles by emitting echo-locating high frequency sounds, almost inaudible to the human ear. They do this through their mouth or nose and sound bounces off objects, which they detect in their large ears; it also allows them to locate flying insects. They not only roost in caves but many, particularly in the eucalypt woodlands, roost in hollows of trees. Megabats, particularly Flying Foxes, eat fruit and nectar but they live primarily in the tropics; there are none on the Nullarbor.

The Red Kangaroo (*Macropus rufus*) is the largest kangaroo and is found throughout the Nullarbor. It requires good green herbage to thrive well but when droughts affect the arid regions, breeding almost stops, with most females ceasing to breed after 3 months of drought. Young in the pouch will often die after 2-3 months of drought. This is nature's way of protecting the healthy adults from losing condition and possible death, letting them survive until the rains next fall and they can breed again with more probability of success.

Birds: There are numerous birds on the Nullarbor, the most conspicuous being the Wedge-tailed Eagle. Do be careful when passing these eagles on the road if they are on a road kill, they digest a fair amount and become sluggish on take off so try and slow down when approaching them.

On the open plains is where you find a very cryptic bird, the Inland Dotterel as well as Cinnamon Quail-thrush (race *alisteri*), Australian Bustard, White-winged Fairy-wren, Samphire Thornbill, Ground Cuckoo-shrike and, after storms, Oriental Plover. In the northern area of the Nullarbor centred around Rawlinna Station wherever the tree called Western Myall (*Acacia papyrocarpa*) grows you will see a restricted parrot, the Blue Bonnet (race *narethae*).

Wedge-tailed Eagle

Chestnut Quail-thrush

Blue Bonnet (race *narethae*)

Shy Heathwren

Sunset on the Eyre sand dunes

Pink Cockatoo

Eyre Telegraph Station set in the mallee below the giant sand dunes

Rob & Alex Bisgrove – hard working wardens at Eyre Telegraph Station

Nuytsland
NATURE RESERVE

The reserve is a long narrow band of land from Israelite Bay in the west to Red Rock Point in the east. It covers an area of 625,332 ha, and a coastline of nearly 500 km. It is the longest stretch of reserve coastline in the whole of Australia. Nuytsland was named by Frans Thyssen, who sailed on the Gulden Zeepaard (Golden Seahorse), after one of the notable passengers on his ship, Pieter Nuyts.

Access in to the western end of the park takes you through Cape Arid National Park to Israelite Bay on a 4WD track.

Eyre Bird
OBSERVATORY

At the north east end of the nature reserve, south of the Cocklebiddy Road house, is a very special place; it is now the Eyre Bird Observatory, but in its formative years it was the Eyre Telegraph Station built in 1897.

The Overland Telegraph line between Albany and Adelaide was a joint project between Western Australia and South Australia. It took just three years to complete and the first full transmission occurred on the 8th December 1877 and continued right up until 1927, when it was replaced with more up to date lines that ran along the railway line, without intermediate relay telegraph stations.

Edward John Eyre with his faithful companion Wylie had experienced on his epic expedition from Adelaide to Albany the most debilitating water shortages. After 5 days walking from Eucla without water, they nearly died but they found some water below the Bealbie Hills. The water was terribly brackish. Some passing Aborigines told them of a soak near the Eyre Sand Dunes and there is water there to this day.

It revived the party of Eyre, Baxter and the three Aborigines Joey, Yarrie and Wylie and they rested for 1 month before starting the next leg of the journey, which they knew would be arduous and without water. Tragically on the 3rd

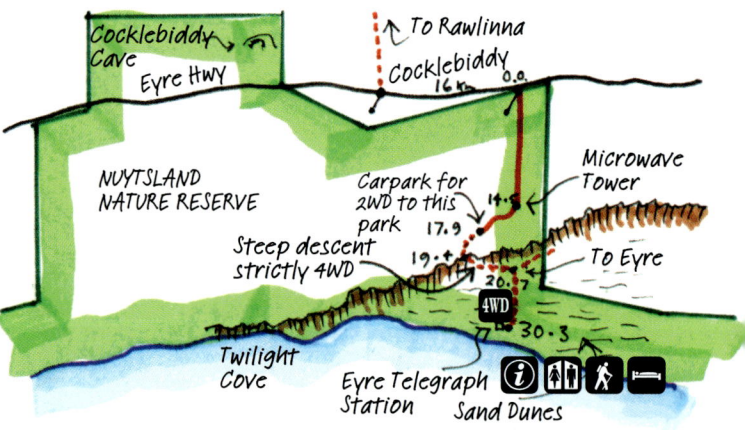

NOTE: Deflate tyres please at base of scarp to 18lbs to negotiate track to Eyre

night Baxter was killed. To this day there is some uncertainty as to whether or not it was one of the Aborigines that shot Baxter or Eyre himself. Joey and Yarrie, however, abandoned the party, leaving Eyre and Wylie with little or no provisions and a 1,400 km journey still to make. Well, make it they did, 5 months later. It was one of the most gruelling overland journeys that any explorer made in Australia.

Getting enough drinking water has always been a problem at Eyre and the early telegraph workers were able to extract fresh water from the sea by using heated condenser units that would take sea water and convert it to fresh water. For every 455 litres of sea water they could extract 273 litres of drinkable water.

Eyre was closed down in 1927 and for 49 years it stood abandoned. The old corrugated roof staying mostly in place, saving the old building.

In 1976 the Royal Australasian Ornithologists Union approached the Post Office Historical Society with the aim of renovating the building into a bird observatory, which they did, and now there is basic accommodation available to all travellers.

Eyre has a remote and peaceful atmosphere as if time has stood still and it was still 1897.

You do not have to be a bird watcher to stay here, even though the observatory is an important place for recording bird movements and running nature based courses. It is available to all who are crossing the Nullarbor or who simply want to get away to a remote area leaving mobile phones and the plastic world behind.

Here, the beautiful Pink Cockatoos come in to drink, the Welcome Swallows make their home, and the Purple-gaped and New Holland Honeyeaters and Brush Bronze wing all come regularly to the bird baths to drink. You can take walks along the never-ending beaches, walk into the mallee scrub and look at Malleefowl mounds and you also may see a Malleefowl, Chestnut Quail-thrush or Western Yellow Robin.

The shoreline is only 1 km away and between it and the homestead are 90 m high pure white sand dunes. A creative photographer could spend days here.

The accommodation is comfortable, although fairly basic. Meals are provided by the resident wardens. Please book your accommodation in advance with the wardens.

You can also attend one of their many nature based courses, or simply visit for the day. To get to the observatory you must have a 4WD, but if you are staying overnight, arrangements can be made with the wardens to pick you up from the top car park above the scarp, where 2WD vehicles can go.

To access the observatory there is a gravel road south of the highway, 16 km east of Cocklebiddy. Sketch map details and information are provided on a covered sign 500 m down the gravel road.

Eucla
NATIONAL PARK

Just west of the South Australian border is the small settlement of Eucla, with fuel, meals and accommodation, including caravan, camping and motel units. It lies adjacent to the small Eucla National Park of 3,560 ha.

There are two major features of interest here—Wilson Bluff, where spectacular views can be seen including the long line of coastal cliffs that stretch into the distance and the pure white sands of the Delisser Dunes. In the dunes lie the last remnants of the old Eucla Telegraph Station, that once had 10 telegraph operators handling calls between the east and west coast. Now all that is visible are a couple of chimneys and parts of the walls, the rest is being covered by ever moving sand dunes. You can access the ruins on a track 4 km west of Eucla, south of the highway with a 2WD.

Not far from here, with the aid of information from local Aborigines, Edward Eyre found water at the base of the dunes, as he did a further 250 km west, near Eyre Bird Observatory and its sand dunes.

Later in 1872, the Muir brothers John, Tom and Andrew, decided to move to the Eucla region from the lush south west near Mount Barker. Part of the reason was that in 1870, the explorer John Forrest had described the area in glowing terms, obviously having seen the land in a good season. The Muir story is one of hardship and toil in these waterless regions and it must have taken its toll as John Muir died in 1878 of pneumonia, at 42 years of age. His wife, Asenath, and their four children moved to Port Augusta. Their grandson, Jim Muir, and his wife, Alison, have written an interesting story of the early history and exploits of the Muir family.

Delisser Sand Dunes

The ruins of Eucla Telegraph Station

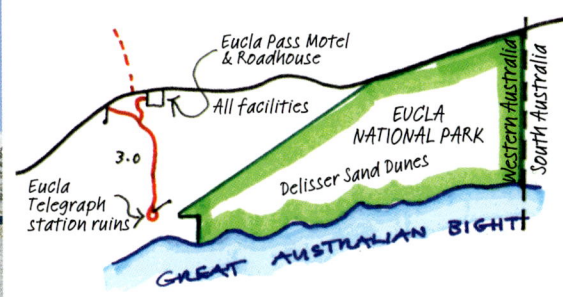

Driving across the Nullarbor

Just a few reminders:
- Try to avoid driving too long, particularly after dark.
- Try to avoid driving close to sunset when driving west as the sun will be in your eyes for quite some time and it's hard to see oncoming vehicles.
- With big trucks do the right thing and keep well to the left as you not only do them a favour but you decrease your chances of getting stone damage; it is only a few seconds lost.
- If you really do have to drive at night, and remember road trains do, play safe; slow right down and if anything pull right over when they are passing as the highway is not that wide. The most serious and potentially dangerous situation is overtaking road trains at night. Seriously think about whether it is worth driving at night on the Nullarbor, as the strain of concentration at night is most tiring.
- Dusk is when kangaroos are most active and on the move to feed, and hitting them at 110 km/hr can be very dangerous for all concerned.
- Always carry water in case of a breakdown, particularly in summer.
- Remember the time changes. SA is 1.5 hrs ahead of WA and 2.5 hrs when they have daylight saving. Also there is Central Western Standard time. When heading eastwards, put timepieces 45 minutes forward at Caiguna.

The Mulga wildflowers in full bloom.

Mid West
REGION

Mid West
REGION

Travelling north from Perth, the Brand Highway passes through Moore River National Park. Like many of the lower mid west parks, its main attraction would have to be the wonderful displays of wildflowers.

The limestone pinnacles in Nambung National Park are always of interest to the newly arrived traveller to Western Australia, and are accessed west of the highway. There are other limestone formations of interest in this area such as the caves at Drover's (no cave access – area for walkers only) and Stockyard Gully.

The parks of Lesueur, Badgingarra, Watheroo, Alexander Morrison and Tathra National Park are all noted for their incredibly rich flora. Mount Lesueur is the third richest park botanically in Western Australia after the Fitzgerald and Stirling Range National Parks.

The central drives through the northern wheatbelt, either via the Moora, Three Springs route or the Wongan Hills, Wubin, Mullewa route, can be very rewarding, particularly if one wishes to get the feel of wheatbelt country towns. There are also quite a few historical towns en route, particularly New Norcia.

Coalseam Conservation Park, between Mingenew and Mullewa, is not a spectacular park but for people who have seen the major parks, this is a lovely small park to visit. It has interesting fossils and gorge country which is quite unexpected after travelling through open farming country.

A major park north of Geraldton is Kalbarri National Park. Not only are the displays of wildflowers here fantastic but the deep gorges cut by the Murchison River are quite magnificent.

Finally in the north of the Mid West is the Shark Bay World Heritage area. The scenery is not spectacular, in fact it can be dry and arid, but there is a beauty in these red sands set against the clear turquoise seas. This region is really noted for being one of the most important marine habitats in the world, hence its being declared as a 'World Heritage' area.

Featherflowers in full bloom at Reynolds Reserve north of Wongan Hills

Moore River
NATIONAL PARK

Situated just 120 km north of Perth is the Moore River National Park with an area of 17,540 ha. It is a day use park only. Its main feature would have to be its variety of wildflowers. Unlike some parks whose flower displays diminish at the beginning of summer, Moore River National Park has perhaps its greatest spread of colour in late November and early December. The bright orange 'Morrison' *(Verticordia nitens)* and the yellow-flowered Slender Banksia *(Banksia attenuata)* and Christmas Tree *(Nuytsia floribunda)* are in full bloom.

One of the best locations to view these flowers is approx. 8 km south of Moore River on the west side of the Brand Highway, just past Red Gully Road. There is a floral Kangaroo Paw sign noting the turn off to the car park.

Here you can walk through open Banksia woodland. As you commence the walk, there is a very restricted Rose Banksia *(Banksia laricina)*, a bush that is only about a metre tall and flowers from April to June with an interesting propeller-shaped fruit.

In spring there is a greater variety of wildflower species here but not so well covered in colour as in November and early December. Look for the lovely red Winter Bells *(Blancoa canescens)*.

A 4WD track runs through the park but it is not easily accessed and it is very overgrown, with a semi-permanent swamp called Nine Mile Swamp in the middle. It is not recommended to drive this sandy track at this stage in the development of the park.

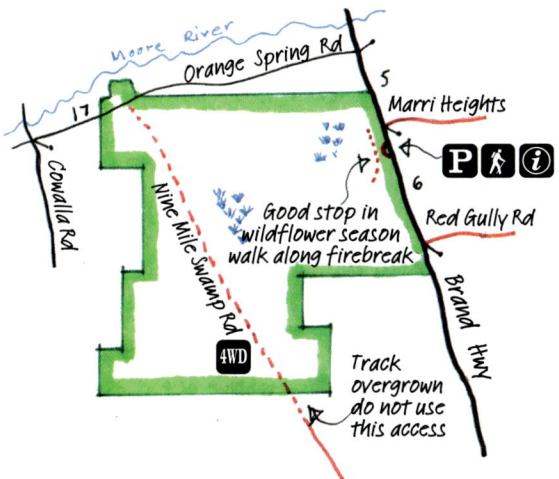

Morrison featherflower *(Verticordia nitens)* in bloom, Moore River National Park

Moganmoganing
NATURE RESERVE
(formerly Old Plains Road Nature Reserve)

In the 1800s there was not a direct road to New Norcia from Perth, only a track that went via Toodyay. It was opened up by the Benedictine monk, Bishop Salvado, of the New Norcia monastery. The road eventually became known as the Old Plains Road.

If one is travelling in this direction, it is certainly worth a detour between late August and early October. There is a small roadside nature strip that runs for approx. 5 km along the old road. Even though the reserve is no more than 60 m wide, it contains a wealth of plants.

A few kilometres south of here is a nature reserve, named in honour of the botanist and historian Erica Erickson. It has open wandoo woodland, good for orchids in early spring as well as some thick dryandra heath.

Roadside wildflowers in full bloom ▶ at Moganmoganing, mid-September

The Pinnacles at sunset   Pinnacles

Nambung
NATIONAL PARK

This is a very popular park and well worth the visit for all travellers. It lies just south of the small seaside town of Cervantes, 245 km by road north of Perth.

Here in the park lie some unique geological rock formations that protrude through the yellow sands, forming a sea of vertical columns.

The first Europeans to sight these tombstone-like pillars, were the Dutch, but being cautious they did not land, knowing that they had previously lost ships such as the Gilt Dragon in 1656 along this coast. They recorded their sightings on early charts, likening the pinnacles to some lost city. Well, when you drive around the 5 km one way track, you can imagine their thoughts looking onto this remote coast in those early days.

The limestone pinnacles rise to 5 m in height. They are located on the coastal limestone belt that runs from Shark Bay all the way southwards past Perth. The sand dune soil is known as Tamala Limestone.

There have been several theories as to how the pinnacles were formed but the general consensus by leading geologists is that in the early stages of their development, there were dune systems that over time stabilised with the growth of vegetation on the capping soils. In the sand, lime was leached to the lower levels by rain seeping through the sands. This cemented the lower levels into soft limestone. The vegetation that grew on the surface created an acidic layer of soil and humus, that helped form an insoluble quartz sand layer of calcrete that covered the softer limestone below. Over time, cracks in this hard capping layer occurred and the plants took advantage of these breaks by sending down roots. The softer limestone below the hard capping was then dissolved by rains and the cracks continued deeper into the softer limestone. The harder quartz sands then filled the cavities leaving the soft limestone columns that exist today.

With the drying out of the continent over the last 25,000 years, some of the top vegetation cover died and the dry continuing winds blew away the top quartz sands and also the quartz sands in the cavities. This left the eroded columns that we see today.

There is more to Nambung than just the limestone pinnacles. Just out of Cervantes is Lake Thetis. It is only a small lake but has some interesting ancient life forms that are known as stromatolites. These small cauliflower shaped structures are at least 2000 years old and are basically a bacterial growth that develops with sand on rock to create these dome-like structures. There are several locations in Western Australia showing these ancient life forms. Those at Hamelin Pool in the Shark Bay region are perhaps the most impressive examples.

There are two beach stops, Hangover Bay and Kangaroo Point, both having picnic tables and gas barbecues. If it is very windy on the coast there is a quiet picnic spot about 10 km out of Cervantes off the main road, with picnic tables below big Tuart trees (E. gomphocephala). These trees only grow on these limestone soils and reach their greatest heights in the Tuart National Park north of Busselton. Near the picnic spot on the main road, you will see masses of Acorn Banksias (Banksia prionotes), which are in full flower from March to May.

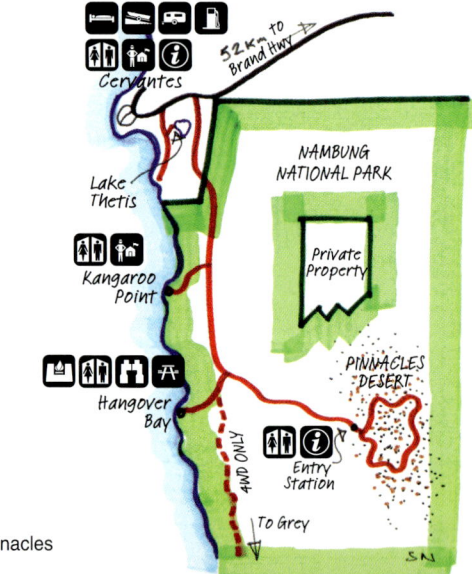

◀ Pinnacles

Cave parks
OF THE MID WEST

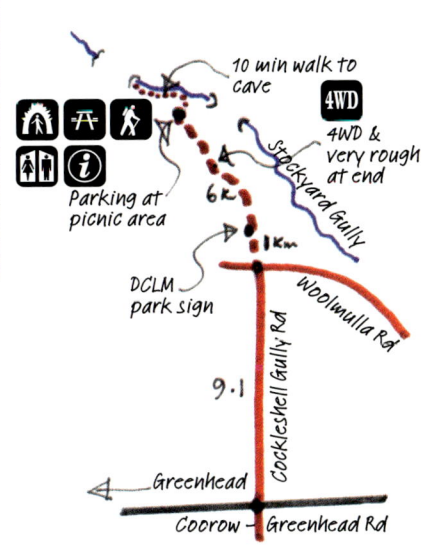

Stockyard Gully
NATIONAL PARK

The road into Stockyard Gully is very rough, traversing large limestone protruding rocks; it is definitely a 4WD track and should be driven in a very low gear. However, when you get to the parking area there is a pleasant picnic spot with tables under large River Red Gums (Eucalyptus camaldulensis).

Walking down down 10 m into a small gully you will pass an information board where a previous flood level has been recorded and it gives you some idea of the flash floods that can channel themselves down these limestone gullies.

When you reach the sandy valley bottom, you can see a small cave on your right (access not recommended by DCLM) but the main cave is in fact to your left. Walking along the valley for 200 m you will come to the entrance of Stockyard Tunnel Cave. There are 3 main caves with open areas in between as you walk along the sandy creek bed. The first cave is about 250 m long, accessible from either end. There is fallen stone rubble at the entrance, so you must negotiate this to get into each cave. Do not try to proceed past the last cave. Be careful after heavy rain, as the sands can appear solid but are in fact like quicksand, containing lots of water. Also caving can be dangerous, so do take care and take back-up batteries when entering caves. Wear good walking boots, note where you came in, and shine the torch back occasionally so you can recognise the rock shapes to assist you on your way back. Do check your headroom. These are precautionary warnings—do not let them stop you enjoying these caves.

Drovers Cave
NATIONAL PARK

Of the two cave systems, Stockyard Gully has more to offer than Drovers Cave in terms of cave size and also has a better picnic site. Both, however, require 4WD and are rough roads to drive on. Just east of the small fishing town of Jurien are some limestone caves located in Drovers Cave National Park. It is a small park of just 2,681 hectares, not well known and little visited, but there are some caves that can be explored. The track into the park is very sandy in places and also rocky from limestone outcrops. It is definitely a 4WD track. In springtime the area is covered with white smokebush and yellow acacia flowers. One of the caves—Hastings Cave has some very large feral beehives suspended right at the entrance, so do be careful if entering the cave system.

UPDATE WALKING ONLY NO ACCESS TO CAVES

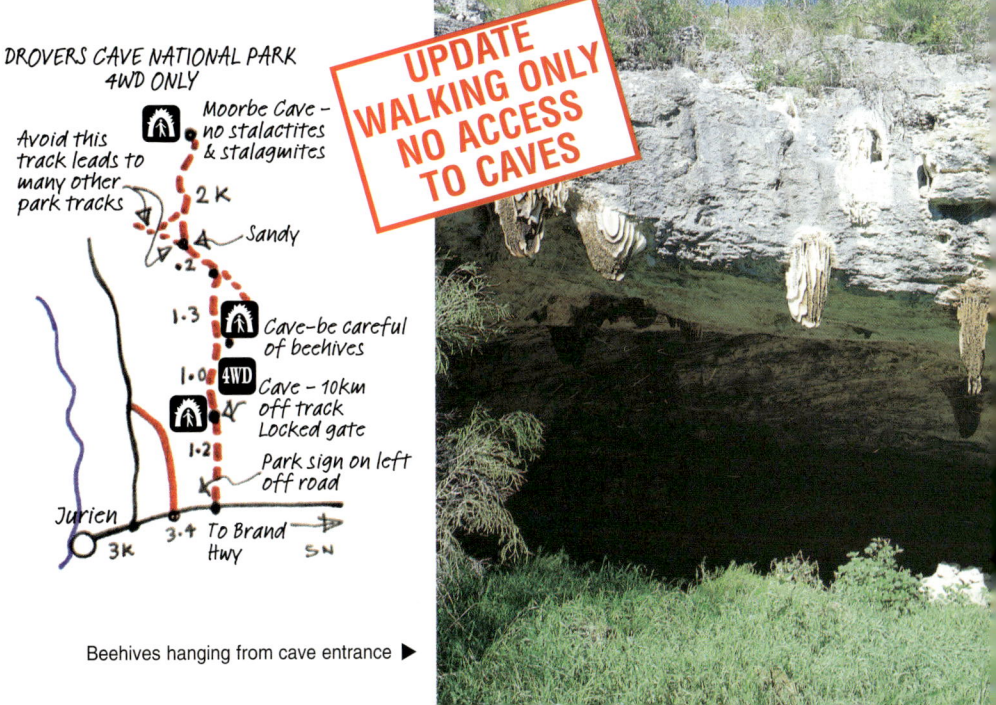

Beehives hanging from cave entrance ▶

THE MID WEST WILDFLOWER PARKS
of Badgingarra, Lesueur, Watheroo, Alexander Morrison & Tathra National Park

Even though all of these parks are totally separate as national parks, they all share one major common attraction and that is that they all contain some of the richest diversity of wildflowers in the state.

Coomalo, South Eneabba, Beekeeper, Lake Logue, and Watto Nature Reserves also have wonderful displays of wildflowers with the highest species numbers being centred on the Mt Lesueur and Eneabba area.

In this region alone, there are over 1,300 species of plants. The banksias, featherflowers, kangaroo paws, myrtles, peas, dryandras, orchids and smokebushes are some of the major groups that make this region so rich and there is always something in flower every month of the year. Botanists call these heathlands 'Kwongan' from the Noongar word for 'sandy plain'.

The soil types have a great bearing on what grows where and here it is the infertile quartz sands and lateritic soils that make the area so diverse in wildflowers. People sometimes wonder, if the soils are so infertile and nutrient deficient, why does the Kwongon heath produce this vast array of plants? One of the reasons is that many of the plants have developed special root systems that have symbiotic bacteria or fungi which extract various nutrients from the soil, as well as absorb nitrogen from the air and fix it to produce a form of fertiliser.

Throughout the Mid West there is something in flower every month of the year, with the main period for all these parks being from June to March, with the highest peak starting from the beginning of August to the end of November. With the mulga region in the east and north east of this region, the best time to see the everlastings, is after good winter rains which can be as early as the end of July and continue until mid October. The displays of everlastings are dependent on good rains and if the winters are dry, which can happen, then little or no displays will occur, so do check before travelling this region.

Where to find the flowers

All of the wildflower parks mentioned are excellent places to visit but you can plan a driving journey that will take you from Moora all the way up to Mullewa and then back down via Morawa, Dalwallinu and Wongan Hills.

These roads not only have very good wildflower roadside verges, but being the older established road systems in the Mid West, there are more historical buildings and early European histories attached to these countryside roads and towns.

▲Burdett's Banksia (Banksia burdetti)

▼Wreath Lechenaulti (Lechenaulti macrantha) in the Mid West.

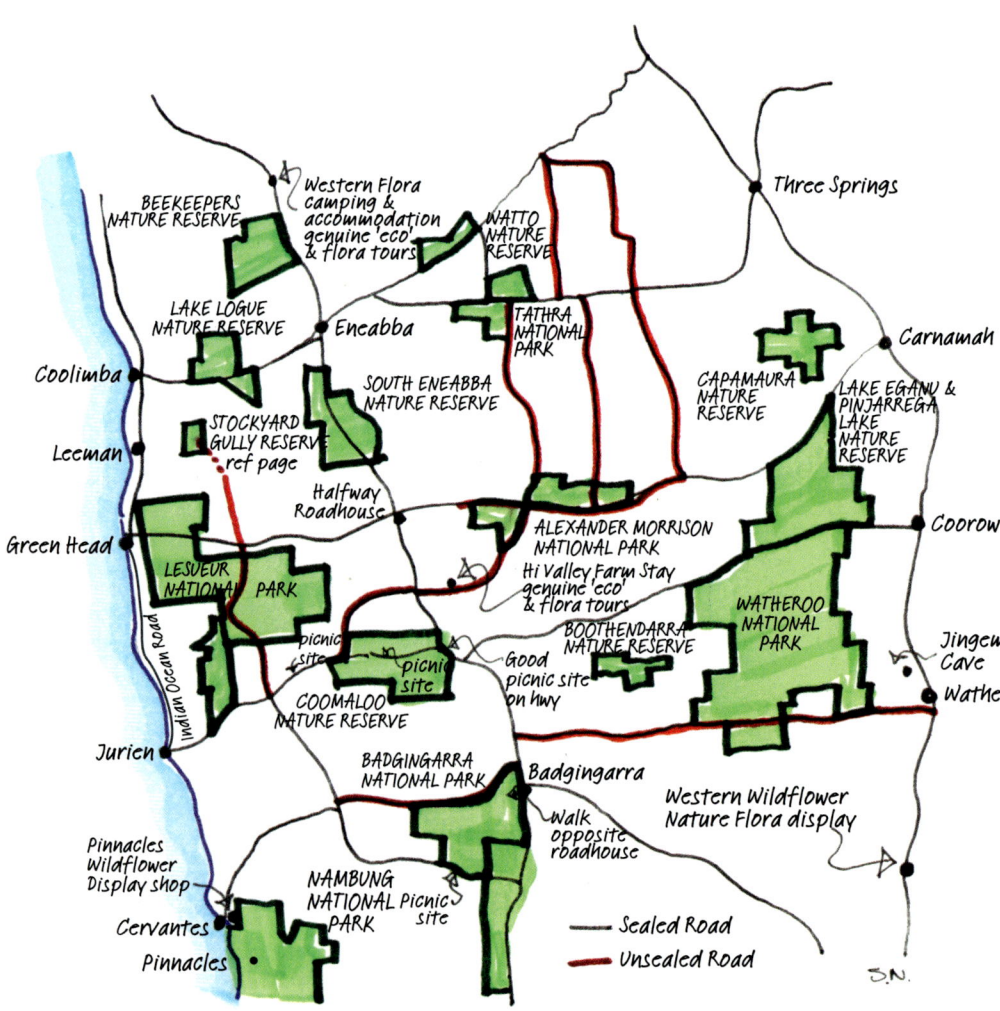

The Central Mid West Parks

Illyarrie (*Eucalyptus erythrocorys*) | Red Pokers (*Hakea bucculenta*) | Shaggy Dryandra (*Dryandra speciosa*) | Morrison Featherflower (*Verticordia noblis*)

Lesueur
NATIONAL PARK

Of all the national parks of this region, Lesueur National Park has the greatest variety of plants, with over 900 species, seven of them very rare plants and nine found only in the park.

Lesueur has the third highest species count of all the state's parks after the Fitzgerald and Stirling Range National Parks. It is hard to imagine that in just a 10 square-metre patch of heath, these soils can support up to 80 plant species.

The park covers an area of 26,987 ha. It was only recently, in 1992, that the Mount Lesueur area became a national park, as there was considerable pressure from the Department of Mines for it to be set aside for the mining of coal.

The landforms include the flat-topped laterite mesas of Mount Lesueur and Mount Michaud and quartz sands overlaying laterite and some sandstone on the lower slopes.

The only vehicle access to the park is off Cockleshell Gully Road and it requires 4WD. The old track from Banovich Road has been closed to prevent dieback spreading into the park. Turn north off Jurien Road onto Cockleshell Gully Road and travel for 8 km, then turn right onto a signposted sandy track which passes through soft sand and hard laterite. It is a lovely drive in spring, passing through heath and woodland. The 6 km track finally terminates at a small car park from which further driving is not allowed. Later this location will be upgraded to have toilets etc.

From here you can look out to the coast and then take the track to the top of Mount Lesueur. First walk approximately 150 m and take the first right track—you will see Mount Lesueur in front of you.

For those who are very keen on flowers, look out for the rare banksia only found in the Lesueur area and called Lesueur Banksia or Pine Banksia (*Banksia tricuspis*) it flowers between March and July. The flowers look like the very common Slender Banksia (*Banksia attenuata*) which is also here, but it flowers between October and February.

The park was named after the French natural history artist Charles–Alexandre Lesueur, who sailed on the 'Naturaliste' off this coast in 1801. The first botanist to collect flowers from here was James Drummond in 1850 and subsequently the industrious botanist Charles Gardner in 1947.

It is a fairly important area for birds with 122 species of birds recorded for the park. Besides the honeyeaters and other birds that feed on the nectar producing plants of the heath, the Wandoo woodlands that grow in the park are very important habitats for the nesting sites of two of our declining parrots, Short-billed Cockatoo and the Western Corella. It must be said that, luckily, there are very heavy penalties for those who deal in the act of taking the eggs and young of our parrots. Reptile diversity in the park is also quite high, with 52 species recorded.

Camping is only allowed in this park by notification to local DCLM staff and is for backpackers only, and on the condition that no open fires are lit.

Looking towards Mt Lesueur

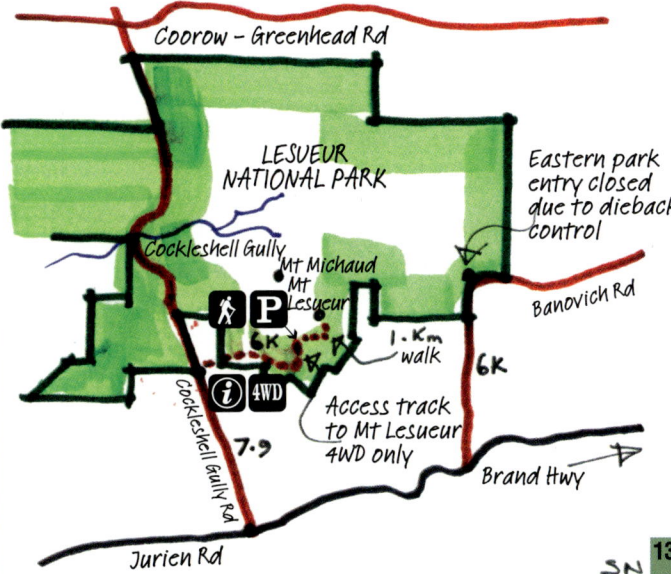

Badgingarra
NATIONAL PARK

The Brand Highway passes alongside this very rich wildflower park. There is a pleasant picnic spot with tables, called 'Drummond' picnic site on Bibby Road that leads to Cervantes. There are many flowers in season around this area. Also, near the junction of the Brand Highway and the turn-off to Badgingarra Road house, there is a DCLM information walk that leads westerly up to the breakaway. The track enters 150 m south of the junction and has a small sign. You can park near the roadhouse and walk back to the highway, but be careful crossing here as cars will be doing high speeds.

On this walk you may see the beautiful Scarlet Featherflower *(Verticordia grandis)*. There are two low bushy banksias here, Round–fruit Banksia *(Banksia sphaerocarpa)* and Propeller Banksia *(Banksia candolleana)*, both common names coming from the shape of their fruit. As you walk up the hill you will see two types of grasstree. Many people just take a glance and think they are all the same, but look at the tops of the grasstrees. One type has a single stem that protrudes from the top, containing hundreds of small flowers, which is the more common type of grasstree. This particular species is *Xanthorrhoea reflexa* not *X. preissi* which occurs in the Perth region. The other has several stems with round flower heads on the end, hence the common name Drumsticks or Kingia, this is a totally different genus, *Kingia australis*.

Not far from here there are stands of the rare Badgingarra Mallee *(Eucalyptus pendens)* as well as the magnificent Mottlecah *(E. macrocarpa)* with the largest flowers of any eucalypt in Australia; it flowers from October to January.

There are two particular kangaroo paws that are quite beautiful in this park, the Yellow Kangaroo Paw *(Anigozanthos pulcherrimus)* and the stunning Black Kangaroo Paw *(Macropidia fuliginosa)*.

The walk to the breakaway from the Brand Highway

Alexander Morrison & Tathra
NATIONAL PARKS

If there were caves, mountains, gorges or large river systems in parks like Alexander Morrison and Tathra, the author would be the first to describe these features to you, but there are none except a 'breakaway' laterite ridge in Alexander Morrison. It is on the Coorow– Greenhead Road about 5 km from the western boundary and provides good views across the plains to the west. These lower Mid West parks are preserved in the main for their incredible diversity of plants.

Alexander Morrison is named in honour of the Western Australian government botanist in the early 1900's. and Tathra is derived from the local aboriginal word for 'beautiful place'. Both parks contain many dryandra species and as well as the taller banksias, they contain the uncommon prostrate banksia, Fishbone Banksia *(Banksia chamaephyton)*, and the low shrub banksia with big round orange-yellow flowers *(Banksia leptophylla var. leptophylla)*. The latter flowers from December to April. If you see a low eucalypt with a corky-looking bark it most probably will be Prickly Bark Blackbutt *(Eucalyptus todtiana)*, flowering from January to April. The lovely pendulous Shaggy Dryandra *(Dryandra speciosa)* and a prostrate darwinia *(Darwinia speciosa)* can be found on the laterite hill tops.

▲ A breakaway ridge in Alexander Morrison National Park

Coomaloo
NATURE RESERVE

Coomaloo is not a national park but, at present, a 'C' class reserve. There are plans to eventually upgrade it to an 'A' class reserve, giving it extra protection for its flora and fauna. It has been included here simply as the picnic site, opposite the junction of Jurien Road and the Brand Highway, is a pleasant place to stop on long journeys. It is currently managed by the Shire of Dandaragan. The surrounding Wandoo woodland is very productive for birds. The wildflowers are also very good, particularly as you walk up the hill from the woodland. In late winter, there are several orchid species to be found below the Wandoo trees in the valley floor.

◀ Coomaloo picnic site

Watheroo
NATIONAL PARK

This is a large park located north west of the township of Watheroo on Midlands Road. In the summer months the park is full of flowering banksias, including Acorn Banksia (*Banksia prionotes*) and Burdett's Banksia (*Banksia burdettii*). Other plants that flower in summer are the Woody Pear (*Xylomelum angustifolium*) and Summer Copper Cups (*Pileanthus filifolius*).

Watheroo National Park straddles the Darling Fault Line. This is an important geological and botanical boundary. On one side is the ancient Western Australian Shield with granite rocks dating back to 2,500 million years old. This region is covered with fertile red soils, with occasional bedrock protrusions through the surface to create important granite outcrops, that have their own flora. Rich Kwongan heaths are interspersed with large areas of mallee country, but with the soil being more fertile, most of it has been cleared for farming.

On the western side of the fault line are the younger rocks and sands of the Dandaragan Plateau where Lesueur, Badgingarra, Alexander Morrison and Tathra are located. Watheroo is the only one that straddles this fault line.

Travelling along the Watheroo West Road you will climb up over the Darling escarpment. The range is low here in the northern part of the Darling Range. You pass through Wandoo and York Gum (*Eucalyptus loxophleba*) woodland and then drop down to a creek system that runs basically over the fault line itself. Then further on, the wildflower-rich Kwongan heath commences. You can return to the Midlands Road via Namban West road in the southern region of the park or via Marchagee Track in the north. Both roads pass through parts of the park.

One small area that is worth a visit is Jingemia Cave, just 5 km north of Watheroo. From Midlands Road turn west down Eagle Hill Road. The rock here is Noondine Chert and very different from the surrounding plains that are predominantly covered with mallees. The cave is located only about 150 m from the car park (there is a picnic table). Be careful of the fallen boulders. It is not recommended you try and enter this cave as there is a vertical shaft that was used for extracting the guano of bats and birds in the 1940s. It is, however, worth looking down into the collapsed cave entrance 20 m below. Taking a careful walk around the chert boulders, you will get good views across Watheroo Park looking west, but be careful when walking on plants as there is a rare rose flower (*Diplolaena* species) growing amongst the boulders.

Jingemia Cave

Ellendale Pool

Ellendale Pool is a small reserve about 40 km southeast of Geraldton. The area is maintained by the Greenough Shire. There is a picturesque pool that lies at the base of a high white cliff that runs alongside the Greenough River. There are barbecue and toilet facilities but it is not recommended that you swim in these waters in the very hot summer months as the water quality is questionable.

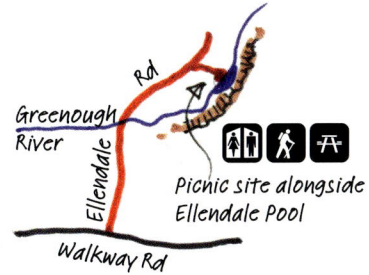

Ellendale Pool

Coalseam
CONSERVATION PARK

Coalseam is a small reserve north of Mingenew. This is a good spot to camp in if you are travelling in the area. In the park is the site of the first mined coal deposit in Western Australia. The Gregory brothers, in 1846, were looking for grazing lands for their sheep, but luckily the area was considered unsuitable. They reported their findings of coal in the park to the authorities and soon after it was mined. It proved, however, to be of a low grade and insufficient quantity to mine profitably.

The Irwin River cuts deeply through the sandstone and shale deposits, exposing coal seams near the base of the cliffs. It is at this lower level on one of the bends of the river below the cliffs that ancient marine fossils can be seen in the siltstone sediments. From the clifftop lookout there is a road that leads down to Fossil Car Park where there are examples of fossil deposits in the cliff face.

Looking down Irwin River

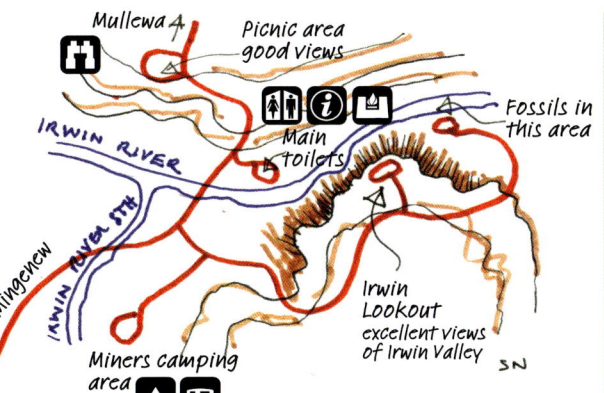

Lake Logue
NATURE RESERVE

This is a good reserve for plants and wetland birds that overlaps the Coolimba-Eneabba Road south west of Eneabba townsite. It protects an uncommon banksia, the Elegant Banksia (*Banksia elegans*). Adjacent to the reserve is Lake Indoon, which has picnic facilities and toilets and is managed by the Shire of Carnamah.

Lake Logue ▶

Stigmodera roei

Temognatha yarreli elegans

Castiarina quadrifasciata

Temognatha tricolorata

Castiarina thurmerae

Curis (species unidentified)

Stigmodera gratiosa

Melobasis (species unidentified)
All photos by David Knowles

Jewel Beetles of Western Australia

What is a Jewel Beetle?
Like all beetles, Jewel Beetles are characterised by having the forewings hardened to form a protective 'shell' over the hind-wings and abdomen. They do not have large prominent jaws or antennae, though their eyes are large and can see well. Their general body-form is elongated and slightly to strongly flattened. Almost all Jewel Beetles have some indication of metallic colouring somewhere on their bodies. Many species combine metallic colouration with bright red, yellow and orange pigments. From the human visual perspective the larger species are easy to classify as the living works of art we know as Jewel Beetles.

How big are they?
Jewel beetles range in size from 2 mm up to nearly 80 mm. The great majority are under 20 mm. Our largest species is *Julodimorpha bakewelli*.

How many species are in Western Australia and Australia?
Australia has approximately 1,500 species which is about one twelfth of the known world fauna. Western Australia has about one half of the known species occurring within its borders.

Where are they?
Jewel Beetles occur in almost all known habitats, from coastal dunes, mangroves, salt-lake margins, grasslands, sedgelands, shrublands to woodlands and forests.

When do you see them?
These beetles may be seen in almost all months of the year in this huge state. However there is a tropical peak of adult activity during and after the northern 'wet' and during spring and summer south of the Tropic.

How do you see them?
Jewel Beetles are most easily observed by humans from ground level up to eye height on foliage and flowers. Many of the larger species in the south can be seen in the mallee regions in summer flying to and from mallee blossom. This is mostly well above human height except in those areas where the mallee trees are low. A wander through a patch of low summer flowering mallee can expose the inquiring observer to one of the most spectacular Australian insect gatherings this country has to offer, especially when the flowers are inspected closely.

What is their ecological role?
Approximately 50% of our species are associated with flowers and the rest with foliage. The greatest number of flower-visiting species are best seen on the low growing members of the family Myrtaceae which includes eucalypts, 'paperbarks' and 'ti-trees'. Leaf-feeding species are most easily seen on acacia and Sheoak foliage. The flower-visiting species are involved with pollination, and have brush-like mouthparts, like many other nectar feeders, adapted to nectar feeding, as leaf-feeding species help control populations of certain plants by pruning. The larval or grub stages are involved in living, dead, or dying, wood recycling.

Are Jewel Beetles protected in WA?
The whole family has been protected in WA since 1978.

Mulga Parrot

Mulga in full bloom

The "Aussie" shearing shed

The Mulga

Inland from Mullewa, Morawa and Dalwallinu is a continuous 1,164 km long by 1.5 m high fence, known as the 'State Barrier Fence'. The fence itself stretches further than the length of the British Isles which gives you some idea of its dimensions. It was initially designed to keep out rabbits that had devastated crops in the Eastern States, and which were on the move west at an alarming rate in the early 1900s. It never succeeded as rabbits managed to get to the other side. It now restricts Dingo's and migrating Emus entering the south west.

The fence in the Mid West almost follows the start of the mulga country, that stretches way out into the edges of the western deserts. It is the demarcation line between where farmlands give way to sheep station country. It is also the demarcation line between the eucalypt dominated south west region and the acacia country. This change is based on the fact that rainfall for the acacia region often receives less than 200 mm of rain a year. When the mulga does receive good winter rains, however, the country can be transformed into a sea of colour. The plants that create these multi-coloured carpets of flowers are of course the 'everlastings', which have papery dry petals that do not dry out in the warm drying winds that occur after the rains.

There are many drives that one can take in the Mid West to experience the displays of everlastings and also numerous sheep stations that have accommodation or camping facilities on them—refer to page 189. This is not only a great way to see the country but one gets to meet station owners who are wonderful people, giving the traveller an insight into outback life away from the urban-dominated world many of us live in.

▲Galahs

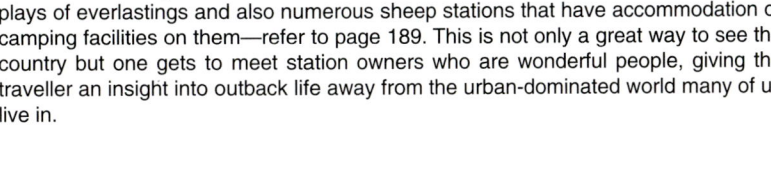
▲Crested Pigeon

▼Chestnut-rumped Thornbill ▼The everlastings in full bloom ▼Lonely grave in Mulga

Sooty Terns over their breeding colony

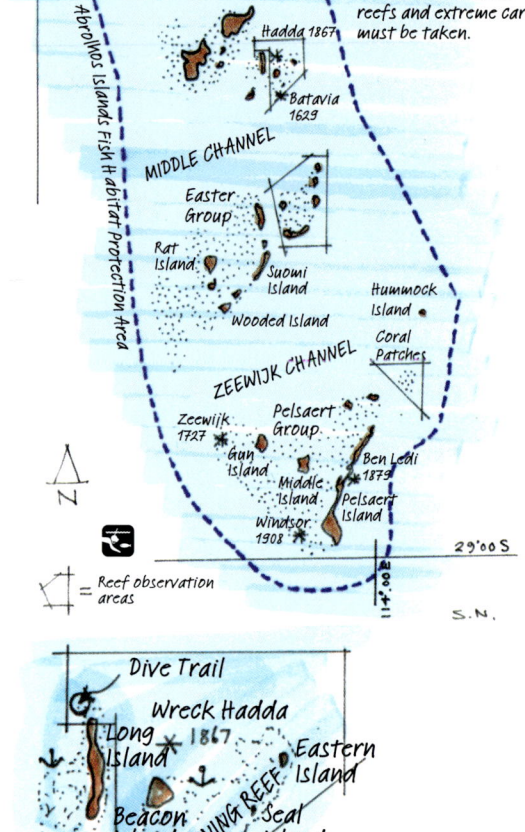

Lesser Noddys resting in the mangroves

Lesser Noddy

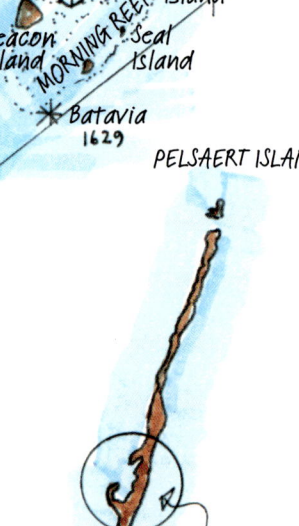

The Abrolhos Islands

The Houtman Abrolhos Islands lie 60 km west of Geraldton. There are 122 islands split into 3 main groups: Wallabi, Easter and Pelsaert Group.

Most of the year these islands remain relatively undisturbed until the months of March, April and May when the rock lobster season commences. This industry is very important to the local fishing industry and the catch in one year can exceed 1,000 tonnes. There are strong controls on the length of the season, the number of available licenses and the areas where people can fish.

Recently, 4 areas have been set aside for conservation and there will in time be areas that become full marine parks. Within these 4 areas, diving for pleasure is allowed but taking of any marine life is prohibited except under conditions relating to lobster fishing. Refer to the sketch map for details, but seek further advice from the Fisheries department and/or DCLM in Geraldton.

The reefs of the Abrolhos occur at these latitudes primarily due to the warm Leeuwin Current that starts in April and finishes in October, bringing with it nutrient-rich marine life as food for fish and lobster alike. It is here that both tropical and temperate marine life cross over.

The Abrolhos are also vitally important as breeding grounds for many species of birds. Some colonies have many thousands of birds. Let's look at Pelsaert Island which the author has visited many times. It is a long, narrow island, being 12 km long and 40-500 m wide, and rises above the high water mark by only a few metres. It is composed of limestone sand, coral boulders and shingle. The island is mostly bare but the more vegetated part in the south, is covered in annual herbs and grasses.

Over 60 species of birds have been recorded for Pelsaert Island alone. One of the most important breed-

Please note this is an "A" class nature and marine reserve – notification should be made to CALM prior to your visitation.

ing colonies on the island is that of the Lesser Noddy. It is confined to the Indian Ocean and is known to breed in two locations, one colony in the Seychelles Islands and the other in the Abrolhos Islands of Pelsaert, Woody Island and Morley Island.

The naturalist John Gilbert recorded the Lesser Noddy colony on Pelsaert Island in 1842, then inexplicably it disappeared in the early 1900s, although there was a very small colony on Woody Island. In 1936 the colony was re-established on Pelsaert and has reached numbers of 27,000 nests. The Lesser Noddy nests in the White Mangrove *(Avicennia marina)*.

Other birds that breed on Pelsaert are Common Noddy, Bridled Tern, Sooty Tern, Roseate Tern, Fairy Tern, Crested Tern, Caspian Tern, Silver Gull, Pacific Gull, Wedge-tailed Shearwater, Little Shearwater, Red-tailed Tropicbird, White-bellied Sea Eagle and Osprey.

Other fauna that can be seen here are the large King Skink *(Egernia kingii)* and the Australian Sea-lion *(Neophoca cinerea)*.

This chain of islands is known also for the many wrecks that have occurred on its reefs and at least 18 wrecks are known. The most published and horrendous story was that of the Batavia which in the early hours of 4 June 1629 ran aground on Morning Reef, near Beacon Island in the Wallabi group. The lookout mistook the white breakers as moonshine on the water. The vessel carried 316 people consisting of crew, passengers and soldiers and a fortune in valuable cargo. This proved to be the catalyst that created the troubles to come. Even though the boat was wrecked, it was possible to get all the passengers onto one of the small islands. While this was occurring a mutiny was being planned by several of the crew. Captain Pelsaert organised the ship's sloop to sail all the way to Batavia (now Jakarta), over 2,500 km to the north, with a small complement of crew and passengers. While Pelsaert was gone on this major journey, the most appalling atrocities occurred, with the rape and murder of 125 of the surviving men, women and children. A courageous resistance was given by Weibbe Hayes and the soldiers on another island to fend off the mutineer.

When Pelsaert returned in the 'Sardam' three months later, his vessel was intercepted by the soldiers who explained the atrocious events that had occurred. Many of the mutineers were tried and executed on the same islands. The mutiny on the Bounty is well known in world terms but the story and drama of the Batavia is far more gripping in terms of events and atrocities that occurred. The book 'Islands of Angry Ghosts' by Hugh Edwards gives a fascinating and chilling account of this tragic story.

There are excellent dive sites on the islands, although many are moderate to difficult dives. Beacon Island has some good dive sites and off the northern end of Long Island in the Wallabi group, there is a marked dive trail with information plaques. These waters can be quite dangerous for boats, particularly as the weather can change so quickly, hence the many wrecks. There are a few dive vessels that leave from Geraldton and most know the waters very well. For more information on the Abrolhos, contact the Geraldton Tourist Bureau.

The Kalbarri Kwongon heath in full bloom

Sunset on the cliffs at Red Bluff

Murchison Gorge

Kalbarri
NATIONAL PARK

Kalbarri National Park is one of the most popular parks in Western Australia and for good reason, as it has some outstanding scenery. It is just under 600 km north of Perth and covers 186,071 hectares, making it one of the state's largest parks.

Here, the 500 km long Murchison River has cut through rocks known as Tumblagooda Sandstone, to create spectacular gorges with multi-coloured sedimentary sands stained by iron oxides. The sandstone was laid down 400 million years ago. It contains some of the finest fossils in the country, giving evidence of our early marine creatures like the amphibious arthropods, which often left footprints in the fossil sandstone beds. On some of the walks, you will see a rippled surface on the sandstone rocks, evidence of tidal waters on the ancient sand beds.

The entrance to the park is 19 km off the North West Coastal Highway and then a further 47 km to the township of Kalbarri on the coast. There are several lookouts that view the Murchison Gorge, including Ross Graham, Hawks Head, Z Bend and The Loop, with the well known rock formation of 'Nature's Window'. The roads at present are sand/gravel and often badly corrugated, so if you can leave caravans at Kalbarri it would help.

You can walk to the base of the gorge at several of the locations and tracks are signposted. At the Loop there is a 1.5 km return walk with stairs to 'Nature's Window' accessible by most people. If you are fit and well prepared, there is a

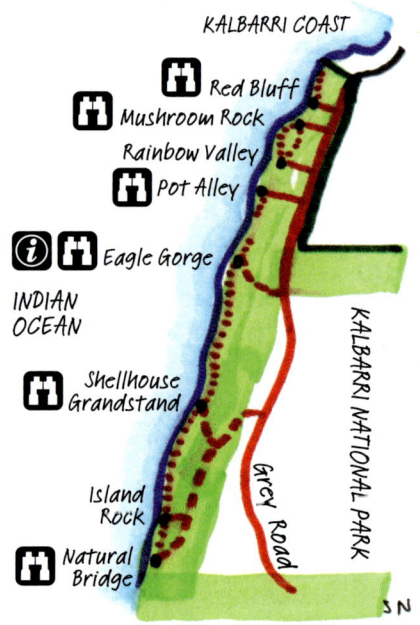
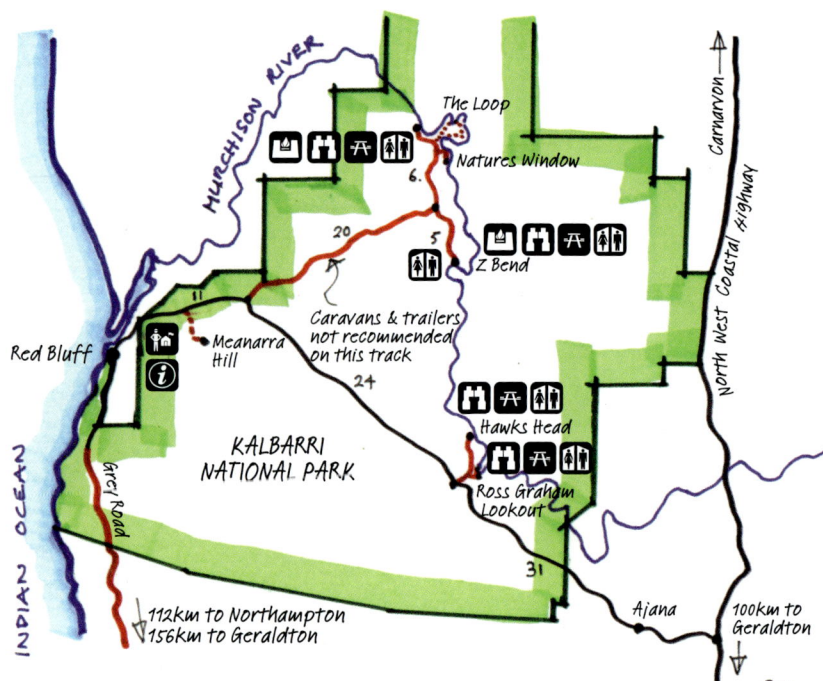

very good walk around the loop and back; this will take 3 hours and is approximately 7 km, and well worth it. At the Z Bend you can carry on down the steep gully to the pools below, but you must be agile to do it. It is a good area to swim on a hot day.

At Ross Graham Lookout there is an easier, shorter walk to the gorge river. Most people, however, are content to enjoy the views from the lookout at Hawks Head.

The coastal drive from Port Gregory an all-weather road and this will makes a wonderful scenic drive. Just south of Kalbarri and in the national park itself are several coastal walks and lookouts and in the evening light the colours on the cliff face make wonderful viewing. You can commence at the first lookout at Red Bluff and then visit several more as far as Natural Bridge lookout. At Mushroom Rock there is a 2 hr nature trail with information along the way. Overnight hiking (no facilities) in the Murchison River gorge is permitted but you must register at the DCLM office for advice and information.

Wildflowers have been discussed at some length in this section of the book but here at Kalbarri some mention must be made, as the park is noted for its exceptional wildflower displays from mid-July through until early October, although there are still many flowers out in the early summer. There are over 800 species in this park, a few being found nowhere else. The winter months are the time to see many of the 40 odd species of orchid in the park. In early spring the kangaroo paws will be out, including the endemic Kalbarri Catspaw (*Anigozanthos kalbarriensis*).

As you drive along the main Kalbarri road, you will pass many long-stemmed White Plume Grevilleas (*Grevillea leucopteris*) as well as other species like Acorn Banksia (*Banksia prionotes*), Sceptre Banksia (*Banksia sceptrum*), the lovely woolly, Lambswool (*Lachnostachys eriobotrya*) and Pink Pokers (*Grevillea petrophiloides*). In late spring, the brightly coloured featherflowers are out, with the pink of the Woolly Featherflower (*Verticordia monadelpha*), the yellow of the featherflower (*Verticordia nobilis*) and the White Northern Cauliflower (*Verticordia polytricha*) making a wonderful display.

Shark Bay
WORLD HERITAGE REGION

Shark Bay was declared a World Heritage area not because it has high mountains or spectacular gorges. It was recognised for the pristine environment of its marine waters and the location of some rare animals and plants on land. When the early naturalists and explorers like Dirk Hartog, William Dampier and Nicolas Baudin made their sweeping statements deriding this coastline, they never would have envisaged that it would become such an important refuge for wildlife and a destination for many tourists.

The country does, however, have a beauty of its own and that is the vista of red sand dunes that meet with the clear blue seas of Shark Bay. It is the sea that holds many of the treasures that make this a very special place. In these waters are some of the most extensive and diverse seagrass meadows anywhere in the world and this makes it a haven for such important creatures as dugongs, turtles, dolphins and many types of fish. At the base of Hamelin Pool is also one of the world's most famous living examples of the ancient life form of stromatolites.

At Monkey Mia one can experience the joy of seeing the amazing interaction between wild Bottlenose Dolphins and people. You can drive into 4WD country at Francois Peron National Park, camp and fish on pristine beaches, often having areas all to yourself.

Boating people will be in their element, sailing the clear blue waters, catching fish and visiting remote beaches. Yes, there are many ways to enjoy this unique region.

Monkey Mia Reserve

Since 1960, both individual and groups of Bottlenose Dolphins (*Tursiops truncatus*) have been coming to Monkey Mia of their own free choice. It started when fishermen, returning with their daily catch, would throw the odd fish to the dolphins. Over the years a dozen or so individuals have been returning on a daily basis, sometimes only one or two a day. The interesting fact is that they are members of a large pod of more than 100 dolphins, yet no more than a dozen adults and young will come in to feed. This may be one of the sub-groups that exist in the pod. Sub-groups have their own feeding range, but members interchange from one group to another, especially for breeding purposes. They also are long-lived, living up to 30 years. We often connect well with dolphins as they speed along in the bow wave of a boat. To watch them suddenly turn in unison and surf on a high wave towards a beach and then pull out at the last minute is truly a magnificent sight. One thing they can do that we cannot without heavy equipment is dive down to great depths, as deep as 500 m, to get fish.

There is an area set aside to view the dolphins on the beach. No boats or swimmers are allowed in this small zone. There is normally a ranger present and he or she guides how close you can be. Also they are the only people allowed to feed the dolphins or they select persons to do so. They welcome sensible questions and are most helpful. There are some basic rules, however, that should be followed.

Follow the instructions of the ranger. Stand in the water to adult knee level. Wait for the dolphins to approach you – do not wade out to meet them. DO NOT TOUCH THE DOLPHINS, even though the temptation is very strong. Try to avoid using sunscreen on your hands and legs whilst with the dolphins as this irritates their eyes.

Dolphins are highly intelligent animals and like human beings can become intolerant or upset, so observe the rangers and heed their suggestions.

Putting the rules aside, it is a wonderful experience to witness this occurrence by such beautiful, intelligent mammals, something you will never forget.

Bottlenose Dolphins range considerably in size from 2 m to 3 m. The Shark Bay individuals are smaller in size than those found in the south west. They are not the only Dolphin to be found in Western Australia waters with at least 9 other species being recorded. The Common Dolphin *(Delphinus delphis)* and the Bottlenose Dolphin are the most numerous.

There is a large camping, caravan and accommodation area adjacent to the feeding beach but it does get full in the high season and the township of Denham has a great selection of accommodation only 25 km away.

In the sand dunes behind the main beach area there is an interesting walk. It is a relatively easy walk of 1.5 km and gives an insight into some of the history and wildlife of the area. There is a lonely grave of young Hilda Johnstone who died on a vessel travelling from Carnarvon to Perth. Her father became Surveyor General for WA in the early 1900s. A lookout gives good views of the blue waters set against the red sand dunes. Besides the common birds that may be seen here, this is the best locality in Australia for seeing a very uncommon species, the Thick–billed Grasswren *(Amytornis textilis)*. It sometimes scurries around the main parking area, quite amazing considering how, in other parts of Australia, Thick–billed Grasswrens, as well as the other 8 species in this genus, are so hard to see.

For the fisherman, there is a main boat ramp and boat trailer parking area. There is also a very good information centre.

Thick-billed Grasswren

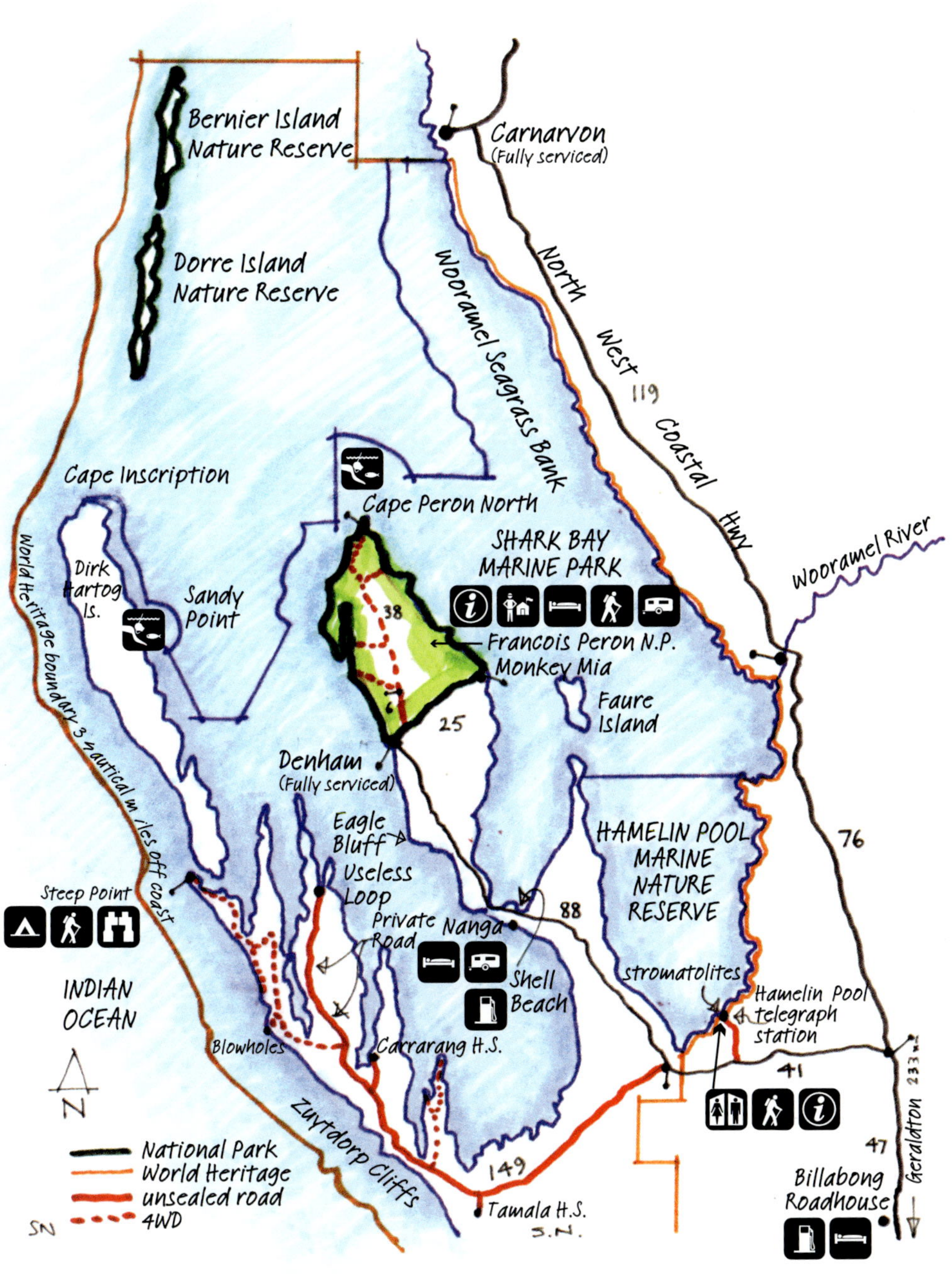

Shark Bay World Heritage Region

Dolphin paying the tourists a visit at Monkey Mia

Francois Peron
NATIONAL PARK

The park is named after the naturalist Francois Peron who sailed on the ship the 'Geographe' under the captaincy of Nicolas Baudin. He visited Peron Peninsula twice, once in 1801 and again in 1803. He was an indefatigable collector, sending over 100,000 specimens back to France.

Peron Peninsula was, until recently, a sheep station which was purchased by the state in 1990. It was gazetted a National Park in 1993, so it is a relatively recent acquisition. DCLM took on the management of the northern 52,500 ha of the station.

You can take 2WD to the homestead itself but the rest of the park is very much restricted to 4WD and tyres should be let down to at least 18 lbs, as there is a great deal of very soft sand on many of the tracks. There is a 1 km walk around the homestead and visitors are allowed to have a dip in the warm artesian pool.

Throughout the park there are claypans known as 'birridas'; do not attempt to drive on them as you may not get out. Underneath the hard-looking surface is often thick soft mud that can be quite deep. You can snorkel at Gregories Reef or fish at one of the many beach locations. No wood fires are allowed.

There are countless beaches ideal for fishing in Francois Peron National Park

Shark Bay Marine Park & Hamelin Pool Marine Nature Park

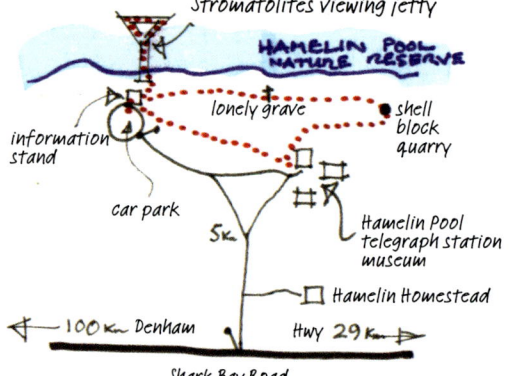

These two marine reserves cover a huge area of 9,510 square km. Within this area there are, the famous dolphins that visit Monkey Mia most days, the stromatolites of Hamelin Pool, the pure white shells on Shell Beach, some wonderful diving and snorkelling sites; and some of the best recreational fishing in Australia. It is no wonder that the existence of this marine environment was one of the major deciding factors for the area being included in the World Heritage List.

The clear, shallow waters of these marine reserves have some of the most extensive seagrass meadows in the world. They also contain the greatest number of seagrass species. Seagrass is not a seaweed but actually an underwater flowering plant with male and female plants. They have a strong root system, unlike seaweeds that have no roots or flowers and in fact are an algae. You may ask what is so important about seagrass. Well, they are the home and breeding ground for many fish and they provide vital food for the Dugong or sea cow, as well as supporting a whole ecology of marine life which is reliant on this type of underwater vegetation.

The Dugong is an almost totally herbivorous marine mammal feeding primarily on the seagrasses. They are timid creatures being mainly solitary, except when with young, and have been recorded to live up to 70 years. They have been hunted for their meat in many parts of the world and close relatives like the Steller's sea cow were hunted to extinction. Here, luckily, they are relatively safe with an estimated population of around 10,000. Shark Bay is the farthest south these mammals can be found. If you are in a boat, do not chase these creatures as they stress very easily. If you wish to observe them, cut your engine and float past, and they may even come up and look at you.

Hamelin Pool and the living fossils, stromatolites

Not far from the North West Highway off Denham/Hamelin road is the southern bay of Hamelin Pool. You will first come across the old buildings of the Hamelin Telegraph Station, established in 1884 as a telegraph repeater station for the Perth to Roebourne line. You can visit the tourist centre and there is also a camping and caravaning site. A few hundred metres from here is the edge of Hamelin Pool, a very shallow, highly saline part of Shark Bay, having twice the salinity of the ocean.

Here there are some of the most interesting structures of stromatolites in the world. DCLM has built an excellent walking jetty with information boards that allows observation without damaging the structures.

Stromatolites, in simple terms, are structures created by minute micro-organisms that slowly over time build up into these dome-shaped structures. The structure consists of several types of micro-organisms and scientists call this a 'microbial community'. Some of the very first life forms similar to those that have created these structures, have been found in the rock structures of the Pilbara region estimated to be 3.5 million years old.

Stromatolites grow at an incredibly slow rate, estimated to be approx. 5 mm per year, so many of the domes here would be up to 1,000 years old. They also vary in structure and content relative to their position at the shoreline, as different groups of micro-organisms work best at different water levels.

Thousands of years ago stromatolites were one of the dominant life forms on earth but now they are restricted to these high saline locations with little water circulation. It is thought that because there are few grazing fish that feed on algae and seaweeds here, due to the water being too shallow and also too saline, the stromatolites are able to survive and grow.

After visiting the stromatolites walkway, you may be interested in looking at the shell block quarry near the Hamelin Pool Telegraph Station.

Stromatolites

Diving & Snorkelling in Shark Bay

The Shark Bay region has some very good dive sites and the Denham Tourist Information centre will be able to assist here with the location and which operators go out to the dive sites. The best time to dive in this region is in the winter and spring months, when the winds are less strong than the summer months, plus temperatures all round are better. Summer brings the added danger of cyclonic weather. Tides in this region are very strong at times, so always dive on a slack tide and unless you are very experienced you should go with the local tour charter boats who know the area well and who know the local water conditions, as well as the best time to dive.

One of the most interesting wrecks in this region is Gudron which was wrecked in 1901. It is the largest wooden vessel sunk in Western Australian waters. There is a fascinating story attached to this, as the ship was sunk by the ship's carpenter, who drilled a hole in the hull and subsequently scuttled the ship.

This site, however, can have strong currents and if you are a novice diver then go with a charter boat. There are several dive sites around Shark Bay and also DCLM have produced two very useful guidebooks on the various dive sites in Western Australia, including this area.

Fishing in Shark Bay

Shark Bay is one of Western Australia's best angling localities but over the last few years there has been a decline in certain fish species, particularly Pink Snapper. Fisheries of WA introduced a new Fisheries Management Plan to rebuild fish stocks in the inner gulf of Shark Bay. So, besides the normal state bag limits, there are specific fish limits and sizes in the Shark Bay area, plus there are waters where fishing is restricted or prohibited. Do check with the local Fisheries Department before commencing fishing, particularly from boats. Notwithstanding the above, there is still great fishing to be had from this fantastic region.

Shell Beach Conservation Park

Shell Beach lies about 45 km south of Denham where the Peron Peninsula forms a very narrow isthmus. It is an interesting beach in so much as it is totally covered in small white shells. It consists almost entirely of the shell of one species named Hamelin Cockle *(Fragum erugatum)*. Some of the beaches in L'Haridon Bight are up to 1 km wide and 8-10 m thick with compressed shells of this particular species and scientists knowing the dimensions and thickness of these shells estimate that it has been occurring over the last 5,000 years.

The reason why so many shells die and accumulate here is that there is a sand bank known as Faure Sill that slowly, with time, restricted access of tidal movements into Hamelin Pool and L'Haridon Bight. This increased the salinity to almost twice that of the ocean and although the cockle could adjust and survive in such saline conditions, the various crabs and other marine life that fed on cockles could not and hence the cockles over the last few thousand years have lived in higher densities.

On the foreshore the shells are loose and can be easily picked up with one's hands but as you go back to the rear of the beaches, the shells have compacted into a solid mass, that is known by geologists as 'coquinite'.

Millions of tiny white cockle shell cover Shell Beach

Project Eden

Just a short distance south of the turn-off to Shell Beach, is a 2.4 m high and 3.4 km electric fence. Why is it here? Well, DCLM has embarked on a major project to eradicate the introduced animals that have decimated the natural Australian fauna. The project aims to keep feral animals south of the fence and out of the Peron Peninsula and to reintroduce those animals that once existed on the peninsula but which have become locally extinct in the last hundred years. The primary culprits for the loss of our fauna are the European Red Fox and the Feral Cat. Both have played a major role in eliminating many of our birds and mammals over the years, so much so that Western Australia has lost 10 mammal species on the mainland. Many of the older Aborigines recognise some of the specimen skins of the now extinct mammals that are held at the Western Australian Museum, and can recall when they were prevalent in the early 1950s.

To assist in bringing back the Peron Peninsula to some resemblance of its original habitat and wildlife distribution, more than 30,000 sheep and goats were removed from north of the fence. This will allow the reintroduced fauna to survive better without having to compete for food with these efficient grazers of the native vegetation.

In 1995, DCLM began a massive aerial baiting program. It decimated the fox population and to a degree affected the cat population. Alas the feral cat is one of the hardest feral creatures to eradicate and special baiting techniques are being developed. With the dramatic loss of foxes, the cat increased, as foxes will take the young feral cats. Another major baiting program was geared towards the cat and it has been fairly successful taking out approx. 70-80% of the cat population at this stage.

The vermin barrier fence that crosses near Shell Beach

Some of the mammals to be returned over time are the Western Barred Bandicoot *(Perameles bougainville)*, Woylie or Brush-tailed Bettong *(Bettongia penicillata)*, Rufous Hare-wallaby *(Lagorchestes hirsutus)*, Shark Bay Mouse *(Pseudomys fieldi)* and Banded Hare-wallaby *(Lagostrophus fasciatus)*. Woylie *(Betonggia pencillta)*, Greater Bilby *(Macrotis lagotis)*. The Malleefowl has also been returned to the peninsula. Hopefully, over the next few years, this country will have some of these animals return, that were almost lost forever.

Looking across Dales Gorge–Karijini National Park

Pilbara
REGION

Pilbara
REGION

This is a land of ancient rocks even older than the Kimberley, rich in minerals such as iron, copper, tin, gold, manganese and asbestos and in many ways, that is what most people think of when they talk of the north west. To many who know it well, it is a land of stark beauty with numerous rugged ranges like the Hamersley Range, Cape Range, Kennedy Range, Collier Range, Chichester Range and the huge monocline Mount Augustus, combined with one of the finest reef systems in Australia.

You can travel this whole region making one grand circular tour.

Starting from the town of Carnarvon head north to Coral Bay; the surrounding country is certainly not breathtaking here but the opportunities to fish, dive and snorkel are fantastic. Unlike Queensland's Great Barrier Reef where you often have to take long boat journeys to get to the outer reef, here you just head off the beach and within minutes you can look down on the clear Ningaloo coral reefs with an amazing variety of fish.

Further up the Ningaloo Reef coast, with more opportunities for fishing and diving, The Cape Range National Park provides the rugged backdrop of Cape Range.

North is the Dampier Archipelago with 42 islands, many being remote and rarely visited. The fishing is exceptional and professional tourist boats can take you to some of these islands.

Numerous rock carvings throughout this region are testament to the long habitation of this land by the Yapurarra and Martuyhinira Aboriginal people.

Leaving the coast south east of Roebourne, you enter the beautiful Chichester Ranges, then off the Wittenoom road is Millstream with its permanent pools lined with the Millstream Fan-palms (Livistona alfredii) and the magnificent Cadjeput trees (Melaleuca leucadendra).

Climbing higher you enter one of the most spectacular parks in Western Australia, Karijini National Park, with its many deep gorges and waterfalls with permanent pools. It also has the highest mountain in WA, Mt Meharry.

From the town of Newman, there are lots of options. For example, either head north via Marble Bar and up to Port Hedland or head south down the Great Northern Highway. For those wishing to travel to the Rudall River, you must have a 4WD and be well prepared and self-sufficient. Notify Newman police and ideally DCLM of your intentions. This park although magnificent is very remote, with numerous internal tracks, and you should be experienced in 4WD driving techniques.

If you wish to complete your circular tour, then you would head west towards Mt Augustus via Three Rivers Station and Mulgul Station. Up until this point most areas can be traversed with 2WD vehicles but now you are on station country. Roads are rough and vehicles are few and far between such that 4WD vehicles are safer here. Care must be taken particularly if rain is imminent. Also, you travel through many private properties with numerous sidetracks, so be careful with your directions and please close all closed gates (ie. leave the gate as you find it).

Mt Augustus is a huge monocline rock greater in volume than Uluru (Ayers Rock) with many interesting walks, one of them to the summit, but it's long and only for the very fit.

Cutting across country you can next visit the Kennedy Range National Park, with its dramatic rock formations below a 75 km long sandstone mesa, with a continuous cliff face over 100 m high.

Finally your journey ends where you began in Carnarvon. Obviously this is an overall guide describing the region in general terms; there are, however, so many different places to visit and routes to take, the options are endless.

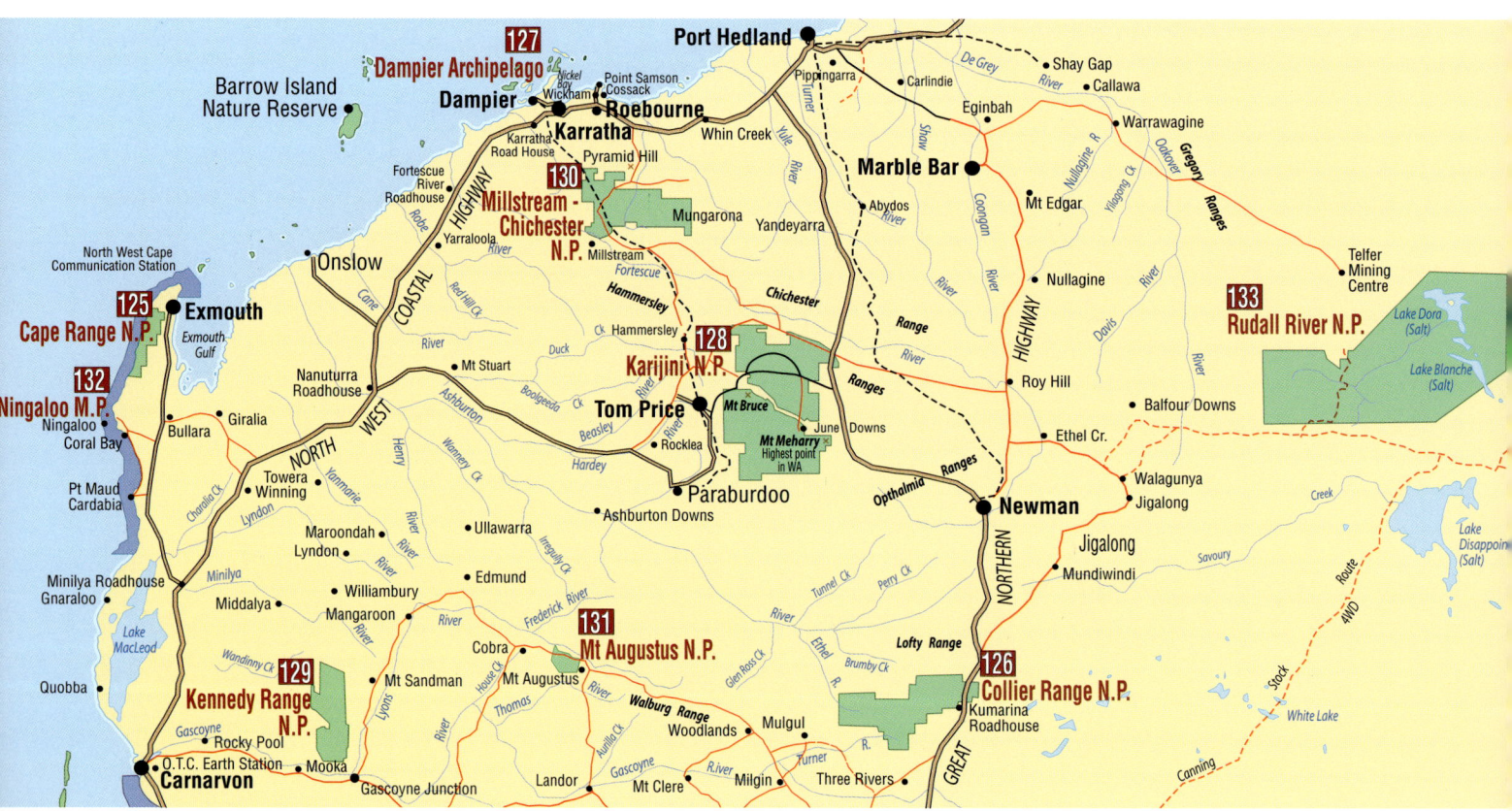

Ningaloo
MARINE PARK

Multi-coloured corals

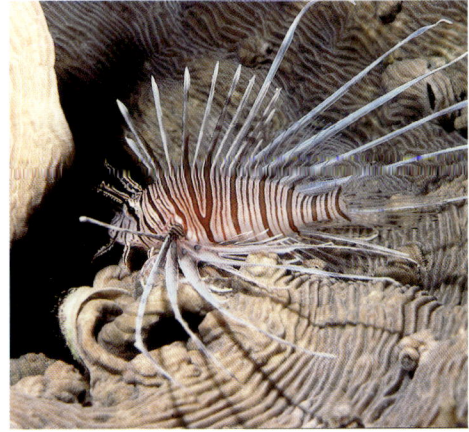
Butterfly Cod or Lion Fish

Whale Shark

Diving over Western Australia's coral reefs

Scorpion Fish

Manta Ray ▶
All photos on this page by Chris Powell

Along the North West Cape, there is a 260 km long fringing barrier reef stretching from Bundegi Reef in the south to just north of Jurabi Point in Cape Range National Park. The reef as yet is not well known in world terms but it will be over time, for there are some magnificent coral reefs that in some places are just a few metres from the shoreline, needing no long boat journeys to see them. It also has the added benefit that there is no major industry or agricultural pollution to damage this fragile environment unlike other reef systems. However, just as our land parks need pro-tection, so too do our marine parks.

Ningaloo Reef is a 224,000 ha marine park that encompasses both State and Commonwealth waters, and there are strong conservation laws in place to protect it. There are 3 managed zones: 1. General Use Zone: This area basically allows for general commercial fishing with appropriate licences and private fishing where Department of Fisheries regulations re bag limit and size apply (refer to their recreational guide to fishing regulations). 2. Recreation Zone: No commercial fishing, only recreational fishing. 3. Sanctuary Zone: There is strictly no fishing of any kind in this zone. It is really like a giant aquarium, where people can view and wonder at the multitude of corals and fish as well as protecting the breeding stocks of all marine life.

Coral reefs are primarily built from 'hard corals' which are microscopic living organisms called polyps. They are carnivorous invertebrate animals that feed mainly on zooplankton. They develop a hard limestone skeletal case to support them and also protect them. Over the years the corals die leaving solid limestone structures from which the new corals have a base to grow.

Besides the main hard corals, there are other forms of coral such as 'soft coral'; these, as the name implies, are soft and do not have the hard outside casing instead having soft stems that are reinforced with a multitude of hard microscopic particles, giving the stems a form of skeletal structure. Soft corals are most impressive at greater depths between 10 and 30 m.

Other wonderful groups of corals exist, such as whip corals, fan corals, lace corals, blue and black corals. In fact there are at least 250 species of coral on Ningaloo reef. There are also 500 species of fish and 600 species of molluscs (sea shells and sea slugs).

For the fisherman the main target species are Northwest Snapper, Coral Trout, Yellow-tailed Emperor, Red Emperor, Baldchin Groper, Black-spot Sea Perch and Sweetlips.

We have discussed some of the smaller marine life forms but what of the larger marine life? Well you cannot get much bigger than whales and the Humpback Whale passes this coastline on its way to breed in the northern tropical waters in autumn. It spends more time at Ningaloo on its return from the tropical waters to the Antarctic around mid-August into September.

Whales, as we all know, are mammals, but there is also a massive fish that frequents these waters and that is the Whale Shark. It is totally harmless to humans feeding on nutrient rich plankton and small fish. They attain lengths of up to 12 m and weights of up to 10 tonnes.

One of the major reasons divers come to Ningaloo, between mid-March and mid-June, is to experience the sheer wonder of swimming with these gigantic, peaceful Whale Sharks, as well as other large fish like Manta Rays.

Off this coast there are nearly 20 shipwrecks dating from the wreck of the 'Rapid', a 366 tonne wooden ship wrecked in 1811, to the Norwegian freighter, Cofuku Maru wrecked in 1931.

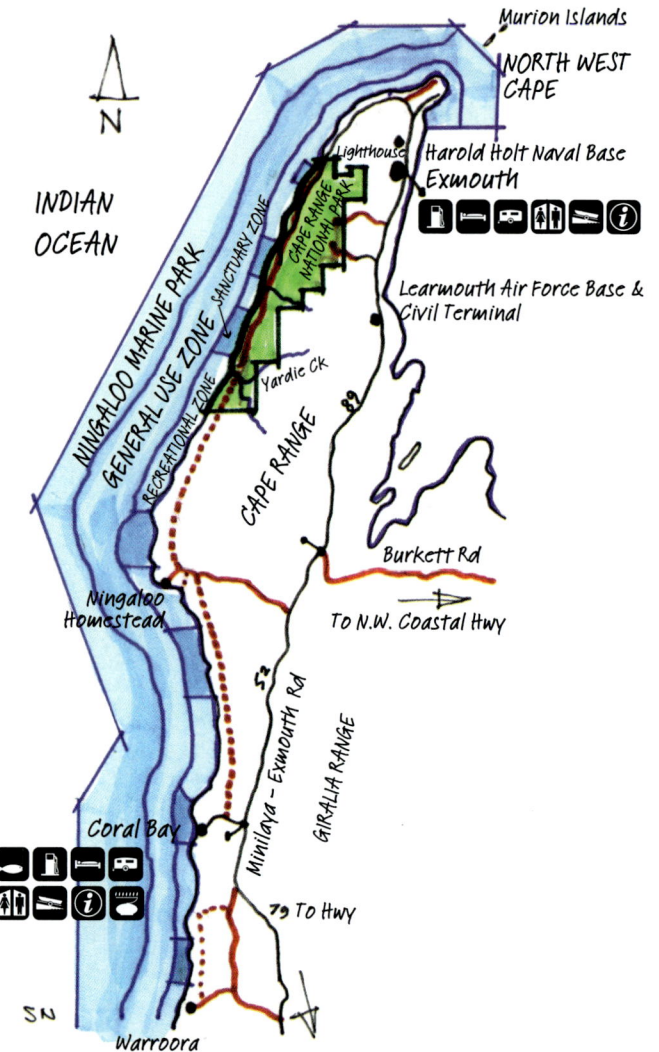

Coral Bay

This is a great place to start your journey on the North West Cape. It is, however, getting very crowded in peak season as so many people wish to stay here. The snorkelling here is easy and well protected from the main outside reef, but do be careful of boats. Also the area is predominantly free of sharks. There are hotel and motel accommodation and caravan parks. There are glass bottom boats for coral viewing and other fishing charter boats, and snorkel gear is available for hire, so there is lots to do here. A DCLM ranger is resident in the high tourist season from April to October.

Cape Range
NATIONAL PARK

The Cape Range is a limestone ridge that rises to 314 m and forms the central spine of the North West Cape. Here, you can enjoy camping on quiet beaches, fish from a boat or shore, snorkel only metres from the beach in the clear blue waters or walk in the many rugged gorges that lead into the central spine of the range.

The southern boundary of the park is 70 km north of Coral Bay and the northern boundary just 39 km from Exmouth. Besides the tourist centre in Exmouth, there is a very good information centre within the park itself at Milyering. Here the DCLM staff can assist you with camping information, walking trails, where you can fish and the best places to snorkel and dive.

Dive sites in the park

Pilgraunna dive site is about 22 km south of the Information Centre; it is an excellent dive for all levels, has easy vehicle access, and there are 6 camping bays.

Even though the reef is only 150 m long and no more than 10 m from the shore, there is very good marine life here.

Turquoise Bay dive site is about 10 km south of the Information Centre. There are 7 camping bays and it is an excellent dive for all levels, with reasonable access – just walk 200 m north from the car park and enter the beach, swimming north parallel with the beach. Here you will see the bombies (massive coral domes, Porites species), swim around them as they are often near the surface.

Lakeside Bombies dive site is near the Information Centre. Just go north from the centre and turn left to T-bone Bay and then left again to Lakeside, park and then walk 500 m south. The first bombies are approx. 30 m out. This site is good for all levels but exercise some caution here as currents can be strong from south to north, so the dive can be difficult if conditions are not good.

Mandu Mandu Creek

Milyering Visitor Centre

Looking into the gorge from Charles Knife Road

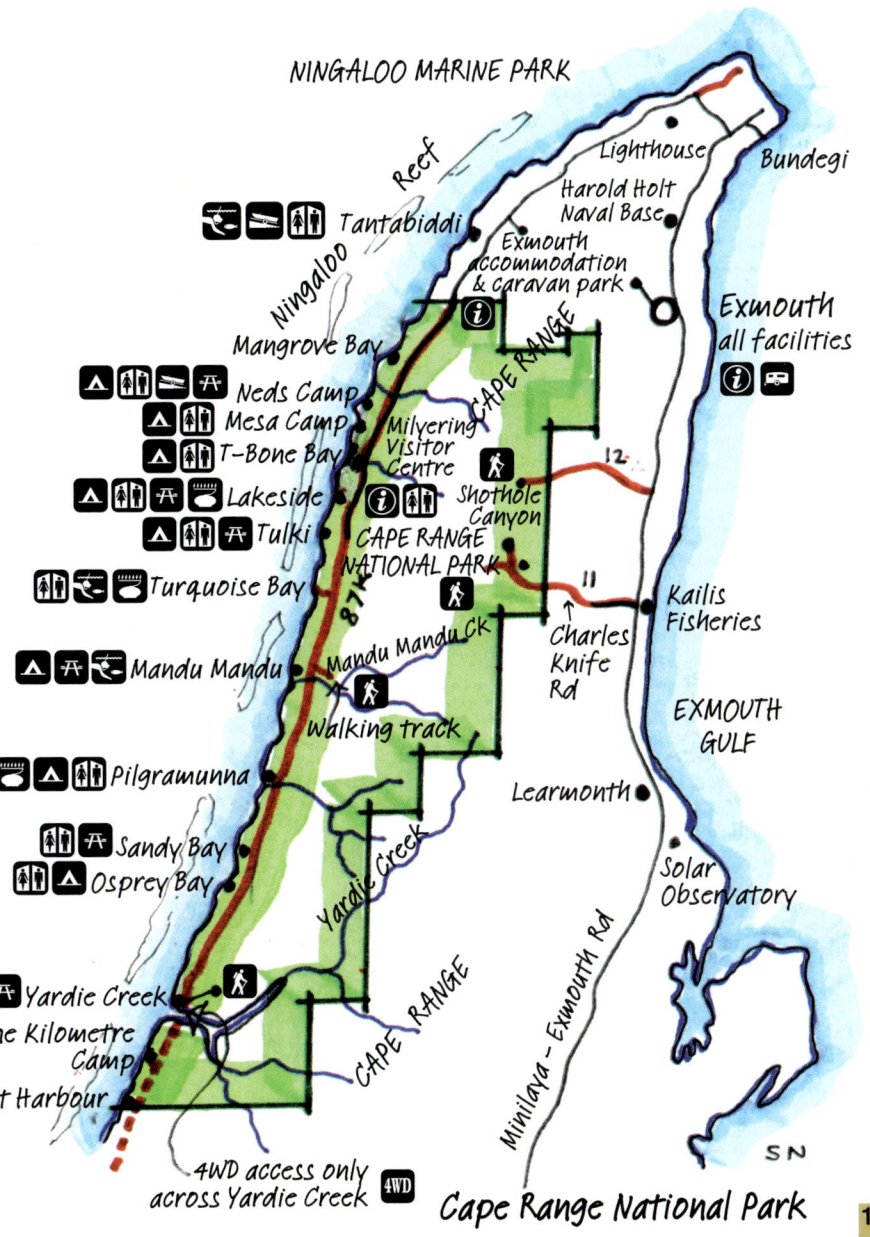
Cape Range National Park

Snorkelling is a fantastic way to see the coral but if you are inexperienced, try and swim with those who are more experienced and never swim alone. Be careful of currents and plan to dive on the slack tide. During an outgoing tide the current strength increases. The Information Centre will help with which areas are safest for beginners. Also, do not touch the coral particularly 'fire coral' because it can sting.

Walking trails

Before you commence any walk in the Cape Range National Park, remember it is waterless, rugged and temperatures can be deceptive even in the winter months, so take plenty of water. It is always wise to drink at least half a litre of water before any walk even if you don't feel like it at the time. All longer walks should only be done between April and September.

Shothole Canyon A 250 m, 3/4 hr return walk. It is a steep climb, so be careful, but it gives great views. To access it, walk from Shothole Canyon Road. The turn-off is 14 km south of Exmouth on the eastern side of Exmouth Peninsula. There are picnic tables at the end of Shothole Canyon Road.

Bird Hide Walk A short 10 min. return walk from Mangrove Bay car park to the bird hide. There will not always be birds here but it is worth a look. It's best when the tide is out.

Yardie Creek Walk This is 38 km south of the Information Centre and 500 m from Yardie Creek picnic area and goes to a limestone ledge. You can continue on a more rugged track which is a 1.5 km return walk on the north side of the gorge. It's a great place to see the Black–footed Rock-wallaby (Petrogale lateralis) on the southern rock face. Stop at the end of the creek and return. Yardie Creek, for many, is the most interesting area to visit in the Cape Range.

Mandu Mandu Walk This is a 3 km return walk, and it is 15 km south of the Information Centre at Mandu Mandu car park. The walk winds its way on the north side of Mandu Mandu Gorge and after a small steep-sided creek that you have to go up and down, the rest is along the gorge edge—be careful. You can look down into the gorge and back out to sea. You then can turn back from the first high area or keep walking until the track takes you into the stony gorge gully, and walk along the dry creek bed. In the early morning you may see Common Wallaroo or Euro (Macropus robustus) on this walk.

If you do not wish to take walks but would like to experience the ridge tops, they can be accessed from south of Exmouth on either the Shothole Canyon Road or the Charles Knife Road. Be careful as the roads are narrow for passing vehicles and the roadsides drop away steeply. However, there are some spectacular views.

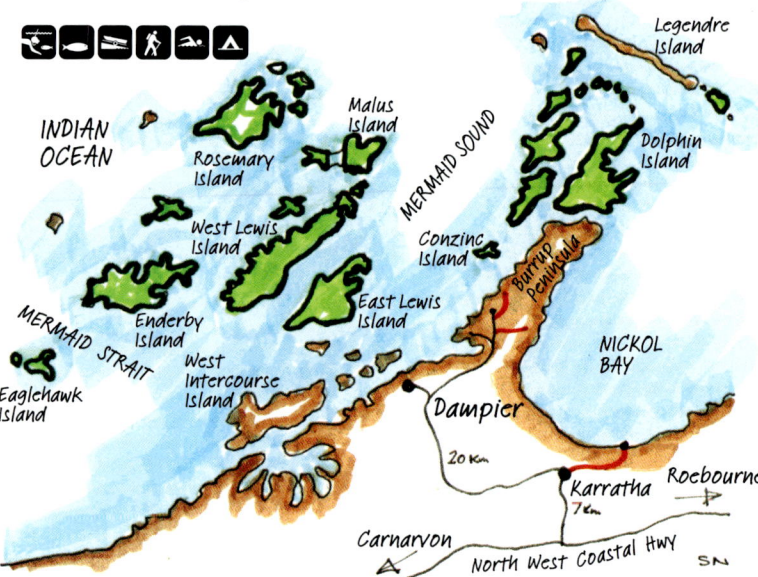

Sturt Peas (*Swainsona formosa*) in the Dampier Archipelago

Dampier
ARCHIPELAGO

This is a chain of 42 unspoiled islands of which 25 are nature reserves (as yet not gazetted as a national park). Many of them are very stony, consisting of granite, dolerite and basalt rocks and the area was the home of the Yapapurra people who were called the 'island people' by mainland Aborigines. They left wonderful rock engravings depicting wallaroos, turtles, birds and human figures, the best examples being on Rosemary and Enderby Islands. William Dampier was the first European to explore this area in 1699. He described Australian flora and fauna as "miserable and impoverished". Well, yes, many of the marsupials are nocturnal and certainly hard to see, and the country may not 'come alive' until winter and spring with the many displays of flowering plants, but hardly what one would describe as "impoverished". His comment was particularly ironic knowing the low number of flora and fauna species of his country of origin, England.

There are a few marsupials on the islands; Northern Quoll (*Dasyurus hallucatus*), Rothschild's Rock-wallaby (*Petrogale rothschildi*) and Common Wallaroo can be found. Marine mammals include the Humpback Whale, Southern Bottle-nosed Whale, False Killer Whale, Dugong, and Risso's, Bottle-nose and Indo-Pacific Hump-backed Dolphins.

There are excellent dive sites on the outer section of the archipelago and great fishing opportunities. Diving and fishing would have to be the main attractions for this region.

Chichester Range at sunset

Python Pool

Millstream-Chichester
NATIONAL PARK

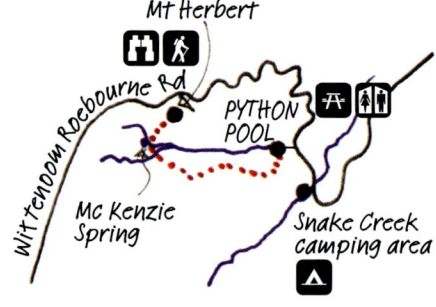

Chichester Range

Looking down from Mt Herbert above the floodplains of the George River towards Pyramid Hill has to be one of the most beautiful vistas in Australia, particularly as the sun sets across the yellow spinifex and red rocks. The rocky hillsides can also look spectacular after good rains when the spinifex turns emerald green and patches of pink Tall Mulla Mulla (*Ptilotus exaltatus*) and red Sturt Desert Pea (*Swainsonia formosa*) add their bright colours to nature's tapestry.

There is a walk from the Mt Herbert car park on the south side of the ridge that takes you along the old camel track of pioneering days to the watering hole of McKenzie Spring—it is 4.5 km return. You can return along the same track or carry on the longer track to Python Pool but it's a hard 16 km return walk. If a fit member of the party wishes to do it, they can be met at Python Pool (8 km one way) but clear instructions and times must be given between all parties.

From the Mt Herbert car park, it is a short walk (600 m return) to the top of the hill, with fantastic views. All these walks are stony and require a moderate level of fitness.

At the base of Mt Herbert is Python Pool, there is a 15 min return walk to the pool from the car park. This is a typical 'plunge pool' which is quite common throughout the Pilbara and Rudall River region, created where there is a higher valley on a raised plateau that falls away to lower plains. The larger waterholes normally have permanent water and were vital to the Aborigines in the hotter months.

The Chichester Ranges as seen by painter Eitan Friedman, fellow traveller

Millstream (Ngarrari)

This is the ancestral land of the Yinjibarndi people and was an important meeting place for various clans as the area was rich in food. Some Yinjibarndi people have been employed as rangers over the last few years.

The first European to explore the area was F.T. Gregory and a pastoral lease was taken out in 1865. Not far from Chinderwarriner Pool is the early homestead of Millstream, now a DCLM information centre. The original homestead was 50 m south west of the present dwelling and it was built in the late 1800s. The amazing fact was that the building timber was shipped all the way from England at the high cost of 1,200 pounds. It was shipped to the early port of Cossack and then carted all the way across these stony plains. A lot of work and a lot of money in those days, particularly as there was plenty of local building material nearby.

The present-day building was built in 1920 and the Gordon family took over in 1925. At one stage they had over 55,000 sheep that grazed over 400,000 ha of land. There was a Chinese gardener who attended the extensive vegetable gardens, there being no shortage of good water. The Gordon family were there until 1964 before it became a tavern, then finally DCLM took over the lease in 1986.

Camping: There are several camping sites - refer to the adjoining map. There are shady campsites in each area but Crossing Pool camping area tends to be a little quieter, as it is off the main track into Millstream Homestead. The pools are great for swimming, although quite cold in the winter months. Drinking water is available at the Visitor's Centre but is not treated–boiling reccommended. Small boats and windsurfers are allowed but power boats are not. At the Millstream Visitor's Centre there are gas barbecues and tables, toilets and a telephone.

Deep Reach Pool

Walks: There is a short 750 m walk from the homestead with interpretive plaques giving an interesting history of the early settlers here.

There is a much longer walk, called the Murlunmunyajurna Track, which is 7 km and approx. 2 hrs return. It takes you through varied country starting from the homestead, and crosses riverine vegetation, groves of Millstream Fan-palms and rocky hillsides.

The restricted Millstream Fan-palm *(Livistonia alfredii)* with its beautiful fan leaves and smooth bark is a feature of this area and not to be confused with the huge Date Palms *(Phoenix dactylifera)*, that have been introduced and sadly have affected much of the surrounding water vegetation near the homestead. DCLM are in the process of removing them because of their effect on the local flora.

The permanent pools derive their water from the continuous springs that draw water up from the underground aquifer stored in the porous dolomite rock.

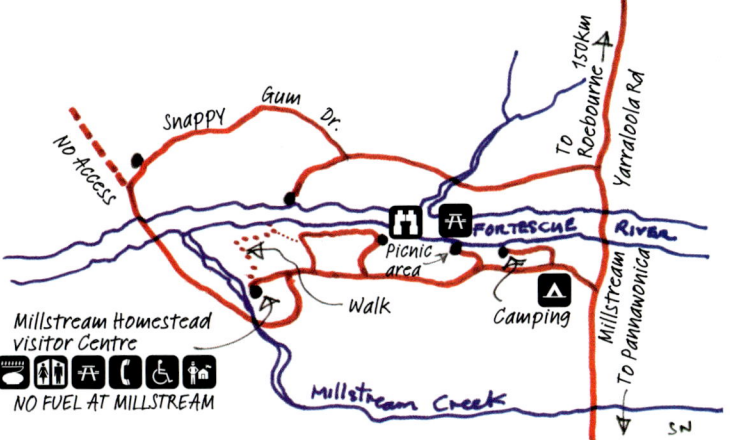

Kalamina Gorge

Karijini
NATIONAL PARK

Karijini National Park lies almost entirely within the Hamersley Plateau, which is the largest area of elevated land in Western Australia. This park covers 627,444 ha and is the second largest park after the Rudall River National Park.

It contains some of the oldest rocks on the Australian continent, with the major rocks being banded ironstones, granite, shales and dolomite.

The origins of the basement rocks date back prior to 2,500 million years in age. These are primarily granite and above this, sedimentary rocks were laid down between 600 and 2,500 million years ago in the ancient ocean of the Hamersley Basin. These sediments were rich in iron and silica. Over millions of years the weight of sediments laid over the existing base sediments created immense pressure and the water contained in these base sediments was squeezed out and the sediments became tough bed rock. With the horizontal movement of continental plates, the rocks developed fault lines and then they were forced up to create the mountain ranges we see today.

The characteristic appearance of the Hamersley Range, having alternate gentle slopes, then a steep cliff and then gentle slopes and more cliffs, is due to the alternation of weak and resistant rocks, the cliffs being the harder iron and the slopes being the shale and dolomite.

You can enter Karijini National Park coming from either Tom Price, Roebourne, Port Hedland or Newman.

There are so many beautiful gorges that one can visit but Dales, Joffre and Red Gorges are very popular. Let's take a look at the main visiting areas one at a time.

Weano recreation area

You enter this area off Banjima Drive. It is 14 km to the main day-use car park. There are very good barbecues and table facilities set under huge canvas awnings, very tastefully done and great for shade.

You can walk from the day use area to the two lookouts. People often wonder what the gates at the lookouts are for. They are there for rescue teams to be able to retrieve people from the base of the gorge in the remote possibility of an accident.

The views are spectacular from the lookout, allowing you to look down 4 separate gorges: Weano, Joffre, Hancock and Red Gorges. Weano is a day use area only.

There is a steep, winding track down to the base of Weano Gorge—600 m, 1 hr return. There are longer walks here for the experienced walker. Contact the ranger for further information.

Joffre (Jijingunha) and Knox Gorge

The turn-off to Joffre is 3 km from the turn-off to Weano Gorge. Joffre Falls is just 1.5 km off Banjima Drive on the left hand side.

It's a short 200 m drive in and a 5 min. walk to a cantilevered steel platform.

Joffre is not a big falls, but the ladder effect of the rock formation with the water trickling down to a small lower pool, makes this a very attractive falls. Another 4 km from here is Knox Gorge. The drive is very picturesque as it makes its way over the stony hills lined with Snappy Gums (*Eucalyptus leucophloia*). It is a short 300 m walk to the lookout, not as spectacular as Oxer Lookout, but still another dimension to the Hamersley Range. There are a series of walks for experienced walkers, into Knox Gorge and the other to Joffre Gorge. Enquire at the visitors centre for information.

Kalamina Falls

It is 6 km to the car park from Banjima Drive, then a short 5 min. walk down a steep track to the base of this small gorge. Most people can make this walk and even though this is not one of the large gorges, it certainly is one of the most picturesque. In front of you is a small permanent pool and just a short walk to your right, along the rock strata, is a magic little waterfall with ferns draping over the edge. For the more energetic, there is a wonderful walk, left of the entry track that goes downstream. The walk is interspersed with long flat ledges and then pebble stone river beds and rock pools. It is a relatively easy walk and takes you past beautiful coloured rock walls, ending at Rock Arch Pool (3 km and 3 hrs return) If you do not have time to walk the deep gorges then at least walk this, as it will give you an idea of how these gorges are structured.

Dales Gorge and Fortescue Falls Recreation area

It is 10 km to Fortescue Falls car park from Banjima Drive and just 0.5 km on to the end car park above Circular Pool in Dales Gorge.

If you have the time and just want to walk on the gorge rim, then drive all the way to the end car park and take the short 5 min. walk to the rim giving you views into Dale Gorge. After this you can walk to your right and take the walking track on the rim back to the lookout at Fortescue Falls (800 m). It is a 1 hr steep return walk to the base of the gorge below the falls.

Circular Pool is a very steep walk (800 m and 2 hrs return). There is a walk between Fortescue Falls and Circular Pool, which leads down creek in Dale Gorge (1.5 km and 3 hrs return).

For those who wish to climb Mt Bruce, it is a long 9 km return walk, allow 6 hrs. This is for experienced walkers. Go as early as you can, and even if it is cold don't take too much gear as it will soon come off when you warm up. Make sure you carry adequate water and only walk between May and September for comfort. The unique award winning Karijini Visitors Centre can provide more information on the park. It also gives visitors an opportunity to meet with and speak with local Aboriginal people if available.

Fauna and Flora

The park has a flora list of 481 species, although, if a thorough study was done over time, it would most probably be closer to 800 species. The acacia species are very prevalent with 53 being recorded to date. The predominant eucalypts are Kingsmill's Mallee (*Eucalyptus kingsmillii*), Snappy Gum (*E. leucophloia*), River Red Gum (*E. camaldulensis*), *E. victrix*, Coolabah (*E. microtheca*) and two bloodwoods (*Eucalyptus hamersleyana* and *Eucalyptus deserticola*).

Of the marsupials, two small endemic marsupials are the Pilbara Ningaui (*Ningaui timealeyi*) and the Little Red Antechinus (*Dasykaluta rosamondae*), found in hummock grasslands. Both are carnivorous.

There is an amazing little rodent, the Western Pebble-mound Mouse (*Pseudomys chapmani*) found in the park. These little creatures carry

Pebble Mound Mouse mound

Kalamina Falls

Pebble mound Mouse (Pseudomys chapmani)
Photo by Greg Barron

Spinifex Pigeon

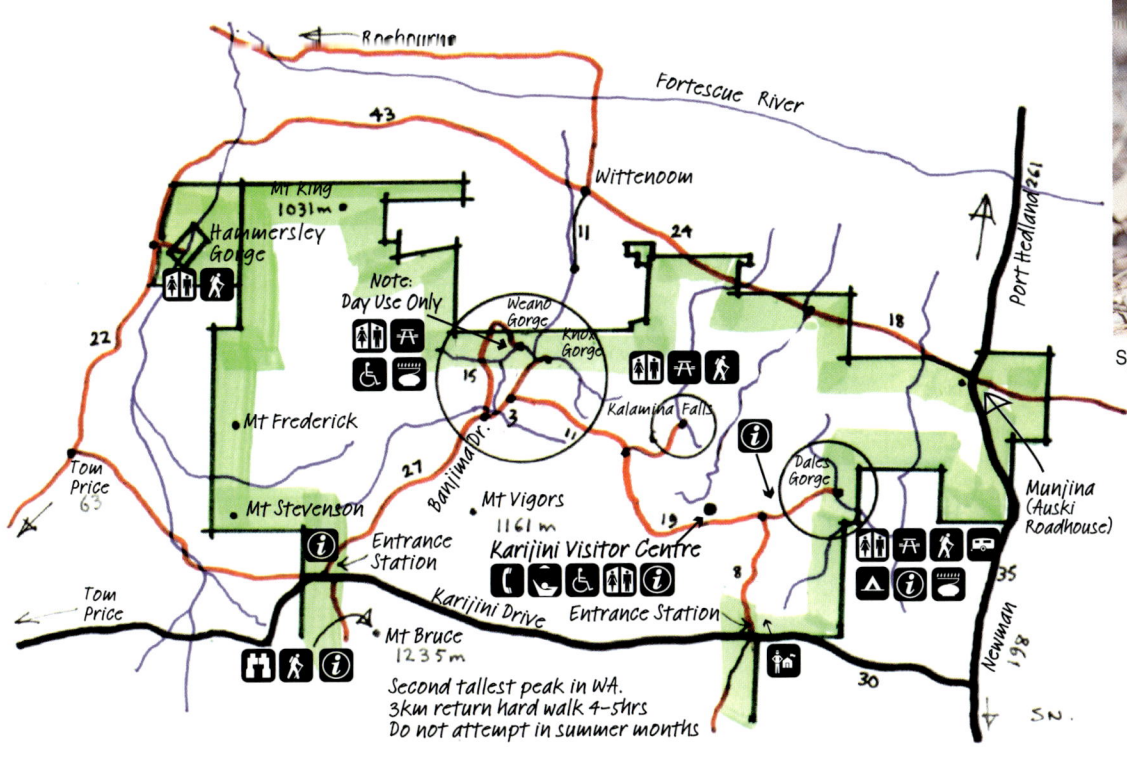

stones, often half their weight and pile them up into mounds and then create nesting chambers below the ground. The mound keep the soil cool and collect moisture. The mice apparently lick the dew off the top of the pebbles. Even though they are small (average body length 60 mm) the mounds can be 500 mm high and cover up to 9 square metres (see photograph on page 162). There are low numbers of Rothschild's Rock-wallaby (Petrogale rothschildi) a species restricted to the Pilbara. On the open plains there are Red Kangaroo (Macropus rufus) and on the rocky hillsides Common Wallaroo (Macropus robustus).

History

There are three main aboriginal language groups that have parts of their tribal lands covering the Hamersley Range. In general terms (remembering that the Aborigines have no equivalent word for border or fence and do not see land as having clearcut boundaries as Europeans do) the northern part of the park is the traditional land of the Panyjima. The southern part of the park is the traditional land of the Yinhaawangka. The western end around Mt Bruce overlaps with both Kurrama and Yinhaawangka people.

The current and future plans for the park are worked in conjunction with the Karijini Park Council which includes the tradtional custodians representing the Aboriginal language groups associated with this region.

In 1863, the surveyor and naturalist F.T. Gregory named this region the Hamersley Range, after his friend and supporter Edward Hamersley.

The park has had few changes, other than on the flat mulga country which has been altered by cattle and present and past mining activity.

Kalamina

Knox Gorge

Above Fortescue Falls

Sturt Pea *(Swainsona formosa)*

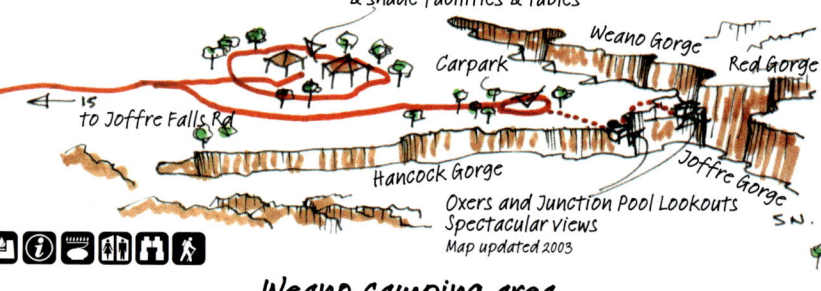
Weano camping area

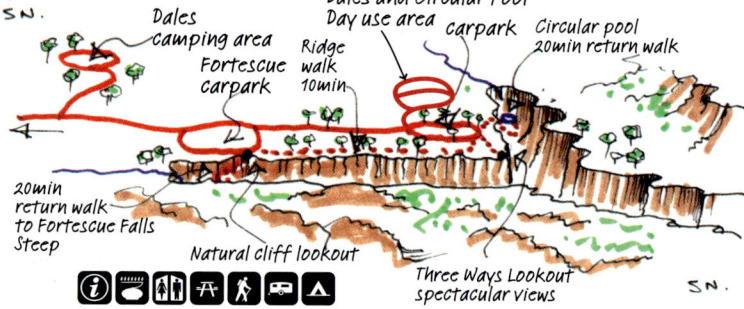
Dales camping area

Collier Range
NATIONAL PARK

The Collier Range National Park covers an area of 235,162 ha and is situated 155 km south of Newman and 245 km north of Meekatharra. Considering its size, this park is little known. We know that where the Great Northern Highway passes through the park, there are low hills covered in spinifex and mulga woodland. On the western side of the park, where the Tangadee Road cuts through the park, there is at first mulga woodland followed by open spinifex plains and low stony outcrops. The centre of the park consists of the Collier Range running from the south east to north west.

There are no access tracks into the park except the two roads mentioned, that pass through part of the park. Pastoral leases adjoin it but other than that it remains a wilderness area.

The little visited western side of the Collier Range

Rudall River (Karlamilyi)
NATIONAL PARK

This park was named after the surveyor and explorer William Frederick Rudall by the explorer and prospector Frank Hann. It gets its Aboriginal name from the Martu people after their name for the Rudall River.

This is a very remote park and covers an area of 1,283,706 ha which makes it the second largest national park in Australia, after Kakadu National Park.

It has a rugged beauty all of its own. There are no huge mountains or large bodies of water, but climb to the top of the ridge near Tjingkuldjjatjarra waterhole at sunset and just survey the 360 degree view—this will give you a greater appreciation of the beauty of this wilderness region.

It must be said at the outset, that this park is a long way from civilisation. It has no signs and no facilities. This region should definitely not be traversed by people who have had no wilderness outback 4WD experience and Newman police should be notified of your impending trip as well as DCLM.

The Rudall River National Park covers 3 basic habitat areas. In the east and north east the park borders the Great Sandy Desert and access is restricted in this part of the park anyway, as there are two Aboriginal communities, Punmu at Lake Dora and Parnngurr near Mt Cotton.

In the south west and far west the park includes part of the Little Desert and if you have travelled from Newman, you will have travelled along the Talawana Track through sand dune ridges with Desert Sheoaks, typical of this desert.

One of the many beautiful pools at Desert Queen Baths

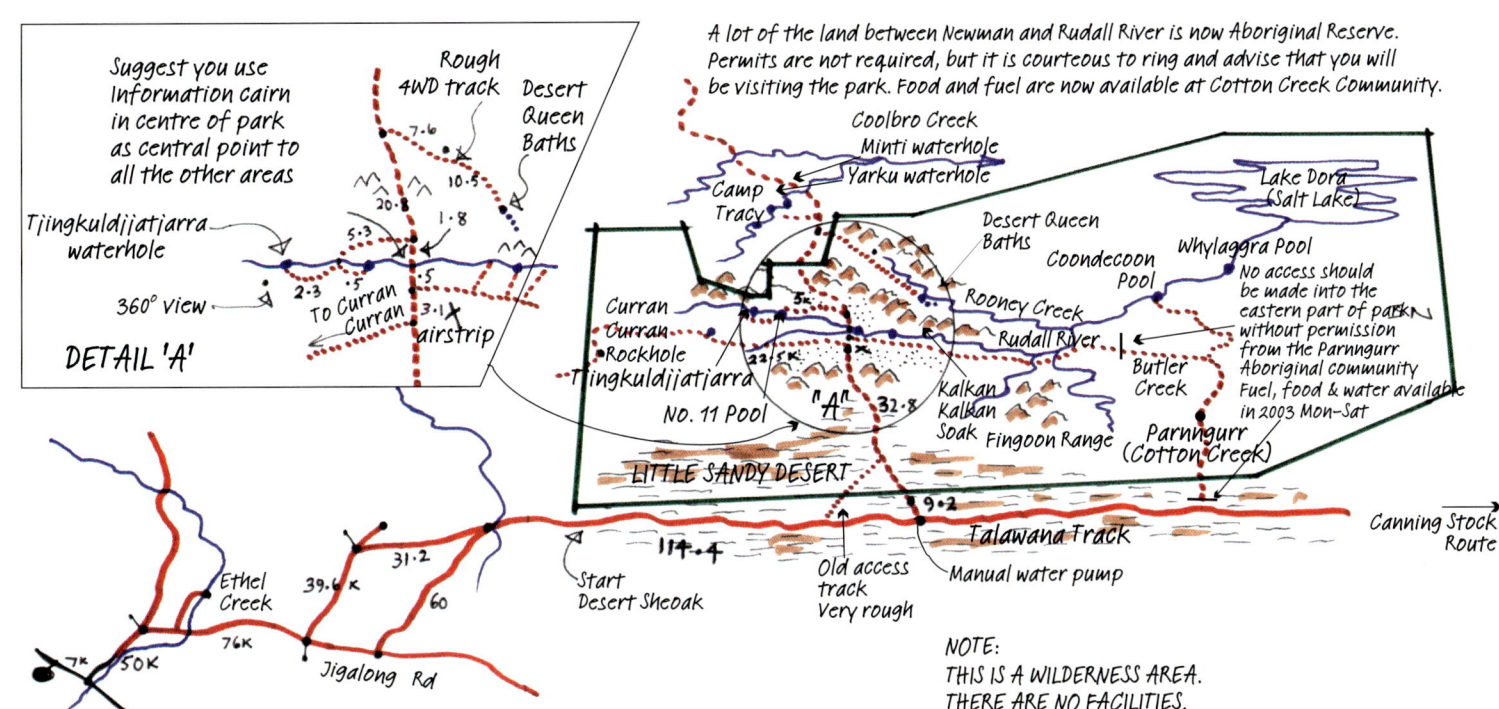

From Newman to Information cairn at Rudall River crossing –316km

Rudall River National Park

The central part of the park is the most accessible and includes the headwaters of the Rudall River and low rugged ranges of the Broadhurst and Fingoon Range. It is within this region that your travels should be centred, as there is so much to see and do here, plus you are respecting the privacy of the Aborigines at the eastern part of the park by not entering their area.

At the start of Talawana/Rudall River Track set the trip-metre to 0.0. At the 9 km mark you will see some lovely River Red Gums with good shade and below them a water pump put in by CRA Exploration. (There was water in August 1999 but none in May 1997). It a good place to camp if you cannot make the park by nightfall. From the 10 km mark on, you will travel through low sand dune country passing Flame Grevillea *(Grevillea eriostachya)*, Wickham's Grevillea *(Grevillea wickhamii)* and Cork Tree *(Hakea suberea)*, with the occasional Desert Bloodwood *(Eucalyptus chippendale)*. If you're travelling in spring the grevillea flowers may be out and Black, Pied and Grey-headed Honeyeaters could be feeding.

At 21.1 km, there is a track back on the left, which was the old access road into the Rudall River National Park. At 37.3 km, you climb between some stony hills before dropping down to the flat, sparse, stony plains before the Rudall River. At 42 km there is a track due west, that goes to Curran Curran Rockhole. It is suggested that you carry on just a little further to the Rudall River (a stony crossing with no water) at 45.5 km. From the Talawana Track to here, is basically a straight track, so no left or right turns should have been taken.

Now you can take all your bearings/distances from this central point and return to it after radiating out in any chosen direction.

Wildlife of the Rudall River National Park

Monitor Lizard *(Varanus panoptes panoptes)*

Our deserts lie in what is known as the 'Arid Zone', to many simply 'the dead heart of Australia', although it certainly is not a dead zone. We only need to walk in the central desert sand dunes to see the many footprints left by the nocturnal fauna.

For centuries, the central deserts of Australia have received little or no rain through each consecutive year. The majority of the rain falls in the summer months from cyclonic rain and some years complete areas like the Rudall will miss out on these rains. When the heavy rains do fall the temporary river pools fill and a few will in fact hold water through the severest droughts, supplementing the water needs of the Red Kangaroo, Common Wallaroo and many birds.

But what of the flora and fauna that exists in the sand dune country—how do they survive when water almost immediately sinks into the desert sands? Well, nature has developed many techniques for survival in these arid lands.

Much of the fauna is nocturnal, which protects it from the excessive heat. Plants have adapted in many ways; have a look at the leaf structure of the hakeas, grevilleas, eremophilas and the Desert Sheoaks—they are often needle-like in shape, and having little surface area they lose less moisture. If you check the leaves of the Desert Bloodwoods, they have a hard leathery feel to them which stops moisture from evaporating. They are often shiny and light in colour, reflecting and absorbing less heat. Some leaves are hairy to hold on to the moisture in the early morning dews that sustain so many inland plants. The everlasting flower petals are mostly dry and brittle and have very little moisture content, but are still bright to attract the various pollinators.

The Desert Sheoak starts its early years growing straight and tall, with all its branches hanging close to the stem, to protect the bark from the searing heat. Then finally when it is mature it spreads its branches to give a broad canopy and to distribute its seeds and protect its lateral root systems from the sun.

What we lack in numbers of mammal species, we certainly make up for in numbers of reptile species. Australia has over 800 species with many specimens still awaiting classification. A brief survey at one location in 1979 found 6 species of frog and 24 species of reptile. The museum now has on record 7 frogs and 52 reptiles. Many reptiles come out at night, thus avoiding the heat. They derive most of their moisture requirements from the prey they catch. The burrowing frogs can survive for a few years

View from the hill above Tingkuldjjatjarra Pool looking east across the vast wilderness of the Rudall River

underground, living in a protective chamber, awaiting the first rains. Like many of the reptiles, most mammals are nocturnal, living down deep cool burrows or in well-sheltered nests, and also many of the small mammals, like reptiles, derive their water needs from what they eat.

They are, however, at the mercy of the feral cat that has depleted so much of the fauna in the desert. Most animals between the large kangaroos and the smaller mammals, like the Sandy Inland Mouse *(Pseudomys hermannsburgensis)* are gone from the Rudall, they include the Western Quoll *(Dasyurus geoffroii)*, Mulgara *(Dasycercus cristicauda)*, Bilby *(Macrotis lagotis)*, Golden Bandicoot *(Isoodon auratus)* and Rufous Hare-wallaby *(Lagorchestes hirsutus)*. The last animal mentioned, the Rufous Hare-wallaby, was mentioned by the naturalist Otto Lipfert in 1931, who described it as common on the Canning Stock Route and one of the principal foods of the desert Aborigines in that area. Luckily it survives on Bernier and Dorre Islands at Shark Bay and DCLM are planning to re–introduce it to Peron Peninsula as part of their very progressive 'Western Shield' project.

Why is the feral camel a problem? Well, they can drink up to 80 litres at one time and a herd

Dingo *(Canis lupus dingo)*

Camel *(Camelus dromedarius)*

Kingsmill Eucalyptus *(Eucalyptus Kingsmillii* - Yellow flowering form)

Bilby *(Macrotis lagotis)* Photo by Michael Morcombe

Flock of Budgerigars drinking at pool

Ground Cuckoo-shrike

Painted Finch

will drink a small water hole dry, and they love our desert acacias and other plants. Alas, the Rudall has a lot of them. They are exciting to look at for the first time but when you realise what damage they do, you will not be so impressed.

Birds are lucky, most can fly over long distances, hence many of our desert-frequenting birds are nomadic, moving to areas where water and food are more prolific. Even so, they still must survive the high temperatures of most of their range and in times of severe drought, they will move into the south west or south east; it is not always just for water but often the lack of a food type. For example, Emu will congregate in their hundreds on the vermin fence in WA, when the desert mulga regions have had lengthy droughts. This is due to the fact that grasshoppers and other insects, as well as fruiting plants, are in short supply and their instinct is always to move deeper into the south west. Sadly, with no water on the east side of the fence, they never make it. Some birds are sedentary like the Spinifexbird which does not need to drink much water. It survives in the Rudall in the gullies and plains that have the biggest dome spinifex, spending most of its time out of the sun, deriving its moisture from insects.

If you camp near one of the pools in the Rudall, check the bird species that come to drink. You may see the beautiful Painted Finch, or walking through the tussock grass to drink there may be a Crested Pigeon, Little Button-quail or the colourful Spinifex Pigeon.

If you see an attractive coloured raptor with a grey back and chestnut coloured belly, long broad wings slightly up-turned, quartering only a few metres above the spinifex, then there is good chance you are looking at a Spotted Harrier, one of our most beautiful birds of prey.

Brief History

The Martu Aboriginal people are the original people of this area. There are four main language groups, the Mandjildjarra, Gardutjarra, Nguilibardu and Warman. Many Aborigines moved out of the desert after the war years and many moved through the Rudall area to Jigalong Mission. During the early 1980s, Aboriginal groups from Strelley Mission started returning to the edge of the Rudall River National Park and around Lake Dora in the north east of the park. Then in 1984 some of the Jigalong group moved back to their tribal lands within the park at Cotton Creek, now called Parnngurr. Permission must be gained to enter these communities.

The first Europeans to enter the park were Wells and Jones in 1896 who explored around Lake Blanche before heading north on their ill-fated Calvert Expedition. They died of thirst near Joanna Springs approx. 300 km north east of the Rudall River. The Calvert Expedition is a tragic but fascinating story.

The first major exploration by Europeans was made by William Rudall accompanied by Herbert Trotman and two Aboriginal trackers nicknamed Cherry and George. It was, in fact, to try to find Wells and Jones, who had perished 300 km north of here. Rudall searched for 3 months for the missing party. He was extremely lucky to make it back to the Oakover, as his camels died south of Joanna Springs, and if it was not for the help of local Aborigines who took them nearly 400 km back via various water holes, they too would have perished.

Frank Hann explored the area at the same time as Rudall and by sheer coincidence bumped into Rudall's search party on the western part of the park near Hanging Rock.

Military Dragon *(Ctenophorus isolepis)* Photo by David Knowles

Bandy Bandy snake *(Simoselaps anomalus)*
Photo by David Knowles

Fat-tailed Gecko *(Diplodactylus conspicillatus)*
Photo by David Knowles

Flame Grevillea *(Grevillea eriostachya)*

Mount Augustus

Mount Augustus (Burringurrah)
NATIONAL PARK

Mount Augustus is 1,105 m above sea level and rises up 858 m from the surrounding stony mulga plains. The park area (9,168 ha) covers the mountain and the land immediately below it. The area of the park was released from the lease of Mt Augustus Station in 1988. There are many comparisons drawn between Mt Augustus (Burringurrah) and Uluru (Ayers Rock) and it is important to keep things in perspective, both in geological terms and descriptive terms.

Uluru is a true monolith, that is 'a single body of rock of uniform quality and considerable size'. Mt Augustus is a monocline, 'a huge body of rock strata uplifted and folded'; it is not a single body of uniform rock (see sketch opposite). The rock covers 4,795 ha, about twice the surface area of Uluru.

In terms of visual impression, they are quite different. Mt Augustus is like looking at any normal mountain range typically covered in vegetation, the main difference being that it rises sharply as a single entity above the surrounding plains, which makes it very impressive. Uluru is a vast single solid rock, that rises almost vertically out of the surrounding plains. It has a singular colour having virtually no vegetation on it whatsoever and is, when seen close up, simply awesome.

However, just like Uluru holds great significance to the Anagu people, so too does Burringurrah hold special significance to the Wadjari people. They have some interesting stories about the origins of Burringurrah, all based on the death of a tribal Aborigine being punished. One such story describes a boy called Burringurrah who could not handle the pain while going through the important ceremony of initiation. He ran away, breaking the strong code of Aboriginal law. He was then chased and punished. He died from his spear wounds and lay with his left leg bent up against his body with the stump of the spear still protruding from his leg. With some visual imagination, you can see these shapes from the south east side of the mountain.

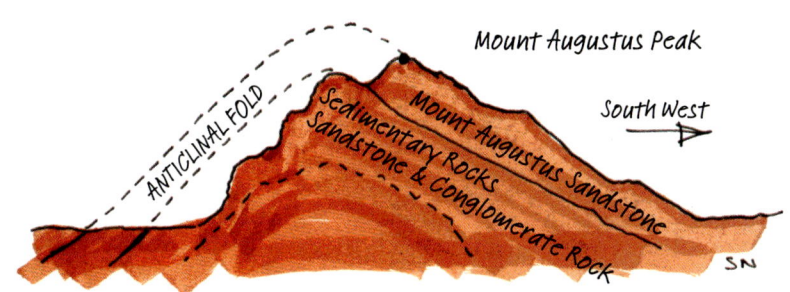

Geologically, Mt Augustus consists of three main rock strata levels; the bed rock was schist and granitic rock, formed between 1,600 and 1,900 million years ago. Above this, formed from ancient sea beds and subsequently compressed, are sedimentary rocks of sandstone and conglomerate rocks laid down over 1,000 million years ago, and then later a final stage of pure sandstone, known as Mt Augustus sandstone, laid over that. With the massive forces of the earth's crust that occurred subsequent to that, the three types of strata were uplifted to form the basic structure we see today.

Francis Thomas Gregory was the first European explorer to climb Mt Augustus in 1858. He named it after his brother, who was on another expedition looking for the remains of the explorer, Dr Leichhardt. In the 1880s pastoralists started to enter this region and Mt Augustus Station was opened up by Samuel James Phillips. It passed through the family until the First World War when Ernest Potts managed it for 35 years until his death in 1955. It has changed hands a few times since then.

You don't need a 4WD to get to Mt Augustus, however, the roads are bumpy and dusty at times and stations few and far between. So your vehicle should be in good shape. Carry spare water. There is a large private campsite at Mt Augustus, with some provisions, fuel, phone, general accommodation and meals. There is also accommodation, camping, fuel and supplies at Cobra Station. There is no camping allowed within the park.

Access can be either from the west via Carnarvon, Gascoyne Junction (you could visit the Kennedy Ranges on the way) and Cobra Station, or from the south east via Meekatharra and Landor Station. If you're travelling from the north via Newman, you can cut across from Three Rivers and Mulgul Station. Be careful here as few people travel this route.

Walking Trails

There is a circular drive known as Burringurrah Drive (part of it being the main Cobra–Mt Augustus Road). All walking trails lead off this. See sketch map for location, walking times and length.

The Summit Trail: Commences at the Beedoboondu car park. This is a long, hard climb, 12 km return, taking at least 6 hrs. You

Goonlinee or Cattle Pool

Rocky pools on part of the summit walk

should be fit and experienced in walking on rocky terrain. Start as early as possible, carrying water and spare food. The mobile ranger is only on site seasonally, usually in the winter and spring. If the ranger is not on site, advise the resort staff that you are attempting to climb and give your expected time of return. Do attempt to see them on your return. However, you do not have to climb to the top to gain an appreciation of the mountain. If you walk up the same trail as the summit walk, there is a walk called the circuit walk which takes you up a lovely boulder-strewn creek bed and then comes around the back of the creek, returning to the car park. Refer to the information boards for location. There is some rock hopping required but it is well worth the walk and with luck there should still be water in some of the pools most of the year.

Other Walks: At Mundee car park there is a short, easy 10 min. return walk that takes you to a sandstone rock face that depicts some early engravings.

At Ooramboo there is a short walk to more Aboriginal engravings and then 100 m past them is Edney Springs. The walk to Edney Lookout is much further (6 km return walk, 2.5 hrs), but it is much easier than climbing to the summit and will still give you great views. There are picnic tables at the car park with good shade, a great place to return and have lunch.

Goonlinee, or Cattle Pool, has been a major permanent waterhole for the Wadjari People. It is a good place to swim but be careful of underlying roots and weeds. There are picnic tables and it is the best area in the region for shade and water combined.

Emu Hill Lookout has been designed to give people a look at the mountain as the colours change with the setting sun. If you have wide-angle lenses, you can get good effects right below the mountain, without the longer drive.

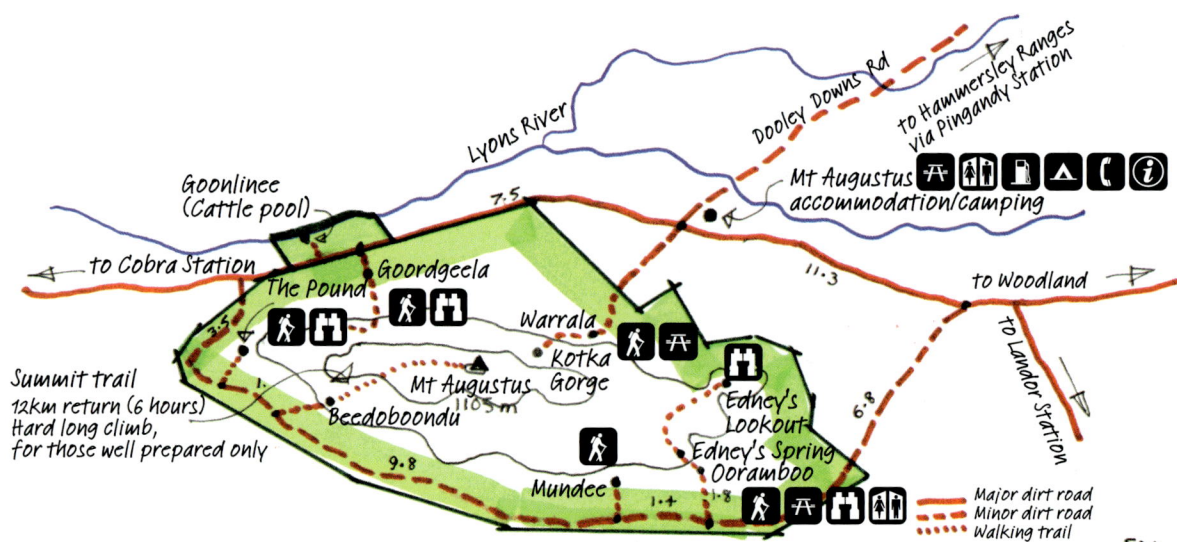

Kennedy Range
NATIONAL PARK

When you drive right up to the base of this massive elevated plateau, you cannot help but be impressed, for not only does the edge of the plateau rise over 100 m right in front you, but also looking north or south, the walls keep going on and on to the horizon. The scarp runs for about 75 km, and the plateau itself is only 12–25 km wide. The top of the range is quite extraordinary as there are red sand dune ridges covered in spinifex and acacia scrubland.

The sandstone was formed like so many areas in the Pilbara by the accumulation of ancient seabed sands being compressed, hardened and then uplifted, and finally laterised. There are some fascinating marine fossils to be found particularly on some of the huge fallen boulders, evidence of the rocks of wetter times. An example of more recent fossils here, is the world's oldest fossilised banksia. Three tribal groups overlapped in this area; the Malgaru and the Maia in the east joined up with the Wadjari, traditional owners of the Mt Augustus region.

The first European to enter this region was Francis Thomas Gregory in 1858, who named the Lyons River and named the Kennedy Ranges after the Governor of Western Australia, Arthur Edward Kennedy. After Gregory returned to Perth, he wrote up his findings and one thing he did mention was the lack of Gastrolobium plants in the north west, the plants that are poisonous to sheep in the south west. In subsequent years many pastoralists moved into the area, one such station Mount Sandiman Homestead, (part of Minnie Creek Station) allow camping and do the occassional tour.

Walking Trails

The Falls Walk: It is a short 500 m return stony walk that passes some impressive fallen boulders. The Falls themselves are mostly dry throughout the year as this region only receives on average 210 mm of rain a year.

Temple Gorge Track: 1.5 km return walk. The track divides near some very large boulders. To the left is a short 500 m return walk. To the right it goes further (1 km return), with good views of the gorge walls. About 200 m before the small creek where you cross to enter the campsite area, is an open stony area and an old 4WD track; walk about 200 m past where vehicles have turned and on the left, where the rubble has fallen down the cliff face. This whole Kennedy Range is a lapidarian (people interested in stones) delight.

Draper's Gorge Track: 3 km return walk. This is a very stony walk in parts and you should be a fit and experienced walker. Keep walking on and you come to a multi-coloured sandstone waterfall (most probably dry), which you can walk around. The track keeps going further up the gorge.

The DCLM requess that people do not climb to the top of the range as rocks are extremely lose and unsafe.

It is 45 km from Gascoyne Junction to the turn-off to Kennedy Range, then 11 km to the entry information board.

Kennedy Range

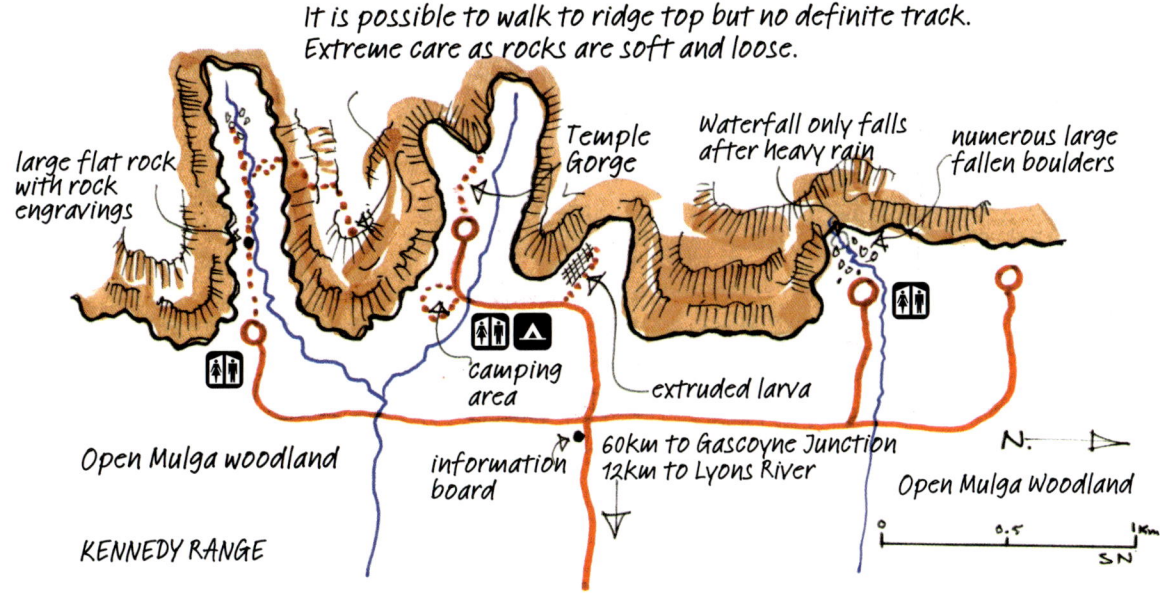

KENNEDY RANGE

Bungle Bungle Range–Purnululu National Park

Kimberley
REGION

Boab tree off the Gibb River Rd

Kimberley
REGION

If you're travelling to the Kimberley for the first time, there is a good chance you will not see all that you had planned; the reason being that the country is so vast and the roads few and far between and there is so much to see and do. The Kimberley covers an area of over 420,000 square kilometres, nearly twice the size of Victoria.

Weather is an important factor when travelling into the Kimberley. Most of the rains fall in December through to March and can range from hardly any rain to massive downpours that will not allow access until well into May. So, most people travel in the winter months. For those who are not used to tropical temperatures, there are only eight weeks that are relatively mild and they are from mid June to mid August, but the downside is that most people travel then.

You will normally enter the region from the west at Broome or the east at Kununurra. If towing caravans the Gibb River Road between the Pentecost River and Gibb River station can be very rough and corrugated and really is not suitable for general caravans, but you should check all details either in Broome or Kununurra. The ideal situation is to leave caravans at either town and travel by 4WD only, as many of the best scenic areas can only be accessed by 4WD.

Travelling the Gibb River Road is the best way to see this spectacular region as you will travel through rugged mountain ranges with access to many beautiful gorges with permanent water holes. I strongly recommend that when planning your trip you contact some of the cattle stations that allow camping or full board accommodation. This allows you not only to meet wonderful people but also gets you off the main tracks, allowing you to experience the beauty of this vast wilderness that few get to see.

If you commence your journey from the east or the west you can make the round trip by travelling along the Gibb River Road and then back along the Great Northern Highway. You will need to allot a good percentage of your holiday if travelling through the centre of the Kimberley, particularly if you are going to travel up the Kalumburu road, as the roads are slower and there is simply so much to see and do. In general, you should require far less time on the Great Northern Highway section, allowing yourself time to at least visit Purnululu, the Halls Creek region and Geikie Gorge.

The town of Broome still has a lot character, even though the pressures of tourism have changed many aspects of this historic pearling town. There is a good tourist bureau with up-to-date information and they can forward much valuable literature prior to your journeys. The region around Broome is called the Dampier Peninsula which was and still is, home to the Bardi People. There are no rugged mountains here but undulating red loamy sandplains covered by grassplains, with sparsely covered eucalypts and dense stands of wattles, often called 'Pindan country' from the Bardi word meaning "arid and waterless".

Leaving Broome and travelling east, you will pass over the mighty Fitzroy River at the 160 km mark. When in full flood, more water passes under the bridges near Willare in one hour than the total volume of water contained in Sydney Harbour. Fifteen kilometres north of the Willare Bridge, you will either turn right on the Great Northern Highway or carry on a further 42 km to Derby and then back to the turn-off leading to the Gibb River Road. If you are travelling in a 4WD one way around Australia, you can visit Derby, back track to the Great Northern Highway and travel to Fitzroy Crossing and visit Geikie Gorge. Then back track just 42 km to the Leopold Downs Road which will lead you to Tunnel Creek, Windjana Gorge and then the Gibb River road itself. Then the options are just endless, until you get to the Wyndham-Kununurra road, where you can turn left and visit Wyndham just 47 km away and then travel to Kununurra. You will find that if you have travelled extensively in the hinterland of the Kimberley, you will be a little travel weary. It is wise to go straight to Kununurra and use it as a base for a few days to rest and take it easy. There are all the facilities you may require there, plus many local areas to visit, and just like Broome, there is a very good tourist information centre. You can then travel down to Halls Creek where there are some interesting historic sights left over from the goldrush days. Then on your return you can make the 4WD journey into the magnificent Purnululu National Park; you will need at the very least two full days to enter and exit this magnificent park. If you were travelling from Kununurra to Broome, then you would just reverse the journey outlined above. If you were travelling Broome to Broome or Kununurra to Kununurra then a circular route would be the ideal, travelling the Gibb River Road and returning via the Great Northern Highway, thus avoiding any back tracking.

The Bungle Bungle Range, Purnululu National Park

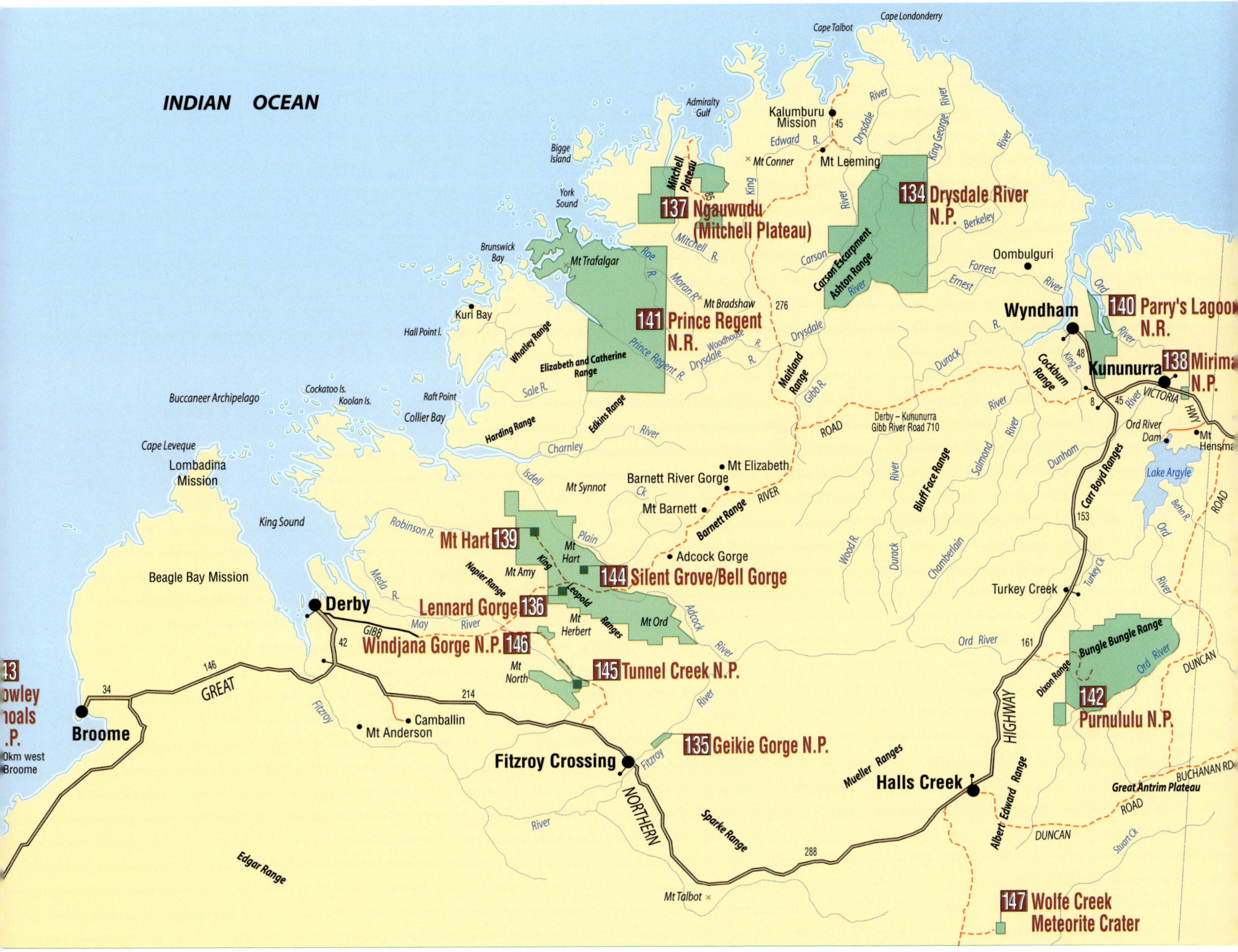

The Devonian Barrier Reef
PARKS

There are three National Parks within the 300 km long 'barrier reef' system: Geikie Gorge, Tunnel Creek and Windjana Gorge. All are located within an ancient limestone reef system of the Napier, Oscar, Geikie and Emanuel Ranges, then further east, near Kununurra, there is an outlier known as the Ningbing Range. They were formed between 350 and 370 million years ago in the Devonian Period, when the main Kimberley Plateau was an island landmass and the Canning and Bonaparte Basins were in fact tropical seas.

Some of the present day limestone walls tower over the surrounding plains up to 100 m high, as at Windjana Gorge. The reef was created by minute organisms that secreted lime, forming honeycomb structure. These organisms include calcareous algae, extinct organisms called stromatoporoids and corals and can be seen in the fossil remains. Although corals are the predominant reef-forming life form today, they were not so important in the structuring of reefs in the past. The barrier reef is exposed on the fringe of the Kimberley Plateau on almost three sides and is presumed to extend into the Indian Ocean and Timor Sea, forming one gigantic circular reef system.

There are many examples of fossil remains within all parks, particularly Windjana, where besides the more prevalent molluscs (shells), there are strange-looking fish, with armour plated exteriors, quite typical of fish of the Devonian period.

Tunnel Creek
NATIONAL PARK

These are Western Australia's oldest limestone caves, being formed over 350 million years ago. Tunnel Creek cave is 750 m long and passes through the Napier Range. It is thought that Tunnel Creek once flowed across the top of the range when the surrounding ground level was much higher and now the creek flows through the range in the wet season, following a fault line in the range. The cave is up to 12 metres high and 15 metres wide.

You can actually walk through the tunnel in the dry season but you will have to remove walking shoes and wade through cool pools, normally not above waist level for adults. Ideally take sneakers to help you climb over the large boulders that litter the entrance to the cave. Take a torch and on a hot day be prepared, it will be a lot cooler than outside. The tunnel has collapsed in the centre allowing additional light to enter the cave.

You can sometimes hear the clicking of bats, as there are several species within this one cave system.

It was also here that the Aboriginal, Jundumurra, known by the early white settlers as 'Pigeon', was tragically killed by a fellow Aboriginal police tracker in 1897.

Please respect any Aboriginal paintings by not touching. If rain is imminent in the area, do not enter the cave, as it is subject to flooding.

Entrance to Tunnel Creek Cave

Geikie Gorge
NATIONAL PARK

The Fitzroy River cuts its way through the longest gorge in the Devonian reef system, being some 14 km long. The force and volume of the water travelling through the gorge in the wet season is so immense that the dark weathered 30 m high limestone walls are polished white up to 15 m above the dry season water level.

The gorge was named in 1883 after Sir Archibald Geikie and in some ways it was quite appropriate as he was Director General of Geological Surveys in the United Kingdom, and he certainly would have been impressed with the geology of this region. However the Bunaba, traditional owners and custodians of this area, call the gorge Darngku, pronounced Darn-goo. The Darlingunaya Aboriginal Corporation, in conjunction with DCLM, run boat tours in the dry season (mid-April to October). You can take a 1.5 hr boat trip up the gorges, learning a little about the history, geology and wildlife of this area, or take a special boat trip with Darlingunaya guides if available.

With the permanent pools remaining all year the wildlife is quite prolific and in these fresh waters are the ancestors of ancient sea life, such as stingrays, sawfish and the Johnston Freshwater Crocodile (*Crocodylus johnstoni*).

The mammals include Agile Wallaby (*Macropus agilis*), Short-eared Rock-wallaby (*Petrogale brachyotis*), Torresian Flying Fox (*Pteropus species*), Ghost Bat (*Macroderma gigas*) and Orange Leaf-nosed Bat (*Rhinonicteris aurantius*). Most snakes are rarely seen but Stimson's Python (*Bothrochilus stimsoni*), Black-headed Python (*Aspidites melanocephalus*), Olive Python (*Bothrochilus olivaceus*), Children's Python (*Bothrochilus childreni*) and King Brown (*Pseudechis australis*) can be seen here.

There are walks available passing through Cadjeput, River Gums and Pandanus vegetation. Look out for the bright orange edible fruit of the exotic vine, about the size of a 10 cent piece.

There are a few walks; the reef walk is approx. 3 km return and takes about 1.5 hrs, and there is a shorter 20 min. walk along the banks of the Fitzroy River to a popular swimming area. The sandbar and junction of the Fitzroy and Margaret Rivers near here is an important area to the Bunaba and Goonian people, as at the beginning of the wet season it is a place for ceremonies for young men.

Entry to the park is during daylight hours from 6.30 a.m. to 6.30 p.m. Entry is restricted or closed during the wet season. The nearest camping and accommodation is in Fitzroy Crossing, just 16 km away. Private water craft are requested not to enter the water immediately prior to the boat tour times. (See Ranger first.)

Birds: In the tall cadjeput and eucalypt woodland, Yellow Oriole, Figbird, Pheasant Coucal and White bellied Cuckoo-shrike can be seen, and along the water's edge, (if you are lucky) you may see the beautiful small bird called the Purple-crowned Fairy-wren moving through the thick pandanus (*Pandanus aquaticus*).

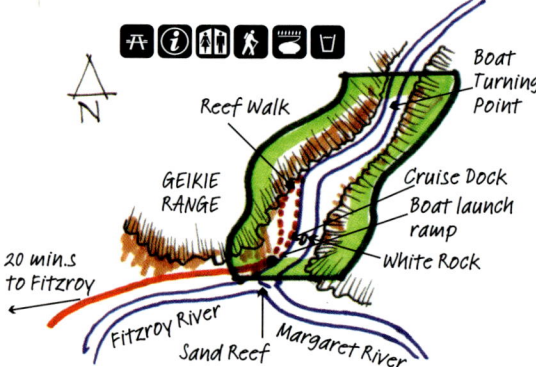

Limestone gorge walls at Geikie Gorge

Windjana Gorge
NATIONAL PARK

While driving across the flat grassplains of the Lennard River floodplain, the vertical 100 m high limestone rock walls are an impressive sight. The Lennard River has cut a narrow 4 km gorge through the Napier Range. Large freshwater pools remain during the dry season and it is perhaps one of the best locations for viewing the Johnston Freshwater Crocodile (although not normally dangerous, parents should exercise caution with children).

It is a short walk from the parking areas to the entry information boards and perhaps the best walk is into the gorge itself; you can either just enter the first part of the gorge or carry on the 3.5 km one way walk. This takes you on the eastern side of the gorge passing alongside the beautiful sculptured walls of the gorge, testament to the power of the water created by the wet season floods. As you walk alongside the pools, large paper-barked Cadjeputs (Melaleuca species) and Leichardt Pines (Nauclea orientalis) give you good shade. Fig trees on the cliff face give food for the Great Bowerbird and Figbird. Past the first pool a large quartz-like white rock named 'Bandingan', the 'baby spirit rock', by the Bunaba people juts out of the river bed. It is only a few hundred metres from here that Jundumurra and Ellemarra, the outlawed Aborigines, with several other Bunaba tribesman killed the two white stockmen, Gibbs and Burke, who were trying to bring cattle into their tribal land. A tragic story from both perspectives, particularly as later, Jundumurra was shot and Ellemarra was hanged.

Besides the strong Aboriginal history linked to this gorge one of the most interesting aspects of this whole area is the geological history, and information boards on the first part of the gorge walk will explain some of the fossils that can be seen in the area. It is not just in recent times that fossils have been found in these remote areas. The Dublin geologist E.T. Hardman, on his 1883 expedition, found the femur bone of the large prehistoric marsupial known as Diprotodon in the gorge. Later, the bones of huge extinct crocodiles and turtles were found. If you are particularly interested in fossils then you should walk to what is called the 'classic face' on an east-facing wall where numerous examples of early marine life can be seen, but you will have to walk at least 2 km into the gorge. Please remember the taking of fossils is prohibited.

There is a short half hour savanna walk that loops from the camping ground, or a longer 3 km walk below the limestone reef wall to the ruins of the historical police outpost station, 'Lillimilura', the scene of the killing of Jundumurra's first victim, police constable Richardson. At the ruins is an outline history of the events that took place in the late 1800s and a memorial plaque to Richardson who sadly died there.

If you are driving into this area in April or early May, check the road conditions as the track can be boggy after a heavy rain season.

Windjana is 150 km from Fitzroy Crossing about 2 hr drive and 145 km from Derby also about two hours.

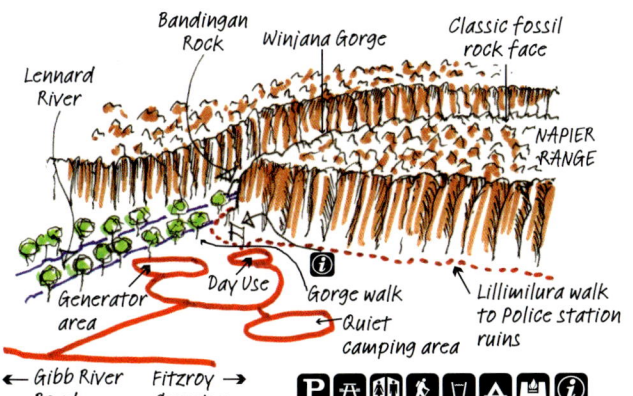

Windjana Gorge through the eye of a camera and through the eyes of painter Eitan Friedman

The Gibb River Road

The Gibb River Road is one of the most exciting drives in Australia. If you are travelling from Kununurra, it is the massive Cockburn Range that greets you as you commence your journey. If you start from the Derby end, it is the vertical jagged cliffs of the Napier Range that alert you to the rugged country that lies ahead.

The road was first opened up as a cattle stock route in the mid 1960s and it is roughly 670 km from Derby to the junction of the Wyndham and Kununurra road. It still is rough in parts and should be done in a 4WD. At the Derby end, there is 60 km of bitumen road, then it's mostly a dirt-formed road to Gibb River Station. Between Gibb River Station and the Pentecost River the dirt track can be quite corrugated and is definitely not recommended for towing caravans. The road often becomes impassable in the wet season and should be travelled only in the dry, between May and November. There are increasing numbers of vehicles travelling in the wet season and yes, you may be alright one day but then it may rain solidly for a week or even longer and you could be stranded for months. The station owners will help in an emergency but they run big businesses and are not there to tow your bogged vehicle out, so do plan your travel dates wisely and check road conditions beforehand. Also be careful on 'jump ups,' it is easy to think you are the only one travelling on these roads but some people now travel at high speeds, so stay well left when passing over a crest.

There are now adequate fuel supplies en route but you should always carry additional fuel.

Boab trees lose their leaves in the dry season, seen here at Yammera Gap in the Napier Range

Leopold Range near Mt Bell showing the massive forces that shaped this mountain range

Boab trees lose their leaves in the dry season, seen here at Yammera Gap in the Napier Range

King Leopold
NATIONAL PARK

Travelling from the Derby end and possibly seeing Windjana Gorge, you will pass through the Napier Range at Yammera Gap.

Approximately 144 km east of Derby you will enter the King Leopold Range National Park, which covers 392,000 ha. The ranges were named by Alexander Forrest in 1879 after King Leopold of Belgium, because of the king's interest in exploration. They lie at the south western edge of the Kimberley Plateau. Massive forces some 560 million years ago, pushed the quartz, sandstone and pebble conglomerate over the underlying granite which can be seen as one climbs up the valley below Mt Bell (744 m high) (see above picture). The highest mountain in the whole of the Kimberley, Mt Ord (937 m high), is in this range, 40 km south east of here.

Mt Hart Homestead

As you wind your way through the hills you pass over Apex Creek and just past this is the turn-off to Mt Hart Station, 186 km east of Derby. Access to the station is along a 50 km 4WD track. There is no camping, only full board accommodation. The homestead was included in the initial purchase of the station by DCLM in 1992. Rather than let the homestead fall into disrepair DCLM appointed managers to run it as accommodation for tourists. From the homestead a short 4.6 km drive takes you to a small gorge with large cadjeput and fig trees with clear pools of running water, and if you are lucky in the early morning, you may catch a glimpse of the Northern Nailtail Wallaby (*Onychogalea unguifera*) amongst the dark dolerite rocks. Remember there are many excellent privately owned homesteads where you can stay while travelling the Gibb River Road (further details refer page 189).

Kimberley
WILDLIFE

Sugar Glider *(Petaurus breviceps)* Photo by Michael Morcombe

▲Northern Quoll *(Dasyurus hallucatus)*
Photo by Greg Barron
▼Agile Wallaby *(Macropus agilis)*

The Kimberley is one of the most biologically diverse region of Western Australia. It contains the greatest number of marsupials and over three quarters of its flora does not occur further south. Many of the plants are closely related to those of southern Africa like the classic Boab tree (*Adansonia gregorii*) and its African relative known as the Baobab (*Adansonia digitata*.) By far the largest plant community is the Poaceae, the grasses. Some like Cane grass or Sorghum (*sp*) attain heights of up to 4 m and if one has ever had to walk through these thick grasses, it's an experience that one does not relish.

When you first visit the Kimberley, you will notice the many types of palm and pandanus trees. Along the many creeks you can see *Pandanus aquaticus, spiralis* and *darwinensis*. There are several Fan-palm of the genus *Livistona*. On the Mitchell Plateau the tall *Livistona eastonii* is as prolific in some areas as the eucalypts. In the far north west there are few stands of the only Banksia of the northern region, *Banksia dentata* commonly known as Tropical Banksia.

The wettest areas in the far north west like the Mitchell Plateau region contain the highest density of marsupials. Amongst the sandstone boulder country can be found the Short-eared Rock-wallaby (*Petrogale brachyotis*) or its diminutive relative the Monjon (*Petrogale burbidgei*). Alongside these marsupials are some birds that only frequent the rock country, like the Black Grasswren, White-lined Honeyeater and the yellow faced form of the Partridge Pigeon. The monsoonal vine thickets not only support unusual plants but in these small remnant patches of vegetation can be found species of birds that are typical of the larger rainforest areas of Queensland, like Spangled Drongo, Yellow Oriole, Figbird, Cicadabird, Varied Triller and Little Shrike-thrush.

The wetlands, particularly around Kununurra have a wealth of bird life and a commercial cruise along the Ord River can be most rewarding.

Estuarine Crocodile: Just a word of warning. Crocodiles frequent most of the coastal waters of the Kimberley. They are very territorial and can move extremely fast whether in water or on land. Do heed the crocodile warning signs and in remoter areas keep well away from the waters edge, particularly near muddy shore lines and mangrove areas.

Frilled Lizard *(Chalmydosaurus kingii)* Photo by David Knowles

Saltwater or Estuarine Crocodile (*Crocodylus porosus*)

▲Freshwater Crocodile (*Crocodylus johnstoni*)
▼Black-headed Python (*Aspidites melanocephalus*)
Photo by David Knowles

Quinine Tree
(*Petalostigma pubescens*)

Grevillea microcarpa

Kapok Bush (*Cochlospernum fraseri*)

Sticky Kurrajong (*Sterculia viscidula*)

Double-barred Finch

Great Bowerbird

Pheasant Coucal

Masked Finch

▲Peaceful Doves

▲Rainbow Pitta

▲Long-tailed Finch

▼Painted Finch   ▼Star Finch   ▼Crimson Finch   ▼Zebra Finch

Finches of the Kimberley

Of Australia's 15 finches, 7 can be found in the Kimberley. This does not include the Mannikins of which there are 4 and the Kimberley has 3 of them. Our rarest finch in this region is the stunning Gouldian Finch, most have black face masks but a quarter have red face masks and a very few yellow. If you wish to see these exquisite birds you must get up early and sit near some of the small pools with little water in them and sandy edges, not the big pandanus lined pools.

The common finches of the Kimberley are the Double-barred and the Long-tailed Finch. Closely resembling the Long-tailed is the Masked Finch with an all yellow beak and black frontal face mask, but it is far less common.

Lennard River
GORGE

The turn-off to the gorge is 194 km east of Derby and there is a sign saying 'Millie Windie Road'. Turn off here and 200 m from the main road take the first track to the right which is signposted to Lennard Gorge. The parking area is 6.3 km from here. If you have an off-road trailer, park just 1 km along the track alongside a small creek which could still have running water in the dry season; unhitch the trailer here. From here the track is very stony. The Gorge is quite spectacular and is only a 5 min. walk from the car park. Be careful here as there are sheer cliff walls down to the base of the gorge, but with care you can walk down to the permanent rock pools below and often in the early part of the dry, the waterfalls will still be flowing. The gorge is 5 km long so you can head upstream or down.

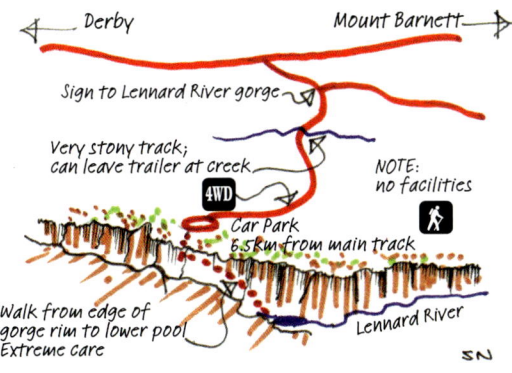

Lennard River Gorge

Bell Gorge & Silent Grove

Heading further along the Gibb River Road, you will pass by cliff faces with gigantic rock strata folds near Mt Bell. Further on you start to descend a long steep hill and just after the bitumen starts there is a parking area on the left, so take time to look out across the plains with Bell Creek below, and over the Isdell Range. The track to Bell Gorge will wind its way to your left in the valley below. At the base of the hill you will be back on the dirt and cross over Bell Creek. The turn-off to Silent Grove and Bell Gorge is 217 km east of Derby. Bell Gorge is one of the most spectacular gorges in the Kimberley and well worth a visit. The drive to Silent Grove passes through flat cane grass floodplains, interspersed with Kimberley White Gums *(Eucalyptus houseana)*. Nineteen kilometres along the track you come to Silent Grove, where the ranger is based during the dry season. This was the site of an outstation, run by Mt Hart Station. There are camping facilities here but if you wish to camp alongside Bell Creek closer to the falls, you must drive a further 6.5 km to the start of the various camping bays. There are individual and group camping areas, with toilets spread out over the next 1.5 km. Fees are collected by the mobile ranger/caretaker on site, but you will need to collect a camp number tag in the high season from Silent Grove before driving to the camping sites along the Bell Creek. It is strongly recommended that you get to Silent Grove by mid-day at the latest if you wish to secure a camping site here.

Bell Gorge Falls

Pool above Bell Gorge Falls

◀ Looking down Bell Gorge from the falls

It is a wonderful location with a freshwater running stream lined with pandanus and large trees such as Wild Plum *(Terminalia platyphylla)* and the Australia-wide River Red Gum *(E. camaldulensis)* giving shade during mid-day. At night the Bush Stone-curlew and both Southern Boobook and Barking Owl may call, while Northern Brown Bandicoots *(Isoodon macrourus)* scurry around in the cane grass. The car park at the start of the walk to Bell Gorge is 11 km from Silent Grove. The start of the walk is steep and stony for 150 m and then you come to a small creek bed. Turn right here and walk down the pebble creek bed, but don't forget to note where you entered, as it is easy to walk straight up the creek here. You will walk past Freshwater Mangrove trees *(Barringtonia acutangula)* and Ironwood *(Erythrophleum chlorostachys)*. After a short 15 min walk, you will come out to an open rock area above the main falls. First head to the left of the falls and look down the valley – from here you will gain a general picture of your location. You can either walk up the rocky hillside to the left and look back at the main falls or, if you are keen, return back to the head of the falls and cross over the rocky part upstream at the top pool. For the agile, you can then climb up the opposite hillside and down to the pools below with care. If you are fit you can continue down the gorge. Refer to sketch map for location of walks.

Mirima (Hidden Valley)
NATIONAL PARK

This small park is just walking distance from Kununurra or a short 5 min. drive and well worth a visit. If you cannot get to the Bungle Bungle Range, then see this park as it is almost a small cameo version of the fractured and disected multi coloured domes at Purnululu National Park. The sedimentary strata within the domes are 350 million years old, but the actual domes were created 20 million years ago by pressures that uplifted the sedimentary rocks. Then, with wind and rain, the quartz sandstone was eroded as water broke through the cracks and faults in the harder laterite capping, thus creating the small valleys and domes that you can see today.

There are a few walks in the park, the harder 1 km return Didbagirring trail takes you up a steep slope that looks across the Ord River floodplain as well as back into the Mirima Range itself. On the ridge tops in the early dry you may see clumps of the pink flowers of Kimberley Heather *(Calytrix exstipulata)* in full bloom and if you are early you may catch a glimpse of the Short-eared Rock-wallaby, or the more common Agile Wallaby. There is a short 500 m walk with information boards on the circular botanical trail, useful in identifying some of the plants you may have seen elsewhere in the Kimberley. DCLM in the height of the season has run short guided walks and also slide nights for visitors to Kununurra; check details with the DCLM Kununurra office.

Rocky outcrops in Mirima National Park resemble those found in Purnululu

Parry's Lagoon (Marlgu Billabong)
NATURE RESERVE

Parry's Lagoon, just south of Wyndham, is a very important 36,000 ha wetland nature reserve for waterbirds and other wildlife. Before the early 1900s the Ord River remained unchecked on its journey to the sea and the natural grasslands were grazed by just kangaroos and wallabies, but soon these plains were to become a vast holding area for cattle before they went to the meatworks in Wyndham. Then after this, the huge Lake Argyle Dam held back the main body of the floodwaters that would normally come down in the wet. Fortunately the wetlands, although reduced, still hold large bodies of water after good rain seasons and the main billabong, Marglu, normally has water remaining even at the end of the dry season. It is not unusual to see several thousand ducks spread out across the flooded lagoons.

DCLM has constructed some of the best bird hides in WA alongside Freshwater Mangroves at the billabong edge. Besides the resident ducks,

◀ Looking over Marlgu Billabong from Telegraph Hill

Marlgu Billabong

Magpie Geese

Plumed Whistling Duck

Yellow Chat

the area is an important feeding ground forsome of our migratory waders that fly all the way down from Asia and Siberia, arriving at the beginning of the wet season. One of our most uncommon shorebirds, the Little Curlew, migrates all the way from the high tundra in Siberia to feed here, and in other parts of northern Australia, at the end of the dry season. Migrating waders can lose up to one third of their body weight after these lengthy flights, but soon recharge the body system with foods from these wetlands. Birds like the Yellow Chat, rarely seen by even the keenest birdwatchers, breed in the centre of the Lignum and Sesbania of the floodplain.

Parry's Lagoon can be accessed from the Great Northern Highway and the main entrance is a dirt gravel road, 15 km south of Wyndham and 85 km north west of Kununurra. There is an information board just 1 km off the highway and just past this a turn-off left to Telegraph Hill and the main wetlands. The view from Telegraph Hill gives you some idea of the extent of the wetlands. From here you can drive down to the bottom of the hill, turning right to the two bird hides, then you can return back out either via the track to Wyndham or the track to Kununurra. Caution: Even though this is a freshwater area, Saltwater or Estuarine Crocodiles are known to frequent the lagoons occasionally, so try and stay back from the water's edge.

Black-necked Stork

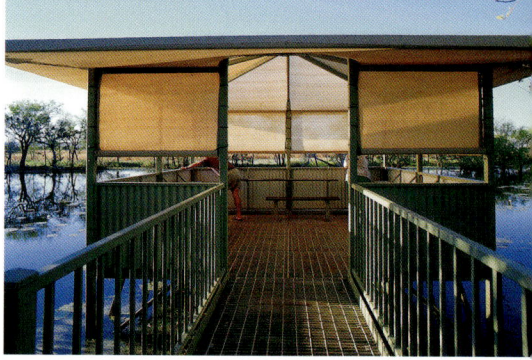

The observation hide of Marlgu Billabong

Drysdale River
NATIONAL PARK

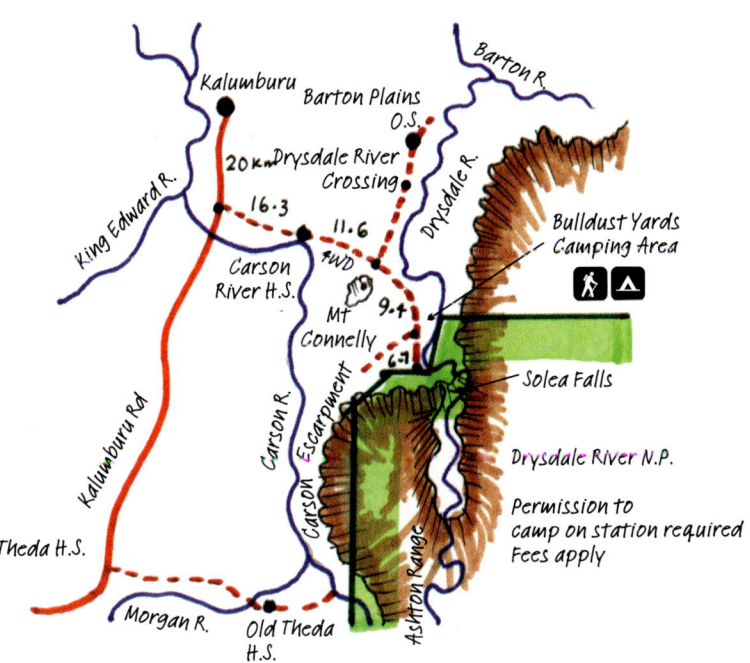

This is a vast wilderness park covering an area of 448,000 ha, the Drysdale and Carson Rivers being the main river systems to pass through this park. There are similarities to the Mitchell Plateau region, although the north west region of the Kimberley supports a higher diversity of flora and fauna due in the main to a higher rainfall. Nevertheless, this region is very important as a conservation area.

All visitors wishing to enter this park must register with the DCLM office in Kununurra and should be well experienced in bush walking in remote areas, or accompanied by people who are. There are no facilities within the park. Access is via a few localities, all on private station tracks that abut the park. Access via Carson River Station is just 0.5 km north of the Carson River crossing on Kalumburu Road heading east. It is then a 16 km drive to the station. Half a kilometre past the station is a sign on the left saying 'Drysdale River National Park 19 km'. The camping ground at Bulldust Yards is on Carson River property 44 km from Kalumburu Road. You must seek permission before planning to enter the park and a fee is charged.

If you have not had experience in four wheel driving and remote bush survival techniques before, it is very unwise to enter this wilderness region where getting lost is very easy due to the nature of the terrain.

Steep Island at Doubtful Bay on the remote Western Kimberley coast

Coast near Broome

Kimberley Coast, Rowley Shoals Marine Park and Prince Regent Nature Reserve

Kimberley Coast

The Kimberley is the most remote and rugged coastline in all of Australia. To sail these waters is a real privilege in an age when cellular phones and fast cars dominate the urban environment. Here there is peace and tranquillity all of its own. To enter the pristine bays and coastal gorges often without another vessel in sight is a wonderful experience. You can sail up gorges with 100 m rock faces either side or land on pristine sandy beaches. However, these are dangerous waters to the inexperienced sailor with some of the highest and strongest tidal movements on the Australian coast, combined with a great deal of uncharted waters. You can be sailing in many fathoms of water and then suddenly there are rocks only a few metres down.

There are, however, quite a few reputable tourist vessels that sail these waters and the tourist centres in Broome, Kununurra and Derby know most of them.

Rowley Shoals

Many divers will tell you that these coral atolls have some of the finest dive sites in Australia. The atolls are certainly some of the most pristine in the world. Unfortunately they are 300 km or 180 nautical miles west of Broome in the Indian Ocean and a costly journey to make from the big cities. However they still say it is well worth the trip.

There are 3 atolls - Clerke Reef, Imperieuse Reef and Mermaid Reef. They consist of an outside perimeter coral reef, enclosing an internal lagoon. Two lower atolls, Imperieuse and Clerke, are managed by DCLM. Mermaid Reef Marine Nature Reserve is managed by Environment Australia with assistance from DCLM.

The water clarity is second to none and the marine species diversity immense, with over 230 species of coral and a staggering 700 species of fish. There are huge giant cod that are quite tame but totally protected. Also many reef systems like the Great Barrier Reef are under pressures, be it pollution, crown of thorns starfish or other reef predators, but here on the Rowley Shoals the reef system is free of such pressures. It is also one of the three breeding sites in Western Australia of the beautiful Red-tailed Tropicbird, a rare sea bird in these waters.

Fishing is not allowed on Mermaid Reef and fishing restrictions apply for Clerke and Imperieuse Reefs. Collecting of shells is not allowed.

There are a few professional dive boat companies that visit these atolls from Broome.

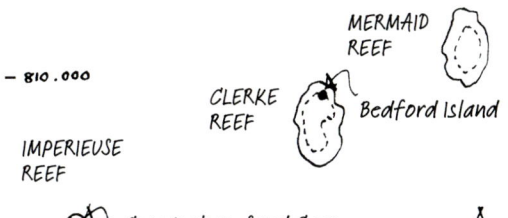

Ngauwudu (Mitchell Plateau)

The whole region is quite spectacular and here, are some of the finest water falls in Australia, particularly when in flood.

The area is a very inportant region for the Woonambal people, most of whom live in Kalumburu but have returned and established a community here.

The DCLM are working closely Woonambal people to protect this important areaq for both visitors and the local people.

Please keep to those tracks marked for visitors.

As the journey to Ngauwudu is a long drive from any major town, one should contact one of the main DCLM offices to check the current status of the tracks and facilities available.

The whole area is full of paintings and important sites. For the experienced walker with an interest in Aboriginal culture, it is not too hard to find them but please respect them by not touching the art work.

Mitchell Plateau is 70 km off the Gibb River /Kalumburu road. It is definitely a 4WD track and as this region has a higher rainfall than southern parts of the Kimberley it is not uncommon for low lying areas to have boggy conditions late into the dry. There are no facilities and you must be totally self-sufficient. If travelling from and returning to Drysdale River Station, you will require a minimum of 550 km worth of fuel for exploring different areas within the plateau.

There are now toilets and a ranger based in the dry season at the end of the Mitchell Falls track. In the main tourist season air charter companies fly into the airstrip and a resident chopper is also based there for scenic flights.

Mitchell Falls track

This is a moderate to difficult 6 km return walk which traverses rocky country. You will come to a small waterfall (Little Mertens Falls) just 500 m from the car park. Note the lush vegetation surrounding the bottom pool. This is one of the many small patches of monsoonal rainforests that can be found in the northern part of the Kimberley. They are remnants of Australia's wetter times and support higher numbers of fauna and flora species than the open woodlands.

Further down the track you will pass through open woodland, rocky hill tops and then along a pandanus-lined creek to a beautiful pool above Big Mertens Falls, be careful of the edge here, it is 2.5 km back to the car park. Across the other side and over the ridge, you will drop down to the impressive Mitchell Falls with its four-tiered set of falls. To gain the best views you will need to cross the river and make your way along the other side, dropping over a side overflow creek, and then up the slope to look back at the magnificent set of falls. It is strongly suggested that you do not attempt to gain access to the lowest pool and definitely do not swim there, as Saltwater Crocodiles inhabit this area.

Surveyors Pool (Aunauyu)

Access to the pool is approx. 21 km north of the turn-off to Mitchell Falls, then down a stony track for 6.5 km. It is then a moderate 8 km return walk from the Surveyors Pool car park.

Crystal Creek and Port Warrender (Closed to public)

Geology

The top surface of the plateau consists of a thin laterite bauxite layer just 2–5 m thick, from which aluminium could be produced and in fact the plateau was well surveyed not too long ago and mining rights are still being held for much of the plateau. Laterite soils always occur in tropical regions of the world and are created by high humidity and rainfall, affecting the underlying volcanic basalt by leaching out elements and leaving an element called gibbsite, from which aluminium is made.

The plateau is 370 m above sea level and the other surrounding country is made up of sandstone and does not have this thin laterite capping.

Flora and Fauna

This region is very rich in species diversity, particularly mammals, with at least 39 having been recorded here. This is the most species for any similar sized area in Western Australia, so it is vital that this region be protected. Many are small and nocturnal like the Red-cheeked Dunnart (*Sminthopsis virginiae*), Butler's or Carpentarian Dunnart (*Sminthopsis butleri*), Golden-backed Tree-rat (*Mesembriomys macrurus*), Brush-tailed Tree-rat (*Conilurus penicillatus*) and Scaly-tailed Possum (*Wyulda squamicaudata*). Most people rarely see these little creatures but you may be lucky in the early morning or late evening and see the Short-eared Rock-wallaby (*Petrogale brachyotis*) or the diminutive Monjon (*Petrogale burbidgei*), the smallest of all rock-wallabies.

The common Fan Palm seen throughout the top plateau country is *Livistona eastonii* and in wet areas the beautiful cycad, *Cycas lane-poolei*, can be found. The common trees are Ironwood (*Erythrophleum chlorostachys*), Darwin Woollybutt (*Eucalyptus miniata*) and Darwin Stringybark (*Eucalyptus tetrodonta*).

Birds Birdwatchers come here to see the endemic Black Grasswren. They can often be seen near Little Mertens Falls, or when walking any of the boulder country with clumps of spinifex. The rare raptor, the Red Goshawk, can be seen, if you are lucky, in the eucalypt woodland, particularly near the King Edward River area. They have a preference for river systems that have large Cadjeput trees (*Melaleuca leucadendra*). The White-quilled Rock-Pigeon is endemic to the Kimberley and is quite common near the Mitchell Falls area. The White-lined Honeyeater can be seen as you walk through the thicker creek vegetation. To see Rainbow Pitta you must walk into the thicker rainforest vine thickets which are not easily accessed from the main tracks.

Mitchell Falls

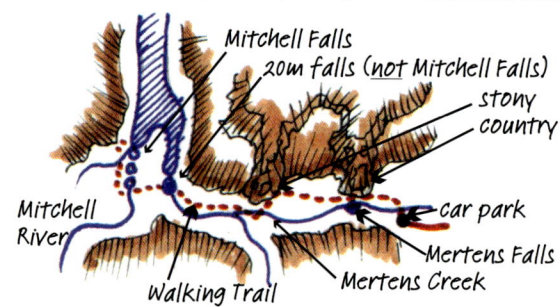

Detailed drawing of Punamii-unpuu area (Mitchell Falls)

The beehive domes of the Bungle Bungle Range — A pool at the end of Cathedral Gorge

Purnululu
NATIONAL PARK

This has to be one of the most impressive parks in Western Australia. It is particularly noted for its stunning dome-like structures with multi coloured bands, that make a spectacular sight in the early morning or evening light.

Europeans used parts of the park as early as the 1900s for cattle grazing and evidence of old stock yards and fencing still exists, but most of the pastoral leases were resumed in 1967.

Generally though, the park was little known until the mid 1980s and was not vested as a national park until 1987.

There are now strong conservation management plans put in place by DCLM in conjunction with the Aboriginal traditional custodians of the region. Radiocarbon dating on artefacts shows that the Aboriginal people have lived in this region for over 20,000 years and people from Warmun (Turkey Creek) still know many of the traditional ceremonial sites.

The name Purnululu means 'sandstone rock' in the Kija language and Kawarra 'cliff you cannot climb'. The word Bungle Bungle is thought to have come from the corruption of the name of the grassfound in the region, called 'bundle bundle grass'.

You access the park off the Great Northern Highway, 51 km south of Warmun. It is 53 km from the entry information bay near the highway to the registration bay opposite the ranger station inside the park. The main three-way junction that accesses all tracks is just a further 500 m in.

To the left is Kurrajong camping ground at 6 km and to the right Walardi camping ground, 11 km.

If you are visiting the park by road, try to get to the highway entry point by at the latest mid-day, so you can have plenty of time to get to your camping site, as the access road will take you some time. Twelve years ago the entry track would take 5 hrs. It is a better track now but it will still take you 3 hrs. It is definitely a 4WD and 4WD trailer track only and the management authorities intend it to stay that way, making the park a wilderness area with low impact tourism (more people fly over the Bungle Bungle than drive in, so getting a flight and seeing the park is not a problem). You will need to have at least 400 km worth of fuel on board to enjoy the park and still be able to return to Warmun. The first part of the entry track runs through the private property of Mabel Downs so stay on the main track, which is always signposted. There is a pleasant stop at Calico Springs, half way along the rough entry track, with water and good shade from the Freshwater Mangroves (*Barringtonia acutangula*), Roughleaf Cabbage Gum (*Eucalyptus confertiflora*) and Cadjeput (*Melaleuca species*). The creek side is lined with Pandanus.

During the summer months this is an extremely hot area so try to visit between the months of May to September. The park is officially closed January 1st to March 31st.

The Bungle Bungle Range is formed by quartz sandstone and conglomerate stone and some siltstone similar to but not quite the same as the domes in Mirima National Park outside Kununurra. These sedimentary formations were deposited into the Ord Basin some 360 million years ago. Surrounding the Bungle Bungle were other mountain ranges such as the Osmond Range. Uplift occurred here and then streams which eroded sands and rocks from these ancient hills were deposited at lower levels, forming broad plains of sandstone. With time and weathering a hard crust of laterite was formed. With further uplift, the natural fault lines were eroded first and with continued water erosion, deep valleys were created as one can see clearly on the walk to Cathedral and Piccaninny Gorges.

The domes look very solid but are in fact very fragile due to the fact that the sand grains of the sandstone are held together by silica cement and although structurally strong, when water breaks through the laterite capping, the grains are easily washed away over time. The more cracks that are exposed the more individual small valleys will be formed. The colourful orange and black bands that one can see in the ranges are caused by the fact that the different alternating layers of strata have different porous qualities and the more permeable layers allow water to seep through and form algal-bacterial growth, which is dark in colour. The harder, less porous layers are covered in thin layers of iron and manganese, creating orange coloured bands. Knowing the fragility of these rocks you can understand why it is important not to attempt to climb the domes.

Besides the 360 million year old sandstone domes there are many other rock systems and you will drive past dark thin ridges of the far older limestone.

Rocky outcrops near Echidna Chasm

Walks

Domes Trail 25 km from the ranger station. This short 1 km walk allows you to wander around the base of the domes and can be done before the Cathedral Gorge walk.

Cathedral Gorge 25 km from the ranger station. This is a must, a wonderful walk and not too long, being 2 km.

Picaninny Gorge 25 km from the ranger station. This is a far longer walk, being 14 km to the 'Elbow' and a 30 km plus walk to the 'Fingers' which requires an overnight back pack camp. These walks should only be tackled by those who are fit and well prepared. You must register with the ranger before setting out.

Echidna Chasm This is in the north west of the park. You walk through a very narrow chasm where you can touch the high 100 m walls on either side. It is an easy to moderate walk of 2 km and on the way you will pass tall slender Livistona Palms (*Livistona eastonii*).

Other Walks: There are other walks such as the 5 km return Mini Palms Gorge Walk, named after the stunted Livistona Palms that grow only a few feet high in the shady gorge and the Froghole Walk, 1 km return. Look for the Rockhole Frog (*Litoria meiriana*), dark brown and only 20 mm long. These two walks are moderate to difficult.

Even though little rain falls in the dry, the park supports over 600 species of plants. The open woodland plains support Silver Leaf Bloodwood (*Eucalyptus collina*), Rough-leaf Range Gum (*E. aspera*), Bauhinia (*Bauhinia cunninghamii*) and Wickham's Grevillea, (*Grevillea wickhamii*). If Wickham's Grevillea is in full flower, then look out for feeding birds such as Black, Pied, and Grey-fronted Honeyeaters. If you see a large flock of birds congregating above the flowers, there is a good chance you will be looking at Masked Woodswallows and maybe a few White-browed Woodswallows as well.

Flights You can fly from Kununurra, Warmun or Halls Creek or take the helicopter flight near Walardi campsite in Purnululu itself. These flights are recommended and if you are in the park, it is still well worth it, as it gives you a great appreciation of the unique dome structures.

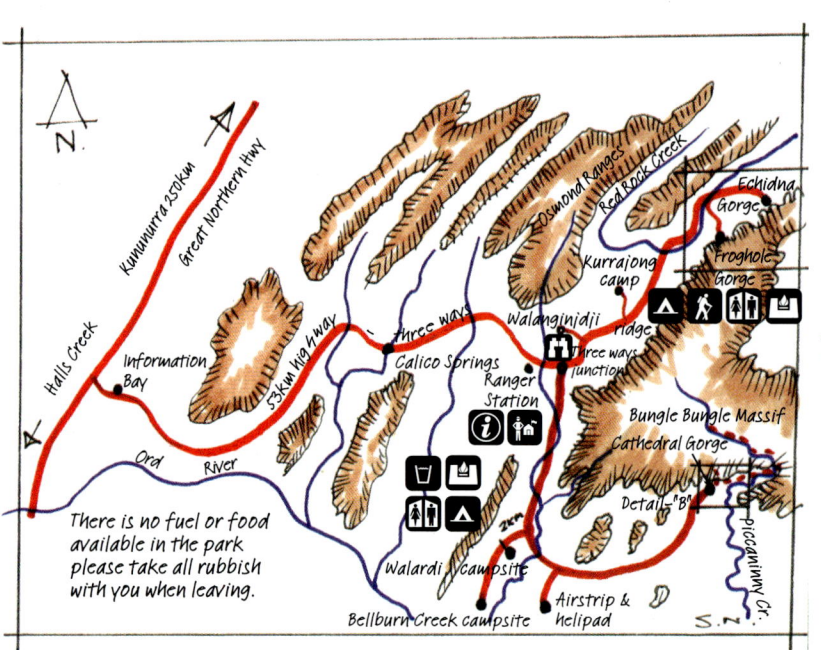

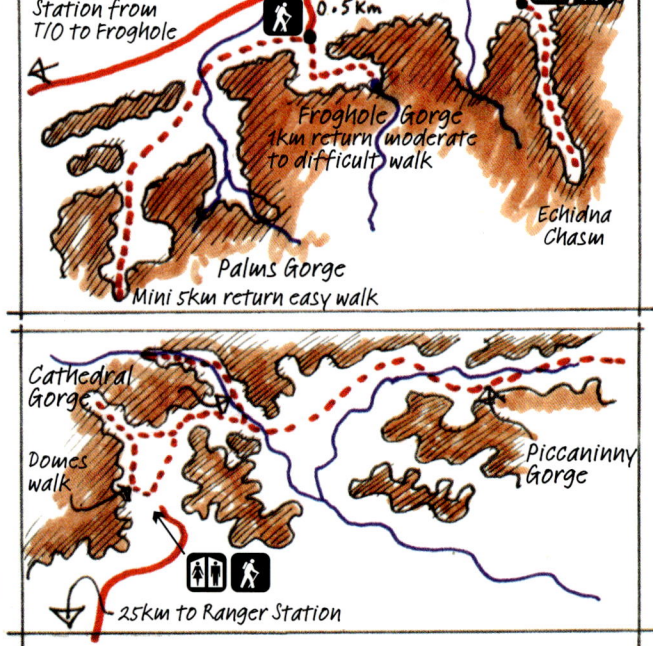

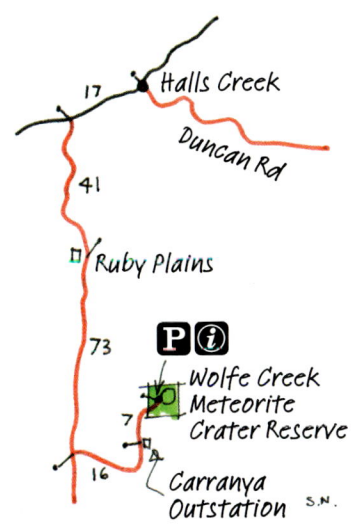

Wolfe Creek Crater

Wolfe Creek Crater (Kandimalal)
RESERVE

Wolfe Creek Crater is the second largest meteor crater in the world after Meteor Crater in Arizona USA. It is located on the north western edge of the Tanami Desert, 145 km by road south of Halls Creek. It was not discovered by Europeans until 1947. They were N.B. Sauve, F. Reeves and D. Hart, while on an aerial survey of the region. Reeves and Hart returned 2 months later to make a more detailed survey. It takes its European name from the pioneer Robert Tennant Stowe Wolfe who travelled to the Kimberley in 1886.

The local Djaru people and their ancestors would have known of Wolfe Creek for centuries; they called it Kandimalal and in their mythology about the origins of the crater, they believed that two snakes cut paths through the desert plains, creating Sturt Creek and Wolfe Creek. One of the snakes emerged from the earth's surface, creating Wolfe Creek Crater.

There are five true circular craters in Australia, the smallest being 'Dalgaranga Crater' north of Yalgoo WA, having a diameter of 25 m compared to that of Wolfe Creek at 950 m. There are other examples of meteorite impacts in Australia, some being much larger, but due to weathering and movements in the earth's surface they no longer have the classic circular crater formation.

The crater forms an almost perfect circle, 950 m across at its widest point, and the crater floor having a diameter of 675 m. It reaches a depth of 55 m from the top of the rim to the crater floor and is at least 25 m below the surrounding plain. The depth of the crater would have been far greater at the time it was formed, but with weathering and wind-blown soils the depth has been reduced.

Scientists estimate that a gigantic meteor made its impact here nearly 300,000 years ago. Small meteorites entering the earth's atmosphere soon burn out, they are the shooting stars we see on clear starry nights. But this massive projectile weighing an estimated 50,000 tonnes would have retained a great deal of its volume after crashing to earth. Also it would retain much of the cosmic velocity it had just prior to entering the earth's atmosphere, with estimated speeds of 15 km per second. That's like travelling from Perth to Sydney in 6 minutes. Obviously the forces created by the speed, weight and impact of such a missile on the earth's surface would substantially alter the flat laterite and quartzite plain it hit. Not only would the impact pulverise the existing rocks but the phenomenal pressures that would occur would create such heat that the meteorite would literally explode out from the impact, sending debris far and wide. Pieces of the meteorite have been found several km away. On the outside rim, besides the fragments of the original laterite and quartzite rocks, are round rocks called 'Shaleballs' which contain minerals previously unknown to science and give us an insight into the fascinating origins of outer space minerals.

It is a fairly long drive to the crater along a dusty track and you would want to think seriously about travelling here, as it will take at least a full day to travel in and out. If you are travelling down the Canning Stock Route or the Tanami track then it is only 17 km off the main dirt track.

Prince Regent
NATURE RESERVE

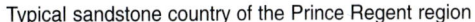
Typical sandstone country of the Prince Regent region

This 635,000 ha reserve contains similar flora and fauna to the Mitchell Plateau area. At present access to the reserve is by permit only. There are no roads into the park and access is via the coast only and permits to walk this country from boats are still required.

▼King Cascade

SECTION 3

A painter reflects on the beauty of Hellfire Bay Cape Le Grand National Park while a young boy enjoys fishing below

Ancillary Information

Included in this section of the book are some general facts on our wildlife, information on various recreational activities that occur in our National Parks, conservation issues and finally contact information regarding accommodation within Western Australia.

Some interesting facts about our lesser known vertebrates—reptiles; and our Invertebrates—spiders, beetles and moths.

Ring-tailed dragon (*Ctenophorus caudicinctus*) Photo by David Knowles

Coastal Bandy Bandy snake (*Simoselaps littoralis*) Photo by David Knowles

Reptiles

What types of reptiles occur in Western Australia?

Western Australia has almost 50% of the Australian reptiles occurring within its borders. WA also has the richest semiarid and arid reptile faunas in the world. Sixteen Families of reptiles occur in this State.

How many species of each Family are represented in Western Australia?

Crocodiles 1 family–2 species–tropical, **Sea Turtles** 2 families–5 species–tropical; **Freshwater Turtles** 1 Family–10 species–mostly tropical; **Snakes** 7 Families–114 species (**Colubrid Snakes** 3 species–tropical, **Elapid Snakes** 50 species–state-wide, **Pythons** 9 species–state-wide, **Blind Snakes** 25 species–state-wide, **File Snakes** 1 species–tropical, **Water Snakes** 3 species–tropical, **Sea Snakes** 23 species–mostly tropical); **Lizards** 5 families–356 species (**Geckos** 67 species–state-wide, **Skinks** 200 species–state-wide, **Goannas** 20 species–state-wide, **Dragon Lizards** 45 species–state-wide, **Legless Lizards** 24 species–state-wide).

How big are they?

The Saltwater crocodile is the largest reptile reaching up to 7 m, and the largest turtle is the Leatherback Turtle reaching 3 m. Our largest lizard is the Perentie Goanna which reaches 2.5 m.

Where are they?

Reptiles occur in almost all known land habitats, from coastal dunes, mangroves, salt-lake margins, grasslands, sedgelands, shrublands to woodlands and forests. Crocodiles, sea turtles, freshwater turtles, sea snakes, file snakes and water snakes are restricted to freshwater and marine habitats

When do you see them?

Most land reptiles are active during the warmer parts of the year. However there is a tropical peak of adult activity during and after the northern 'wet' and during spring and summer south of the tropic.

How do you see them?

Crocodiles are usually observed basking on riverbanks. Freshwater turtles, sea turtles and sea snakes are most commonly observed from high places like large boats, cliffs, jetties and bridges. The larger snakes and lizards are most commonly encountered on roads during the day and night. Many thousands are killed each year by traffic. Turning debris in station and country dumps can also reveal many species.

What is their ecological role?

The great majority of our reptile species are predators controlling populations of a wide variety of animals from mammals, birds, amphibians, fish, other reptiles, spiders, insects and other invertebrates.

Snakes

How many Families of snakes occur in Western Australia?

Western Australia has 7 families and 114 species of snakes occurring within its borders.

How many snakes of each Family are represented in Western Australia?

Colubrid Snakes (2 Tree Snakes and the Keelback) 3 species–tropical; **Elapid Snakes** (venomous land snakes) 50 species–state-wide; **Pythons** 9 species– state-wide; **Blind Snakes** 25 species–state-wide; **File Snakes** (Water snakes)1 species–tropical; **Water Snakes** (Mangrove snakes and Freshwater snake) 3 species–tropical; **Sea Snakes** 23 species–mostly tropical.

How big are they?

Western Australia's longest snake is the Pilbara Olive Python which is reported to reach over 5 m. The smallest snakes are all small species of blind snakes. At around 15 cm these snakes are often confused with worms, however the small eyes, forked tongue and spur on the tip of the tail will define them as snakes.

Where are they?

Snakes occur in almost all known land habitats, from coastal dunes, mangroves, salt-lake margins, grasslands, sedgelands, shrublands to woodlands and forests. Sea snakes, file snakes and water snakes are restricted to freshwater and marine habitats.

When do you see them?

Most snakes are active during the warmer parts of the year. However there is a tropical peak of adult activity during and after the northern 'wet' and during spring and summer south of the Tropic.

How do you see them?

Sea snakes are most commonly observed from high places like large boats, cliffs, jetties and bridges. The larger snakes are most commonly encountered on roads during the day and night. Many thousands are killed each year by traffic. Turning debris in station and country dumps can also reveal many species.

What is their ecological role?

All snakes are predators controlling populations of a wide variety of animals from mammals (eg. Taipan and larger pythons), birds (eg. Rough-scaled Python), amphibians (eg. Keelback, Tiger Snake and Short-nosed Snake), fish (eg. Sea snakes, file snake and water snakes), other reptiles (eg. Black-headed Python and Whip Snakes), crabs (eg. White-bellied Mangrove Snake) and insects (blind snakes). Blind snakes are specialised feeders on ant pupae, larvae and eggs, as well as all stages of termites.

Snakes also provide food for a range of other creatures from humans, mammals, birds, other reptiles, fish, to insects and parasites.

Banksia Moth (*Danima banksiae*) — Photo by David Knowles

Ground Beetle (Family Carabidae) — Photo by David Knowles

Moths

What is the difference between a moth and a butterfly?
This commonly asked question is usually answered by a generalisation. Moths do not usually have clubbed antennae, male moths have distinctly more feathery antennae than females, most species are nocturnal, and they tend to have hairier bodies and more muted wing colouration. Their caterpillars tend to be hairier as well.

How big are they?
Moths in Western Australia range in wingspan from 5mm up to 240mm. The great majority are under 30mm. Our largest species is the female Wattle Goat moth of the arid inland that has a body that weighs more than a mouse and a wingspan of 240mm. These are the heaviest moths in the world.

How many species are in Western Australia and Australia?
Australia has approximately 20,500 named species in 77 families, which is about one fifth of the known world fauna. Western Australia has about one quarter of the known species occurring within its borders. Many species remain to be discovered and named.

Where are they?
Moths and their caterpillars occur in almost all known habitats, from coastal dunes, mangroves, salt-lake margins, grasslands, sedgelands, shrublands to woodlands and forests.

When do you see them?
Adult moths may be seen in almost all months of the year in this huge State. However there is a tropical peak of adult activity during and after the northern 'wet' and during spring and autumn/early winter south of the tropic.

How do you see them?
Moths are most easily seen fluttering around lights, including camp lights. service station and caravan park lights surrounded by bush are good places to see a wide variety of species, many remaining on the walls the following morning. Entomologists use light traps to collect moths. They use a variety of light sources to attract different species, including ultra-violet, mercury vapour, and actinic lights.

Why are moths attracted to lights?
Moths navigate by keeping the angle of reflected light from the moon constant. If a human light source gets between the moon and the moth the brighter source will be favoured and the moth will spiral towards it maintaining its angle.

What is their ecological role?
Being metamorphic insects dictates two ecological roles. The larval role for moths is mostly plant population control by pruning leaves, buds and flowers. Other moth larvae are recyclers of living, dying, or dead wood. An important role for the caterpillars of some Australian moths is to process the millions of tonnes of dead gum leaves that daily fall on the ground. Adults of most moths are nocturnal and provide pollination services to many plants. Both larvae and adults provide food for a huge range of predatory organisms and parasites.

Predatory beetle

What is the difference between a predatory beetle and other beetles?
Although there are a number of predatory beetle families represented in Australia most belong to the family *Carabidae* which are commonly known as Ground Beetles and Tiger Beetles. Almost all are predators and have usually prominent jaws. Many are ground-based and have lost the ability to fly, and the thorax is often strongly differentiated from the head and abdomen. Many species of Ground beetles are black or dark brown, with or without metallic body margins. Some species are completely metallic with green being a common colour. Most Tiger Beetles are partly or wholly metallic with one group of beach and salt lake specialists combining metallic colouration with white wing cases.

How big are they?
Ground and Tiger Beetles in Western Australia range in body length from 2 mm up to 70 mm. The great majority are under 20 mm. Our largest species occurs in the arid zone north of the Tropic.

How many species are in Western Australia and Australia?
Australia has approximately 1,800 named species. Western Australia has a diverse Ground Beetle and Tiger Beetle fauna, especially in its huge semi-arid and arid zones.

Where are they?
Predatory beetles and their larvae occur in almost all known habitats, from beaches, coastal dunes, mangroves, salt-lake margins, grasslands, sedgelands, shrublands to woodlands and forests. The majority of species are associated with drainage and water bodies in the arid and semi-arid zones. Two main groups of Tiger Beetles are strongly associated with salt lakes.

When do you see them?
Adult beetles may be seen in almost all months of the year in this huge State. However there is a tropical peak of adult activity during and after the northern 'wet' and during spring and summer south of the Tropic.

How do you see them?
These beetles are most easily seen running on the ground beneath lights, including camp lights. Service station and caravan park lights surrounded by bush are good places to see a wide variety of species, many remaining on the ground the following morning. Some species, including the widespread metallic green 'stink' beetle can occur in huge numbers after good rains. A night walk around a salt lake in summer or autumn can also be productive.

What is their ecological role?
Being metamorphic insects dictates two ecological roles, in the case of predatory beetles the roles are the same for larvae and adults, although different prey items may be involved. Collectively they control populations of mostly herbivorous invertebrates. Both larvae and adults provide food for a huge range of predatory organisms and parasites. They are good indicators of ecological health—diverse prey equals diverse predators.

Photo by David Knowles — Red and Black Spider (*Nicodamus sp.*)

Spiders

What types of spiders occur in Western Australia?

For the purposes of this book there are two main divisions within these Arachnids. The so-called 'primitive' spiders have jaws that work with a stabbing action, and are represented by Tarantulas, Trapdoors and Mouse Spiders. The so-called 'modem' spiders have 'scissor-action' jaws and include almost all web-building spiders, Huntsman, Wolf spiders, Jumping spiders and White-tailed spiders.

How many types of spiders occur in Australia and Western Australia?

There are simply not enough people employed in this arachnophobic country to process our rich and interesting spider fauna. Approximately 2,000 species contained in many families have been described with easily double this amount of species sitting, unnamed, in bottles in Museums.

What types of habitats do spiders occur in?

Spiders occur in almost all land habitats from the wettest to the driest and the lowest to the highest. Indeed the young spiders of some species disperse by 'ballooning'. This involves the spider exuding a long filament of silk into the breeze, which may carry them to great heights and over great distances.

Do all spiders use silken snares to catch their prey?

No 'primitive' spider builds a snare to catch their prey, though they still use their silk to make sperm webs, egg sacs, line their burrows or shelters, make trip wires and balloon (some only). Many 'modem' spiders do not use silk to snare their prey and are active or ambush hunters. These include Huntsman, Wolf spiders, Jumping spiders, White-tailed spiders and Crab spiders.

What is the size range of Western Australian Spiders?

Our smallest spiders will easily fit onto the head of a pin. Our largest spiders have legs that will span an average human hand, and both are restricted to the Kimberley Region. The largest and heaviest spider is a Tarantula and the largest web-building spider is a Golden Orb Weaver.

Do spiders have courtship rituals?

Male spiders indulge in some extremely complex courtship rituals. The most complex are seen in male Peacock Jumping spiders. They use a combination of gem-like colours, special display flaps, an elongated and ornamented third pair of legs and dance to woo their mates.

How do spiders mate?

Male spiders and female spiders have genital slits beneath the base of the abdomen. Both sexes have two short leg-like appendages either side of the jaws. In the mature male spider the tips of these 'palps' are modified to take up, store and deliver sperm into the female. He first makes a small web beneath him and exudes two droplets of sperm onto the silk. The tip of a palp, at this stage, resembles a deflated balloon containing a coiled straw. The spider protrudes the right straw and sucks up the droplet and does the same for the left. He is now ready to find a mate and deliver the sperm into her abdomen. His inflated palp tips look like boxing gloves. Mating can be a risky business for some types of spiders, which may lose life or limb in the process. Surviving males usually die of starvation after the act of mating because the appetite for food is turned off.

How do spiders grow?

Hatchling spiders absorb the yolk and cast their first skin before they can feed. Some species may only cast their skin about five times before reaching maturity whereas female 'primitive' spiders moult throughout their whole lives.

How long do spiders live for?

Most 'modem' spiders have an annual life cycle like the Garden Orb Weaver, whereas the primitive spiders like female Tarantulas have been recorded to live over 20 years.

What type of ecological services do spiders provide?

All spiders are predators that control population levels of the largest group of land animals—the insects. Like any small predator they also provide food for other creatures from bacteria, fungi, and parasites right up the line to humans.

Jumping Spiders

Photo by David Knowles — Karri Peacock jumping spider (*Maratus sp.*)

What features define a Jumping spider?

These small (less than 20 mm) diurnal hunting spiders have eight eyes. The central pair of eyes at the front are distinctly enlarged. They jump using their hind limbs and many species are excellent mimics, mainly of ants.

What do Jumping spiders do and where do they occur?

Jumping spiders surround us from the highest mountains to the seashore and from the wettest rainforest to the driest desert. They provide a virtually invisible insect control service for the environment, but for most of us, they remain undetected. The limitations of human eyesight, in combination with lack of desire, shield us from a world of wonder and some impressive statistics.

How many types of Jumping spiders are in Western Australia and what size are they?

Only one percent of Western Australian spiders bear formal scientific names. Universities need to address this gross deficit urgently. Fingernail-sized Jumping spiders are the most successful group of spiders if the number of species is used as a measure of success. They are currently represented by less than 5,000 described species on a world-wide level, but it is possible that this figure could easily be doubled with a little time and a microscope.

How far can they jump and why have such good eyesight?

Aside from being able to jump up to 40 times their own length, these little diurnal hunters have evolved the best eyesight among the spiders. Their enlarged central pair of anterior eyes are visible to the naked eye. It is this pair of eyes that has led indirectly to their Family name Salticidae. The name is derived from the Latin salto 'to dance with pantomimic gestures'. The witness to 'the dance' must have eyes to see.

Why do jumping spiders dance?

The 'dance' in Jumping Spiders is primarily employed by mature males as a precursor to mating. As with human dance, with its focus on a combination of limb and body movements and bright costumes, many jumping spiders employ similar communication techniques to ensure the reproduction of the next generation.

Recreational activities in our parks

4WD Driving

Having driven 4WDs for nearly thirty years, I guess I could write a lot about them but the subject is too immense for this book. There are some very good 4WD clubs; many of them specialise in driving the make of vehicle you may possess, which is useful in terms of getting to know the do's and don'ts of your vehicle. They are, however, generally quite happy to have other brands tag along. The Four Wheel Drive Club of WA, however, is a bigger club and reading one of their trip notes, there were 5 Patrols, 4 Landcruisers, 3 Discoverys, 2 Pajeros and 1 Bravo, so it was a good mix. Contact: Four Wheel Drive Club of WA (Inc) PO Box 109, Northbridge, WA 6865.

The Toyota Landcruiser Club of WA is very big and as you can see above, is taking a very responsible attitude to our countryside. Whilst on this subject, there is an Australia-wide organisation called 'Tread Lightly Australia'. Here in WA, the 4WD Association has lists of all the 4WD clubs. The main thing is that all clubs affiliated to this organisation must adhere to the 'Tread Lightly Australia' code which in general covers the main rules for protecting the countryside by

4WD clubs like the Toyota Landcruiser Club of WA are taking a very responsible attitude to their activities

Before travelling into remote areas, it's wise to gain experience and join a 4WD club

not driving off tracks, wrecking sand dune vegetation, driving on granite outcrops, etc. (as depicted on page 187), It is a great step forward and a credit to those who enforce it.

The 4WD Association of WA will let you know which clubs are affiliated and nearest to your locality.

Contact: PO Box 6029, East Perth, WA 6829. Ph. 08 9243 6839. www.space.net.au~wa4wd

Fishing

More Australians fish than any other recreational pastime. It is a real pleasure to catch your own fresh fish and cook it over an open fire. Western Australia has the largest coastline by far of any other state, having over 12,500 km of coastline, but even with our small population some areas are being over-fished. Some of the best fishing areas in Western Australia, like Shark Bay, have stock levels of Pink Snapper at an all time low and Fisheries of WA are having to take strong measures to protect them. Do remember state bag and size limits apply.

I think most fishermen now realise that there are not unlimited fish out in our vast oceans. Since 1988, the total world population of fish has been on the decline; people know this, it is a fact, and still they come from some countries to our southern waters and take millions of tons of fish, and we kid ourselves it's going to last. Well, this book is not about gloom and doom but in our own way Australians are becoming more responsible. We don't throw dynamite in coral seas to kill fish, nor use other irresponsible techniques. Lets start at home by just getting a simple feed and use some of the 'Catch Care' rules when returning undersize fish or keeping to bag limits.
- Treat fish gently, to reduce stress and damage.
- If possible, avoid lifting fish out of the water to unhook.
- Try to wet hands before handling fish and remove the hook carefully.
- If the fish has swallowed a hook, cut the line rather than pulling a hook from the gut or gills.
- Stick to the bag limits and only take enough for your family to eat. Remember fish for the future of all.

Fishing in Cape Arid National Park

Regarding where to fish, the subject is far too big for this book and there are many books on fishing and where to go. As a rule the more remote the region, the better the catch. If you are lucky enough to sail the Kimberley coastline, you will certainly catch some mighty big fish; also the beaches east of Esperance have some of the best beach fishing in the state—enjoy your fishing.

Canoeing & Rafting

Canoeing is great fun. You can simply paddle down quiet waters like the Canning River or do serious 'white water' canoeing down rivers like the Avon or Murray River. You can do sea kayaking near Penguin Island. However, it is very important that you at least know the very basics about canoeing, particularly if you are going to enter moving water systems. There is equipment you must have, however, as a minimum requirement when starting canoeing.

Flat water
- A canoe in good condition with adequate buoyancy and end ropes or handle for pulling the canoe.
- Good strong paddles.

Moving or white water rivers
- If canoeing on moving or white water rivers, you must have approved helmets and be able to swim fairly well.
- Canoe with others, unless you are really experienced and even then it is not a good practice to canoe alone.
- Use an approved buoyancy vest (Personal Flotation Device -Type 2)

It is very wise to do a canoeing course, as you do not have to purchase equipment, as it is included in the hire/course fee, and you will learn so much and find what great fun it is. From basics, you can develop your skills into white water canoeing and kayaking, which is very exciting.

The organisation Canoeing Western Australia Inc. runs courses like 'Getting started', 'Moving on to moving water' and 'Mastering white water rafting'. They can give you a list of canoeing clubs and also reputable canoeing operators who run courses and tours.

There are grade ratings placed on each part of the main canoeing rivers, ranging from easy grade 1 to grade 4 for the very experienced. Do not attempt to enter rivers with a high grade until you are experienced.

The canoeing season is relatively short in the northern south west from June to September, but can last longer in the deep south west.

The main 'flat water' rivers are the Swan, Canning, Serpentine, lower reaches of the Murray and Moore Rivers. The main 'white water' rivers are the Avon, Murray, Blackwood,

Frankland, Warren, Collie (good in summer) and Deep Rivers.

In the north, the Murchison can also be canoed by those who are experienced and there are tour operators that can take you.

White water rafting is also very popular and there are tour operators who run rafting tours down the Avon.

The Department of Sport and Recreation has produced some useful pamphlets on the major canoeing rivers showing where you can start and finish a canoe trip.

Useful addresses: Canoeing Western Australia, PO Box 28, Wembley, WA 6014.
Website: canoewa.asn.au Phone: 9285 8501.

'Learning the ropes'

Diving

To snorkel above the clear waters of Ningaloo Reef or even close to Perth on Rottnest Island is a wonderful experience. If you take it further and dive with scuba gear, you have a hobby that gives untold pleasures. Below the sea surface lies another world, full of beauty with a combination of colours that you rarely see on land.

Western Australia has some great diving localities and on the map on page 189 are some of the localities.

There are some basic rules even for snorkelling:
- Always inform someone of your dive site and ideally swim with a friend.
- Establish not only where you will enter but also where you will exit the water.
- Establish what the tides are like and the speed and direction of currents, if any.
- Know your swimming limits; swim only as far as you know you can return from with ease.
- Be careful of swimming too close to coral–even a simple scratch can turn septic.
- As well as the snorkel and mask, use fins (flippers) as they assist you in currents and make your swim far more relaxing.
- Always check the weather forecasts, as weather conditions can change very quickly on open waters.

It is imperative that you complete an accredited scuba course before using scuba gear, as lives have been lost through inexperience and not carrying out standard procedures for scuba diving.

Although scuba diving is potentially dangerous if certain rules are not obeyed, it is, however, relatively safe and opens up a world beyond belief.

There are many reputable diving schools and most run not only good beginners' courses but great tour packages for short destinations like over to Rottnest Island, as well as more exotic destinations.

This book in no way should be used as a guide for diving localities. They are mentioned in the body text to let you know they exist. DCLM produce very good snorkel and diving site books which have a great deal of detail. There are also many good manuals on diving but the first thing you should do is visit a quality diving school and seek advice before you do anything.

Bushwalking

This is the most common activity in parks and requires little equipment and gives so much pleasure. However, if you intend to do more than just a simple stroll, there are some things you must have and be aware of.

The most essential item is a good pair of walking boots that cover the ankles. Go to a quality camping/bush walking store (many stores that sell camping gear, do not sell quality walking boots) and seek advice. If you are going to do short walks, there are lighter walking boots. If you intend to do serious long distance walking then get top boots that cover and give support to the ankles. Have adequate thick woollen/nylon socks. Try the boots with these socks and really make sure they are not too loose and definitely not too tight. Here is a basic list of items to take on longer walks:
- Strong walking boots.
- Quality long socks.
- You can wear shorts but you may get badly scratched so it is best to wear long trousers unless you know you will not get scratched. In the Kimberley use jeans and cut out large holes in the back to air the legs. Cane grass can cut you to bits on rugged overland walks.
- Wear a long sleeved shirt, and take a pullover with you if it looks cool.
- Wear a hat to protect you from the sun but still carry blockout cream.
- Take a small backpack containing light rain gear, matches, small first aid kit, at least 1 litre of water (2 on hot days), back-up high energy food, maps and a compass.

Do inform people of where you are going and when you plan to return. Drink at least half a litre of water before you start a long walk. You may not feel like it but you will find that you will drink far less during the day, particularly when it is warmer. Avoid really hot days and check the weather forecast. Ideally, walk with another person.

There are a few bush walking clubs and the government department Ministry of Sports and Recreation should be able to assist with further information on 08 9387 9700. DCLM's Hills Forest Activity Centre also has organised walks (contact 08 9295 2244). Also, Perth Bushwalkers Club Inc. has very good walks in the Perth hills and other areas. It is a great way to meet people who like the outdoors and keeping fit. However, if your interest lies in knowing more about fauna and flora in the bush, then I suggest you join one of the other natural history groups mentioned below. Perth Bushwalkers address is PO Box 8321, Perth Business Centre, WA 6849. Phone 08 9362 1614.

Climbing

Another challenging hobby is rock climbing and abseiling. It is one thing to abseil with ropes that are attached from above but to climb up a sheer rock face is a daunting thought to the uninitiated. Those who do it though love it and develop nerves of steel. We have some good climbing rock walls in many of our national parks such as on Peak Charles, the Stirling and Porongurup Range, West Cape Howe, Torndirrup and on the coast near Margaret River.

DCLM has some hobby classes regarding simple abseiling techniques through the Hills Forest Activity Centre (Phone 08 9295 2244).

The Ministry of Sports and Recreation (Phone 08 9387 9700) can assist with who to contact in the Climbing Association of Western Australia. They can inform you where you can attend a basic climbing course. Needless to say, do not attempt any form of rock climbing without some training and use up-to-date gear; old ropes, particularly if worn can be fatal if you fall.

Also, if you do choose to climb in national parks, it is your total responsibility if accidents happen, even if there is no adequate signage warning you of potential hazards.

Reputable stores in Perth or Fremantle can give you some advice on where to go for climbing courses and advice on the relevant climbing gear required.

Permits to cave and rock climb in national parks and reserves must be obtained from DCLM.

Wildlife viewing

Wildflowers

We are privileged to live in the richest part of Australia in terms of our flora. There are over 10,000 species in the South West Botanical Province alone (not to be confused with this book's region headed South West Region). That is a staggering figure. To travel the south west in spring is a sheer delight, particularly in the high flora-rich parks like Mt Lesueur, Stirling Range and Fitzgerald River National Park. As there are so many species to see and identify the challenge can be quite daunting but you can develop an interest in, say, one genus. The Western Australian Herbarium needs dedicated amateurs to assist them in their monumental task of slowly building up a flora base. There is a very good society called the Wildflower Society of Western Australia. The Perth head office is at Perry House, 71 Oceanic Drive, Floreat, WA 6014. Ph. 08 9383 7979. Website -www.ozemail.com.au-wildflowers.

The society has branches in a few localities in Perth and throughout Western Australia. Besides having regular meetings they have field trips into the bush. There is also the Western Australia Orchid Society—more details can be obtained from the above groups.

I have written a guide book on where to find wildflowers in this state, with over 900 species illustrated, called 'A Guide to the Wildflowers of South Western Australia'. It is not a book for the serious botanist but is designed to assist the traveller on what species can be found in the South West. It is available at all Angus and Robertson and Dymocks bookshops, as well as other bookshops.

Looking at wildflowers in Tuttaning NR

Bird watching

It is hard to believe that in the UK for example, there are over 1 million members in the Royal Society for the Protection of Birds. That's almost the population of Perth who are interested in our feathered friends. It is a hobby that is growing—you only need a pair of binoculars and you are ready to go.

For some, the enjoyment comes from finding new species. Australia has nearly 800 species of birds that either reside here or visit this island continent.

In each different habitat zone lives different species of birds and people travel to all corners of Australia to try to see them, particularly the rare species. There are very good guide books available on the birds of Australia. One of the most up-to-date and informative is by the Perth-based naturalist, Michael Morcombe, titled Michael Morcombe Field Guide to the Australian Birds.

There is a bird society called Birds Australia. The Western Australian branch address is Perry House, 71 Oceanic Drive, Floreat, WA 6014. Ph. 08 9383 7749. The society holds regular meetings as well as day and extended bush trips, some as far as our desert regions.

General wildlife

Besides ornithology (study of birds) and botany (study of plants), there are of course other fields of study that one can gain an interest in. One of the largest fields in the natural sciences, that is least known or studied, is that of entomology—the study of insects. The world has over a million species. Here in Australia there are countless species collected that have not even been classified by taxonomists. It is an area wide open for the amateur to delve into and enjoy and those scientists who are approachable are more than willing to help those who take up the challenge.

Sea watching at Point Anne in the Fitzgerald NP

Our mammal world in Australia is unique and the reptile world even more diverse. All these various groups of animals fall under the umbrella of the natural sciences and one particular society, the Western Australian Naturalist Club has an interest in all aspects of the natural world. Their meetings can be based on any topic and they have field trips to many areas throughout Western Australia. Besides holding meetings in Nedlands, they have several other meeting places in the metropolitan and country areas.

The fascination of seeing a new specie for the first time

Photography in National Parks

Recording one's holiday, be it with a video camera or still camera, can be most rewarding and form life-long records when our memory often forgets what we saw, when and where.

Like anything in life there are ways to get things right or improve on technique.

Most 35mm cameras will give you adequate shots and with improved technique can give even better results.

Most people are aware of camera shake and mistakenly buy very fast films like 400 ASA etc, but the quality of these films does not compare with slower films of around 50 ASA. To avoid camera shake use a tripod as it allows you to free your hands up and compose your photograph. It also allows you to set a small aperture, say around f16 or f22, to get good depth of field if wanting your foregrounds and backgrounds in focus.

The tripod allows you to take sunsets or sunrises where the light may be low and the speed reading very slow.

While we are on sunsets aim the camera away from the sun and take a reading to the side and then fix that reading and shoot at the setting sun. You may need to waste two or three shots to try the best reading.

With landscapes try and take most of your shots at the beginning or end of the day. The low angled sun will give you softer and more impressive light.

With composition, try and look at vertical formats occasionally they can be impressive with certain subjects. Also try with landscapes to have interesting subjects in the foreground as it may add strength to the overall quality of the shot.

If things are relatively similar in tone in the shot, say lots of yellow sand with green colours, try and have a bright red flower or brighter colour in the foreground to lift the subject matter. Obviously this can not be done all the time.

If you wish to take birds or animals you will have to invest in telephoto equipment, this can be very expensive if you want good gear and should only be undertaken by those who wish to invest lots of time and money in this area.

On a more technical note, one of the major problems is that the automatic built-in light meters are designed to meter grey tones or neutral toned objects. With subjects that have lots of neutral colours in them it's fine, but if you are photographing say a sandy beach with lots of sunlight reflecting off the water, then the camera reads this light as extremely bright and will incorrectly over compensate for the brightness, with the result that you will get underexposed photos.

It is always wise to buy a camera with which you can control the auto metering system. So for example if you are photographing a neutral toned red or light blue flower the meter will give you a correct reading, but if you have lots of white or bright yellow flowers in full sun the meter will underexpose trying to compensate for the brightness. The yellow itself is not really bright in terms of colour, it's simply yellow, but with the compensation it will come out dark yellow.

You get over this in two ways, either meter on a more neutral area, say medium toned greens, and check the light reading, or set the meter manually to that reading and point it back to the bright subject and take the shot.

Or if say the shot reads 120 seconds at f8 on the bright subject, reduce the speed say to 60 seconds.

If the subject is very dark and you have a tripod and you are on f11 at speed of 8 seconds, slow down the speed to 4 sec and let just a bit more light in.

Don't forget to take spare camera batteries, spare film and make sure you have tried the camera out before making a long journey, many people think "holiday—I need a new camera" and buy one the week before without any time to check it out.

Avoid leaving camera equipment and film in a closed car in full sun as the temperatures can cook film.

Animal tracks

A cross section of the tracks of the major groups of mammals found in Australia are represented here as an aid to differentiating one mammal from another. The sketches illustrated show the perfect profile of a track but when you are in the wild it is not easy to get a perfect footprint, but with time you can start to identify the main features that differ from one print to another.

In the early morning, particularly in sandy areas, is the best time to look before the wind blows the main features off the track, and the low angle of the sun picks up the profile much easier.

Macropodoidae (Kangaroos and other marsupials)

The Macropods are the largest group of marsupials in Australia and all macropods have 5 toes on the front foot. The hind foot is totally different, being much longer, hence its family name Macropodidae, macropod meaning large foot. In all macropods except the eastern states Musky Rat-kangaroo, the first toe no longer exists. The second and third toe are smaller, being joined together, except at the top joint where they split, having two small claws that are used as the primary grooming toes. The third and forth toes are both strong and are the only ones that touch the ground when the animal is moving.

Kangaroos and wallabies have two main forms of locomotion. One is basically a slow gait used when grazing. This allows all four feet to touch the ground as well as the tail, which is used as a basic support when the hind feet follow through to meet the front feet. The other locomotion is when the animal is hopping, when neither the front feet nor the tail touch the ground.

Although Bettongs are small macropods, they still share the same basic locomotion movements as kangaroos and wallabies.

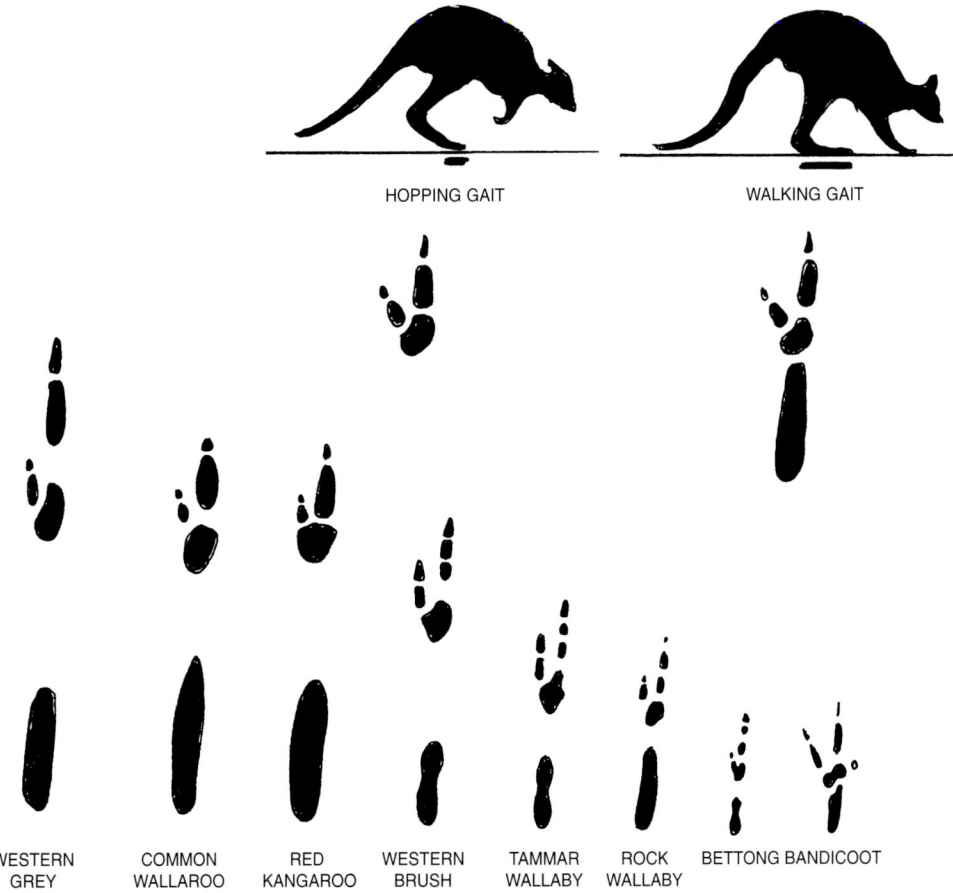

HOPPING GAIT · WALKING GAIT

WESTERN GREY KANGAROO · COMMON WALLAROO · RED KANGAROO · WESTERN BRUSH WALLABY · TAMMAR WALLABY · ROCK WALLABY · BETTONG BANDICOOT

Echidna

The front claws are quite broad and strong, designed for digging into termite mounds. Some of the hind claws are particularly long and allow the Echidna to groom itself between the long body spines.

Possum

In the possum, the front foot has five strong toes and a technique of spreading the toes when walking which makes them easily recognised. The hind foot also has five toes but the first toe has no claw and like humans, is joined to the second toe, which aids the possum when climbing trees.

Their rolling gait when walking produces the distinct tracks where the hind toe angles away from the body.

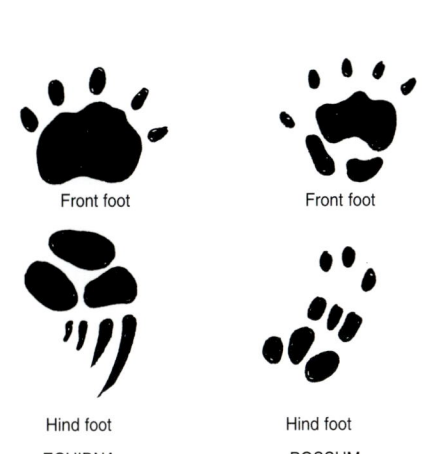

Front foot / Front foot / Hind foot / Hind foot
ECHIDNA · POSSUM

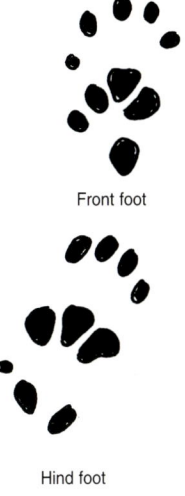

Front foot / Hind foot
QUOLL

Front foot / Rear foot
WOMBAT

Desert sandunes are a great place to look for animal tracks

Wombats

You are certainly lucky if you see the footprints of the Hairy-nosed Wombat in Western Australia as it is now quite rare, but once seen you will have no problem identifying the large footprints, particularly the large front pads that split into three triangular shapes.

Bandicoot

Bandicoots make similar tracks to potoroos. They have an unusual locomotion where the front two feet move forward alternately but the back two come forward together. They do not hop like macropods so all four feet will be seen as tracks.

Dingo, European Red Fox and Cat

All three carnivores show four toes on each foot with distinct pads. Both the Dingo and Fox have extended claws when walking but the cat retracts its claws. A Dingo's footprint differs from a Fox by two basic features. Firstly, as the illustration shows, the back two pads of the Dingo pass the rear of the front two pads but in the Fox the front of the back pads align with the rear of the front pads and secondly, the overall shape of a Dingo's footprint is circular in shape while that of the Fox is oval.

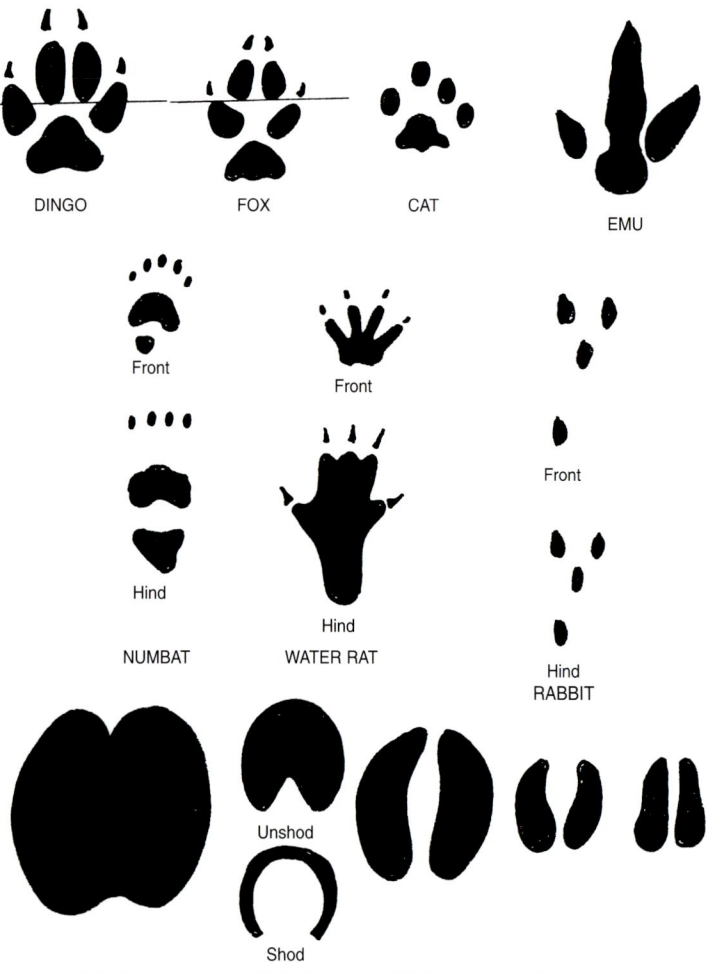

Drawings are not true to size and are not proportionate to each other – guide only

Conservation of our parks and the environment

Within the pages of this book I have endeavoured to pass on as many facts to you the reader as possible with the intention of developing a greater appreciation for the wonders and beauty of this vast state.

In doing so, I have tried to temper my strong desire to explain some of the damaging long term environmental problems that exist for us here in this Western Australia and indeed the world. This book is not about gloom and doom and it is certainly not intended as a forum for political debate.

Suffice to say that the following comments are my views only and are certainly not everybody's but if we work together and find middle ground, beneficial changes can occur.

I am fortunate to travel around Australia each year visiting many corners of this fantastic country but sadly each year I see the regular logging trucks flying down the country roads of Tasmania. I see a few more acres of virgin rainforest cleared on the Atherton Table Lands, Queensland, home of the beautiful Tree Kangaroo and countless other animals. I see in our own state Kwongan heath rich in wildflowers cleared for additional paddocks and I say to myself when will it end ? What do we do to stop this desire to clear more and more land. When is enough, enough?

Many of us are tired of talking about conservation just as the international aid workers are experiencing burn-out going from one human tragedy to another, or the 'WA 1999 Policeman of the Year' who tried to quit his job as the pressure of mediating between opposing factions in the deep south west over the 'old growth forests' was simply just too much to bear. It is not an easy road to tackle the environmental problems that confront us and we can easily brush these problems under the carpet, hoping they will go away.

There are no easy answers or quick fixes but the reality is that if we do not start to combat salinity, curb the desire to clear land for greed and short term gain, stop clear felling etc, then the planet will slowly take its toll on us. The ozone hole over the Antarctic is growing by the day, world temperatures are on the rise, the world's fish population is on massive decline, so things are happening around us but we can in our own way start to try and turn the tide.

We are quick to blame farmers for the massive land clearing program of the 30's to the 60's but there were insane Government policies that demanded that the majority of land be cleared to retain right of ownership. We are quick to point the finger at timber workers but for generations they have worked in the forests and only now with the massive demands of modern times are we experiencing clearing at an unprecedented rate. We blame DCLM or local shires when a tragedy occurs and cry that there was inadequate signage to tell us that there are rocks under the water, or that branches can fall from trees, or when a German tourist decides to wander in the mid day summer sun at Kata Tjuta (the Olgas) and tragically dies and then the German Government has the temerity to slap a $1 million law suit on the Australian National Parks Service. Who gains from all of this ?, well, the lawyers are having a ball and the international disease of suing your fellow man spreads. We should all take responsibility and be accountable for our own actions, no more so than with our fragile environment.

The following illustrations highlight some of the sad things that occur in our parks and state, they are not often shown in books as publishers feel that people don't want to see them. Well sorry folks but I'm the publisher and I'm sure you can handle a few not so beautiful shots as those that have gone before.

Powder Bark Wandoo clear felled alongside an an 'A' class reserve

We do not have a lot of old growth Karri forest and what remains is extremely precious. To clear fell virgin forests like the Karri opposite, is a real sad state of affairs. We must slow this process down and plant more trees especially indigenous trees that our endemic invertebrates can exist in and feed on, in turn our birds feed on them and so the natural chain turns the full circle.

The rubbish left by people never ceases to amaze me, often it is left by people far too drunk to even think straight let alone envisage protecting our environment. Our penalties for littering are rarely enforced, try doing it in Singapore, it's a whole new ball game there. I have resigned myself to the fact that some people will never change and wherever possible I clear up rubbish even if it is simply to help the over worked park rangers.

The white tree in the foreground is Powder Bark Wandoo. If you run your hand down the bark you will see a white powder film on your hands unlike the more common Wandoo tree that has no powder on the surface. There are not too many woodlands with good stands of Powder Bark Wandoo left.

The clear felled woodland (on the previous page) was one of the few uncleared woodlands that lay alongside an 'A' class reserve. The local shire said it should not be cleared. The Environmental Protection Authority said it should not be cleared. With persistence, it went to ministerial level—it was cleared in more ways than one. One man gains in the short term, the flora and fauna are destroyed in the short term and we suffer in the long term. The land we protect today is a biological storage centre that can greatly affect the quality of our life in the future and once cleared can never be replaced.

Vandalism takes on many forms, either burning down an ablution facility made by hard working carpenters. or driving over our fragile granite rock systems such as here in the Goldfields at Victoria Rock. These wheel ruts will stay like this for over 50 years thanks to a five minute fun ride. The only way is for people to stand up to this form of vandalism. Much of it lies in educating the young to impress upon them the need to preserve things.

Let's start to think about the quantity of chemicals that are poured into our soils and the produce we subsequently eat from them. Do we need to overstock areas that are marginal lands. The choice is ours.

Don't give up trying to turn things around, your planet needs your help, however small.

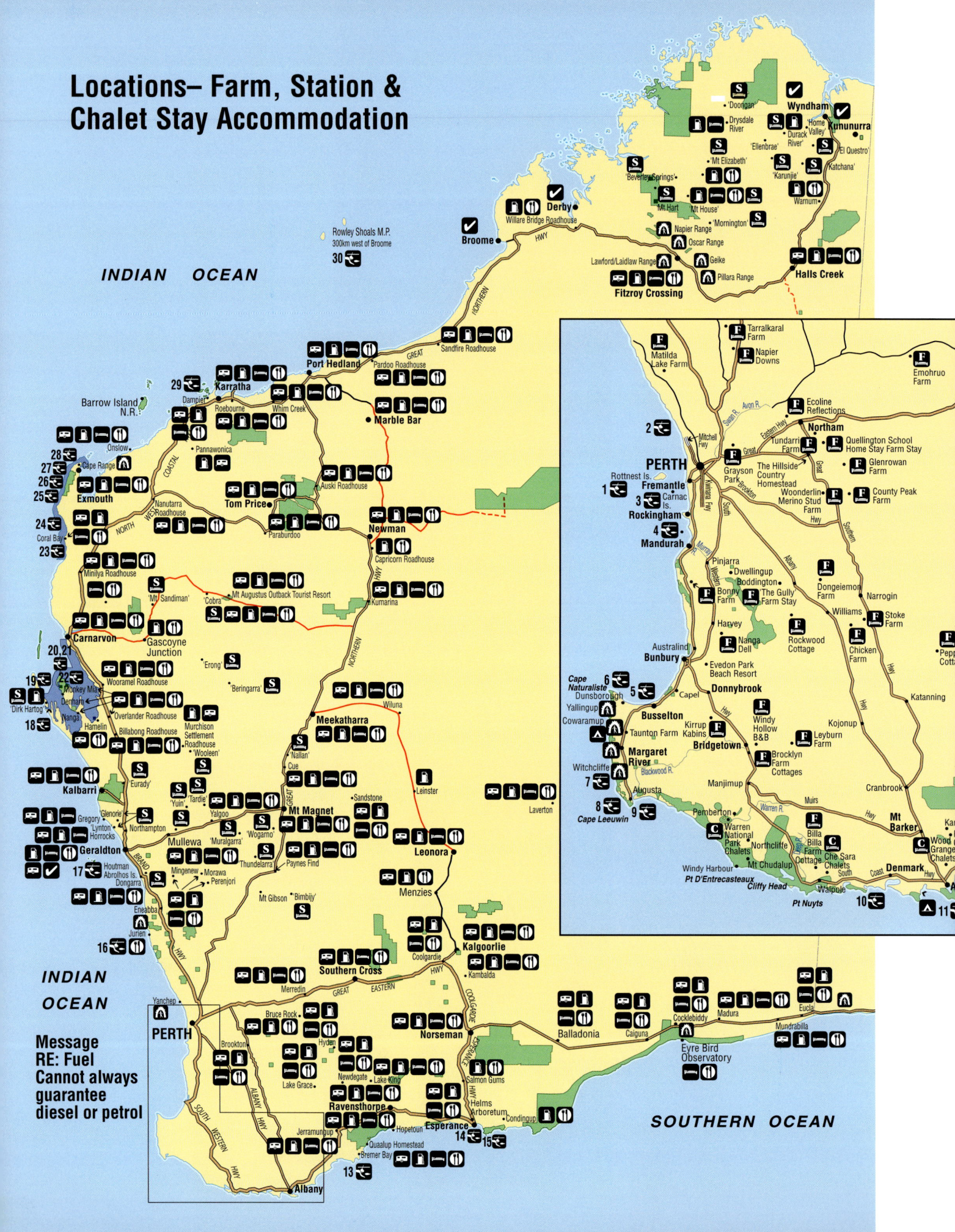

Farm, Station & Chalet Stay Accommodation

SYMBOLS

- ✓ All facilities
- Meals
- Fuel
- Caravaning
- Accommodation
- F Farm Stay
- C Chalet Stay
- S Station Stay
- Caving
- Dive sites

Dive Site Locations

1. Rottnest Island
2. Marmion Marine Park
3. Carnac Island
4. Penguin Island & Shoalwater Marine Park
5. Busselton Jetty, Busselton
6. Bunker Bay–Near Dunsborough
7. Hamelin Bay–Near Dunsborough
8. Cosy Corner–Near Augusta
9. Flinders Bay Bombies–Augusta
10. Madfish Bay–William Bay
11. Mistaken Island–Albany
12. South Point & Coffin Island
13. Little Boat Harbour–Bremer Bay
14. Artificial Reef & Woody Island–Esperance
15. Rossiter Bay & Lucky Bay–Cape Le Grand
16. Boulinger Island & Jurien Beach–Jurien
17. Abrolhos Islands
18. Monkey Rock–Shark Bay
19. Gregories Beach–Shark Bay
20. The wreck of the Gudron–Shark Bay
21. Broadhurst Corals–Shark Bay
22. Bottle Bay–Shark Bay
23. Coral Bay
24. Paradise Beach–Coral Bay
25. Piligramunna–Cape Range N.P.
26. Turquise Bay–Cape Range N.P.
27. Lakeside–Cape Range
28. Oyster Stacks
29. Goodwyn & Angel Island–Dampier Archipelago

Refer to CALM book 'Dive & Snorkel Sites in Western Australia'

FARM & STATION STAYS

SOUTH WEST & SOUTH COAST

Ambergate Acres
RSM 345, Busselton
(08) 9753 1132
Woodridge

Beulah Downs
RMB 62 Kojaneerup,
Manypeaks
(08) 9847 7032

Billa Billa Farm Cottages
PO Box 146, Walpole
(08) 9840 1131

Blackwood Inn
South Western Hwy,
Mullalyup
(08) 9764 1138

Bonny Farm
PO Box 347, Pinjarra
(08) 9530 3203
Tackenup Road, Napier
(08) 9844 3446

Brooklyn Farm Cottages
PO Box 67, Bridgetown
(08) 9761 9064

Cairnhill Homestead
PO Box 28, Yallingup
(08) 9755 2828

Chambejo Farm
PO Box 95, Ravensthorpe
(08) 9835 7015

Che Sara Sara Chalets
Hazelvale Road, Walpole
(08) 9840 8004

Evedon Park Bush Resort
c/- PO Burekup
(08) 9726 3397

Ferguson Farm Stay
c/- PO Dardanup
(08) 9728 1392

Jerramungup Farm B&B
South Coast Hwy,
Jerramungup
(08) 9835 1002

Kalpara Farmstay
RMB 136 Orchid Valley via
Kojonup
(08) 9832 3016

Karribank Country Retreat
Porongorup Road,
Porongorup
(08) 9853 1022

Kerriley Park Farm
Yelverton North Road, via
Busselton
(08) 9755 7524

Kirup Kabins Farm Stay
Mailman Road, Kirup
(08) 9731 6272

Leyburn Farm
RMB 138 Boyup Brook
(08) 9761 7506

Lucieville Farm Chalets
RMB 390 South West Hwy,
Bridgetown
(08) 9761 1733

Marri Lodge
PO Box 818, Margaret
River (08) 9757 3293

Nanga Dell Farmstays
PO Box 303, Harvey
(08) 9726 9202

Newlands Farm Holiday
PO Box 282, Donnybrook
(08) 9731 6261

Nooraglen
PO Box 161, Ravensthorpe
(08) 9838 1072

Northlands
RMB 153 Boyup Brook
(08) 9765 1098

Pemberton Farm Chalets
Vasse Highway, Pemberton
(08) 9776 1290

Pump Hill Farm Cottages
Pump Hill Road,
Pemberton

Rannoch West
RMB 1117 Denmark
(08) 9840 8032

Sandyknowe Bed & Breakfast
Miamup Road, Cowaramup
(08) 9755 5336

Stirling Range Retreat
Chester Pass Road via
Borden (08) 9827 9229

Taralea
PO Box 1147, Bunbury
(08) 9728 1252

Taunton Farm
PO Box 33, Cowaramup
(08) 9755 5334

Valley Views B&B
PO Box 815, Margaret
River (08) 9757 4573

Warren National Park Chalets
PO Box 100, Pemberton
(08) 9776 1188

Windy Hollow B&B
PO Box 129, Bridgetown
(08) 9761 2523

Woody Grange Chalets
RMB 9570A Willyung
Road, Albany
(08) 9844 3458

Yardup Cottage
Chester Pass Road,
(08) 9827 9209

WHEATBELT

Anne Hathaways Cottage
PO Box 398, Armadale
(08) 9497 3942

Bimbiji Station
PO Box 44, Beacon
(08) 9667 1022

Catton Hall Country Homestead
Wilkins Road, Mt Helena
(08) 9572 1375

Chuckem Farm
PO Box 181, Narrogin
(08) 9885 9050

County Peak
PO Box 65, Beverley
(08) 9646 4026

Dongiemon
RMB 814 Congelin-
Wandering Road,
Williams
(08) 9884 5235

Egoline Reflections
PO Box 1026, Northam
(08) 9622 5811

Emuhroo
PO Box 26, Yelbeni
(08) 9682 5013

Glenrowan
PO Box 327,
Doodenanning Road, York
(08) 9641 7051

Grayson Park
Bailup Road, Woorooloo
(08) 9573 1219

Kievi Farm Lodge
RMB 853 Marradong
Road, Williams
(08) 9885 6026

Matilda Lake Farm
Lot 1484 Telephone Road,
Gingin West
(08) 9575 7657

Napier Downs, Wannamal
North Road, Wannamal
(08) 9655 9015

Peppercorn Cottage
PO Box 48, Dumbleyung
(08) 9864 1012

Quellington School House Farm Stay
Quellington via York
(08) 9641 1343

Rockwood Cottage, Springhills Farm
Zilko Road, RMB 625
Williams
(08) 9885 7092

Rosedale Farmstay
PO Box 23, Beverley
(08) 9648 1031

Southglen Estate
PO box 66, Glen Forest
(08) 9298 8617

Swan Valley Holiday Cottages
10070 West Swan Road,
Henley Brook
(08) 9296 1007

Stoke Farm
RMB 702 Great Southern
Hwy, Narrogin
(08) 9885 9018

Tarallcaral
RSM 603 Gillingarra West
Road, Gillingarra
(08) 9651 5023

The Gully
RMB 828 Williams
(08) 9884 1076

The Hillside Country Homestead
PO Box 12, Forrest Street,
York
(08) 9641 2076

Tundarri
PO Box 1127, Northam
(08) 9622 1950

Woolpack Farm
RMB 593 Crossman Road,
Boddington
(08) 9883 8305

Woonderlin Merino Stud Farmstay
PO Box 3, Beverley
(08) 9646 1239

Woorabbin Springs
PO Box 99, Cunderdin
(08) 9635 1042

MID WEST & PILBARA

Cobra Station
PMB 28 Cobra Station via
Carnarvon
(08) 9943 0565

Dirk Hartog Island Station
Shark Bay
(08) 9948 1211

Erong Springs Station
via Mullewa
(08) 9981 2910

Glenorie Lookout Lodge
Swamps Road,
Northampton
(08) 9935 1017

Kachana
PO Box 779, Kununurra
(08) 9161 4346

Lynton-On-Sea
PO Box 169, Northampton
(08) 9935 1040

Muralgarra Station
PO Box 17, Yalgoo
(08) 9963 7994

Nallan Station
PO Box 24, Cue
(08) 9963 1054

Obawara
PO Box 190, Brand
Highway, Dongara
(08) 9927 1043

Thundelarra Station
via Wubin
(08) 9963 6574

Yuin Station
Yalgoo
(08) 9963 7982

Wogarno Homestead
PO Box 525, Mt Magnet
(08) 9963 5846

Wooleen
Murchison via Mullewa
(08) 9963 7973

KIMBERLEY STATION STAY

Beverley Springs Station
(08) 9191 4646

Drysdale River Station
(08) 9161 4326

Durack River Station
(08) 9161 4322

Ellenbrae Station
(08) 91614325

El Questro Station
(08) 9161 4318

Karunjie Station
(08) 91614322

Mt Barnett Station
(08) 91914652

Mt Elizabeth Station
(08) 91914644

Mt Hart Station
(08) 91914645

Mt House
(08) 91914649

Mornington Station
(08) 91917035

Caravan Parks in Western Australia

PERTH REGION & ENVIRONS

Hillside Garden Village
270 South Western Highway,
Armadale
Lakeside Caravan Park
Mandurah Road,
Baldivis
Burns Beach Sunset Holiday & Leisure Village
35 Ocean Parade, Burns Beach,
Iluka
Carine Gardens Caravan Park
Old Balcatta Road,
Carine
Perth Holiday Park
91 Benara Road,
Caversham
Forrestfield Village
351 Hawtin Road,
Forrestfield
Perth International Tourist Park
186 Hale Road,
Forrestfield
Coogee Beach Holiday Park
Cockburn Road,
Coogee
Fremantle Village Chalet Centre
Lot 1, Cockburn Road,
Fremantle
Woodman Point Holiday Park
Cockburn Road,
Munster
Riverside Gardens Estate
2462 Albany Highway,
Gosnells
Swan Valley Tourist Village
6581 West Swan Road,
West Swan
Karrinyup Waters Resort
467 North Beach Road,
Gwelup
Banksia Tourist Caravan Park
Lot 219 Midland Road,
Hazelmere
Springvale Village
161 Maida Vale Road,
High Wycombe
Jandakot Caravan Park
11 Hammond Road,
Jandakot
Kelmscott Caravan Park
80 River Road,
Kelmscott
Lake View Terrace Caravan Park
Cnr Lake Road & Lakeview Terrace,
Kelmscott
Kingsway Tourist & Caravan Park
Cnr Wanneroo Road & Kingsway,
Landsdale
Midland Caravan Park
2 Toodyay Road, Middle Swan
Mundaring Caravan Park
Great Eastern Highway,
Mundaring
Crystal Brook Caravan Park
Kelvin Road,
Orange Grove
Bakers Hill Roadhouse
Great Eastern Highway,
Bakers Hill
Kenlorn Caravan Park
224 Treasure Road,
Queens Park
Quinns Rock Caravan Park
Lot 211 Ocean Drive,
Quinns Rock
Central Caravan Park
34 Central Avenue,
Redcliffe
Cee & Cee Carapark
Rockingham Road,
Rockingham
Rockingham Holiday Village
147 Dixon Road,
Rockingham
Rottnest Camping
Rottnest Island
Starhaven Caravan Park
Pearl Parade,
Scarborough
Serpentine Falls Caravan Park
South West Highway,
Serpentine
Cherokee Village Mobile Home & Tourist Park
10 Hocking Road,
Kingsley
Wanneroo Caravan Park
off Wanneroo Road
Club Capricorn
Two Rocks Road,
Yanchep

COUNTRY AREAS

Albany Happy Days Caravan Park
Lot 21 Millbrook Road,
Albany
Albany Tourist Village Caravan Park
550 Albany Highway,
Albany
Cheynes Beach Caravan Park
Via Manypeaks
Emu Beach Holiday Park
Medcalfe Parade, Emu Beach,
Albany
Frenchman Bay Caravan Park
Frenchman Bay Road,
Albany
Kalgan River Chalets & Caravan Park
RMB 8634, Nannup Road,
Albany
King River Palms Caravan Park
Chester Pass Road,
King River
Middleton Beach Holiday Park
28 Flinders Parade,
Albany
Mt Melville Caravan Park
22 Wellington Street,
Albany
Oyster Harbour Caravan Park
Elizabeth Street,
Lower King (Albany)
Panorama Cottages & Caravan Park
106 Frenchman Bay road,
Albany
Rose Gardens Caravan Park & Chalets
41 Mermaid Avenue,
Emu Point, Albany
Doonbanks Chalets & Caravan Park
Augusta
Flinders Bay Caravan Park
Albany Terrace,
Flinders Bay
Molloy Caravan Park
Fisher Road,
Kurdardup (via Augusta)
Turner Caravan Park
Blackwood Avenue,
Augusta
Holiday Homes Caravan Park
Old Coast Road,
Australind
Leschenault Inlet Caravan Park
Lot 52 Cathedral Avenue,
Australind
Waddi Farms Caravan Park
Koonah Road,
Dadgingarra
Balingup Transit Facility
South Western Highway,
Balingup
Ballidu Caravan Park
Wallis Street,
Ballidu
Beacon Caravan Park
Main Road,
Beacon
Bencubbin Caravan Park
near Mukinbudin
Bencubbin
Beverley Caravan Park
Vincent Street,
Beverley
Binningup Beach Caravan Park
31 Portland Drive,
Binningup
Boddington Caravan Park
Wuraming Avenue,
Boddington
Bolgart Caravan Park
George Street,
Bolgart
Flax Mill Recreation Camp & Caravan Park
Flax Mill Road,
Boyup Brook
Bremer Bay Caravan Park
at river mouth
Bremer Bay
Fishery Beach Tourist Park
Cnr Wellstead & Point Henry Peninsula Roads,
Bremer Bay
Bridgetown Caravan Park
South West Highway,
Bridgetown
Brookton Caravan Park
Brookton Highway,
Brookton
Broome Caravan Park
Great Northern Highway,
Broome
Broome Vacation Village
Port Drive,
Broome
Cable Beach Caravan Park
Millington Road,
Broome
Palm Grove Caravan Resort
Cnr Cable Beach Road & Murray Road, Cable Beach,
Broome
Roebuck Bay Caravan Park
Walcott Street,
Broome
Roebuck Plains Roadhouse
Great Northern Highway,
Broome
Tarangau Caravan Park
Millington Road,
Broome
Brunswick Caravan Park
South West Highway,
Brunswick
Bunbury Accommodation Village
Bussell Highway,
Bunbury
Bunbury Glade Caravan Park
Timperley Road,
Bunbury
Koombana Bay Holiday Resort
Koombana Drive,
Bunbury
Punchbowl Caravan Park
Ocean Drive,
Bunbury
Riverside Caravan & Cabin Park
5 Pratt Road,
Eaton
Waterloo Village Caravan Park
South West Highway,
Bunbury
Acacia Caravan Park
Bussell Highway,
Busselton
Amblin Caravan Park
Bussell Highway,
Busselton
Beachlands Holiday Park
10 Earnshaw Road,
Busselton
Busselton Caravan Park
163 Bussell Highway,
Busselton
Busselton Holiday Village
118 Peel Terrace,
Busselton
Four Seasons Holiday Resort
Lot 33 Caves Road,
Busselton
Kookaburra Caravan Park
66 Marine terrace,
Busselton
Lazy days Caravan Park
452 Bussell Highway,
Busselton
Mandalay Holiday Resort & Tourist Park
Geographe Bay Road,
Busselton
Sandy Bay Holiday Resort
2 Norman Road,
Busselton
Siesta Park Holiday Resort
Caves Road,
Busselton
Geographe Bay Holiday Park
525 Bussell Highway,
Busselton
Peppermint Grove Holiday Park
Peppermint Grove Beach,
Capel
Carnamah Caravan Park
McPherson Street,
Carnamah
Carnarvon Caravan Park & Units
Robinson Street,
Carnarvon
Carnarvon Tourist Centre Caravan Park
Robinson Street,
Carnarvon
Marloo Tourist Caravan Park
Wise Street,
Carnarvon
Mt Augustus Outback Tourist Resort
Via Carnarvon
Norwesta Caravan Park
12-20 Angelo Street,
Carnarvon
Plantation Caravan Park
Robinson Street,
Carnarvon
Startrek Caravan Park
North West Coastal Highway,
Carnarvon
Wintersun Caravan Park
546 Robinson Street,
Carnarvon
Wooramel Caravan Park
North West Coastal Highway,
Carnarvon
Pinnacles Caravan Park
Aragon Street,
Cervantes
Collie Caravan Park
Porter Street,
Collie
Mr Marron Holiday Village
Porter Street,
Collie
Coolgardie Caravan Park
99 Bayley Street,
Coolgardie
Haven Caravan Park
Lot 34 Great Eastern Highway,
Coolgardie
Coorow Caravan Park
Station Street,
Coorow
Bayview Coral Bay
Robinson Street,
Coral Bay
Peoples Park Caravan Village
Robinson Street,
Coral Bay
Corrigin Country Caravan Park
Corrigin
Cranbrook Caravan Park
Mason Street,
Cranbrook
Bruce Rock Caravan Park
Dunstall Street,
Bruce Rock
Cue Caravan Park
Austin Street,
Cue
Cunderdin Caravan Park
Lot 74 Olympic Avenue,
Cunderdin
Dalwallinu Caravan Park
Great Northern Highway,
Dalwallinu
Transit Caravan Park
Dampier
Darkan Caravan Park
Coalfields Road,
Darkan
Blue Dolphin Caravan Park & Holiday Village
Hamelin Road,
Denham
Shark Bay Caravan Park
4 Spaven Way,
Denham
Boat Harbour Chalets & Camping
Boat Harbour Road,
Denmark
Ocean Beach Caravan Park
Ocean Beach Road,
Denmark
River Bend Chalets & Caravan Park
East River Road,
Denmark
Rivermouth Caravan Park
Inlet Drive,
Denmark
Rudgyard Beach Holiday Park
Rudgyard Beach Road,
Denmark
Wilson Inlet Holiday Park
Lot 6 Ocean Beach Road,
Denmark
Kimberley Entrance Caravan Park
Rowan Street,
Derby
Willare Bridge Roadhouse & Caravan Park
Great Northern Highway,
Derby
Dongara Denison Strata Caravan Park
123 Point Leander Drive,
Dongara
Dongara Denison Tourist Park
George Street,
Dongara
Seaspray Caravan Park
81 Church Street,
Dongara
Dowerin Motel & Caravan Park
Dowerin
Dumbleyung Caravan Park
Harvey Street,
Dumbleyung
Dunsborough Lakes Holiday & Caravan Park
Commonage Road,
Dunsborough
Dwellingup Caravan Park & Chalets
Del Park Road,
Dwellingup
Eighty Mile Beach Caravan Park
between Port Hedland & Broome
Halfway Mill Roadhouse & Caravan Park
Brand Highway,
Eneabba
Udale Caravan Park
Three Springs Road,
Eneabba
Western Flora Caravan Park
Brand Highway,
North Eneabba
Bathers Paradise Caravan Park
Westmacott Street,
Esperance
Bushlands Holiday Village
Collier Road,
Esperance
Crokers Park Holiday Resort
817 Harbour Road,
Esperance
Esperance Bay Caravan Park
162 Dempster Street,
Esperance
Esperance Seafront Caravan Park
Goldfields Road,
Esperance
Orleans Bay Caravan Park
Duke of Orleans Bay,
Esperance
Pink Lake Caravan Park
Pink Lake Road,
Esperance
Exmouth Accommodation & Caravan Park
Exmouth
Ningaloo Caravan Park
Murat Street,
Exmouth
Lighthouse Caravan Park

Vlaming Head,
Exmouth
Frankland Caravan Park
Moir Street,
Frankland
Tarunda Caravan Park
Forrest Street,
Fitzroy Crossing
Fortescue River Roadhouse & Caravan Park
North West Coastal Highway
North West Coastal Highway
Batavia Coast Caravan Park
Cnr Lot 3 Hall Road,
Geraldton
Belair Gardens Caravan Park
Wilcock Drive,
Geraldton
Drummond Cove Holiday Park
North West Coastal Highway, Drummond Cove,
Geraldton
Greenough Rivermouth Caravan Park
4 Hull Street, Cape Burney,
Greenough
Separation Point Caravan Park
Cnr Wilcock Drive & Port Way,
Geraldton
Sunset Beach Holiday Park
Bosley Street, Sunset Beach,
Geraldton
Mt Barnett Station
Gibb River Road,
Gibb River
Goomalling Caravan Park
Throssell Street,
Goomalling
Green Head Caravan Park
9 Green Head Road,
Green Head
S Bend Caravan Park
Brand Highway,
Greenough
Guilderton Caravan Park
Dewar Street,
Guilderton
Halls Creek Caravan Park
Roberta Avenue,
Halls Creek
Hamelin Bay Caravan Park
Hamelin Bay Road,
Hamelin Bay
Camp Mornington
off South Western Highway,
Harvey
Lake Brockman Tourist Park
Logue Brook Dam Road,
Harvey
Rainbow Caravan Park
Kennedy Street,
Harvey
Hopetoun Caravan Park
Spencer Street,
Hopetoun
Horrocks Beach Caravan Park
Via Northampton
Wave Rock Caravan Park
Wave Rock Road,
Hyden
Jerramungup Caravan Park
Moorshead Road,
Jerramungup
Jurien Bay Caravan Park
Roberts Street,
Jurien
Anchorage Holiday Village

Anchorage Lane,
Kalbarri
Kalbarri Tudor Caravan Park
10 Porter Street,
Kalbarri
Murchison Park Caravan Park
Grey Street,
Kalbarri
Red Bluff Caravan Park
Red Bluff Road,
Kalbarri
Boulder Accommodation Village
Lane Street,
Boulder
Golden Village Caravan Park
406 Hay Street,
Kalgoorlie
Goldminer Caravan Park
cnr Great Eastern Highway & Atbara Street,
Kalgoorlie
Kalgoorlie Accommodation Village
Burt Street,
Boulder
Prospector Holiday Park
Great Eastern Highway,
Kalgoorlie
Kambalda Caravan Park
Gordon Adams Road,
Kambalda
Balmoral Holiday Park
Balmoral Road,
Karratha
Karratha Caravan Park
Mooligunn Road,
Karratha
Rosemary Holiday Park
Rosemary Road,
Karratha
Sunbeam Caravan Park
Cornwall Street,
Katanning
Kellerberrin Caravan Park
Connolly Street,
Kellerberrin
Kirup Caravan Park
South West Highway,
Kirup
Kojonup Caravan Park
75 Newstead Road,
Kojonup
Kondinin Caravan Park
Gordon Street,
Kondinin
Koorda Caravan Park
Scott Street,
Koorda
Kulin Caravan Park
Rankin Street,
Kulin
Hidden Valley Caravan Park
Weaber Plains Road,
Kununurra
Ivanhoe Village Tourist Park
Ivanhoe Road,
Kununurra
Kimberleyland Holiday Park
Duncan Highway,
Kununurra
Kona Lakeside Tourist Park
Lakeview Drive,
Kununurra
Kununurra Town Caravan Park
Konkerberry Drive,
Kununurra
Lake Clifton Caravan Park
Old Coast Road,
Lake Clifton

Lake Grace Caravan Park
Mathers Street,
Lake Grace
Lake King Caravan Park
Varley Road,
Lake King
Lancelin Caravan Park
Hopkins Street,
Lancelin
North End Caravan Park
Bootoo Street,
Lancelin
Desert Pea Caravan Park
Weld Avenue,
Laverton
Ledge Point Caravan Park
Robertson Road,
Ledge Point
Snag Island Leeman Caravan Park
29 Thomas Street,
Leeman
Leonora Caravan Park
Rochester Street,
Leonora
Aqua Caravan Park
647 Pinjarra Road,
Mandurah
Belvedere Caravan Park
153 Mandurah Terrace,
Mandurah
Dawesville Holiday Village
Old Coast Road, South Mandurah
Estuary Caravan Park
25 Olive Road,
Falcon
Lucky Caravan Park
20 Henson Street,
Mandurah
Mandurah Caravan Park
603 Pinjarra Road,
Mandurah
Miami Caravan Park
Lot 2 Old Coast Road,
Falcon
Peel Caravan Park
637 Pinjarra Road,
Mandurah
Peninsula Caravan Park
Ormsby Terrace,
Mandurah
Timbertop Caravan Park
6 Peel Street,
Mandurah
Waters Edge Caravan Park
Old Coast Road,
South Mandurah
Yalgorup Eco Park
Henry Road,
Melros Beach, Mandurah South
Fonty's Pool Caravan Park
Seven Day Road,
Manjimup
Manjimup Caravan Park
South Western Highway,
Manjimup
Warren Way Caravan Park
South Western Highway,
Manjimup
Marble Bar Caravan Park
264 Contest Street,
Marble Bar
Gracetown Caravan Park
Cowaramup Bay Road,
Margaret River
Margaret River Caravan Park
36 Station Road,
Margaret River
Prevelly Park Beach Resort
Walcliffe Road,
Margaret River
Riverview Caravan Park

8 Wilmott Avenue,
Margaret River
Taunton Farm Cottages & Caravan Park
Bussell Highway,
Cowaramup
Meekatharra Caravan Park
Great Northern Highway,
Meekatharra
Menzies Caravan Park
Shire Offices, Shenton Street,
Menzies
Merredin Caravan Park
2 Oats Street,
Merredin
Mingenew Caravan Park
Lee Steere Street,
Mingenew
Monkey Mia Dolphin Resort
Monkey Mia Road,
Shark Bay
Moora Shire Caravan Park
Dandaragan Street,
Moora
Morawa Caravan Park
White Avenue,
Morawa
Mount Barker Caravan Park
Albany Highway,
Mount Barker
Mount Magnet Caravan Park
Hepburn Street,
Mount Magnet
Mukinbudin Caravan Park
Cruickshank Street,
Mukinbudin
Mullewa Caravan Park
Main Road,
Mullewa
Myalup Beach Caravan Park
Myalup Beach Road,
Myalup
Balingup Road Caravan Park
Balingup Road,
Nannup
Nannup Caravan Park
4 Brockman Road,
Nannup
Nanutarra Caravan Facility
North West Coastal Highway,
Nanutarra
Narembeen Caravan Park
Latham Street,
Narembeen
Narrogin Caravan Park
Williams Road,
Narrogin
Capricorn Caravan Park Roadhouse
Great Northern Highway,
Newman
Dearlove's Caravan Park
Newman Drive,
Newman
Newman Caravan Park
Kalgan Drive,
Newman
Valley Of The Giants Eco Park
South Coast Highway,
Nornalup
Gateway Caravan Park
Lot 1175 Prinsep Street,
Norseman
Mortlock Caravan park
Great Eastern Highway,
Northam
Northampton Caravan Park

North West Coastal Highway,
Northampton
Port Gregory Caravan Park
Port Gregory via Northampton
Windy Harbour Camping Area
Windy Harbour via Northcliffe
Ongerup Caravan Park
Walker Street,
Ongerup
Ashburton Travellers Park
Onslow
Beadon Bay Village
PO Box 50,
Onslow
Onslow Ocean View Caravan Park
Second Avenue,
Onslow
Peaceful Bay Caravan Park
Peaceful Bay
Pemberton Caravan Park
Lot 1 Pump Hill Road,
Pemberton
Perenjori Caravan Park
Crossing Road,
Perenjori
Pingelly Caravan Park
Sharrow Street,
Pingelly
Pinjarra Caravan Park
95 Pinjarra Road,
Pinjarra
Solveig Caravan Park
Sampson Road,
Point Samson
Porongorup Range Tourist Park
Porongorup Road,
Porongorup
Blackrock Caravan Park
cnr North Circular Road & Stanley Street,
South Hedland
Cooke Point Holiday Park
Taylor Street,
Port Hedland
Dixons Caravan Park
North West Coastal Highway,
Port Hedland
South Hedland Caravan Park
Hamilton Road,
South Hedland
Port Smith Caravan Park
140 km south of Broome
Preston Beach Caravan Park
Mitchell Road,
Preston Beach
Quairading Caravan park
McLennan Street,
Quairading
Ravensthorpe Caravan park
Elston Street,
Ravensthorpe
Ravenswood River Resort Hotel & Caravan Park
Pinjarra Road,
Ravenswood
Harding River Caravan Park
De Grey Street,
Roebourne
Sandstone Caravan Park
Irvine Street,
Sandstone
Seabird Caravan Park
Williams Way,
Seabird
Nanga Bay Resort

PO Denham,
Shark Bay
Southern Cross Caravan Park
Coolgardie Road,
Southern Cross
BP Roadhouse Caravan Facility
Railway Road,
Three Springs
Tom Price Caravan Park
Central Road,
Tom Price
Hoddywell Caravan Park
330 Clackline Road,
Toodyay
Toodyay Caravan Park
Avonbanks Railway Road,
Toodyay
Trayning Caravan Park
Sutherland Street,
Trayning
Wagin Caravan Park
Arthur Road,
Wagin
Coalmine Beach Caravan Park
Coalmine Beach Road,
Walpole
Lake Navarino Forest Resort
Inverell Road,
Waroona
Waroona Caravan Village
Logue Street,
Waroona
Wickepin Shire Caravan Park
7 Fisher Street,
Wickepin
Williams Caravan Park
Brooking Street,
Williams
Wiluna Caravan Park
Lennon Street,
Wiluna
Auski Tourist Village Roadhouse
Karijini National Park,
Wittenoom
Wongan Hills Caravan Park
Wongan Road,
Wongan Hills
Wyalkatchem Caravan Park
Goomalling-Merredin Road
Three Mile Caravan Park
Baker Street,
Wyndham
Wyndham Caravan Park
Baker Street,
Wyndham
Yalgoo Caravan Park
Stanley Street,
Yalgoo
Caves Caravan Park
Yallingup Beach Road,
Yallingup
Yallingup Beach Caravan Park
Valley Road,
Yallingup
Yealering Caravan Park
Sewell Street,
Yealering
Mt Bakewell Caravan Park
Eighth Road,
York
Murray River Caravan Park
South Yunderup Road,
Yunderup
Tathams Caravan Park
South Yunderup Road,
Yunderup

Index of Parks

Abrolhos Islands 136	Ellendale Pool 133	Lennard Gorge 169	Shoalwater M.P. 27
Alexander Morrison N.P. 132	Ellis Brook Reserve 46	Leschenault Peninsula N.P. 58	Silent Grove/Bell Gorge 169
Araluen Park 48	Esperance Lakes N.R. 91	Lesmurdie N.P. 46	South Ledge 45
Avon Valley N.P. 40	Eucla N.P. 123	Lesueur N.P. 131	Spectacles N.P. 31
Badgingarra N.P 132	Fernhook Falls 75	Mandalay Beach 69	Star Swamp Reserve 33
Beedelup N.P. 69	Fitzgerald River N.P. 87	Manning Reserve 30	Stirling Dam 61
Bell Gorge 169	Forest Heritage Centre 60	Marmion M.P. 25	Stirling Range N.P. 84
Bibbulmun Track 53	Forrestdale N.R. 32	Millstream / Chichester N.P. 148	Stockyard Gully N.P. 129
Bibra Lake 30	Francois Peron N.P. 140	Mirima N.P. 171	Stokes N.P. 90
Bickley Brook 47	Frank Hann N.P. 111	Mitchell Plateau 174	Sues Bridge 62
Bold Park 38	Fred Jacoby Park 46	Moganmoganing N.R. 127	Sullivans Rock 49
Booragoon Lake 31	Geikie Gorge N.P. 164	Monkey Mia 138	Swan Estuary M.P. 34
Boorabbin N.P. 114	Gleneagle 53	Moore River N.P. 127	Tathra N.P. 130
Boulder Rock 51	Gloucester N.P. 66	Mount Augustus N.P. 157	Thomson's Lake N.R. 31
Boyagin Rock N.R. 105	Goongarrie Station 115	Mount Dale C.P. 51	Torndirrup N.P. 80
Buckleys Breakaway 105	Gooseberry Hill 42	Mount Frankland N.P. 75	Tree Top Walk 77
Bungendore Reserve 47	Hamelin Pool Marine N.R. 140	Mount Hart 166	Tuart Forest N.P. 59
Burra Rock N.R. 112	Herdsman Lake 32	Munda Biddi Trail 52	Tunnel Creek N.P. 164
Canebrake Pool 62	Hills Forest Discovery Centre 45	Nambung N.P. 128	Two Peoples Bay N.R. 81
Canning River R.P. 34	Hoffman Mill 61	Ningaloo M.P. 145	Valley of the Giants 76
Cape Arid N.P. 93	Holland Track 116	North Ledge 45	Victoria Rock N.R. 113
Cape Le Grand N.P. 92	Humps N.R. 107	Nuytsland N.R. 122	Walpole-Nornalup N.P. 76
Capel Wetlands 58	Hut Pool 62	Parrys Lagoon N.R. 171	Walyunga N.P. 41
Cape Range N.P. 146	Jaurdi Station 114	Paruna Sanctuary 44	Warren N.P. 66
Cave Hill N.R. 112	John Forrest N.P. 43	Peak Charles N.P. 113	Watheroo N.P. 133
Centre Road 74	John Rate Lookout 76	Penguin Island N.R. 22	Wave Rock Reserve 107
Chapman Pool 62	Kalamunda N.P. 42	Porongurup N.P. 82	Waychinicup N.P. 82
Christmas Tree Well 48	Kalbarri N.P. 137	Prince Regent N.R. 177	West Cape Howe N.P. 79
Churchman's Brook Dam 52	Kalgoorlie Arboretum 117	Purnululu N.P. 175	William Bay N.P. 78
Coalseam C.P. 133	Karijini N.P. 150	Recherche Archipelago N.R. 91	Whiteman Park 38
Collier Range N.P. 152	Kennedy Range N.P. 159	Rottnest Island 23	Windjana Gorge N.P. 165
Coomaloo N.R. 132	King Leopold N.P. 166	Rowles Lagoon C.P. 115	Wolfe Creek Crater 177
Conspicuous Bay 77	Kings Park 37	Rowley Shoals M.P. 173	Woodman Point 27
Dampier Archipelago 148	Karakamia 44	Rudall River N.P. 153	Woody Island 91
D'Entrecasteaux N.P. 70	Lake Logue N.R. 133	Serpentine N.P. 50	Wungong Dam 52
Drovers Cave N.P. 129	Lane Poole C.P. 60	Shannon N.P. 71	Yalgorup N.P. 57
Dryandra Woodland Reserve 98	Langford Park 48	Shark Bay World Heritage Area 138	Yanchep N.P. 35
Drysdale River 173	Leeuwin-Naturaliste N.P. 63	Shell Beach 141	Yellagonga R.P. 33

References

Bennett, E. 1995, *Common & Aboriginal names of Western Australian Plant Species*, Wildflower Society of WA.

Brooker, M. & Kleinig, D. 1990, *Field Guide to Eucalypts,* vol. 2, Inkata Press, Melbourne.

Bush, Maryan, Browne-Cooper & Robinson 1995, *A Guide to the Reptiles and Frogs of the Perth Region*, University of Western Australia.

Christidis, L. & Boles, W. 1994, *The Taxonomy & Species of Birds of Australia & its Territories*, RAOU, Melbourne.

Erickson, E., George, A., Marchant, N. & Morcombe 1986, *Flowers & Plants of Western Australia*, Reed, Sydney.

Hoffman & Brown 1992, *Orchids of South West Australia*, University Press, WA.

Johnstone, R. & Storr, G. 1998, *Handbook of Western Australian Birds,* vol.1, Western Australian Museum.

Kawalilak, R. (ed.) 1990–1999, *Landscope,* Department Conservation & Land Management, WA.

Kawalilak, R. (ed.) 1992, *Perth Outdoors*, Department of Conservation and Land Management, WA

Kawalilak, R. (ed.) 1997, *Dive & Snorkel Sites in Western Australia*, Department Conservation & Land Management, WA.

Kawalilak, R. (ed.) 1998, *More Dive & Snorkel Sites in Western Australia*, Department Conservation & Land Management, WA.

Moon, R. & Moon, V. 1999, *The Kimberley an Adventure Guide*, Kakirra Adventure Publications, Vic.

Nevill, S. 1998, *Guide to the Wildflowers of South Western Australia*, Simon Nevill Publications, Perth.

Scott, J. 1999, *Walking the Capes*, Cape to Cape Publishing, Perth.

Storr, G. & Johnstone, R. 1999, *Lizards of Western Australia 1. Skinks*, Western Australian Museum, Perth.

Strahn, R. 1998, *The Mammals of Australia*, New Holland Publications, Sydney.

Tyler, M., Smith, L., & Johnstone 1994, *Frogs of Western Australia*, Western Australian Museum.

Wilson, K. & Knowles, D. 1998, *Australias Reptiles*, Collins, Sydney.

York Main, B. 1967, *Between Wodjil and Tor*, Jacaranda Press, Melbourne, & Landfall Press, Perth.